Waste Recycling for
Energy Conservation

Waste Recycling for Energy Conservation

David Kut and Gerard Hare

THE ARCHITECTURAL PRESS: LONDON
HALSTED PRESS DIVISION
JOHN WILEY & SONS, NEW YORK

First published in 1981 by The Architectural Press
Limited: London
Published in the USA by Halsted Press,
a Division of John Wiley & Sons, Inc, New York
© 1981 David Kut and Gerard Hare

British Library Cataloguing in Publication Data

Kut, David

    Waste recycling for energy conservation.
    1. Recycling Waste, etc.) – Great Britain
    I. Title II. Hare, Gerard
    604'.6'0941   TD 794.5   81-80645
ISBN 0-85139-707-7 (British edition)
ISBN 0-470-27178-7 (United States edition)

Set in Quadritek Baskerville 11 on 12 point
Printed and bound in Great Britain by
Mackays of Chatham

Contents

Preface

The recent explosion in the cost of gas and oil, combined with the continued escalation in the prices of the major raw materials, have highlighted the relatively new activity of 'recycling'. The intense coverage of new recycling plants, or advances in recycling technology, in the daily press provides evidence of a growing public awareness and interest in resource and energy conservation.

This book is intended for public authorities, for architects and engineers, and for plant operating and supervisory personnel. It explains the philosophy and practice of resource and energy recovery; it provides practical guidance for everyone involved in recycling and recovery procedures.

Particular attention is directed towards mechanical sorting and to the classification of urban and industrial refuse; to refuse-derived fuels and their storage, handling and incineration; and to the operational procedures which apply to recycling plants of all kinds.

Carefully selected case histories describe important industrial recycling applications which function in Europe and in the USA; these highlight the benefits and the financial returns which can be achieved by thoughtful recycling.

The authors are confident that this book will stimulate much further interest in a comparatively underexplored sector of our modern consumer society, promote action towards a cleaner environment and encourage the more efficient use of our resources and energy.

David Kut BScEng, CEng, FIMechE, FCIBS,
MInstE, MConsE, FInsArb
Gerard Hare CEng, MIMechE, FIHVE, MRSH

Acknowledgements

The authors acknowledge and appreciate the assistance obtained from the following persons and firms in respect of information relating to their products or research which have been incorporated in this book:

Dr P. Birch, Dr J. G. Chesters, Mr J. Harger, Mr J. Preston, Mr R. D. Leaver, Nordisk Pladerorsfabrik A/S, Robey of Lincoln Ltd, John Thompson Wilson Ltd, G. W. B. Boilers Ltd, Bristol Automation Ltd, Honeywell Controls Ltd, Satchwell Control Systems Ltd, Short and Mason Ltd, Brannan Thermometers Ltd, Bailey Meters and Controls Ltd, John Stein and Co, Kaiser Refractories Ltd, Christy and Norris Ltd, Hahn and Co Ltd, Vigers, Stevens and Adams Ltd, W. C. Youngman Ltd and The American Conference of Governmental Industrial Hygienists.

Thorn Lighting Ltd, Hoval Farrar Boilers Ltd, Wormald International (UK) Ltd, Robert Jenkins Systems Ltd, Mrs F. Beak (BRE), How Fire Protection Ltd, Raytheon Services Company, Sound Attenuators Ltd, Chemical Engineering Construction (Pensett) Ltd, BEWT (Water Engineers) Ltd, Spur Engineering Ltd, NEI International Combustion Ltd, Imperial Machine Company Ltd, Bosari and Co, Kitson's Insulation Contractors Ltd, The '600' Group Ltd, The Energy Equipment Co Ltd, M. Beaumont (F. E. Beaumont Ltd), Publications Officer Building Research Establishment, Commission of the European Communities (in respect of the Cresta Report information) – current copyright. The photographs relating to the RDF (WDF) pellets and to the Warren Spring Laboratory's equipment are reproduced by kind permission of the Director, Warren Spring Laboratory.

The authors also thank Miss Katy Vize of David Kut and Partners and Mrs Eileen Sheppard of Gerard Hare (Engineers) Ltd, who so ably assisted in the preparation of the manuscript, Mr Gerry Glover of David Kut and Partners who oversaw the drawing of the illustrations and Mr Maritz Vandenberg of the Architectural Press Ltd for his helpful guidance towards the publication of this book.

1
Trends in
Waste Generation

1.1 WASTE IN A CHANGING SOCIETY

Waste is a part of the human condition of existence: the higher we
soar above the basic level of survival, the greater and more diverse
the rejects of civilised living. Waste management and the recycling
of waste are rapidly achieving major importance for essentially
these two reasons: to maintain an acceptable environment free
from excessive pollution on the ground and in the air; to conserve
ever scarcer and more costly raw materials and energy.

The underlying philosophy of efficient waste management can
be summed up briefly:

- recycle re-usable material
- recover maximum energy from the combustible portion
- dispose the residue in a manner which will cause least harm to
  the environment.

1.2 PROCESSING PHILOSOPHY

The nature of waste product or waste accumulation can vary widely;
one may be dealing with municipally collected domestic rubbish,
discarded motor vehicles, or with waste products resulting from
manufacturing processes. There is thus a great variety of waste
which has to be recycled or dumped by methods most suitable to
particular environmental and economic parameters.

The permissible limits of pollution are set by public opinion,
health hazards and often by government or local authority regulations and codes. The extent of feasible recycling of waste depends
not just on the desire for conservation, but on a realistic assessment
of the capital and energy resources required to achieve worthwhile

results by employing one method rather that another. For example, a local authority will not incinerate or pyrolise its refuse if there are adequate sites available to accept rubbish tipping and there is little demand for any recycled heat or products.

Some industrial processes are embarrassed by a high proportion of waste production which can cause serious disposal problems. unless in-house waste distribution, with or without recycling, can be provided.

Substantial schemes of waste recycling generally involve major plant and buildings, making it advisable to assemble a professional team to advise on the overall feasilibity and on the execution of the scheme. Such a team may include architects, engineers, cost accountants, quantity surveyors and clients briefing officers (see chapter 2).

The commonly used term waste recycling embraces a number of clearly defined methods or classifications as follows:

Direct recycling
Indirect recycling
Re-use
Volume reduction
Baling
Compaction
Crushing and comminution
Extrusion
Pulverisation
Composting
Briquetting
Mechanical sorting
Incineration
Pyrolisis and fluidised-bed processing.

The American Solid Waste Disposal Act 1965 was introduced only because of public alarm at air pollution levels. The British Clean Air Act 1968 and its equivalent in other countries has made it an offence in law to excessively pollute the atmosphere. However, much remains to be done with regard to stricter control methods, particularly related to the balance of oxygen, ozone and other key elements in order to ensure that the atmosphere continues to provide all the goodness and variation of matter previously taken for granted. Most river authorities now have strict water pollution and conservancy laws, but the international high seas still remain a favourite target for waste dumping. Even at the present time some so-called civilised countries dump untreated solid waste into the seas. By the time under-developed countries achieve decent plumbing and a weekly bath, pollution control should be a prime topic of conservation.

Controlled land-filling with municipal waste is now fairly standard, even though uncontrolled tipping has not been entirely phased out. There is still little co-operation between governments, municipalities and state control boards in what has traditionally been a local problem. There is seldom any directive or encouragement for the ordinary householder to separate waste into recyclable lots to benefit the community and to reduce the quantity of waste left over for eventual disposal.

1.3 TYPICAL WASTE COMPOSITION AND ITS USES

Experience shows that the quantity and constitution of domestic refuse generated in a particular location depends on the size of the population and on its standard of living. In the prosperous USA, the average output of refuse per person has increased in 50 years from about 0.91 kg per head in 1920 to over 2 kg per head at the present time. In the less affluent UK, the current average is 1 kg per head. About three million tons of domestic refuse are collected every year in the area of Greater London; that collected in the whole of England and Wales in the 1960s was in the region of 14 million tons per annum, enough to cover the whole of the square mile of the City of London to a height equivalent to that of a block of flats 11 storeys high—a truly fearful vision!

Tables 1.1–1.4 (on pp 18 ff) show the composition of typical refuse as collected from domestic, office, commercial, hospital and holiday resort premises. It is predicted that the trend of consumer packaging will cause an increase in the volume of refuse over the next decade, but that the average weight of the refuse per household will diminish. It is suggested that the foreseeable increase in the plastics content of refuse will be quite moderate, but could be very considerable if the plastic milk bottle were to generally replace the glass bottle.

The great volume of refuse presents a daunting problem in handling and transportation to the disposal area/plant. In the collection of domestic refuse, many local authorities employ refuse vehicles which incorporate refuse compaction equipment, so that a greater weight of refuse can be collected on each trip.

Household waste
Contents of household waste, such as non-returnable glass bottles,

tin cans (mainly aluminium) and metal objects are virtually indestructible by natural processes. Bacterial clean-up agents are unable to break down many synthetic chemical products, such as plastics and detergents. It is not uncommon for public or municipal cleansing departments, with or without separation plant facility, to deal with dead cats, food wastes (squashed tomatoes, rotten apples, plate leftovers etc) leaves and lawn clippings, magazines and old newspapers, food and beverage cans and bottles, old clothes and wrappings, disposable cups, plates, razor blades and diapers, broken small appliances and busted toys, paint cans, cosmetic jars and tubes, rags, rugs, vacuum cleaner sweepings, building debris, and many other forms of almost inseparable rubbish. Less than 50 years ago a certain amount of voluntary waste separation took place, as the children from poor families separated rags and other scraps from rubbish tips.

There was also much less reclaimable material to be found in household waste. The recent upsurge in living standards has produced considerable lowering of our awareness of what is being thrown away. When disposed, the mingling of organic and inorganic household waste matter breaks down to the following basic constituents:

%	
35	paper
16	yard wastes
15	food wastes
10	metals
10	glass
2	textiles
4	plastics
3	rubber and leather
5	miscellaneous

Municipal waste composition varies according to the size and location of each community, type of neighbourhood, time of year and climatic conditions. Rural communities, for example, usually have more food and yard wastes, but less paper; metropolitan and urban areas have a larger percentage of old newspapers. In late December there is more packaging and wood (Christmas trees). In the autumn there are obviously more leaves, twigs and rotting vegetation.

Waste as fuel
Table 1.4 lists typical industrial and commercial wastes with

significant heat value as used for fuel. When such waste materials are available, careful consideration should always be given to the economics of heat recovery provision combined with incineration. See also chapter 7.

Waste for sale
In many locations, market research will pinpoint the potential users of recycled waste products which relate to the local industries. The particular product(s) depend on the adopted methods of waste sorting and/or manipulation. The following examples illustrate the general scope:

Glass
Bottles and other items can be used in glass manufacturing. The market research must establish likely users of the glass within a reasonable transporting distance from the plant. The required condition of the glass must also be considered (eg cleaned, broken glass, complete bottles, types of glass, etc).

Ferrous metals
These metals are of interest to scrap dealers, steel works, etc. The metal waste is relatively dense and can be transported economically. Discarded tinned food containers (tins) become valuable at times of high tin commodity prices and are of value to the steel industry. Processes exist for the separation of the tin from the containers, so that the tin can be separately marketed, though the economic viability of such processes is still being developed.

Non-ferrous metals
Such waste from metal working shops and factories is valuable; it is usually melted and reshaped (brass, copper, zinc, etc). In North America, aluminium beer cans are widely used and there is some scope for the sale of such discarded cans sorted from municipal refuse.

Waste-derived fuel
The manufacture and use of waste-derived fuel is a potential growth industry. The fuel is a fairly dense solid material in nodule form. It is not worthwhile transporting this over large distances as the transport cost would then outstrip the intrinsic value of the fuel; an economic balance must therefore be established. Power stations and other users will require a detailed specification of the waste-derived fuel to ensure that the burning of such fuel can be carried out safely in their boilers and furnaces.

Compost
This is for soil enrichment. A market is likely to exist in agriculture, horticulture and garden maintenance.

Paper
Waste can be used in the manufacture of new paper and of cardboard. A market research study must be made to ascertain the condition in which the paper can be used by local paper making industry (eg clean paper, pulp, cardboard, newsprint).

Plastic
Waste can be used in the production of coarse plastic articles; there are also processes for the recovery of the plastic raw material. Market research must establish the likely users and their detailed requirements.

Steam or hot water
Steam or hot water can be produced from incinerated waste which is passed through waste heat boilers. There may be scope for a limited heat supply to premises adjoining the waste plant or for more ambitious schemes of group or district heating. Several examples of the latter exist in England and in other developed countries, where municipal waste is fed into incinerators which provide steam or hot water to district heat networks.

  The economic viability of the re-use of recycled material has to be proven. It is unlikely that a municipal waste sorting or incineration plant can operate a profitable recycling business, but the income from the waste products may appreciably reduce the overall cost of operating the plant and there will be a contribution towards the conservation of resources.

1.4 WASTE RECOVERY METHODS

Mechanical sorting
Mechanical sorting systems are in use and further developments are progressing urgently for the recovery of usable commodities from bulk, municipally collected, household wastes. The technology involved appears to have good prospects of contributing materially to the solution of some of the difficulties which beset the disposal of household wastes and to the conservation and recycling of valuable resources. The chief objects of recovery by mechanical sorting are glass (for re-use in the glass making industry), paper fibre (to be recycled as coarser paper products), tin cans (recovery of expensive tin or re-use in steel making), combustible portion (compressed

into transportable fuel pellets), plastics (reconstructed into coarse products or re-used as raw material), compost (farm or horticultural use) and others. The effort and expense invested in the recovery of a particular waste component must depend on the available market for such material in the locality of the mechanical sorting plant.

It is a fallacy to believe that collected refuse, even after separation, is immediately suitable for incineration and energy recovery. Refuse may be very wet; it may have to be dried before pelletising or shredding to suit some basic form for use as a low grade waste fuel. It is important to understand that refuse-derived fuel (RDF) presents many problems to the combustion engineer in terms of low calorific value, plastic, high ash and moisture content and flue gas corrosive properties. Standard available incineration plant is not really suited because of the exacting nature of most Clean Air Laws.

If all the discarded refuse in the UK amounted to 18 million tonnes each year, then, at most the quantity of combustible matter would be 4.5 million tonnes. Because it would be feasible to process RDF only from the largest communities, the estimated energy contribution should then only be in the order of 1 million tonnes coal energy equivalent. Nevertheless this would be a significant contribution.

In the long term RDF must be burnt in purpose-designed plant. Regardless of volume and content, it is the responsibility of each local authority to handle these non-productive 'negatives' in the most efficient, least costly and most environmentally sound manner possible.

Timber resources
Timber resources are of universal importance, being valuable for ship and boat building, light flooring, interior and exterior joinery, window frames, sills, stair treads, fire-proof doors, laboratory benches, furniture, carvings, marine uses such as piling, dock and harbour work, paper making and sliced veneer. Probably less than 50 per cent of a felled tree is actually used for these purposes, the waste being generated from bark stripping, sawing, plank trimming etc. It can thus be readily accepted that wood waste is an important alternative fuel in timber growing areas, and particularly in areas which have no other fuel readily available.

It is well known that the rain forests of Brazil and other tropical climates provide most of the oxygen balance for the atmosphere of the earth. It is less well known that wood from trees possesses a calorific value of at least half that of best quality coal and the value of wood waste as a fuel is of this order. Wood with plant material provides the equivalent of about 200 million tonnes of coal each year or approximately 2.5 per cent of the total fuel supply of the world.

Proteinaceous feeds are a new possibility in this field using microbial techniques for the conversion of carbohydrate wastes, such as wood waste, paper and agricultural crop residues.

Other waste forms exist, but they have significantly less total energy recovery potential.

Tyres
The burning of tyres does have certain economic and technical problems. Pyrolised fuel from this high calorific value waste source may present a better commercial proposition.

Lubricating oils
When 'spent' lubricating oils should be centrifuged and/or recycled if possible. After suitable filtering this waste may, however, provide a high calorific value fuel easily burnt in an adapted conventional oil burner.

Sewage
Sewage burning has been practised for many years when economic and technical considerations permit.

Methane digestion and bio-gas production in general may become more feasible with better techniques and equipment.

Chicken manure
Chicken manure, like other products of poor animal digestive systems, is generally high in protein value and could be recycled. Such wastes present reasonable low grade fuel being usually relatively dry and with low ignition temperatures.

Mushroom compost
The difficulty of burning mushroom compost like other vegetation waste forms means that it may be better to use the natural process of decomposition as a method of handling and processing organic wastes which can then be used as soil conditioners or as top dressing for refuse disposal tips.

Industrial chemical wastes
These may be recyclable or combustible, but a special examination of such wastes is necessary.

Distillates
These originate from plant produce and other inflammable spirit sources, which because of their high calorific and octane values may be readily used for internal combustion engines.

1.5 WASTE RECYCLING METHODS

Direct recycling
Direct recycling is commonly adopted in the factory where the article is manufactured. Thus, misshapen glassware is returned to the furnace for remelting and re-use; rejected precious metal objects are remelted and recycled for new products; in plate glass manufacture, the recycling of a certain proportion of broken glass is an essential feature. Whether or not such recycling is adopted, depends on the relative cost of the required procedures and energy requirement as compared to the cost of the original product (eg the glass or metal) or of the virgin material (eg gold or silver). Direct recycling may be classfied as *in-house* recycling.

Indirect recycling
With this method some properties of the material are recycled. Examples:

- The recovery of heat generated in a wood waste or tyre incinerator and use of this for space or process heating
- The reconstruction of wood working wastes in chipboard manufacture
- The incorporation in road building construction of power station waste in the form of clinker and pulverised fuel ash
- The conversion of waste plastic containers into coarser products, such as fence posts.

There are numerous other examples of such indirect recycling.

Economics dictate that the cost of indirect recycling must compare favourably with that of obtaining the same benefit by other means, eg heat recovery provision with an incinerator plant will only be viable if the related capital and operating costs are less than those of raising the heat in a conventional boiler installation. Incineration, or pyrolisis with or without heat recovery, of municipal waste must be proved more convenient or cheaper than tipping into a suitable rubbish dump (not always locally available).

Re–use

The article is recycled for repeated use. This may apply to containers (such as returnable bottles), to timber, glassfibre or steel shuttering used on building sites, scaffolding, etc. Re-use will only be adopted where the cost of transport and handling is cheaper than the purchase of the factory delivered new article and where the condition of the material is suitable for satisfactory re-use.

Volume reduction

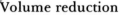

In supermarkets and in shopping centres, a great bulk of refuse is generated, mainly in the form of empty containers, cartons, packing materials, etc. It is clearly desirable to reduce the volume of this waste before transportation from the premises.

A number of alternative systems and equipment are available and are briefly described below.

Baling

Baling is suitable for dry materials only. The tied bales may be stored fairly compactly before collection off site. Where the waste comprises a mixture of wet and dry refuse, baling is not generally suitable, as the wet waste must be separated from the dry waste and handled in some manner other than baling. Plate 1 shows an industrial baling plant operating with wood waste. (Plates appear in the two illustrated sections.)

Applications:
Dry materials only.
Where adequate dry storage available.

Suitable for:
Shops, supermarkets, warehouses.

Compaction

Compaction equipment is available to reduce the volume of the refuse by as much as 8 to 1, though a lesser reduction of, say, 4 to 1 is more general with most commercially available compactor equipment. For shopping centres and supermarkets, mechanical compaction of the refuse is the most attractive method, as the materials do not require sorting or handling, other than collection at a suitably located central waste centre and subsequent placing into a compaction machine. Whilst the refuse may be placed directly onto the compactors by the shop personnel, this is beset with difficulties, particularly relating to the safety aspects. It is a much better procedure for each shop unit to be allocated a refuse container for subsequent collection either for in-house compaction or for disposal in a central refuse compaction centre (see also chapter 8, compactors).

Plate 2 shows a medium-sized compactor unit.

Application:
Dry and wet material.
Where high degree of compaction is required.
Minimum storage availability.
For individual or central compaction.

Suitable for:
Shopping centres, canteens, hotels, restaurants, refuse collection.

Crushing and comminution
Machines are available for crushing small bottles or for cutting tin cans of up to 20 l capacity. This equipment may be used on a smaller scale, such as for restaurants which must handle a large volume of non-returnable bottles.

Industrial hoggers are available for shredding timber off-cuts and various types of shredders may be used for special purposes. This equipment reduces the individual pieces of waste material to process a material which is more readily conveyed to storage (eg wood waste into a silo) or more easily compacted when tipped, as well as being less unsightly than bulk waste. Excessive noise generation is possible and must be allowed for.

Application:
Bottles and tins.
Hogging of off–cuts into chips.

Suitable for:
Restaurants, hotels, woodworking industries.

Extrusion
Extruders employ a hydraulic ram or Archimedean screw to simultaneously crush and compact the refuse by forcing it through a tapered tube or against a spring-loaded plate. A very high volume reduction is feasible of up to 15 to 1. Noise and vibration is likely to be associated with this method.

Application:
To increase collection capacity.

Suitable for:
Direct use on refuse collection trucks.

Pulverisation

Pulverisation of refuse is currently carried out almost exclusively using a high speed mill which breaks down the materials by impact and shredding. Waste is typically pulverised to such a size that 80 per cent of the material will pass through a 50 mm mesh, with a top size of approximately 200 mm when preparing the refuse for tipping.

A newer pulverising process employs a twinshaft slow speed mill which *cuts* the refuse. Several such machines are in use working on materials such as tyres, bulky refuse of a general nature and domestic refuse. The material discharged from the mill is typically 80 per cent less than 50 mm with a top size of 200 mm.

Application:

For conditioning bulk refuse prior to incineration or recycling.

Suitable for:

Mechanical sorting plants, municipal and other large scale incinerators.

Briquetting

There is a fairly low limit on the quantity of wood waste which can conveniently and economically be stored on the premises, whether in the form of off-cuts in a dump or as chips/dust contained in a silo. The matter becomes particularly acute in schemes of energy recovery for space heating in temperate climates, as the recovered heat will not generally be required during the summer. The choice then presents itself of either bypassing the heat recovery equipment and discharging the hot gases directly into the chimney (assuming that the chimney construction is suitable for this) or to continue heat recovery and dissipate the unwanted heat to atmosphere. Whichever is adopted, the recovered energy is lost. In some cases, it has proved practicable to install a briquetting machine, through which the wood waste chips and sawdust are compressed and processed during the off-heating season into briquettes which are placed into store for firing in boilers during the winter. Off-cuts may also be so processed after having been hogged into chips. Briquetting presses operate at high pressure and are noisy vibratory machines; they must be carefully located to avoid a nuisance. The storage arrangements for the briquettes are critical as they easily crumble and revert to wood dust. The use of briquetting installations is particularly popular in Switzerland and in Scandinavia.

Application:

Mainly for the briquetting of wood dust.

Suitable for:
Woodworking industries

Composting
In composting, the organic constituent of the solid waste material is subjected to biochemical degradation to provide as the end product a humus-like mass which is suitable for soil conditioning and enrichment.

Before the composting process can commence, the refuse must be reduced. Composting can only be achieved on the organic refuse; selection by screening and magnet is therefore necessary. The non-compostable, combustible element may be destroyed by incineration with, or without, heat recovery. The volume reduction that can be achieved by composting is in the order of 2 to 1. The advantage over pulverising system is that the material is of a soil-like consistency and does not expand when tipping.

Application:
For volume reduction (2 to 1).
Preparation prior to tipping.

Suitable for:
Local authorities involved in tipping of rubbish, landscape and farming soil enrichment.

1.6 ENERGY RECOVERY METHODS

Incineration
In the process of incineration, the waste material is combusted and thereby reduced by up to 90 per cent in volume, and by up to 60 per cent in weight. The residue, being ash, is much more easily and cheaply transported and dumped than the original bulk material.

It is feasible to recover the energy generated in the combustion by adding a waste heat boiler or warm air furnace to the incinerator, the very hot gases discharged from the incinerator giving up most of their heat in these heat exchangers before entering the chimney.

Table 1.5 lists typical industrial and commercial wastes with significant heat values and fuel potential. In some manufacturing industries, such as furniture and other timber-derived articles, there is a large output of wood waste in the form of chips, off-cuts, wood dust and sanderdust—in the order of 20 per cent plus of the weight of the original timber brought into the factory. The handling of the waste then becomes a major manufacturing concern and can only be realistically tackled by including an incinerator plant as an extension of the production line.

The process of incineration must be strictly controlled to avoid pollution of the environment. The investment required for even quite small-scale commercial incineration plants is costly and a disproportionate amount of space can be taken up with the incinerator building and with the associated storage facilities. It is vital to achieve the most efficient flow of the waste into and out of the storage area, as well as the smooth disposal of the incinerator ashes.

The siting, height and termination of the chimney is a major concern to obviate the danger of creating smoke, sparks or noxious effluent nuisance to the neighbourhood. The local authorities' bye-laws and codes must be consulted through all stages of planning an incinerator plant.

Application:
Destruction of waste to ash.
Heat recovery from waste.

Suitable for:
Municipal authorities, hospitals, manufacturing industries faced with combustible wastes (such as sawdust and off-cuts), tyre and solvent disposal.

Pyrolysis

This is a recycling process which relies on the physical and chemical decomposition of organic matter under the influence of heat in an atmosphere which is deficient in oxygen. Pyrolysis is achieved by heating the waste in a retort at a high temperature in the absence of adequate oxygen for full combustion. Temperature levels actually employed depend on the particular process and on the required end product. In the pyrolysis process, the refuse can be converted into various forms of useable solid, liquid or gaseous materials. Non-combustible items such as glass and metal are removed from the equipment by automatic means for subsequent re-use or disposal. The resultant liquid and/or gaseous fuels may be stored for use when required or be fired into an associated waste heat boiler, offering a major advantage over the incineration process which must utilise the released energy instantly.

Pyrolysis is a relatively novel procedure; commercial scale plants are on offer in the USA and in England, though the process has not yet been widely adopted. It holds out considerable promise for the future.

Application:
Destruction of difficult wastes such as tyres and plastics.
Where minimum pollution is essential.
For heat recovery from waste.
Can provide gas for gas turbine operation.

Suitable for:
Municipal authorities, hospitals, abbatoirs, producers of organic
waste, tyre disposal, plastic disposal.

Fluidised bed combustion

A system of combustion, in which fuel or waste is burnt continuously in an atmospheric fluidised bed which offers much flexibility in that it can accept a wide range of low grade fuel with
associated high heat transfer rates. The fluidised bed is relatively
compact and operates at low temperatures. With the addition of
limestone, the process can desulphurise the combustibles, effecting
extremely low emissions of the polluting sulphur dioxide. The
fluidised bed process has not yet widely progressed into commercial use, but it appears to have much potential applicable to
waste destruction.

Application:
Where high rates of heat transfer are required.
Where low sulphur emission is essential. For heat recovery from
waste.
Can provide gas for gas turbine operation.

Suitable for:
Hospitals (waste destruction), abbatoirs, incineration in city centres,
producers of organic wastes.

Table 1.6 summarises the various waste disposal recycling and
manipulation methods, indicating their main uses and advantages
and disadvantages.

1.7 WASTE DISPOSAL METHODS

Method 1: dumping

The waste is collected from the premises (domestic, commercial or
manufacturing) and is dumped into an authorised rubbish tip or
landfill site.

Suitable for:
Municipalities which have adequate landfill or rubbish dumping sites under their control.
Can assist land reclamation.

Method 2: recycling
The waste is collected and taken to a mechanical sorting centre. The various constituents of the waste are separated prior to sale, recycling or eventual disposal.

Suitable for:
Municipalities which have inadequate sites for dumping of rubbish.
Areas in which there is a reasonable demand and acceptable for the products of mechanical sorting.

Method 3: incineration
The waste is collected and taken to an incinerator. The metals in the waste are usually separated from the waste; the remainder is incinerated.

Suitable for:
Municipal authorities and other large producers of combustible waste/rubbish. Preferably, such application should permit associated generation of energy (hot water, steam or warm air) for electricity generation, process heating or district heating.
Specialist waste disposal contractors in the field of tyre, plastics, solvent, etc disposal, preferably with associated recycling of constituents and heat recovery.
Woodworking industry.

CHECK LIST

Check: whether the waste product is suitable for: mechanical sorting and recovery; direct recycling; indirect recycling; re-use; baling; compaction; crushing and comminution; extrusion; pulverisation; briquetting; composting; incineration; pyrolisis or fluidised bed process.

Ascertain: waste quantities; fuel value of waste; local markets for recovered materials; local regulations and codes concerning waste tipping, air pollution, etc. Facilities offered by local authority, such as conveying, disposal which may affect decision.

TABLE 1.1 DOMESTIC REFUSE: COMPOSITION AND YIELD (AS A PERCENTAGE OF WEIGHT)

	Fine dust or cinder	Vege- table bone etc	Paper and rag	Metal and glass	Misc (incl plas- tics)	Av household/ week		
						Weight	Volume	Density
	%	%	%	%	%	kg	m^3	kg/m^3
1935	57	14	16	7	6	17.0	0.058	291
1963	40	14	25	16	5	14.1	0.071	200
1967	31	16	31	16	6	12.9	0.081	161
1968	22	18	39	18	3	13.2	0.084	158
1969	17	20	40	20	3	12.7	0.089	143
1970	15	25	39	18	3	13.5	0.092	146
1972	21	19	33	19	8	11.8	0.077	153
1973	19	18	36	19	8	11.5	0.076	152
1966*	10	24	43	14	9	19.1	–	–
1975†	18	13	53	12	4	16.8	0.13	130
1980†	12	17	46	18	7	14.5	0.12	120

* typical town in USA
† estimated

TABLE 1.2 RESORT WASTE (US DATA)

Situation	Output	Unit
	kg/day	
Campground	0.57 ± 0.04	Camper
Rented cabin with kitchen	0.66 ± 0.14	Occupant
Restaurant	0.32 ± 0.18	Main meal
Residence	0.97 ± 0.24	Occupant
Observation site	0.02 ± 0.01	Vehicle
Swimming beach	0.18 ± 0.01	Swimmer

Note: Likely to be comparable with areas outside the USA for similar resort activities

TABLE 1.3 COMMERCIAL REFUSE

	Typical bulk density	Multiple stores	Department stores	Super-markets	Hotels	Offices
	kg/m^3	%	%	%	%	%
Folded news-paper, card-board packed or baled	500					
Loosely crump-led paper, office station-ery	50	81	65	50	8	80
Wastepaper (loose in sacks)	20					
Mixed general refuse similar to domestic (no solid fuel residues)	150	13	31	40	55	16
Separated food wastes, un-compacted vegetable waste	200	4	2	-	33	4
Well compact-ed, moist pig swill	650					
Salvaged bones and fat	600	2	2	10	-	-
Empty bottles	300	-	-	-	4	-
Yield per week, kg		1.0[1]	0.54[1]	1.8/5.8[*1]	3.0[2]	1.68[3]

*Supermarkets, judged by their output of refuse, fall into two categories

[1] Per m$_2$ of sales area; 6-day week
[2] Per head staff and residents; 7-day week
[3] Per employee; 5-day week

TABLE 1.4. TYPICAL INDUSTRIAL AND COMMERCIAL WASTES WITH SIGNIFICANT FUEL VALUE

Liquids	Fuel grading	Average heating value (as fired) kJ/kg
Industrial sludge	Depends on composition generally poor	8 600-9 770
Black liquor	Poor	10,230
Sulfite liquor	Poor	9 770
Dirty solvents	Depends on composition may be explosive	23,260-37,220
Spent lubricants	Good	23,260-32,560
Paints and resins	Depends on composition generally difficult to burn	13,960-23,260
Oily waste and residue	Very good	41,870
Solids		
Bagasse	Good when dry	8 370-15,120
Bark	Good when dry	10,470-12,100
General wood wastes	Good	10,470-15,120
Sawdust and shavings	Good	10,470-17,450
Coffee grounds	Good when dry	11,400-15,120
Nut hulls	Good	17,900
Rice hulls	Good	12,100-15,120
Corn cobs	Very good	18,600-19,300
Refuse-derived fuel	Good	6 980-11,630

Note: The effectiveness as a fuel depends generally on the form and composition of the material: in some cases (wet or explosive material) the heat value cannot be realised

TABLE 1.5 HOSPITAL WASTE

Function	Output/bed
	kg/day
Long stay	0.2
Mental	0.7
General	1.9
Maternity	3.8

Note: Estimated to increase at the rate of 10% per annum

TABLE 1.6   SUMMARY OF MAJOR METHODS OF WASTE DISPOSAL

Process	Extensive land required	Major plant investment	Causes pollution	Limits pollution	Reclaims resources	Eases transportation	In-house process
Direct recycling		Possible			*	*	*
Indirect recycling		Possible			*		*
Re-use					*	*	
Landfill	*		*				
Baling					*	*	*
Compaction					*	*	*
Crushing and comminution					*	*	*
Extruders					*	*	*
Pulverisation					*	*	*
Briquetting					*	*	*
Composting	*				*	*	
Incineration	Possible	*	*				
Incineration with boiler	Possible	*	*		*		
Pyrolysis	Possible	*		*	*		
Fluidised bed	Possible	*		*	Possible		
Mechanical waste sorting	*	*		*	*	*	

Noisy operation	Vibratory operation	Costly	Requires market research for product	Comments
				Many possible methods—see 1.5—suitable for industrial users in appropriate circumstances
				Ditto—see 1.5—suitable for industrial users in appropriate circumstances
				Ditto—see 1.5—suitable for packaging firms, building industry, etc
		*		Suitable for land reclamation—see 1.7
				Dry materials only—see 1.5—suitable for shops
*	*			Suitable for stores and shops—see 1.5
*	*			Suitable to deal with small bottles, cans off-cuts —see 1.5
*	*			Offer volume reduction of up to 15 ot 1—see 1.5
*	*			Suitable for tyres and bulk refuse—see 1.5
*	*			Suitable for wood chips and similar—see 1.5
		*	*	Suitable for soil enrichment—see 1.5
		*		Suitable for waste destrection—see 1.6
		*		Suitable for waste destruction with heat recovery —see 1.6
		*		New process under development and pilot use. Suitable for destruction of hospital and other organic wastes with or without heat recovery—see 1.6
		*		Suitable for destruction of hospital and other organic wastes with or without heat recovery—see 1.6
		*		Offers variety of recycling possibilities for municipal authorities —see 1.4

2
The Team

2.1 ORGANISATION

When the management of a waste producer have decided to evaluate the feasibility of a waste disposal proposal, with or without recycling, they must then consider the particular manner in which the matter can best be advanced.

To progress a scheme from inception to completion, a number of defined stages can be identified and must each be explored and completed (see text below and figs 2.1, 2.2 and 2.3).

Stage 1
Establish quantities and types of waste being produced. Identify quantity for each type, where there is a variety of waste production. Verify the rate of production; observe this over a specific period of time on an hourly basis and record the results of this survey methodically over an appropriate length of time. Analyse the pattern of waste production and draw attention to random cyclic swings.

Stage 2
Consider how the waste, or proportions of it, should be handled. Certain waste products are notoriously difficult to incinerate or dump. Identify preferred method of destruction or disposal. Is separation and recovery of certain waste constituents required?

Stage 3
Research the most suitable methods applicable to the particular site and waste products.

Stage 4
Consider the environmental aspects, including pollution, noise generation and fire protection. Consult with the local or governmental bodies, as appropriate, to establish, at the earliest stage, likely limitations which may be imposed be them

Stage 5

View some existing installations which process similar waste and quantities to get a 'feel' of the scope of the required works and seek relevant operating experience.

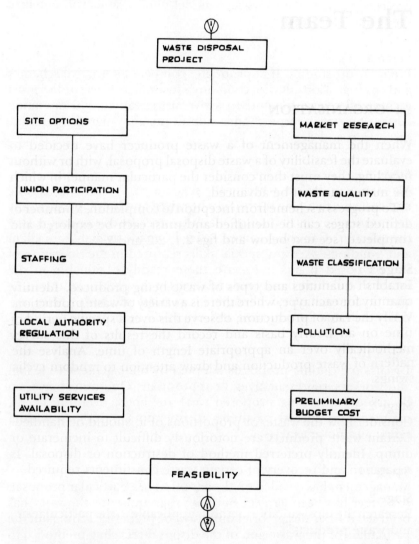

2.1   *From inception to feasibility*

Stage 6

List possible options as regards alternative processes and inst-allations. What standby facilities will be necessary?

Stage 7
Seek out manufacturers of the required equipment. Prepare preliminary layouts and establish availability of space, access and utility services (such as gas, electricity and water). For the larger projects, perspective views and model photographs will enhance the technical report.

Stage 8
Prepare cost studies. If appropriate, compare alternative schemes and costings. Consult with company's insurance. Cost studies must include all relevant factors to arrive at the capital and operating costs. Prepare a report and submit to the management for discussion and decision.

Stage 9
Management decides whether the scheme, or a scheme, is feasible and cost effective. Can the finance be raised and how? Are there any government grants or loans available to meet the cost or part-cost of the scheme? Can the required space be made available for plant and buildings? Are any special skills required in the operation of the proposed plant; if so, are these readily obtainable in the locality? Will there be any redundancies in the present labour force due to automation or changes in working methods? Must additional labour be recruited and can same be obtained.

Stage 10
Discuss the outline proposals adopted by management with staff and workers' representatives, as appropriate. Questions may then be asked concerning proposed work methods, overtime needs, maintenance, special payments to operators, health, pollution, safety and noise aspects.

Stage 11
Management has decided on the adoption of a particular proposal. A budget has been agreed; outline programme for the work has been set. A basic design brief must now be prepared, setting out the particulars of the waste and of the disposal/recycling method(s) to be adopted.

Stage 12
Decide the means by which the design brief can best be translated into the required complete plant.

Select one of the following alternative arrangements:

(a) in-house
(b) package deal with selected manufacturer(s)
(c) professional design team
(d) a combination of the items a to c.

Stage 13
Select the required equipment.

Stage 14
Prepare layout drawings and allocate spaces.

Stage 15
Check structural implications.

Stage 16
Obtain all necessary approvals concerning environmental matters, chimney heights and planning permissions for the proposed plant buildings and enclosures.

Stage 17
Prepare working drawings, detailed specifications and bills of quantities and tender documentation for agreed works. Firm up the installation programme; allow adequate commissioning time within the overall programme. Should performance be tied to a penalty clause for programme over-run? Are tenders required on the basis of firm prices or fluctuations to compensate for inflation? If the latter, then establish basis for costing fluctuations.

Stage 18
Obtain estimates for the required works, either from a particular firm with specific experience relative to the project, or through selective tendering by a number of firms, each of which must be financially and practically capable and competent of carrying out the works. In the latter case, it is essential that each firm tenders on an identical basis and set of drawings and specifications.

Stage 19
Analyse the tenders and compare with the original budget. Check that the tenderers have all quoted on same basis. It is likely that alternative materials and/or methods may be offered by some of the tenderers; evaluate to establish whether these offer advantages over the specified items.

Confirm that one of tenders is acceptable, but do not automatically accept the lowest tender, especially if there is a wide gap between the tender amounts, without establishing that there are no major errors which would cause the contractors to inevitably lose money and sour relations during the course of the project. If a financial error is identified, one has to consider all the implications. It is not always fair to permit a contractor to upgrade his tender to allow for a known error, *after* he has learnt the other tender figures.

Stage 20
Appoint contractor(s) to carry out the work on clear–cut terms.

Stage 21
Supervise the work in progress and continuously monitor performance against intended programme. Agree extensions of contract time for reasons of bad weather and/or delays which are not due to the contractors' lack of performance. Check on concealed aspects of the installation before these are covered up. Hold site and progress review meetings at regular intervals and maintain minutes of same. Keep meticulous records of variations to the original work content and of the related extra costs or credits. Certify appropriate progress or staged payments.

Stage 22
Inspect major equipment assemblies (eg control panels, hoggers, etc) at the manufacturers' works before dispatch to site and witness tests on same.

Stage 23
Agree practical completion of the work when the plant can be put to practical use.

Stage 24
Prepare defect schedules for remedial action by the contractors.

Stage 25
Check the details of the plant commissioning; all relevant data should be recorded and retained. Accept the fully commissioned installation on behalf of the owner.

Stage 26
Obtain and check owners' manuals operating and maintenance instructions prepared generally under the terms of the contract. Do

not certify the final payment to the contractor until these essential documents have been received and approved.

Stage 27
Train operatives in the efficient operation and maintenance of the plant.

Stage 28
Check that the defect schedules have been satisfactorily cleared by the contractors.

Stage 29
Obtain clearance for the completed plant from the local authorities.

Stage 30
Set up routine maintenance and emergency procedures.

Stage 31
Agree the final account with the contractors. If there are major disputes, legal or arbitration proceedings may arise and have to be processed.

2.2 PROJECT TEAM

Selection
Having looked at the overall planning and supervision requirements of the project, one must revert to Stage 12 and consider the selection and composition of the project team in some depth. The project falls essentially *into* two parts, which may be considered jointly or separately — the preliminary work which leads to the formulation of the design brief; the execution of that brief to completion of project. Some managements have the in–house resources to prepare a firm design brief. Others may call upon suitably qualified professionals to carry out the surveys and researches necessary to establish the design brief. Relatively few firms will have the expertise to follow-up the design brief, nor will they be able to direct the operation with the competence necessary to complete the overall project. They have to call in the experts.

When opting for the 'Package deal', one ties oneself to one firm of equipment suppliers or contractors in whose expertise full confidence is retained. However, it is unwise to forgo *all* control and some means should be arranged to check regularly on the progress and quality of the work to ensure that the specified installation and

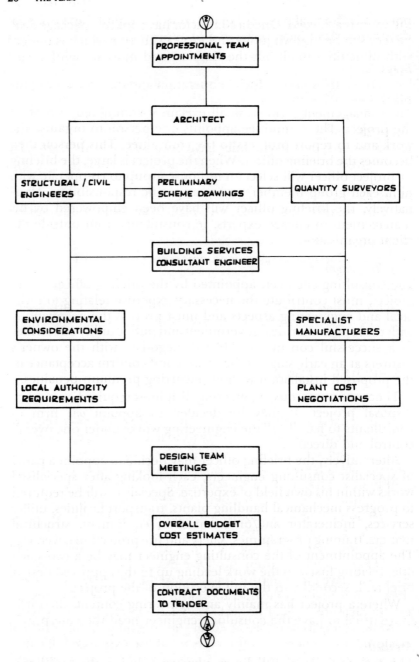

2.2   From appointment of professional team to the completion of the contract documents for tender

full value is achieved. Once a contractor has booked a package deal, he tends to be his own judge and jury, a situation which is fraught with difficulties in all but the simplest and most straightforward cases.

The executive committee

The management forms a small executive committee to oversee the project. The committee appoints one person to organise the work and to report progress to the committee. This person then becomes the briefing officer. When the project is large, the briefing or project officer will select an in-house group to co-operate with him, each group member having a specific responsibility. Alternatively, the briefing officer will have been empowered by his management to engage experts, ie consultants from outside the client organisation.

Consulting engineer:

The consulting engineer, appointed by the briefing officer of the project, must contribute the necessary expertise relating to technical and engineering aspects and must process the negotiations with the local authorities, government and public utility authorities to a successful conclusion. He will negotiate with the owner's insurers at an early stage of the project and confirm acceptance of the proposed installation without incurring premium penalties.

There are numerous engineering disiplines required on a waste disposal project. It may be decided to appoint *one* firm of consultants to handle *all* the engineering works under one overall control and direction.

Alternatively, the briefing officer may decide to appoint a panel of specialist consulting engineers, each looking after specialised works within his own field of expertise. Specialists will be required to progress mechanical handling plants, transport facilities, utility services, incinerator and/or compaction equipment, structural matters, training programmes, safety and fire protection cover, etc. The appointment of the consulting engineer may be a two-stage one, relating firstly to the work leading up to the approved design brief and, secondly, to the full execution of the project.

Where a project has mainly an engineering content, then it is more usual to have the consulting engineer head the enterprise.

Architect:

The architect's brief will be to plan and design the buildings, access to them and advise on associated aspects of the projects. On large schemes, it is not uncommon to introduce a specialist

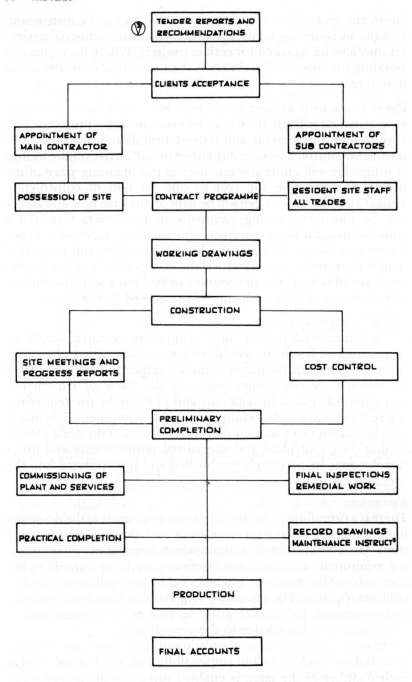

2.3   *From reports on tenders to the final accounts*

landscape architect to blend the new buildings and constructions into the surrounding landscape. Interior and/or industrial designers may also be required for certain projects. Where the contract is building-intensive, the architect is the most suitable leader of the design team.

Quantity surveyor or building cost accountant:
Such an expert will join the design team on the larger projects which have numerous elements and require overall and, possibly complex, cost control. The quantity surveyor will advise on the budget costings. He will guide the architect in the planning stage of the buildings, evaluating the cost of one method of construction against another. A close eye will be kept on the cash flow and advice will be given concerning payments to the contractors. On a conventional building contract, the quantity surveyor's major function is the production of a bill of quantities and associated tender documents against which the competitive tenders for the work are obtained, the negotiation of fair rates with the various contractors, and the conclusion of the agreed final account.

Supplier of major equipment:
On a commercial project, little equipment research would be carried out, as few firms would wish to install untried plant. It is therefore likely that the major items of engineering equipment will be selected by the design team on the basis of experience, inspection of related installations and possibly by pre-tendering, where there is available a choice of suitable equipment. The major suppliers must be brought under the umbrella of the design team, so that their individual and specialised requirements and programmes may be accurately established and incorporated into the overall scheme.

Contractors:
There is a prevailing philosophy in some quarters that the designers design and the contractors construct and the twain shall never meet. On a sophisticated contract which involves much engineering equipment and specialised services, such an attitude is not acceptable. The contractors, whether they are builders or services contractors, should be selected on the basis of known competence and experience for similar work, as well as on a willingness to contribute their knowledge to the general good.

However a design team is constituted, it is most essential that clear lines of leadership and responsibility are established, so that each member of the team is enabled to contribute as part of a close-knit and well-disciplined team.

CHECK LIST

Ascertain: full details of waste problems.
Decide: basic method of waste recycling.
Consider: all environmental and safety aspects relating to method and site.
Decide: specified/proposed recycling processes.
Decide: feasibility of proposal and cost effectiveness.
Consult: with work force on relevant aspects.
Settle: design brief.
Set: overall programme for project.
Decide: composition and selection of project design and supervisory team.
Implement: design stage to tender invitation.
Obtain: approvals.
Obtain: tenders and report on same.
Appoint: contractor(s)
Supervise: progress of work, standard of workmanship adherence to construction programme.
Inspect and test: major sections of completed works.
Agree: practical completion and prepare defect schedules.
Commission:| complete plant and check commissioning data.
Check: completion of defects remedial work.
Check: operative training scheme and schedules.
Check: approval of completed plant by local authority.
Check: operating and maintenance manuals.
Arrange: routine maintenance and emergency procedures.
Approve: contractor(s) final accounts.

3
Buildings and Structures

3.1 PROTECTION OF EQUIPMENT

Equipment such as incinerators, boilers, turbines, air classifiers, hoggers and electric control panels must be protected from unauthorised interference and the effects of weather. Protection may also be required to inhibit the spread of fire into, or out of, the plant areas. In certain locations, precautions must be taken to exclude dust and dirt infiltration to the equipment. Thus, building enclosures must be designed to suit the specific requirements of a scheme. The designer, most commonly a qualified architect, requires to be briefed as to the following aspects:

Internal areas of the building
These must be designed to suit the intended equipment content. Before finalising the areas and heights, the closest attention must be paid to the spaces necessary around the plant for safe and efficient maintenance procedures.

Access provision
This must be allowed for with regard to the installation and subsequent replacement of equipment. Consideration should be given to the need for lifing beams, knock-out wall panels, platforms and ladders.

Drainage needs
These may involve simple gullies, with or without covers, and/or purpose made blowdown pits, petrol or oil interceptors, sumps, condensation and drainage channels, roof drainage, toilet and washing facilities, etc.

Precautions against the spread of inflammable liquids
The presence of inflammable liquids such as petroleum or fuel oil

may involve special enclosures and bung walls, as well as suitable oil-proof (or other) rendering of the walls to partial or full height.

Weight of equipment

For the location of equipment on floors and/or roofs, corresponding structural designs and facilities for lifting the equipment should be produced. Design of roof and weathering is crucial.

Bases for plant

Special provision may be necessary within the base constructions to minimise noise, vibration and heat transmission. Pits may be required for settlement or sediment purposes.

Gas meter room

This will require ventilation to a specified standard. If a gas booster set is necessary, anti-vibration and sound proof enclosure should be considered.

Electrical requirements

Intake and switch rooms are generally required. There may be associated cable entry pits and service duct requirements. Will the facility of stand-by emergency generation be required? If so, to what extent? Is main electricity available for all requirements or will private generating plant be required? Is the supply required at high voltage, low voltage etc?

Communications

These may include telephones, paging, music and loudspeaker facilities, some of which will require builders-work provisions

Ventilation

Natural ventilation: are there to be opening windows, air supply and/or extract louvres? Mechanical ventilation: particulars of structural and other openings through walls and roofs must be known, so that the openings may be formed during construction and be correctly trimmed. The forming of holes (small) and openings (large) *after* construction is a troublesome and costly exercise.

Air conditioning/cooling

This may be required to maintain the comfort of personnel or the dissipation of heat gains which cannot be achieved without cooling of the air.

Water services

Water services are likely to be necessary, involving the provision of water meter and stopcock facilities with associated pits and ducts. Many localities require substantial water storage capacity to be provided on site particularly where there is a sprinkler installation. Ascertain requirements and provide space and structural strength for tanks and supports. Where the water storage needs are very large, say above 20,000 gal (90,900 l), consider tile-lined underground storage tankage (see plates 3 and 4).

Explosion risks

Relief doors may be called for.

Duct and pipe services

It is preferable to pre-plan all major holes for the ducts and pipes which fit between the plant area and the other parts of the complex. This is particularly important where structural concrete walls are employed and openings cannot be provided without much difficulty after construction.

Traffic approach

Establish route for fire-engines to plant area. Ensure that adequate design slab and surface accordingly. Decide whether manholes should be heavy duty traffic-bearing or otherwise.

Fire-engines

Extablish route for fire-engines to plant area. Ensure that adequate turning circle is provided for fire-engines.

Pre-mixed-foam, etc

If pre-mixed foam, Halon gas or similar installations are required, allocate space and enclosures for the cylinders and associated equipment.

Sprinkler protection

There is a likelihood of sprinkler protection being required in certain areas of the plant/offices/car park areas of the complex. Consult with insurance company and local authority concerning the extent of the required cover; this will depend upon their assessment of the fire hazard.

A sprinkler plant may be of the 'dry' or 'wet' type. The dry sprinkler installation incorporates an air compressor by means of which the pipe installation is filled with air under pressure. In the wet system, the whole sprinkler system is, at all times, full of water. The dry system is required in applications where there is a risk of freezing of the sprinkler pipes: it is usual in climates where there are warm seasons, followed by frost conditions, to maintain the sprinkler system dry only during the season of frost, changing over from wet to dry at a pre-determined time each year, and, similarly, from dry to wet.

Plate 6 shows a typical sprinkler installation. The sprinkler valve chamber must be located so that it is accessible to the fire-fighters at all times, with direct access off the highway.

Drenchers may be required for certain high-risk areas. A fully labelled chart, showing the location of all the sprinklers, is required and must be displayed prominently.

In the UK and in some other countries, the sprinkler system has to be fed either off adequate water storage available at the site or be connected off two separate incoming water mains. The specific requirements will depend on the degree of hazard to be protected. Where site water storage is required, one must be prepared for major expense and space allocation.

Sundry fire-fighting provisions

Specifications must be made as to the required types of hydraulic hose reels and their location. These hose reels will be required for first-aid fire-fighting before the fire brigade arrives at the premises. The reels are bulky and must be designed to fit (and blend) into the building.

The type and location of water hydrants is a further consideration. These will be located outside the buildings and will provide water supply connections for the fire-fighters. The use of wet fire-fighting methods is not suitable in certain areas such as in rooms housing electronic equipment, electrical switchgear, computers, etc. Smoke or heat detectors may be provided in such areas to raise the alarm when dangerous conditions arise or to activate automatic fire-fighting equipment. Such detection systems usually incorporate central visual display panels or consoles for quick identification of the danger area. See plate 5.

Hand-held portable fire-fighting appliances, usually of the foam type, will be required in locations specified by the fire-fighters. Water buckets and sand buckets will be placed in appropriate positions.

Fire-fighting risers

These are likely to be required in the stair wells of tall buildings. The (dry) riser will have a connection at the landing level of each storey fitted with a padlocked cap for eventual connection by the fire-fighters in the event of a major fire. Such a riser (or risers) considerably simplifies fire-fighting, as the fire brigade will then simply connect their water supply to the bottom inlet of the riser and deal with the fire-fighting on the affected floor off the branch connection.

Fire alarms
An appropriate arrangement of fire alarm fittings and electric wiring will be required. These should be of a scope suitable to the hazard being protected and the use and occupation of the building.

Emergency lighting
Arrangements of emergency lighting will be necessary to mark exit and escape routes, fire doors, etc. Such a system may consist of a centralised battery-charged installation; alternatively, self-contained rechargeable battery lights are used.

Maintenance areas
Are on-site maintenance facilities, such as workshop, tool racks, spares store, etc required? For large and complex recycling plants such provision is essential.

Staff facilities
What requirements are there for toilets, washhand basins, showers, changing rooms, drying rooms, etc?

Mechanical handling
Establish requirements for cranes, conveyors, etc; allocate space and design supports and foundations.

Chimney
Decide on size and method of construction (see also chapter 11). If the chimney is of metal construction, then many local authorities will insist on an annual inspection and licensing arrangements — provision must be made to allow for this. Design foundations. If the chimney is to be guyed, locate guy support positions.

Lightning protection
Requirements for lightning protection must be ascertained. If necessary, it may be suitable to locate the lightning conductor on The chimney, terminating above chimney terminal. Provide base pit for conductor.

Security

Establish the need for site or plant building enclosure and decide on extent and type. Adequate external security lighting systems must be available. See plates 8 and 11.

Illumination and lighting

Is natural light required in the plant area? Lighting levels should be adequate to permit safe operations within the plant areas — a minimum of 300 lux is recommended for plant areas. Is floodlighting required external to the building for operational, safety or anti-vandalism reasons? Are facilities for hand-held inspection lamps required and, if so, should these be operated at low voltage?

Special requirements for uncommon processes

Check whether any such requirements exist and obtain details.

Battery driven vehicles

Are such to be provided? If so, then charging areas must be allocated, with adequate access for the type of machinery to be employed

Gas turbines

Are these required for waste heat recovery or other purposes?

Co-ordination

The architect has to work closely with the consulting engineers and with the other members of the team to produce and execute a fully detailed brief.

Major structures

Major structures may be required for the following plant and machinery: chimney; water tank towers; storage silos and supports; filter chambers and supports; gas washing plants and supports; crane gantries; lifting beams or frames; access gantries for overhead lights; platforms and gangways; fuel stores and delivery shutes; weighbridge; special structures for uncommon applications.

Plates 7, 9 and 10 show external views of three different buildings.

Plate 12 shows a multiple-boiler installation and plates 13 and 14 are examples of access and support structures.

CHECK LIST

Check: required building enclosures for plant; required internal areas; access provision; drainage needs precautions against spread of inflammable liquids; weight of roof or floor mounted equipment; required plant bases; requirements of public utility companies; availability of adequate electric supplies; requirement for private or stand-by generation; availability of mains gas services; requirement for gas (calor or methane) storage; communications; ventilation requirement (natural or mechanical?); air-conditioning requirement (personnel comfort or process requirements?); provision for explosion relief; duct and piped services; traffic approaches; access for fire-engines; requirement for particular methods of fire-fighting and protection; specification for maintenance and staff facilities; provision for mechanical handling equipment; chimney provision; lightning protection; site and building security; illumination and lighting requirements; battery driven vehicle charging booths; major structures external to buildings.

4
Recovery of Waste Materials

4.1 PAPER RECOVERY

In most locations, paper is an abundant and potentially valuable constituent of household waste: there is therefore a strong incentive for its recovery.

Most existing paper fibre recovery systems are based in part on air classification, to provide a paper-rich concentrate for further upgrading (see chapter 5 for a description of this method). Development work is in progress on methods of separating plastics film from paper, which are less costly in terms of capital equipment and energy consumption than existing methods, and on the selective detection and removal of specific constituents from a paper-rich concentrate.

4.2 PLASTICS RECOVERY

The recovery of paper fibre will normally result in the production of a by-product which is rich in plastics film. In some countries, plastic bottles are a significant constituent of household wastes; these can also be separated as a product.

The size and nature of the potential market for plastics products recovered from household wastes varies considerably between different countries. In some areas, it might be possible to sell a mixed plastic product, while in others, segregation of polymer types will be necessary. Similarly, requirements for reclaimed polymer for use in moulding or film blowing applications will vary.

Several processes are available for the manufacture of products from mixed waste polymer, though there is scope for further development work on the feedstock formulations required for specific end-products and on the effect of additives on product quality.

Various contaminants inhibit the use of reclaimed polymer in standard moulding or film blowing equipment. There exists the possibility of developing new chemical additives to counteract the degradation of secondary polymers during moulding.

A firm in the Netherlands offers a recycling process whereby any old plastic, clean or dirty, can be mixed with a small proportion of waste paper, chopped into small shreds, fed into an extruder, and emerges as a round or square post of any specified diameter — or length — of up to 4m for use as fencing, shore reinforcement, frontage panelling etc.

On the farm, the posts can be used for fencing (no insulators are required for electrified barriers since the posts themselves act as insulators) and they do not rot, have no knots or splinters, are resistant to acids, salts, strong winds, water and frost. They are impervious to attack by pileworm or insects, too, and are said to have a virtually unlimited lifespan.

Posts available at the present time are dark to black in colour, weighing between 700 and 800 kg per m³: like wood, they can be nailed, drilled, sawn and planed.

4.3 ENERGY RECOVERY

High on the present list of priorities is energy conservation relating to the energy or fuel content of the waste. Development work is progressing on the use of both shredded and densified waste-derived fuels.

Experience in the UK suggests that, for industrial use, a densified fuel product is most likely to have adequate storage and handling characteristics, pointing towards the continuous mass production of fuel pellets or briquettes. Methods of handling such densified waste-derived fuel are needed and extended firing trials are in progress to determine the effect of firing waste-derived fuel on corrosion, fouling of boiler tubes and atmospheric emissions. Consideration is being given to the possible use of additives to the fuel from the point of view of increasing its calorific value, prolonging its storage life, reducing its susceptibility to water and inhibiting biological activity.

4.4 WASTE-DERIVED FUEL

There is a close relationship between the extraction of waste-derived fuel and paper fibre from waste because air classification generally forms the basis for separation of a preliminary concentrate. The principles involved in the design of air classification systems apply equally to the separation of either type of product. In the case of fuel, however, removal of plastics is unnecessary, unless a very high PVC content is present which would result in undesirably high levels of chlorine in the fuel. Although care is need in air classifier design for fuel production, the problems are less severe than those associated with fibre recovery.

The biggest problems arise in the conversion of the light combustible fraction from an air classifier into a marketable fuel product which is capable of use in existing boiler installations with minimum modification of existing plant, minimum adverse effect in terms of boiler corrosion and atmospheric emissions and maximum energy conversion efficiency.

In the use of waste-derived fuel, an area of particular concern to the plant operator would be the slagging or clinkering potential of the ash. Table 4.1 lists the fusion temperatures of the residues and non-combustible constituents commonly found in the ash from incinerated solid wastes. With the exception of the glass fraction, the remaining components have ash fusion values within the range commonly encountered with most coals.

A study of temperatures in table 4.1 highlights the important requirement that the fuel should not be contaminated by glass which has a low fusion temperature. Early operating experience in the USA showed that hammer milling of the incoming refuse tended to produce fine glass particles, which were carried over into the air classifier light products, with subsequent operational difficulties (such as blockage of the air spaces between the furnace grate bars by molten glass) when burning this fuel.

Waste-derived fuels differ significantly from coal so that maximum combustion efficiency will not be achieved by burning this in equipment designed to burn coal. There is thus a need for studies of the combustion data for the design of suitable combustion equipment or for the modification of existing industrial burners. For ease of transport, storage and handling, a densified fuel product may be preferred by industrial users, but much research and development is required to provide and specify suitable techniques for the production and use of pelletised or briquetted waste-derived fuel.

4.5 FERROUS METAL RECOVERY

For many years, magnetic separators have been employed for extracting the ferrous content from household waste. The recovery efficiency of such systems has generally been low; often no higher than 25 per cent from raw waste and 50 per cent from pulverised

apply equally to the separation of all types of product. In the case of their however, removal of plastics is unnecessary, unless a very high PVC concentration, which would result in undesirably high levels of chlorine, is obtained. Although some ferrous plastics design has had problems... several... associated with them.

The biggest problems arise in the conversion of the light combustible fraction from an old classifier into a marketable fuel product which is either... some of the installations with additional modifications... a quantitative use effect in terms of boiler corrosion and atmospheric emissions and maximum energy conversion efficiency.

In the use of waste... a particularly concern to the plant operator... the erosive potential of the ash. Table 4.1 lists the fusion temperatures of the residues and some combustible constituents commonly found in the ash from incinerated solid... discharge... of the glass fraction. The remaining combustible constituents... in the range commonly encountered with most coals.

A study of temperatures in table 4.1 highlights the important requirement that low fuels should not be contaminated by glass which has a low fusion temperature... pilot scale apparatus in the USA showed... combustion of incoming refuse tended to produce... glass particles, which were carried over into the air classifier light products, with subsequent operational difficulties such as... in the... furnace grate bars by molten glass, inhibiting the heat transfer.

Waste-derived fuels differ significantly from coal so that maximum combustion efficiency will not be achieved if burning this in equipment designed to burn coal. There is therefore a need for studies of the combustion data for the design of suitable combustion equipment for the modification of existing industrial boilers... of transport, storage and handling, a densified fuel product to be preferred by industry users, but which research and development is required to provide a properly serviceable technology... and use of prepared or prepared waste...

FERROUS METAL RECOVERY

For many years, magnetic separation has been employed for extracting the ferrous content from household waste. The recovery efficiency of such systems has generally been low; often no higher than 25 per cent from raw waste and 30 per cent from pulverised

TABLE 4.1 ASH FUSION TEMPERATURES

Constituent	Initial deformation		Softening		Fluid	
	°C	°F	°C	°F	°C	°F
Clear glass	805	1481	918	1684	1005	1841
Brown glass	882	1620	949	1740	1138	2080
Green glass	893	1640	982	1800	1138	2080
Ash from: mixed waste	1105	2021	1172	2142	1205	2201
cardboard	1127	2060	1183	2161	1227	2241
paper	1183	2161	1261	2302	1361	2482
textiles	1116	2040	1194	2181	1227	2241
plastics, rubber, leather	1150	2102	1216	2221	1261	2302
bones and shells	1539	2802	1539	2802	1539	2802
coal	1140	2084	1200	2192	1330	2426

waste. Shredding or sizing, as carried out in a waste sorting plant, enables a uniform feed with low depth of burden to be presented to the magnetic separator. Several effective magnetic extraction

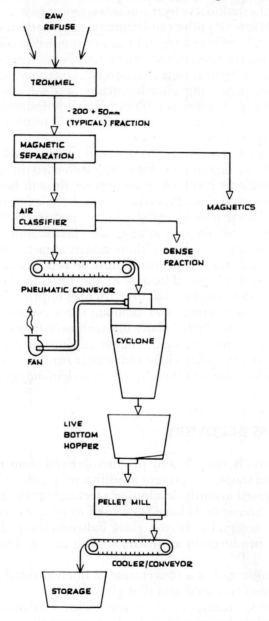

4.1   *Simplified flow-sheet for the production of refuse-derived fuel pellets*

systems have been developed, and 80 to 90 per cent recovery of ferrous metal should be attainable.

The most popular type of separator is the Overband, which consists of a stationary electro-magnet, around which a moving belt is fitted. Magnetic pulleys and drums are also used in some systems, but normally only as a second stage to remove small quantities of ferrous material from other concentrates, or to increase the overall efficiency of ferrous metal recovery. Overband separators are capable of producing effective magnetic field intensities across operating gaps as great as 1000 mm, but it is desirable to minimise the belt-to-belt distance because of the cost in relation to weight and power requirements.

Markets for recovered ferrous metal from household waste are restricted by contaminants associated with used tin cans. There are severe problems involved in recovering tin and high grade steel scrap from used cans. Procedures have been explored, but so far none has been proved to be wholly successful. Shredding will be achieved by water washing, air classification of shredded material, attrition (with or without added abrasive) or burning. In the latter case, the temperature must be kept below about 300°C (572° F) to minimise diffusion of the tin into the iron lattice. Cryogenic fragmentation has been tried, to improve size reduction, increase seam opening and facilitate the separation of dirt and aluminium from the tin-plate, but with only limited success.

Modern can-making technology is moving into the manufacture of two-piece cans, which have only one seam. The preparation task for detinning cans will therefore be less demanding in the future.

4.6 GLASS RECOVERY

Whilst glass is not a major product derived from the sorting of household waste, it is present in sufficient quantity to justify much effort devoted towards developing a technology for its recovery. In general, two methods have been used to produce a glass product which is acceptable to the glass industry from glass-rich concentrates produced in a primary sorting circuit. These are:

Froth flotation: giving a concentrate of finely divided glass which is a mixture of coloured and flint glass.
Optical sorting: transparency sorting yields a mixture of coloured and flint glass, but by adding a colour sorting stage the product can be separated into flint, green and amber fractions.

The nature of the feed to the glass recovery plant depends upon both the composition of the household waste being treated and the type of primary sorting circuit employed. The size range of the material is particularly important in determining the choice of glass recovery method to be adopted. By way of example, the application of the WSL sorting process to UK waste may be considered (see chapter 5). A typical composition of the feedstock to the glass recovery plant would be:

	Dry weight %
Glass	60
Plastics	2
Ferrous metal	1
Non-ferrous metal	2
Putrescible	2
Ceramics, brick, stone, etc	32
Combustible	1
	100

The size range of this material is +20 to −70 mm. Tests have shown that it is possible to use either froth flotation or optical sorting to extract a high-grade glass product.

4.7 NON-FERROUS METALS RECOVERY

Preliminary sorting of the waste involving removal of paper, organics and ferrous metals generally produces a heavy concentrate containing non-magnetic metals, such as aluminium (usually the major constituent), copper and its alloys, stainless steel, die-cast materials and very low concentrations of precious metals. Most of the work on extracting individual non-ferrous metals has concentrated on aluminium. The greatest degree of interest has been shown in the USA because of the high concentration of aluminium beverage cans in the waste.

Separation techniques currently being tested make use of either the density or the conductivity of the non-ferrous metals compared with that of the contaminant, namely glass, stones, organics, rubber, leather, etc. The simplest system (technically) makes use of the density differences in a standard mineral jig. Non-ferrous concentrate is fed into a pulsed wet jig in which the various materials stratify into separate layers. Appropriately placed splitters float off organics, remove glass and aluminium foil and the heaviest fraction, which comprises the non-ferrous metals, collects at the base of the jig. Water is continuously recycled, but make-up water is required to replace that lost with the products. Experimenters have indicated that they expect some scale-up problems in the use of higher throughput machines and these may preclude their use at large scale or involve extensive water treatment.

Other wet systems which have been investigated and could be applied to heavy non-ferrous separation are rising-current, heavy media and magnetic fluid systems. The rising-current principle employs the differences in the falling velocity of particles in a liquid, usually water, in which an effective density greater than that of still water is created. The sink fraction consists of metals and glass, which would have to be further processed for complete separation.

Heavy media separation relies on a sink-float separation in a suspension of a finely ground mineral (eg ferrosilicon, magnetite) in water. The density of the liquid suspension is controlled by the amount of mineral present. Heavy media processing may follow a rising-current separator and multiple passes at different densities can be used to separate out a desired product. Magnetic fluid separation is a similar technique, but in this case, the fluid is a colloidal suspension of magnetic material (usually magnetite) in water kerosene. The apparent density of the fluid is adjusted by control of a magnetic field and this permits a very wide range of densities to be obtained. Both methods have given rise to problems in content of the fluid densities and subsequent product cleaning, and of course the separated products are wet which may reduce their value or necessitate a drying stage.

In general, dry methods of separation based upon the electrical properties of the metals have proved to be more popular than wet methods. Eddy current separators have attracted the most attention, particularly in the USA. In such an arrangement, the waste stream containing non-magnetic metals passes through a magnetic field on a conveyor. This causes eddy currents to be generated in the metal particles. By making the magnetic field vary as a function of time, the eddy currents interact with it to produce a force which levitates the metal particles and carries them along in the direction of the magnetic wave. The effect can be used to deflect the metals from the conveyor; suitably placed splitters can then provide a concentrate of the desired product.

The concentration of non-ferrous metals in European household waste is probably not high enough to merit extensive costly development work, but this may not apply to the USA because of the widespread use of aluminium cans there.

4.8 USE OF RECYCLED PLASTICS

A plastics concentrate is an inevitable by-product of paper fibre recovery from an air classifier light fraction. (With air classification, the term 'fraction' is employed to specify the position within the overall weight of the particular classifier output present.) Several techniques have been developed in Europe, Japan and the USA to use mixed plastics waste directly for the production of finished articles. In general, polyolefins are preferred for these processes, but proportions of other thermoplastics are acceptable and some thermosets and contrary materials are permissible. In some cases, materials such as paper wastes and sawdust are intentionally added to the plastics to improve properties. The materials produced by such methods are in most respects inferior to virgin plastics in their physical properties and the properties of products from any one process, or even any one machine, will vary as the nature of the wastes used varies. For this reason, they are suitable only for non-critical applications and for those where the relative weakness of the material can be compensated for by the use of thick sections.

Alternatively, one can separate mixed plastics into individual polymers and clean them, so that they can be re-used in conventional moulding or film blowing applications. Processes have been devised to achieve this.

It is not known, however, whether such techniques could be applied to the plastics fraction of household wastes to recover polymer of sufficiently high quality to be acceptable to the plastics conversion industry.

4.9 ORGANIC RESIDUE

The organic portion of the waste becomes concentrated as other more valuable consituents are extracted. The main outlets for an organic residue (apart from landfilling) are animal feed production, either by direct sterilisation of the organic materials or by production of single cell protein, composting, or methane generation by anaerobic digestion.

4.10 COMPOSTING

The principle of this method is to stabilise organic waste by exploiting the action of the accompanying micro-organisms.

Composting is basically an aerobic-thermophilic process. Following stabilisation, the material presents organoleptic features similar to those of humus, and the mineral salt content and physical nature make it utilisable as a fertiliser.

The stabilised material or compost prevents erosion of the soil by water and wind and increases the permeability of the ground. From the chemical viewpoint, the part played by oligo and nutritive elements is still to be appraised.

The composting process is associated with a reduction in the initial bacterial complement as a result of the chemicophysical transformation and of the thermal action consequent on the heat that develops during the composting process.

The transformation process can be carried out either:

naturally: the material to be composted is piled up in the open and is turned over periodically with a power shovel;
artificially: a choice of techniques, generally patented, which involve homogenisation and mixing of the material in rotating cylinders (rotary fermenters) and subsequent maturation in piles on the threshing floor.

CHECK LIST

Note methods of: paper recovery; plastics recovery; use of recycled plastics; production of waste-derived fuel; ferrous metal recovery; non-ferrous metal recovery; glass recovery; organic residue and its use; composting and its use.
Check: carefully that the waste-derived fuel is not contaminated with glass.
Note: the adverse effect on the operation of boilers and furnaces of using glass-contaminated fuel due to the low fusion temperature of glass.
Monitor: progress in the research and development of improved waste-derived fuel pellets and briquettes.

REFERENCE

Raw materials, pp 4-26, issued by the Commission of the European Communities, January, 1979.

5
Separation and Recycling of Waste

5.1 PRINCIPLES

Many of the constituents of household refuse differ from one another quite markedly in size. Thus, most of the dirt, dust and ashes in refuse will pass easily through an aperture of 13 mm; most of the kitchen wastes will pass through a 50 mm aperture; most of the tin cans and bottles (together with much of the paper) will fall through a 200 mm aperture. These differences in size can be exploited to bring about a partial separation of refuse into its constituents. Thus, in the experimental pilot plant erected at Warren Spring Laboratories, England, to investigate such possibilities, a large rotary screen fitted with punched plates having apertures of 13, 50 and 200 mm forms an important part of several possible flowsheets. See fig 5.1 for a typical flow-sheet.

5.2 SEPARATION

Before the refuse can be sized, it has to be discharged from the paper or plastic sacks used by many of the local authorities. The tumbling action in the rotary screen helps to empty the sacks, particularly, after they have been torn open by being passed through a screw compactor fitted with suitable knives. The fine fraction (−13 mm) separated by the rotary screen consists mainly of dust, dirt and ashes, and is discarded without further treatment. Its elimination at this early stage in the process reduces dust collection and effluent treatment problems in subsequent stages.

The medium-sized material separated by the rotary screen (−50 + 13 mm) contains not only much of the putrescible material in the refuse (such as food wastes), but also a significant proportion of

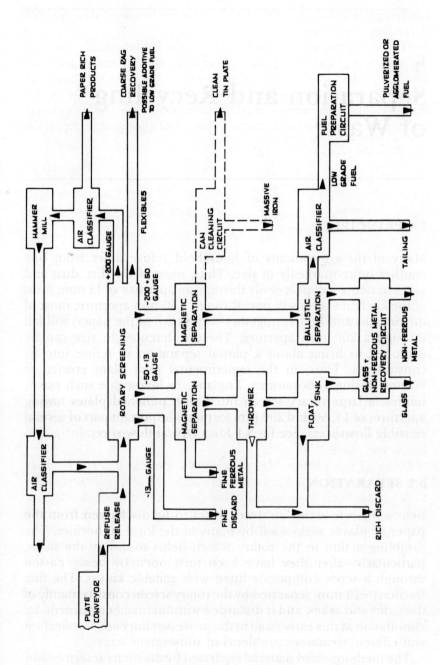

5.1   *Typical flow-sheet of mechanical refuse sorting plant process*

broken glass and other relatively dense materials, including a small percentage of metal.

After the ferrous metal has been recovered magnetically, most of the putrescences are eliminated using a thrower separator, a device originally developed at Warren Spring for processing shredded car scrap. It incorporates a high-speed conveyor which projects the mixture of putrescences — glass, etc — against a suitably orientated slider-plate. Dense objects, such as pieces of glass and metal, slide

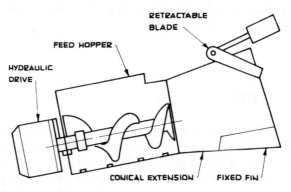

5.2 *Diagrammatic section through a screw compactor employed as a liberating device*

across the plate relatively easily, whereas the less-dense, often moist, putrescibles and other light materials, tend to come to rest on the plate soon after projection and fall into the reject skip located below the plate.

Some of the putrescibles consist of spherical objects, such as Brussels sprouts, small potatoes, etc which tend to roll across the slider-plate, thereby contaminating the dense, glass-rich fraction. Such contaminants are eliminated by floating them away from the glass, metal, etc in a tank full of brine.

The glass and metal in the sink fraction can be separated by exploiting the brittleness of the glass and the malleability of the metal. When the mixture is crushed, the glass tends to break into smaller fragments than the metal, which can then be collected by sizing. Finally, a pure mixed-glass concentrate can be produced by froth flotation — a process already widely used to purify some glass sands prior to their use by the glass industry.

After passing under a magnet to remove ferrous material many of the non-magnetic, dense objects in the coarse size material which have been separated by a rotary screen (−200+50mm) (including the glass bottles) are further separated by taking advantage of the different trajectories of the various components as they are discharged from the relatively high-speed conveyor. A rotating drum is used as a self-cleaning splitter to separate the more dense items like the bottles from the less-dense items with a relatively short stopping distance, such as paper and plastic film. The dense fraction can then be combined with the sink product from the brine tank to recover the metal and glass.

The light fraction from the drum, consisting largely of paper, board and plastic is still contaminated with shoes, plastic bottles, wet newspaper and coarse food wastes, etc. These are separated from most of the paper and plastic film in the horizontal air classifier.

5.3 AIR CLASSIFIER

Basically, this consists of a blower, a rotating drum fitted with an internal helix and a large disengagement chamber, see 5.3 and Plate 15. A current of air is directed along the drum and the sized feed is allowed to fall through the air steam, so that any paper and plastic in the mixture are carried along the drum and into the disengagement chamber. The dense objects fall through the air stream and are conveyed to the opposite end of the drum by the internal helix. Because the majority of the 'fines' have been eliminated from the feed to the separator earlier in the circuit, it is considered that a minimum of gas cleaning will be required before the air from the disengagement chamber can be discharged into the atmosphere. Various types of air classifiers are available, all of which have the object of efficient material separation by air stream.

5.4 SCREENING

An additional fraction produced by the rotary screen at the beginning of the process is made up of all the material larger than 200 mm in size. Earlier in the development of the Warren Spring process, it was found that the largest apertures tended to become blocked by coarse oversize material. Indeed, operation of the screen had to be curtailed within a few minutes of start-up in order to clear these apertures. This problem was overcome by suspending a cable through the screen on to which coarse items of clothing, etc (which plugged the apertures) were caught and pulled free as the screen continued to rotate. Since this modification was carried out, it has not been necessary to clean the screen, except to periodically remove lengths of wool, rubber, etc wound around its exterior.

5.5 HAMMER MILL

The material larger than 200 mm is passed through a hammer mill to reduce it in size and is then returned to the feed end of the rotating screen, eventually to find its way through the streams for separation as already described. Thus, a circulating load is built up between the hammer mill and the rotary screen. It was found that much of this circulating load consists of relatively clean paper, which can be deflected from the conveyor feeding the hammer mill by a gentle air stream.

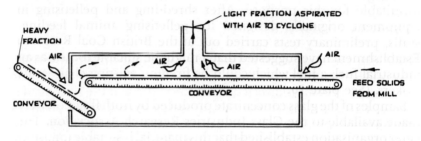

HORIZONTAL AIR CLASSIFIER

5.3   Principle of the Enadimsa horizontal air classifier

5.6 FLOW-SHEET

Considered as a whole, the process shown on fig **5.1** demonstrates how the Warren Spring process has been designed to keep power consumption to a minimum. For example, only a small proportion of the feed is pulverised in a hammer mill, which is a particularly energy-intensive unit operation. Air classification is carried out on a relatively coarse, but narrow, size range of feed, thereby maximising the efficiency and minimising gas cleaning requirements. Wherever possible, an investment of energy required for one purpose (eg maximising the efficiency with which ferrous material is removed) has also been used to bring about a second separation (eg ballistic separation). Many of the unit operations employed are already well-established and readily available; for example, rotary screens and magnetic separators have been used for many years for processing refuse. The staff at Warren Spring have extended the range of such equipment and have demonstrated the conditions under which it can be used most efficiently.

5.7 PRODUCTS OF RECYCLING

Table 5.1 describes some of the products from the Warren Spring process. Many of these materials have been submitted to a number of potential users for assessment. Of the two paper-rich fractions, at least one company considered the material separated from the hammer mill feed to be suitable for use in boardmaking operations. The mixture of paper and plastic film recovered from the disengagement chamber was, however, generally deemed to be unsuitable for this purpose. After shredding and pelletising in equipment originally designed for pelletising animal feeding-stuffs, preliminary tests carried out at the British Coal Research Establishment have suggested that it might be suitable for use as an industrial fuel; a fuel which could be fired on existing chain-grate stokers. (See plate 16.)

Samples of the glass concentrate produced by froth flotation were made available to the Glass Industries Research Association. The latter organisation established that this material is suitable for use in the manufacture of green bottle glass.

The ferrous concentrate separated from the refuse is suitable for use directly in the iron foundry industry.

Another possibility, investigated at Warren Spring, is to separate the tin cans from the mixed ferrous concentrate, shred them and then clean them by attrition. The clean tin-plate produced in this way was submitted to a company which already separates tin electrolytically from clean tin-plate scrapped, for example, during the manufacture of tin cans. The residue left after the tin has been recovered is suitable for re-use by the steel industry. The company's technical staff commented favourably on the tin-plate recovered from refuse and cleaned at Warren Spring Laboratory. Work is continuing on the non-ferrous metal fraction separated by selective comminution; aluminium appears to be the main constituent in this mixture.

5.8 FUTURE PROSPECTS

Experiments are being carried out at Warren Spring on the various reject fractions to assess the possibility of obtaining some additional return. Thus, the possibility is being investigated of generating methane by anaerobic digestion of the putrescible material–food and vegetable waste. Alternatively, this material might be used to increase the humus content, in eg colliery spoil heaps, to assist in their revegetation. The fine fraction may find use as a top cover for waste tips.

TABLE 5.1 PRODUCTS FROM EXTENDED WASTE SORTING CIRCUIT

Product	Typical/ approximate weight as percentage of feed	Description	Comments
Materials capable of immediate utilisation			
Combustibles	30	Mainly paper, plastic film and textiles	Possible use as supplementary fuel in existing solid-fuel-fired boilers? After additional processing, might eventually prove suitable for use as feedstock to board-making operations
Paper-rich fraction	10	Mainly (85%) paper but plastic film, textiles, feathers and fine dust also present	Can be produced in coarse or shredded forms by separation before or after pulverisation. Additional processing required before acceptable for use in boardmaking. (Some marginal improvement in quality of shredded product possible by additional screening)
Tin-plate	5	Mainly (95%) discarded tin cans with adhering labels, lacquer linings and traces of original contents	Commercially acceptable to iron founders. Could be shredded and subjected to additional cleaning producing material acceptable for detinning for the recovery of tin metal and steel

'Massive iron'	1	Discarded kitchen utensils, household goods, car components etc.	Commercially acceptable as low-grade scrap iron
Non-ferrous metal concentrate	1 •	Mainly aluminium but zinc and copper also present	Recovery and cleaning circuits under development. Insufficient material available to date for reliable analysis or assessment
Glass-rich fraction	6	Overwhelming preponderance of white glass but significant proportions of amber and green glass also present	Flotation concentrate — 16 BS mesh + 100 BS mesh. Suitable for use in the manufacture of green bottle glass. Possibility that flotation tailings might be used as sand extender in non-critical building applications

Materials which might be utilised after development of a suitable processing technique

| Putrescible-rich fraction | 20 | Vegetable and animal food wastes, some wood, plastic, paper and glass | Might eventually be used as feedstock for methane generation by anaerobic digestion, or for production of single cell protein suitable for incorporation in animal feedstocks |

Material unlikely to be utilised

| −13mm discard | 15 | Fine dust, dirt and grit | Possibly useful as fill |
| Process rejects | Balance | | |

CHECK LIST

Check: products which may be separated from the available household (or other type) of waste.

Check: the economics of such separation.

Carry out: market research to establish what markets exist within the area of the plant location for the marketing of all, or some, of these products.

Evaluate: the cost of transport and handling to establish customers total economic cost.

Decide: whether to subsidise the sales of recycled products and, if so, at what level.

Note: that various investigations are progressing into possibilities of separation and recycling. Check into the situation current at time of project decisions.

Establish: flow-sheet and plant arrangements to achieve the operational objectives.

REFERENCE

The New Prospectors, Warren Spring Laboratory, Department of Industry, HM Stationery Office, 1976.

6
Case Histories of Recycling Applications

6.1 INTRODUCTION

Many different types and arrangements of waste recycling plants and processes are known and in operation. Almost daily, the technical and popular press describe further applications of these developing techniques of recycling and there is clearly scope for much wider conservation of materials by recycling methods.

This chapter describes a number of interesting case histories, taken from a broad spectrum, with the object of illustrating current achievements in this field.

6.2. FISH-FARMS AND HORTICULTURE

Source and use of low-grade heat
Power stations generating only electricity reject about 70 per cent of the energy input to the boilers to the condenser water-cooling towers. (Electricity is generated by turbines which are steam-driven, taking in steam at the high boiler pressure and discarding it to the cooling towers at a low pressure — the function of the cooling tower is to condense the low pressure steam into warm water, which is then fed back into the boilers.)

The outlet temperature from the condensers varies, taken over a typical year, within the range of about 15 to 35°C (51 to 95°F). It is thus very low-grade heat at a temperature of about 15 to 20°C (27 to 36°F) above the ambient air temperature; water at such a low temperature cannot be used directly for conventional heating purposes, such as district heating or hot water supply.

It has been established that water at the condenser discharge temperature can be used in fish-farming and in horticulture. Since it would seldom be economic to convey the warm water over long distances, the fish-farms and/or horticultural establishments (such as the tomato grower) require to be located close to the power stations.

In the UK Central Electricity Generating Stations are state owned. Rather than diversify into the fish-farming or horticultural business, the CEGB is currently developing joint ventures with private enterprise for the exploitation of the low-grade heat available at the power stations.

For some time, there has been much discussion concerning the operation of district or group heating systems in conjunciton with electricity generating stations as a means of exploiting low-grade waste heat. Although there are several such joint ventures in the UK, the matter essentially remains in the state of preliminary discussion.

Examples of use

At Hinkley Point nuclear power station in Somerset, 'Marine Farms' is farming seed oysters and eels on an independent commercial basis. At Draw coal-fired power station in Yorkshire, the Board, together with Ranks, Hovis, MacDougall, is expanding an eel-farming scheme on a commercial scale. At Wylfa nuclear power station in North Wales, a subsidiary of British Oxygen is undertaking a pilot scheme for raising turbot.

In 1976, the Board, in consultation with the Central Generating Board and the British Ministry of Agriculture, set up three experimental greenhouses at Eggborough coal-fired power station in North Humberside to investigate the possiblity of growing tomatoes and lettuce. As a result of this experience, the Board is now evaluating, with the Express Dairy Foods Group, a large-scale horticultural operation at Drax. A greenhouse covering half an acre has been built there and proving trials with tomatoes will shortly begin.

Follow-up

The authors consider that each and every electricity generating station should closely follow the above, and similar, reports of the successful use of low-grade power station heat. There is an on-going and growing demand for land-bred fish and for horticultural products which can benefit materially from the measure of energy recycling.

6.3 THE ST LOUIS, MISSOURI RESOURCE RECOVERY PROJECT

Background

Energy recovery from municipal waste in the form of steam generated in waste-heat boilers had been proposed numerous times for the St Louis, Missouri area and such installation was seriously considered in the 1940s and 1960s. However, the idea was rejected as impracticable because of the technical operating problems then associated with this type of system.

The basic concept of the present St Louis system was developed in late 1967 during an informal luncheon involving personnel of the Union Electric Company and Horner and Shifrin, Inc, Consulting Engineers, at which a discussion took place concerning the quantity and characteristics of the fuel fired to the utility's facilities and the possibility of utilising densified solid waste as a supplementary fuel. The City of St Louis (the only local agency which maintained control of the collection and disposal of large quantities of solid waste in the metropolitan area) indicated interest in the proposed study and applied for, and received, a partial grant-in-aid from the Environmental Protection Agency to study the process. Horner and Shifrin, Inc, were retained by the City to conduct this investigation in close co-operation with the Union Electric Company. The resulting comprehensive study report concluded that coal-fired boilers are not without operating problems and that these problems would not be significantly increased, if at all, by burning properly prepared refuse as a supplementary fuel.

The operator

The Union Electric Company displayed its interest in the project by offering the use of one, and eventually two, of its major boiler units for full-scale testing of the process, as well as finding the capital expenditures to meet the cost of its portion of the prototype facilities required on its property. The City of St Louis then submitted another application to the Environmental Protection Agency for a grant-in-aid to develop a prototype installation and received approval of this grant on 1 July 1970. Operation of the study facility was initiated during April 1972.

Following these preliminaries, an investor-owned utility in the USA began, for the first time, to burn municipal solid waste as supplementary fuel for the direct production of electric power.

The waste

Solid wastes currently utilised as supplementary fuel in St Louis consist of mixed municipal refuse generated in residential areas. No industrial, commercial, or bulky waste materials are being processed; however, certain selected industrial and commercial wastes may be processed at a later date.

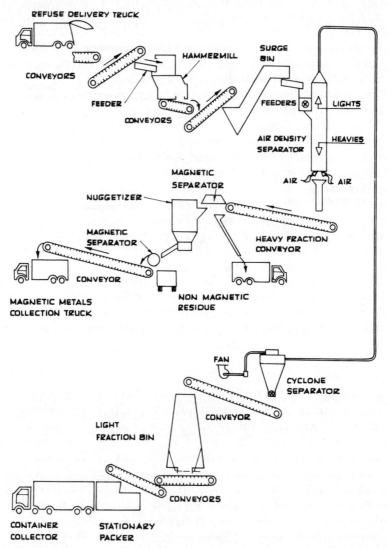

6.1   *St Louis, Missouri (USA) – diagrammatic flow-sheet of mechanical sorting operation*

The plant
The initial refuse preparation occurs at city-operated facilities.

The process

Refuse to be processed is discharged from packer trucks to the floor of the raw refuse receiving building and is then pushed to a receiving conveyor by front-end loaders. From there, the refuse is transferred to an inclined belt conveyor and then to a vibrating conveyor which feeds a hammer mill. This hammer mill is a

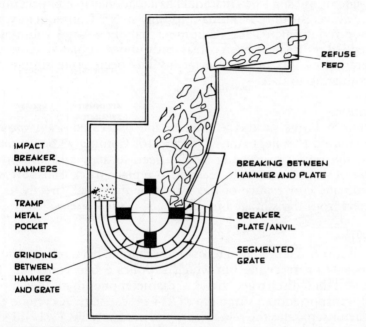

6.2   Arrangement of typical hammer mill as used in mechanical sorting plant

conventional mill with a horizontal shaft, and possesses a hammer circle of approximately 1.52 m and an interior rotor length of about 2 m. Power input to the hammer mill is supplied by a direct-connected, 1250 hp, 900 rpm motor. All refuse entering the hammer mill is reduced to a particle size of less than 38 mm.

The shredded solid waste is transferred by means of a vibrating conveyor leading to the prepared refuse storage bin. Magnetic metals are recovered from the solid waste stream at the head pulley of the inclined belt conveyor and discharged to trucks for shipment to ferrous metal buyers. The processed refuse is then conveyed from the storage bin to a stationary compactor for loading into self-unloading trucks for transport to the power plant facilities.

This initial preparation process was designed to be as uncomplicated as possible to minimise subsequent operational problems associated with refuse processing. Most of the operating problems

that have occurred during the first several years of refuse preparation
system operation have been of a mechanical nature, and are mainly
due to the peculiarities of milled municipal refuse.

Storage and handling

The storage and handling of milled solid waste has required special
consideration, since this material has a tendency to compact under
its own weight into a laminar, springy mass. Consequently, the
power requirements for equipment handling large volumes of
shredded refuse have been consistently underestimated. However,
operation of this processing facility has been quite simple and
encouraging to date.

Transport

In the St Louis prototype system, the processed solid waste is
transported 18 miles to the Union Electric Company's power plant.
Had the refuse processing facility been located near the power
plant, it would have been feasible to replace truck transport with
pneumatic conveyance of the supplementary fuel directly to the
boilers from the storage bin.

Reception

The transported prepared refuse is discharged from self-unloading
vehicles to a receiving bin which supplies a belt conveyor. The
refuse is then discharged to a .3 m diameter pneumatic feeder pipe
and transported to a surge bin of 244 m³ capacity. A cyclone dust
collector separates the refuse from the transport air. Embedded in
the 12.2 m diameter concrete bin floor slab are four drag chain
conveyors, each of which feeds refuse to its own pneumatic feed
system for transport to one of the four refuse burners. Crude
metering of the refuse feed to the boiler is accomplished by varying
the speeds of the drive ring and conveyor drag chains. The
supplemental fuel is fired independently of the normal boiler fuel.

Burning refuse-derived fuel

The prepared refuse is burned in two 20 year-old tangentially-fired
Combustion Engineering boilers located 213 m from the storage
bin. These boilers have a nominal rating of 125 megawatts each
with a maximum gross output of approximately 142 megawatts.
Although the steam systems of these boilers are not 'modern', the
furnace and burner design is basically the same as the newer units
now being put into service. Four pulverisers each feed a level of four
burners, one in each corner. Between each level of coal burners is
located a pair of gas burners, one over the other. All burners are

tiltable. The furnaces are about 8.5 m by 11.6 m in cross-section, with a total inside height of 30 m.

Precautions
There is some inherent risk in mixing the prepared refuse with coal in the feed system because of the possiblity of spontaneous combustion in the pulverisers and the potential for disrupting the operation of the combustion control system. Therefore, space was provided for the installation of refuse burners by removing one of the gas nozzles in each corner of the furnace. The gas flow required to carry a full load of gas — with four of the 24 nozzles removed — was maintained by increasing the load gas header pressure to about 0.14 bar(g). The four resulting refuse burners are similar to 254 mm Combustion Engineering pulverised coal burners, except that the refuse burner contains no grid work at the burner mouth.

Throughput
Prepared refuse is fired through these burners at a rate equal to 10 to 15 per cent, by heat value, of the full load fuel requirement of the unit. This 10 per cent firing amounts to about 12.5 tons of refuse per hour or 300 tons per day. Since the City collects, processes and delivers refuse to the power plant 5 days per week, no provisions have been made to supply refuse fuel to the power plant on weekends.

Coal or gas firing
The prepared refuse is fired to the boilers at a constant rate; the rate of coal or gas firing may therefore be varied to accommodate fluctuations in the boiler heat requirements. If, for any reason, the boiler is suddenly taken out of service, an electrical interlock immediately stops the refuse feed, whilst the pneumatic blowers continue to function in order to clear the ⸝ipelines of any refuse remaining in them.

Operating experience
Since refuse firing was initiated in April 1972, no discernible adverse effects on the boiler furnace or convection passes have been noticed in use by the technical personnel. No significant effect on the stack discharge has been observed. There has been evidence neither of carry-over of unburned particles into the back passes of the boiler, nor of slagging due to the firing of refuse. The performance of the boilers when firing refuse *and* coal has been identical to the performance of the unit when fired *only* with coal. Data are not currently available regarding long-term corrosion

effects of the refuse on the boiler pressure parts. The low sulphur content of domestic refuse may tend to decrease corrosion potential, whereas the higher chlorine content may have an opposite effect.

All the operational problems which have been experienced to date are associated with the 'heavy' fraction of the prepared refuse stream, ie non-metallic metal, glass, wood, etc. These larger and denser particles have resulted in a milled refuse possessing highly abrasive qualities which has caused excessive transport pipe wear and feed stoppages. Pipe wear has been concentrated at the pipe bends and elbows and appears to be a result of abrasion rather than impact. No significant straight pipe wear has been observed.

Another operational problem associated with the refuse 'heavy' fraction has to do with bottom ash handling capability. Since the firing of refuse was initiated the quantity of bottom ash has approximately doubled; however, no problems have been experienced with regard to handling this increased volume.

Since all the refuse is passed through a hammer mill at the commencement of the process, the authors would be concerned about the likely adverse effect of the low fusion temperature of the ash resulting from refuse with a fair glass content on the boiler grates and fire bars. The ash is likely to fuse and clog the primary air passages, causing overheating of the grates andsubsequent damage.

REFERENCE

J.B Pavioni, J.E. Meer Jnr, D.J. Hagerty, *Handbook of Solid Waste Disposal,* pp 346-56, Van Nostrand Reinhold Co, 1975.

6.4 THE RESOURCE RECOVERY FACILITY AT MONROE COUNTY, NEW YORK, USA

History
The City of Rochester and surrounding communities have depended upon landfilling as the primary means of solid waste disposal. By the late 1960s, several of the landfill sites had been exhausted, while others had been closed for violations of New York State sanitary codes. A 1970 engineering study increased awareness of the growing solid waste problem, predicting that the generation of solid waste in Monroe County would approach 2000 tons per day by the end of the decade. Public dissatisfaction with the continuation of the landfill concept was growing.

A long-range solid waste management programme was initiated to fulfil future disposal needs and ultimately to reduce and/or eliminate the need for landfill sites. Under a study contract entered into between the County and Hercules, Inc, a basic resource recovery system design was formulated and a detailed market analysis was conducted. This confirmed the availability of markets to accept products to be recovered by the system for resource recycling, including ferrous and non-ferrous metals, glass, sand and a refuse-derived fuel which could be used as a supplemental boiler fuel.

Legal framework

The County's commitment to resource recovery was exemplified initially by the Solid Waste Management Law enacted in 1973. This law was contested, but ultimately upheld by the State of New York with enabling legislation in 1975. The new law enacted in late 1977 gives the County the authority to direct the hauling and disposal of all solid waste within the County.

Implementation

A request for proposals for a resource recovery plant was issued by the County in 1974 and a three-phase contract was negotiated with Raytheon Service Company (RSL) in early 1975. Services to be performed under each phase were:

Phase 1 design and construction supervision
Phase 2 start-up
Phase 3 operations.

Phase 1 was sub-divided into two distinct parts: design and construction supervision, so that the market values of output products, as well as the capital cost of construction, could be firmly established by competitive bidding before construction contracts were awarded. The detailed system design was approved by the County in August 1975 and the actual 24-month construction phase was given the go-ahead in 1976.

Capacity

The Monroe County Resource Recovery Facility is capable of receiving and processing municipal, commercial and light industrial waste at a rate of approximately 140 tons per hour — equal to 2000 tons per day (520,000 tons of solid waste per year). Plant operations were planned for a two shift, 16 hour, 5 day per week basis. A daily third shift and a Saturday shift are devoted to maintenance activities.

The principal resources recovered by the Facility are by percentage of weight:

	%
Refuse-derived fuel	66
Heavy combustibles	5
Ferrous metals	7
Aluminium	0.35
Heavy non-ferrous metals (copper zinc)	0.05
Mixed colour glass	9
Sand	3
Residual product for disposal	9

The Facility incorporates many design features which provide for technological and economic reliability. For example, each equipment item within the process was designed with at least 25 per cent excess capacity to accommodate surges in the feed rate or variations in the composition of the wastes. Reliability is also assured by 'built-in' redundancy, material bypasses, adequate spare parts inventory, systems for fire and explosion prevention and control, and overall system monitoring and control. Emergency landfill provisions are included in the design, so that the tipping floor can act as a 500 ton per day transfer station if necessary.

Monroe County's Resource Recovery Facility is the first of its type and size in the State of New York and the first major facility to be constructed with State Environmental Quality Bond Act Funding. The total capital and engineering investment for the programme is $50.4 million which consists of $31.9 million invested by the County and $18.5 million assistance by the New York State Department of Environmental Conservation. The cost of operation, including revenues from products, is comparable with current landfill costs.

Site features
The Resource Recovery Facility is situated on 44,300 m² in the south-west corner of the City of Rochester. The site is bounded to the north by Emerson Street, to the east by West Street, to the south by the New York State Barge Canal, and to the west by Lee Road, plate 18. The administration building, which fronts on Emerson Street, contains the main lobby, administrative offices, maintenance shops and storage facilities for spare parts and supplies.

Refuse receiving and handling
The Facility accepts refuse from packer trucks, transfer trailers, or

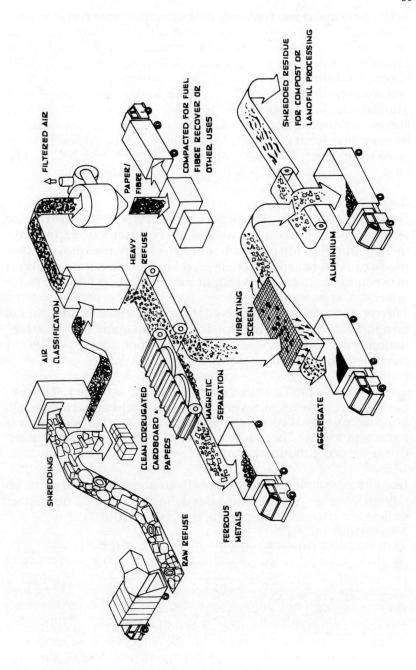

6.3   Resource recovery at the Monroe County Facility

open trucks and trailers. All vehicles approach via the entrance gate. A two-scale system automatically weighs the incoming waste and also records and maintains business transaction data. Vehicles then proceed to the tipping area and back into one of ten 6 m wide tipping bays. Refuse is discharged into a storage area 3.65 m deep and capable of storing 2000 tons. Both tipping and storage areas are fully enclosed within the building in a space 116 m long and 33.5 m wide. From the storage floor, the refuse is manoeuvred by front-end loaders onto in-feed conveyors and carried into the processing plant. The process system is described below. The empty refuse trucks are weighed at the West Street exit.

Output product handling
Products produced by the Facility are delivered to storage bins or portable containers. Up to a full day's production can be stored on the site and on adjacent rail sidings. Transportation of output products is by rail and truck. Typical handling and transportation procedures for the various output products are as follows:
Refuse-derived fuel:
This is pneumatically conveyed from the process area to the compactor building which houses six compactors fed by a 'live-bottom' silo. Here, the RDF is compacted into transfer trailers or containerised unit railcars for delivery to customers.
Ferrous metals:
Ferrous metals can be shipped either by rail or by truck. They are transported by belt conveyor to elevated steel hoppers. Separate hoppers are provided for the storage of light ferrous and heavy ferrous products. These are discharged directly either into open trucks or into gondola railcars.
Glass:
Glass is pneumatically conveyed from the process area to an elevated storage silo. Either closed hopper railcars or hopper trailers are used for transporting the glass product.
Non-ferrous metals
Aluminium is conveyed to a storage silo which feeds into either freight cars or trucks. Other non-ferrous metal products are stored in standard portable containers on site. These can also be loaded onto railcars or trucks.
Heavy combustibles, sand, light waste:
These are conveyed to open trucks stationed under hoppers located under the water process module. As the trucks fill, they are moved and replaced by empties. Surge storage is provided to allow for changing trucks. All output product vehicles are weighed at the Lee Road exit weighbridge upon leaving the Facility.

Traffic control
All yard movements, both by truck and by rail, are monitored from the traffic control centre, either visually or by closed-circuit television. Output product weights and destinations are automatically recorded by a computer which aids in vehicle weight control and information management.

Process system control
The operations control centre is located against the wall separating the storage and process areas. This position provides line-of-sight observation of the processing system as well as of the tipping/storage area. A central display and control unit is located in the centre providing status indication and start/stop functions for process equipment.

The process
The overall process system consists of four subsystems: baseline process, residue recovery, ferrous refining and non-ferrous refining. The baseline process handles all the incoming waste in two parallel lines, producing refuse-derived fuel, ferrous scrap, heavy combustibles and a residual fraction. The residue recovery system receives the residual fraction and separates it into mixed-colour glass, sand, mixed non-ferrous metals and light waste. The ferrous refining subsystem cleans and densifies the ferrous scrap. The non-ferrous sybsystem recovers aluminium and heavy non-ferrous metals as separate products.

To assure adequate capacity, as well as continuing system reliability, two or more units of certain process equipment items are installed. However, this description is written in terms of a single unit.

Baseline process
Figure 6.4 shows the process flow-sheet and illustrates the following text.
1 Primary shredder
Reduces the incoming waste to less than 750 mm in size. Only coarse shredding is necessary, reducing the amount of fine glass produced and minimising shredder maintenance costs. The shredder is protected against internal explosions and fires.
2 Skim classifier
Removes an initial small quantity (15 per cent) of light combustible materials (paper, plastic and dust) from the coarse shredded refuse, and controls dust from the primary shredder.

72

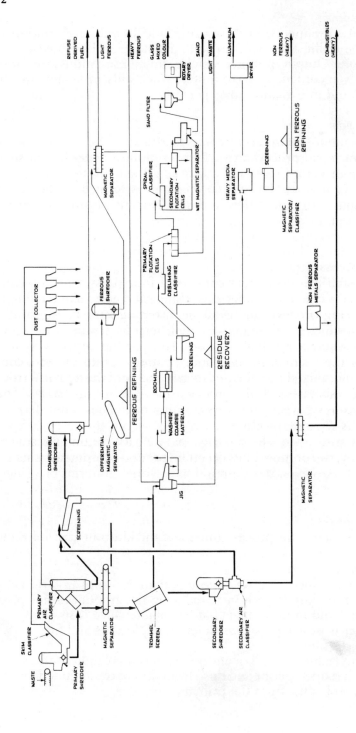

6.4 Monroe County Facility — baseline process flow diagram

3 Primary air classifier

Separates shredded feed material into light and heavy fractions. The rotary drum air classifiers obtain high separation efficiency by dropping the material through an air stream numerous times. The heavy fraction which is to be further processed, consists of putrescibles, glass, metals and heavy organics. The light fraction, primarily paper and plastic, is further processed to produce refuse-derived fuel.

4 Magnetic separator

Removes ferrous metals from the air classifier heavy fraction.

5 Rotary trommel screen

Removes a glass-rich fraction from the non-magnetic discharge of the magnetic separator. This screen undersize fraction is made up of putrescibles, glass, non-ferrous metals and heavy organics to be further processed in the residue recovery subsystem. The oversize fraction is of similar composition but larger particle size, and contains very little glass.

6 Secondary shredder

Reduces the rotary screen oversize material to approximately 50 mm particle size to facilitate maximum recovery of combustibles and to liberate as much non-ferrous metal as possible.

7 Secondary air classifier

Separates the light combustible materials liberated by secondary shredding. These lights are then combined with the light materials from the primary air classifiers.

8 Magnetic separator

Removes the weakly magnetic materials from the secondary air classifier heavy fraction. The remaining heavy fraction consists of wood, leather, rubber, corrugated board and non-ferrous metals.

9 Non-ferrous metal separator

Removes non-ferrous metals from the heavy combustible materials. Approximately 70 to 80 per cent of the non-ferrous metals in the feed stream are recovered having a product purity of 85 to 95 per cent. The metallic fraction becomes feed for the non-ferrous refining subsystem, while the heavy combustible residue is either discarded to landfill or utilised as a fuel.

10 Screen

Removes fine glass, grit and dirt from the light fraction of the air classifiers. This screen undersize will supply the residue recovery subsystem.

11 Combustible shredder

Fine shreds the screen oversize from screen (10) to 90 per cent less than 20 mm, discharging refuse-derived fuel which is pneumatically conveyed to the compactor building for storage and loading.

12 Dust collector

Removes dust from the process air. Dust is added to the light combustibles, becoming part of the refuse-derived fuel fraction.

Residue recovery

13 Jig

Removes light organic matter from the incoming glass-rich feed material, leaving a heavier inorganic glassy aggregate fraction. The wet organics are dewatered and discarded to landfill.

14 Coarse material washer

Dewaters the glassy aggregate. The overflow wash water, which contains a proportion of inorganic fines, is recycled to the jig, while the coarser aggregate is further processed for glass and sand separation.

15 Rod mill

This is used for size reduction of the glass and glass-like particles which form the aggregate.

16 Screen

Processes the rod mill's output. Screen undersize, rich in glass, is fed to the desliming classifier (17); oversize particles are largely metallic and are combined with the discharge of the non-ferrous separator (9).

17 Desliming classifier

Further treats the glass recovery feed by removing very fine material as a mud or slime to be piped to the water treatment system.

18 Primary flotation cells

Separate the glass from contaminants by a froth flotation process in which glass particles adhere to floating air bubbles, while non-glass material such as brick, stone and ceramics sinks. This latter material is pumped to the water treatment system where the non-glass material is recovered as a sand-product.

19 Spiral classifier

This is similar to the desliming classifier (17). It divides the glass-rich discharge of the primary flotation cells into two fractions containing finer and coarser particles respectively. The coarser portion goes to the secondary flotation cells (20), while the fines go to the magnetic separator (21).

20 Secondary flotation cells

Reclean glass particles by the froth flotation process described above, prior to treatment by magnetic separation.

21 Wet magnetic separator

Removes residual fine ferrous material from the glass bearing feed stream. This small quantity of ferrous residue is pumped to the water treatment system.

22 Sand filter
Dewaters the wet magnetic separator discharge, which is a slurry consisting of water and a sand-like material of high-purity, mixed-colour glass. At discharge from the sand filter, water content has been reduced to 10 per cent. Removed water is pumped to the water treatment system.

23 Rotary dryer
Further dries the glass to 0 to 1 per cent moisture before pneumatic conveying to the storage hopper for shipment.

Ferrous refining
24 Differential magnetic separator
Separates the ferrous discharge of the magnetic separators (4) into light and massive fractions, using a magnetic drum to selectively pick up light-weight pieces, such as can, bottle caps and wire. Heavy pieces are conveyed directly to holding bins for shipment to purchasers, while the light fraction feeds the ferrous shredder.

25 Ferrous shredder
Reduces cans and similar objects to flakelike fragments with a minimum of 'baling'. This material is suitable for detinning and is handled separately from the ferrous scrap.

26 Magnetic separator
Further refines the ferrous shredder output stream by removing non-ferrous material for delivery to the residue recovery subsystem described above. The ferrous fraction is conveyed to a storage hopper for shipment.

Non-ferrous refining
The non-ferrous refining subsystem operates on the discharge of the non-ferrous separator (9) and on oversize material from the residue recovery screen (16). This subsystem uses a wet process and has the following equipment:

27   Heavy media separator
Separates aluminium from other non-ferrous metals, using a heavy liquid (a ferro-silicon suspension in water) in which aluminium floats while other metals sink.

28 Screen
This is a two-deck vibrating type unit in which the separation medium is washed from the recovered metals for recycling in the separator. The heavy metals are conveyed to a storage bin for shipment.

29 Magnetic separator/classifier
Purifies the ferro-silicon medium for re-use by removing solids — particularly ferrous material.

30 Dryer
Reduces the water content of the recovered aluminium to 1 per cent before its delivery to storage for shipment.

Water process module
This module treats the process water for recycling in wet process systems thereby drastically reducing the plant's process water requirement.

TABLE 6.1 DAILY MATERIALS BALANCE*

Product	Output-TPD	Output as % of input
Refuse-derived fuel	1326.0	66.3
Light ferrous	133.0	6.6
Heavy ferrous	8.5	0.4
Mixed colour glass	174.0	8.7
Aluminium	6.5	0.3
Heavy non-ferrous	1.0	0.1
Heavy combustibles	103.0	5.1
Sand	71.0	3.6
Light waste	167.0	8.4
Subtotal	1990.0	99.5
Moisture loss	8.5	0.4
Solids to sewer	1.5	0.1
Total	2000.0	100.0

Note: TPD denotes tons/day
* based on a 2000 TPD solid waste input and 1407 TPD of fresh water input to the wet process system of which 1399 5 TPD is recycled

Organisation and history of construction
The construction phase of this project was similar to other large municipal public works projects in New York State. Although State Law requires only four prime contractors on such projects, the bid

documents were prepared with alternative bid arrangements in order to obtain the best possible construction price. These alternatives included the four standard bid packages (general building, heating/ventilating, air conditioning, plumbing and electrical) as well as an alternative that divided the general building package into three separate packages (general building, structural steel and process equipment). The bids received on 15 July 1976 showed that the six contract arrangement was the least costly. The total bid price was $28.4 million.

The contractual relationships between the parties involved in the construction phase were clearly defined. Although the owner, Monroe County, has contractual control of the contractor, Raytheon Service Company (RSC) has been designated in the construction documents as the owner's agent for this work. Thus, RSC and its subcontractor, United engineers and Constructors Inc (UE& C) are performing the standard architect/engineer functions during the construction phase. The majority of the engineering work is actually being performed by UE&C under RSC direction, but RSC has been heavily involved in the process equipment area, as well as the contractual aspects of all the construction contracts.

Construction of the project actually commenced in October 1976, not the most desirable time to start construction work in a colder climate, such as that of the Monroe County area. The clearing and grading work was completed and foundation work started during the autumn and early winter, but not much progress was made during the midst of winter. By the middle of March 1977, the administration area foundation was only partially complete and only one primary shredder pad had been poured.

With the onset of the warmer weather, the pace increased substantially; by mid-May the foundation work for the process area had been completed, and structural steel erection started in the administration area. The perimeter foundation work was essentially completed by the end of July, and roof decking work was initiated in the administration and process areas in late August. The first piece of process equipment, a primary shredder, was set on its foundation in late August. By late October 1977, the roofing on the administration and process areas had been completed and the siding work was initiated. Work had also begun on the installation of the third of seven shredders. The first section of the process area floor slab was poured in mid-November.

At the end of 1977, the process and administration areas were essentially enclosed with a combination of siding and polyethylene. This permitted concrete work, block work and equipment installation to continue inside. As soon as the winter weather eased, the rate of progress increased substantially. In March 1978, work began on the detached water process module, site work resumed, and the interior process area slabs were completed. Work also was initiated on the last of the seven shredders, the first of the rotary drum air classifiers and the motor control centres. The storage area floor slab was poured in May, and the built-up roofing over the tipping and storage area was started in May.

During the summer of 1978, equipment installation proceeded rapidly in both the main process building and the water process module. Foundation work was initiated on the compactor module (RDF holding bin), the on-site rail spurs were installed, and the site paving was started. By late 1978, the process equipment installation in the main process area and water process module was essentially complete, with the exception of the conveyors and trommels. Work also was underway on the installation of the compactor module equipment, and the electrical wiring of motor control centres was nearing completion. Site power was turned on in September 1978, permitting the process equipment contractor to begin his no-load cycle testing. The process equipment contractor concentrated on conveyor installation, piping of the wet process area equipment, wiring of equipment and, most importantly, no-load cycling testing. The electrical contractor continued his wiring, including the wiring from the control centres to the main control room. The main process control panel was delivered in February 1979 and the wiring and testing of the unit has continued since that time.

The process equipment contractor then had to correct the deficiencies that were discovered during no-load cycle testing, complete the individual equipment no-load cycle tests, conduct integrated no-load cycle tests which demonstrate the ability of the equipment to run as part of the system, and perform his functional testing. The functional, or loaded, testing was specified to demonstrate the ability of the process equipment to process 2000 tons of solid waste in 16 hours for two, five-day weeks. This testing was scheduled to be complete by October 1979. Upon successful demonstration of his equipment, the process equipment contractor's work would be complete, with the exception of punch list items that develop during the testing.

Finance
Approximately $28.8 million of the total $29.3 million present (1979) contract value has been expended. The present contract value reflects an increase of about 3 per cent over the original $28.4 million bid value, and this could increase to about 8 to 10 per cent ($30.6 to $31.2 million), before the project is complete. These

increases reflect the variation orders that were issued to the contractors for additional work and to overcome the possibility of voiding various equipment and contractor warranties.

Commissioning

Following the completion of the process equipment contractor's functional testing, RSC will assume the responsiblity for the operation and maintenance of the Resource Recovery Facility. The first objective of this start-up phase will be to 'fine-tune' the process equipment in order to meet the stringent specifications of the output product buyers.

As soon as RSC and the County agree that the Facility is ready for testing, RSC will initiate its acceptance testing. The objective of these tests is to demonstrate the satisfactory design/operation of the Facility. The acceptance test programme recently agreed upon by RSC and the County will be carried out in three parts as follows:

Part 1 will demonstrate the ability to process acceptable solid waste on a single shift basis for a four week period of time at the design capacity, while producing output products of the specified quality and quantity.

Part II will demonstrate the ability to operate each line at two shifts per day for a separate one week period for each line at the design capacity, while producing output products of the specified quality. Additionally, the ability of the glass recovery/refining and water treatment systems to process materials at the design capacity, while producing output products of the specified quality, will be demonstrated for a single two shift period at full plant capacity.

Part III will demonstrate the ability to process all incoming acceptable solid waste (to the maximum quantity specified) for a period of six months.

Plant operation

Following the successful completion of the acceptance tests, RSC will enter the commercial operations phase. Initially, the operation will be limited to a single operating shift with maintenance performed on the third shift. As the incoming tonnage increases above the 1000 TPD (tons/day) level, the amount of necessary overtime will increase. At some specific point, it will become more economical to add a second operating shift for a single process line; eventually, the second shift will be expanded further to allow for the operation of both process lines. As shown in table **6.2** the anticipated total manning level for a single shift operation, which includes a maintenance shift, is 68 employees, and for two shifts, 111 employees. The organisational structure for the plant personnel is shown in fig 6.5. This figure also shows the number of employees in each category required for one and two shift operation, respectively.

TABLE 6.2 TOTAL MANNING SCHEDULE

Category	One shift operation	Two shift operation
Exempt	11	14
Office clerical	4	4
Plant clerical	6	10
Plant operation and maintenance	47	83
Total	68	111

Summary

The implementation of a major resource recovery project as described is a complex, time-consuming and costly venture. It is anticipated that by the time commercial operation has been established a period of over nine years will have elapsed since the initial studies, and in excess of $40 million will have been spent. If the refuse-derived fuel receiving facility is taken into consideration, the time will be over ten years and the cost in excess of $50 million. However, investments of this kind are becoming necessary in many areas where land disposal sites are not readily available. It is anticipated that the total annual cost of the one shift resource recovery operation in Monroe County will be competitive with transfer hauling, and remote tonnage increases. So too, as the oil and virgin materials which the Facility outputs replace become more and more costly, the economics will improve considerably.

6.5 THE DONCASTER PLANT, SOUTH YORKSHIRE

Background

As a result of a thorough appraisal of the wast disposal needs of the Doncaster district in South Yorkshire the county council decided that a modern refuse transfer station should be constructed and that this plant should be operational by 1979.

This decision arose out of the study carried out by the Local Government Operational Research Unit in 1974. This study —

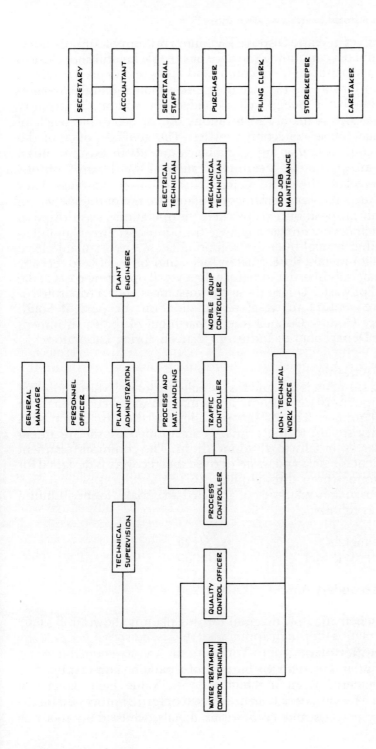

6.5 *Monroe County Facility — personnel manning schedule*

'Alternatives in Waste Disposal for South Yorkshire County Council' — identified a continuing shortage of suitable landfill sites close to the main urban areas of the county and a progressive need to rely on bulk transfer stations to reach the more remote mineral extraction voids, the latter being well provided for within the country boundaries, but mainly in locations out of economic reach of individual refuse collection vehicles. The general policy of the county council is that any capital investments in waste disposal should incorporate as a cardinal feature of the design a serious effort to reclaim the useful materials in the household refuse. They were aware that waste reclamation plants are not of themselves an economic proposition, except where the operational waste disposal circumstances encourage a change from low-cost direct landfill to some other capital-intensive solution. Then, given suitable local markets for metals, fibre, glass or fuel it may be feasible to reclaim these materials in order to reduce the overall operating costs of the disposal of waste. Out of these circumstances grew a tripartite co-operative venture in waste reclamation on the part of South Yorkshire County Council, the Department of the Environment and the Department of Industry's Warren Spring Laboratory.

Design parameters

Initially, the plant is designed as a single stream unit with a nominal throughput of 10 tonnes/hour and a maximum weekly throughput of 1250 tonnes. The design provides for the installation of a secondary stream to the primary core to increase the treatment capacities eventually to 20 tonnes/hour. The common treatment equipment for glass and waste-derived fuel recovery is designed for the 20 tonnes/hour throughput.

Approximate quantities of recycled materials (tonnes/annum) will be as follows:

Ferrous metals	3 125
Waste-derived fuel	10,000
Glass	3 125
Paper (secondary fibre)	1 250

The schematic flow diagram for this plant is shown in fig **6.6.**

Air classifier plant

The classifier is used for the purpose of separating non-combustible heavy material from the high calorific value light paper-rich fraction. Heavy material can be rejected or further processed for the recovery of glass and non-ferrous metals, whilst the paper-rich fraction can be subsequently shredded for the production of waste-derived fuel, either in the 'fluffed form' or pelletised condition for use as a fuel supplement.

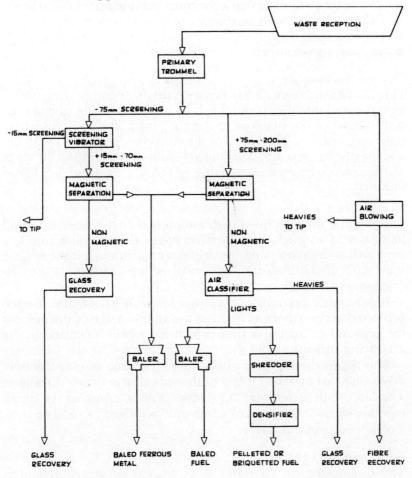

6.6   Doncaster Plant — process flow diagram

The classifier unit, as shown in plate 21, is the full-scale unit for a 1250 tons per week refuse treatment plant currently under construction at Doncaster for the South Yorkshire County Council.

Design of the unit is based upon data obtained from test work carried out in the pilot plant facility at the Department of Industry's Warren Spring Laboratory. After successful performance testing at the Laboratory the plant is now erected at the Doncaster Plant.

The air classifier plant comprises the following main components:

- classifier feed conveyor
- rotating drum with drive
- disengagement chamber
- disengagement chamber collecting conveyor
- delivery air fan with nozzles
- exhaust fan
- supporting steelwork.

Classifier feed conveyor

This is a flat conveyor, 2.5 m between driving centres, designed to eject the feed into the classifier at high velocity, thereby giving even distribution of the material to the air stream and to optimise on trajectory velocity. The speed of the conveyor is infinitely variable and the discharge pulley is arranged for adjustment within the entry of the classifier drum. A variable speed drive unit of 1.5 kW is installed.

Rotating drum

The rotating drum is fitted with an internal circumferential scroll helix at 1.38 m pitch, with the first stage of the scroll acting as a contra-flow discharge unit for the heavy material, and the second stage unit discharging the lighter paper-rich fraction to the disengagement chamber.

A screening section, complete with dust cover and Castell protected access doors, is fitted in the second stage of the unit for the removal of dust and fines which have been liberated in the classifying process.

The drum driving gear comprises a variable output 'friction' drive unit, arranged to drive both ends of the drum through a 'Cardan' shaft assembly. A torque limiter coupling is fitted, together with a speed control 'servo-unit' arranged for local control, with speed read-out facility.

Disengagement chamber

The disengagement chamber is of airtight construction and is provided with an internal baffle arrangement to enable classified light material to fall out of suspension. The bottom of the chamber is fitted with an internally mounted collecting conveyor.

'Pressure' detection equipment is supplied and connected to and between the disengagement chamber and the exhaust duct damper control unit to promote efficient evacuation of the air and to maintain a negative pressure condition within the chamber.

For fire protection, a heat-rise detector unit will be incorporated in the chamber; in the event of actuation, the delivery and exhaust fan will stop and a fire alarm will sound.

Disengagement chamber collecting conveyor
This conveyor collects the classified light paper-rich fraction from the disengagement chamber. The conveyor is of the flat belt type, 1.07 m nominal width by 5.2 m between driving centres, with the skirt plates being formed as an integral part of the disengagement chamber hopper bottom. The conveyor is off-set at a co-axial line through the up-side of the classifier rotating section. A fixed speed drive unit of 1.1 kW is installed.

Delivery fan
For the purpose of supplying air to the nozzle assembly situated at the feed conveyor discharge, a centrifugal-type, electrically driven forced-draught fan is provided. Controlled air is fed to the main nozzle box at a speed of 60 ft/s, with secondary air being directed into an auxiliary 'clean-up' nozzle.

The fan impeller is of the overhung backward airfoil design type and directly driven through a flexible coupling and 11 kW motor.

The facility to control the air quantities being passed to the main nozzle box assembly is vested in a motorised control damper.

Exhaust fan
The exhaust from the classifier will be discharged to the atmosphere by an induced draught fan. The fan is to the same design as the delivery fan described above, but will include a 7.5 kW motor.

The facility to control the pressure conditions within the disengagement chamber will be incorporated and vested in a motorised control damper fitted to the inlet of the fan. Both the delivery and exhaust fans incorporate a design margin on volume and pressure.

Supporting steelwork
An integral supporting steelwork for the unit is provided, complete with access platforms and walkways around the whole of the unit, together with all handrailing, kick-plates and access ladders.

Technical data

| Design throughput | 5 tonnes/hour (minimum) |
| Bulk density | 130 kg/m³ (average) |

Dimensions of drum

Overall length	5.550 m
Inside diameter of drum	2.100 m
Length of screen section	2.500 m
Outside diameter driving rings	2.425 m
Drum screen material	6 mm steel plate, stiffened
Drive unit — variable speed friction	4.5 kW installed

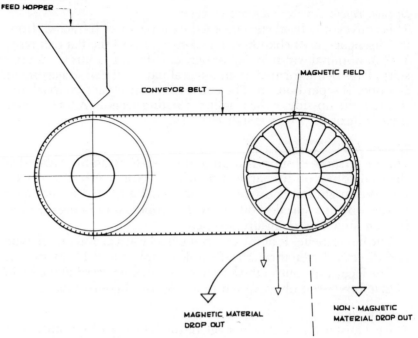

FEED HOPPER

CONVEYOR BELT

MAGNETIC FIELD

MAGNETIC MATERIAL DROP OUT

NON - MAGNETIC MATERIAL DROP OUT

6.7   Magnetic separator — conveyor belt arrangement

Dimensions of disengagement chamber

Overall length	5.500 m (adjustable)
Overall width	3.000 m
Height from floor	7.700 m
Chamber material	3 mm steel plate, stiffened
Total installed load	25.6 kW
Total absorbed load at design	20.0 kW
Process cost electrical power	4 kW/tonne

Magnetic separators
Figures **6.7** and **6.8** show two types of magnetic separators which are used in mechanical sorting plants.

Recycled products
Initially, the products of the Doncaster process will be waste-derived fuel, ferrous metal and glass. Facilities will be incorporated to produce the fuel in either baled or densified forms. Shredding and densification is a relatively expensive process, but it will make the product more attractive as a supplementary fuel by improving its handling and storage characteristics. The recovery of paper fibre from this paper-rich product, rather than using it as fuel, is still

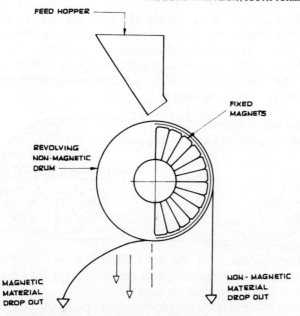

FEED HOPPER

FIXED
MAGNETS

REVOLVING
NON-MAGNETIC
DRUM

MAGNETIC
MATERIAL
DROP OUT

NON-MAGNETIC
MATERIAL
DROP OUT

6.8   Magnetic separator — magnetic wheel type

under investigation. So also is recovery of cardboard and paper from the primary trommel oversize by controlled air blowing.

Costings
The economic aspects of the Doncaster plant are detailed below:

Capital cost
An estimated cost of the Doncaster plant at February 1977 prices is £2.227 million (US $4.677 million) made up as follows:

Plant and installation	**£** **(Sterling)**	**$** **(USA)**
Primary sorting and waste-derived fuel	723,000	1,518,000
Metal recovery	60,000	126,000
Glass recovery	90,000	189,000
Paper baling	40,000	84,000
Compactors (1 for residue removal 2 on standby in case of plant breakdown)	20,000	42,000
Design, development and supervision	207,000	434,000
Sub-total	1,140,000	2,394,000
Building and civil engineering	1,087,000	2,282,000
Total	2,227,000	4,676,000

The total capital cost estimate of £2.23 million ($4.68 million) includes provision for administration, accommodation, weigh-bridges, roads, car parks, landscaping, etc, but not for the purchase cost of the land. When comparing the capital cost of the plant with another, care must be taken to ensure that similar cost components are specified.

Labour and utility requirements
Labour requirements are as follows:

	Plant capacity	
	10 tonne/h	20 tonne/h
Foremen	2	2
Shift operators	8	12
Day men	2	2

Total power requirements
These are estimated to be 40 kWh/tonne of input waste. 10 kWh/tonne are for shredding and pelletising the fuel product and 5 kWh/tonne are for glass recovery.

Aqueous effluent from the glass recovery plant will be 2.6m^3/tonne of input waste. Assuming 80 per cent recycle after thickening, make-up water and effluent to sewer will both amount to 0.52m^3/ tonne. The concentration of solids in the aqueous effluent will be 29 g/l (1.05×10^{-3} lb/in^3).

Recoveries
Pilot scale trials at Warren Spring Laboratories on waste of a composition close to the national average indicate that the following rates of recovery are achievable:

Fuel (pelletised)	30% of input
Ferrous metal	7% of input
Glass	5% of input
Paper	5% of input (90% paper)

Operating costs

Plant capacity	10 tonnes/h		20 tonnes/h	
Waste input	31,000 tonnes/y		62,000 tonnes/y	
Capital cost	£1.47 m - $3.09 m		£2.23 m - $4.68 m	
Working capital	£0.02 m - $.042 m		£0.03 m - $.063 m	
Annual costs	£/y	$/y	£/y	$/y
Capital charges	196,000	411,600	297,000	623,700
Wages	45,000	94,500	60,000	126,000
On-costs	17,000	35,700	23,000	48,300
Manager	5 000	10,500	9 000	18,900

	£/y	$/y	£/y	$/y
Administration	31,000	65,100	41,000	86,100
Maintenance	59,000	123,900	89,000	186,900
Electricity (40 kWh/tonne)	29,000	60,900	57,000	119,700
Natural gas for space heating	6 000	12,600	10,000	21,000
Water	2 500	5 250	5 000	10,500
Chemicals	500	1 050	1 000	2 100
Residue disposal (56% of input)	25,000	52,500	50,000	105,000
Total	416,000	873,600	642,000	1,348,200

Revenues

	£/y	$/y	£/y	$/y
Ferrous metal at £12/tonne ($25.2)	26,000	54,600	52,000	109,200
Fuels at £7/tonne	65,000	136,500	130,000	273,000
Glass at £8/tonne	12,000	25,200	25,000	52,500
Paper at £15/tonne	23,000	48,300	46,000	96,500
Total	126,000	264,600	253,000	531,300

Net operating cost	£290,000	£609,000	£389,000	£816,900
	or £9.3/tonne		or £6.3/tonne	

If glass recovery were not included it is estimated that the capital cost of a 20 tonne/h plant would be £2.0 million ($4.2 million) and the operating costs would be as follows:

Annual costs	£/y	$/y
Capital charges	267,000	560,700
Wages (1 man/shift less)	53,000	111,300
On-costs	20,000	42,000
Manager	9,000	18,900
Administration	37,000	77,700
Maintenance	80,000	168,000
Electricity	50,000	105,000
Natural gas	10,000	21,000
Residue disposal (61% of input)	55,000	115,000
Total	581,000	1,220,100

	£/y	$/y
Revenues	228,000	478,800
Net annual operating cost	353,000	741,300
or	£5.7/tonne	

To compare the above operating costs with those located outside the UK, one must allow for the differences in cost of labour and utility services.

CHECK LIST

Note: the Doncaster Plant has been commissioned following a major governmental study of the local waste disposal needs. The plant has an initial capacity of 10 tonnes/hour with scope for upgrading to 20 tonnes/hour. Recycled products will be waste-derived fuel and glass. Recycling of paper fibre is being investigated. The air classifier is the heart of the plant. It is described in detail. Special care is taken to ensure that the waste-derived fuel is free from glass contamination. The economics of the plant complex are detailed.

6.6 HOUSEHOLD WASTE RECYCLING COMPLEX, ROME

Introduction
The three million inhabitants of Rome generate annually approximately 750,000 tons of refuse. This volume of refuse is collected and processed every day of the year, including Sundays.

For this purpose, the City is sub-divided into four sections, each of which is equipped with a separate disposal plant. Three of these plants utilise Sorain-Cecchini recycling processes. The fourth plant is a composting unit.

The householders' refuse is deposited in disposable plastic bags, usually suspended inside metal holders stored near the entrance of the buildings. These bags are collected by municipal garbage trucks; these are, almost exclusively, compacting systems which optimally compress the refuse without size reduction of the material. Each truck makes two daily pick ups and transports approximately 3,500 kg per pick up.

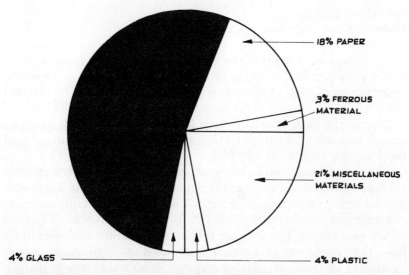

COMPOSITION OF MUNICIPAL WASTE IN PERCENTAGE

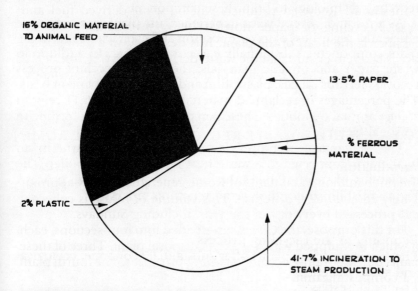

MATERIAL RECOVERED IN PERCENTAGE

6.9   Rome recycling complex — composition of the waste

In addition to household refuse, waste from public markets, street sweepings, commercial and industrial wastes are also collected by the municipal trucks.

Recycling plants

There are two recycling plants in Rome:

One plant in the west of the city which has a processing capacity of 600 tons per day. It began functioning in 1964 and occupies an area approximately 11,000 m² with a building volume of 110,000 m³.

One in the east, which is capable of processing 1,200 tons per day. It was constructed in 1967, covers an area of 25,000 m² and the building volume is 250,000 m³.

The processing capacity of these plants is based on operating two shifts per day, though some of the departments, such as incineration, animal feed production, and paper pulping operate continuously.

Flexibility has been provided in both plant layouts to permit future expansion. The average refuse composition is shown in fig **6.9**. The presence of considerable quantities of waste paper products, as well as that of organic materials (which usually constitute the major portion of the refuse), has directed the recycling technology to both these components.

As a result of several years experience, the plants recycle refuse efficiently, regardless of its composition and even where one of the main components substantially exceeds the other. In addition to waste paper and organic materials, the Sorain-Cecchini process recovers ferrous metals, plastic film and glass on a pilot plant basis. The percentages of reclaimed materials shown in fig **6.11** refer to *average* annual quantities. These percentages can vary according to seasonal factors.

The percentage of non-reclaimable material is burnt in an incinerator connected to a waste heat recovery steam boiler. The availability of steam reduces the fuel costs of the overall process. Figure **6.10** illustrates the overall recycling process.

Economy of the recycling process

The Rome recycling plants offer substantial economic, ecological and social benefits.

Economic results:

● reduced costs in the disposal of urban solid waste for the local authority and therefore for the individual citizen. Depending on the composition of refuse, the saving is of the order of 30 per cent, or in favourable circumstances, even up to 100 per cent, when compared with other conventional systems of waste disposal;

● an improvement in the balance of payments. Italy, suffers from a serious deficiency of precisely those products which are salvageable from refuse: paper, ferrous metal, animal feed, oil (plastic);

- substantial energy savings by exploiting the heat potential of the non-reclaimable matter for in-plant use (sterilisation, reclamation, drying processes), as well as for other uses (steam for neighbouring industries, provision of hot water for local housing, electrical power, etc).

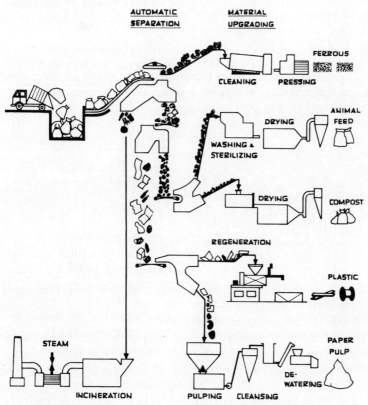

6.10   *Rome recyling complex — overall system*

Ecological effects:
- conservation of scarce natural resources, such as oil, timber, minerals etc,
- a diminution of sources of ground, air and water pollution, compared with other systems of disposal (sanitary landfill, total incineration etc).

Social effects:
- the creation of jobs, both directly and indirectly, to a much

greater extent than other systems, the costs of which are already taken into account in the overall budget;
● research, development and disposal commercial exploitation of new and original technology.
There is also a spin-off to matters outside the immediate field of solid urban waste disposal.

Flow of waste

Reception of the solid waste
On arrival at the recycling complex, refuse trucks can unload at several points: directly onto automatic conveyors of the primary selection lines; into side receiving pits; into the receiving pits of the incinerators (for that portion of the waste destined for immediate incineration); into the receiving pits of the composting section (for that portion of the waste collected in food markets or for the street sweepings suitable only for composting).

All of the receiving pits are equipped with overhead cranes and electro-hydraulic grapples to move the refuse. The receiving pits are capable of receiving and storing up to two days' refuse, thus allowing for plant shutdowns over one day holidays and necessary large scale repairs.

The primary selection lines are of two technically similar types, with a capacity of either 12 tons/h, or of 20 tons/h, and they differ only in their rated capacity. The waste is fed to the plant by conveyors with a special feed mechanism which maintains a constant flow of refuse and prevents bulky items eg refrigerators, mattresses, etc, from entering the system.

Plastic bags are torn open and emptied. The bags are then removed, since they would interfere with subsequent automatic dry selection sections. The operations of feeding at constant rates, elimination of bulky items, opening and emptying of the bags, are essential to the later selection processes, because only by processing a homogeneous loose waste at constant flow, can recovery with satisfactory results of quality and quantity be obtained.

Automatic selection
Once the bags have been torn open and emptied, the automatic selection process can begin. Each selection line is independent and modular (12 or 20 tons/h). This guarantees efficient functioning of the system in that maintenance and unexpected breakdowns only affect a fraction of total capacity.

The machines which segregate the different materials make use of those characteristics which distinguish one material from another,

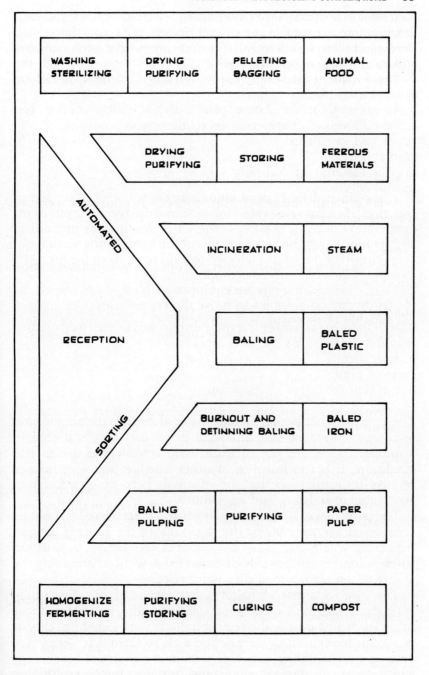

6.11   *Rome recycling complex — diagrammatic flow presentation*

their *physical* properties (weight, fragility, electromagnetic qualities, flexibility, resilience etc) as well as their *static* ones (size shape, etc). To exploit these characteristics, the machines have been designed and manufactured specifically for this application, although the basic principles have been employed in other industries for a long time.

At present, in the Rome plants, the selection process has achieved levels of commercial recycling production for:
paper and cardboard
animal feed
organic material for compost
ferrous metals.

As far as plastic film and glass are concerned, pilot plant recovery is being achieved.

Process flow-chart
The following six products emerge from the automatic selection lines:

bales of paper
coarse organics, suitable for tranformation into animal feed organic material destined for use as compost
ferrous metals
bales of plastic
non-reclaimables for incineration.

The 'products' like paper, organic material, ferrous metals, etc have obvious commercial potential, but given that they still contain impurities, they are not of immediate commercial use in this condition. It is the function of other satellite plants to further remove impurities, so that the materials become of a standard acceptable to industry and agriculture.

The percentages of the materials which are recovered, should be considered average values: the flexibility of the process permits bypassing where necessary any product recovery in a situation where a market temporarily does not exist, without impairing the ability to maintain a total disposal service.

The 'non-reclaimable' matter is that portion of the refuse which consists of materials considered unsalvageable, or part of those materials which during the selection phase were either not easy or economic to recover, or were deliberately rejected. Incineration of such non-reclaimables, disposes of them as a source of heat energy which services the transformation processes. Since this heat substitutes for oil as a fuel, it has an economic value. The installations are so designed that, where desirable and economically feasible, steam can be converted to electricity. The required technology already exists.

Paper
Selected baled paper and cardboard cannot be commercially exploited until the contaminants, mainly rags, plastic, polystyrene, etc have been removed.

Techniques have been developed to remove these contaminants by soaking and wetting in a pulper, removing extraneous material, pressing and sterilisation. The final product is a pulp containing 60 per cent water. The most delicate and complicated part of the operation is the cleansing stage. The water used in this process is recycled. This is made possible because make-up water is required which is shipped out in the pulp product. The resulting waste from the cleansing process is incinerated after having been dehydrated. The quality of the product has shown a consistency regardless of seasonal factors.

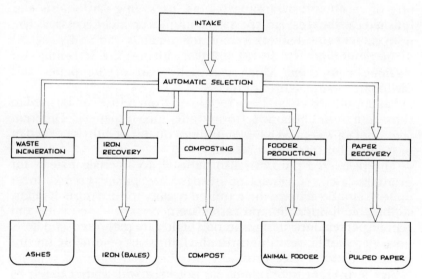

6.12 Rome recycling complex — process flow-sheet

The need for an inventory of bales between the selection and pulping sections is due to the fact that the pulping plants are considerably more efficient if material is pre-pressed, rather than fed in loose, since the latter is more voluminous. The two operations can remain independent, making it possible to carry out selection on two shifts and pulping on a continuous basis.

Paper pulp

In the Rome recycling plants, it is possible to produce approximately 200 tons of paper fibre per day (based on the moisture content of the received material). This received volume is enough to make a significant contribution to paper mills.

The main purposes of the plants concerned with the upgrading of paper recovered from waste are the elimination of contaminants of various kinds (plastic, polystyrene, heavy substances, glues, waxes, fat etc); the achievement of the quality standards demanded by the market; sterilisation; the reduction of effluent problems at the paper mills; a reduction in the need to remove solid contaminants at paper mills; and a consistent quality control for paper mills with consequent predictable processing conditions.

Even whilst maintaining those quality standards already laid down and meeting public health requirements, it is possible to carry out the process at different levels of quality taking into consideration the respective final uses of the pulp.

Where the highest quality is not required, such as in the manufacture of cardboard, wrapping papers, packaging cardboards and finished cardboards, etc, special techniques are not necessary. The pulp, after removal of waxes, bitumens and fats, can be dispatched to the paper mills, which are equipped with the usual screening and cleaning equipment which is usually part of the paper and cardboard manufacturing process.

Paper pulp which has been reclaimed from refuse can be used to substitute fibre obtained from trade mixed papers. Different techniques are applied where a superior quality of pulp is needed in order to substitute for wood pulp.

The recovered pulp can also be used, to a certain extent, for products such as newsprint, rotogravure paper, creped toilet papers, etc. To achieve the required quality for use in such fields, sophisticated upgrading processes are necessary — de-inking and refining — resulting in significantly higher upgrading costs. These, however, should be offset by the higher prices obtainable for this better quality recycled product.

At the present time, plants do not exist which are capable of upgrading paper recovered from waste, whether manually or through source separation, into de-inked pulp. However, recent experiments have brought to a successful conclusion research directed at the solution of this problem, with encouraging results.

Plans are now underway for an industrial plant capable of producing 50 tons per day of 'urban' pulp, already treated and ready for the uses mentioned, in addition to the pulp presently produced for packaging papers.

Animal feed

Coarse organic matter obtained from refuse, fruit, vegetables, and other food remnants, is used to produce animal feed. The process involved is particularly complex because of the high hygienic and veterinary standards required in the final product.

The most important stages are: washing; removal by flotation of coarse inorganic substances still present; sterilisation by means of autoclaves; drying to 6 to 8 per cent moisture content; removal, in various stages, of any small inorganic particles still remaining; pulverising; pelletising; bagging.

The product obtained has a nutritional value equivalent to 70 per cent of corn meal and contains 14 to 17 per cent proteins and 7 to 9 per cent fats.

The sterilisation and drying processes make use of the steam produced by the incinerator, in which the contaminants removed in this process are burnt. The water used for washing is purified in a plant which is an annexe to the main installations. In six years of experience, there has been a consistency of quality in the product and there have been no marketing problems.

The most important and delicate stage of the process is sterilisation through the use of modified autoclaves, where the material has to remain for a certain time at a specific pressure and temperature to complete biological sterilisation. Laboratory analyses maintain continuous quality control of the animal feed.

Use of animal feed:

The animal feed obtained from the organic content of the municipal solid waste is directly utilised by livestock breeders. The percentage fed to the livestock varies depending on the type of animal, the purpose for which they are bred and the size of the individual operation.

For many years now, because of the successful results obtained, this type of feed has been chiefly used with cattle, both for fattening and for milk production.

One of the fundamental characteristics of this feed is its appetising smell of fruit and vegetables.

For cattle being fattened, the ratio of conversion is 100 to 15, ie in order to obtain 15 kg of meat, 100 kg of this feed has to be given as a fraction of the total food intake.

If the large Italian centres alone (consisting of some 15 million inhabitants) were to recover the best organic content of their refuse, it would be possible to manufacture 100,000 tons annually of animal feed, which would then produce about 15,000 tons of meat a year. The lower cost of production, considering it as a part of a disposal process, compared with that of other animal feed, and taking into account the relative nourishment potential, could justify widespread use of selected dried animal feed obtained from refuse, particularly in those countries where it is necessary to import raw materials for feeding livestock.

Ferrous metals

The ferrous metals are extracted from the waste by means of electromagnets which function continuously. The separated materials contain the following impurities:

external labels

residual internal contaminants

plastic, paper and rags caught up in the electromagnet selection process

small percentages of tin, undesirable to the steel mills.

In addition, ferrous metal recovered from refuse poses particular transport problems, due to its volume being made up of 80 per cent cans.

In order to produce a marketable end-product, the Sorain-Cecchini plant provides controlled combustion of impurities in a rotary kiln which eliminates labels, remnants and other extraneous matter and melts a good part of the tin. After emerging from the furnace, the material is subjected to a water-cooling process and then enters a hydraulic press which reduces the total volume. The resulting bales, measuring roughly 50 × 50 × 60 cm and weighing 150 kg are stored in hoppers from which they are loaded into trucks by means of a magnetic disc. The greatest use of this recycled metal is in the production of iron rods for reinforced concrete construction.

The most important quality of the product is its pliability as it improves the priming of fusion processes, thus reducing the wear on the furnace.

Plastic film

A significant percentage of plastic film is salvaged from Rome's solid waste. It is made up of low density polyethylene which is the material used in the manufacture of refuse bags and similar plastic bags for commercial use. Other types of plastic, found in smaller quantities, are not recovered. The plastic film, salvaged and baled, is at present sold to the injection and compression moulding plastic industry because no other more refined reprocessing is as yet available.

After numerous tests made over the past five years in an installation especially designed for obtaining data regarding the upgrading of plastics in general, Sorain-Cecchini is planning shortly to build a completely automatic industrial plant, equipped for all the phases of upgrading, including dry and wet processes.

The aim of this proposed plant is to convert the recovered plastic film from solid urban waste to granules. The granules will have sufficient purity to allow blending up to 50 per cent with virgin resin for the production of plastic film.

Other types of plastic could be reutilised, but research is still in its initial stages and the difficulties involved are considerable.

In Italy, and in Rome particularly, these form only 20 per cent of the total plastic in the refuse stream; therefore in terms of quantity, the problem is almost negligible.

Compost

Three types of refuse reach the composting section: that which has not been sent to recovery lines because of its composition — street waste, refuse from the central and local food markets; that collected by vehicles equipped with a shredding mechanism which, therefore, is indiscriminately mixed and already in a state of deterioration; that which the selection process has assigned to compost.

This section is made up of a series of prefermentation homogenisers operating slowly in a continous unit operation.

In these machines only the organic parts are broken up and begin a process of aerobic fermentation. When it has left the prefermentation homogeniser, the material is screened: that part composed of smaller pieces is sent to the maturing yard, whilst the coarse fraction goes to the incinerators. After a certain period of maturing, the material, which has a high organic content, is then sold to a farmer.

Due to the seasonal nature of compost application, large storage areas are required. Further drawbacks to compost obtained through prefermentation in the homogenisers include the presence of other materials, such as glass, china, plastic, wood etc; the characteristic odour which makes it difficult to use in populated areas; the cost of transportation, storage and distribution resulting from the low ratio of usable organic content to total weight (1 to 2.5 including moisture).

Dry organic matter

After many years of experience, Sorain-Cecchini have developed a process capable of overcoming those problems which arise in the conventional production of compost. The plant comprises the following processes:

The product is dried to 10 per cent moisture content, with

subsequent sterilisation, due to the product remaining for more than an hour in contact with air heated to 110°C (230°F).

Mechanical screening out of extraneous matter — glass, china, plastic etc.

Optional blending of the product with suitable additives to increase and improve the overall plant nutrient content.

Pelletising and bagging.

While still in the experimental stage, this plant is of a commercial size. Excellent results have been obtained from tests made in domestic gardens and greenhouses, as well as in large scale market gardening.

It is anticipated that shortly it will be practicable to convert all the material relegated to compost into this new product which is attracting much interest.

In view of the fuel potential, Sorain-Cecchini is also building an experimental plant in which the dried product will be used as fuel. When the ash handling problems are overcome, this use whould prove to be a viable alternative. The thermal/energy value of the product can be used in the generation of hot water, steam, electricity with advantages over the incineration of raw refuse.

Incineration

The incineration section of the recycling complex consists of modular units which can burn 100 tons per day each, a total six units in the East plant and three units in the West. A boiler is attached to each furnace which when combined produces about 50,000 kg/h of steam at a pressure of 8 bar. The sizing of the individual units is determined by the maximum total steam demand of the plant, as well as providing for a guaranteed steam flow during scheduled shutdowns or during unforeseen break-downs. Two basic functions have established the need for the incineration section of a recycling plant:

1 disposal of the refuse which cannot be recycled,
2 production of the steam necessary for in-plant use.

The incinerators are subjected to less severe conditions than those for which they were designed. In fact, they do not burn 'raw refuse', but simply what has been discarded, which is almost completely free from wet organic matter and is homogeneous and well-mixed.

The ash is quenched in water, stored in silos and then taken into a sanitary landfill. The flue-gas is scrubbed with water before entering the atmosphere.

Water re-use
All the water used in the processes of the various sections of the recycling plant receives primary and secondary treatment before re-use in-plant.

Glass
The recovery of glass from the urban refuse is still at the experimental stage.

The heart of the plant consists of an optic-pneumatic system to separate the glass from other materials. The material to be treated, has to be prepared in such a way as to have certain physical characteristics, with glass representing the highest proportion. The same machine, appropriately adjusted, is then able to sort out the glass into its various colours, clear, green and amber.

After more than a year of experiments, modifications are being made to the system, which will make glass recovery technically and economically viable.

Non-ferrous metals
The percentage of non-ferrous metals (aluminium, copper, brass, lead, etc) in refuse collected in Rome is almost negligible and insufficient to justify its recovery. However, the technology is available for the recovery of non-ferrous metals, should circumstances warrant this.

CHECK LIST

Note: the Rome Waste Recycling Complex is a major group of recycling plants.
The plants produce the following recycled products:

paper pulp of different qualities
animal feed
ferrous metal
plastic film
compost
dry organic matter.

The refuse components which cannot be recycled are fired in a large incinerator section which operates in conjunction with a heat recovery steam boiler. The steam is employed in the recycling operations.
Water is recycled after treatment.

The recovery of glass is carried on in a relatively small scale. This is due to be expanded.

Non-ferrous metals could be recovered if adequate quantities of them were present in the refuse.

6.7 SCRAP FRAGMENTATION PROCESS

Scope

Over 52 per cent of all the steel produced in Great Britain comes from scrap; similar proportions apply to the other industrialised countries. Around 75 per cent of all cast steel, 50 per cent of all cast iron, 80 per cent of all wrought iron and 60 per cent of all refined pig iron comes from scrap. These figures put into perspective the size and scale of the British scrap industry and its importance to the national economy. Ferrous scrap makes an immense contribution to the balance of payments — saving the cost of importing many millions of tons of iron ore each year — and can be ranked alongside coal as one of the indigenous raw materials basic to Britain's industrial prosperity.

To stress the importance of the scrap industry to the economy, analogies have been made between mining for coal and 'mining' for ferrous scrap in the industrial conurbations, which are particularly well endowed with this basic raw material. Whilst this analogy may adequately make its point — ignoring the vast difference between mining technology and scrap processing — it completely fails to make another, equally important, point: namely, that all mining operations *remove* an asset and create scars in the form of either an open-cast quarry or a spoil tip. The scrap industry, however, *creates* an asset, as all scrap iron and steel that lies idle is, at best an encumbrance and, at worst, a dangerous eyesore.

The process of scrap fragmentation in effect serves the community on two levels. It provides industry with a vital raw material in a clean, cheap and easily processed form and it protects the environment from the accumulative clutter of unwanted and out-dated buildings, machinery, equipment and the assorted hardware of 20th-century society.

There have been radical changes over the past ten years, during which time scrap handling has been transformed from a labour-intensive merchanting business into a capital-intensive processing industry, backed by a new and rapidly expanding technology.

Cars

The need for a thriving scrap industry is highlighted by the presence of abandoned cars littering city side streets and open spaces whose fume-filled petrol tanks are a constant, lethal fire and explosion hazard for inquisitive children. A decade ago these scrap cars were a menace. Today, due entirely to the introduction of modern scrap fragmentation processes, redundant cars have become a valuable source of high grade clean steel scrap.

Ferrous Fragmentisers Scrap Fragmentation Factory

Located at Willesden in west London this factory incorporates a revolutionary process which can convert up to 400,000 old and discarded cars a year into high-grade scrap metal — it takes only seconds to reduce the average family saloon to fist-size pieces of clean steel. (See plates 19 and 20.)

This factory copes with cars and other consumer durables, such as enamelled washing machines, refrigerators, cooking stoves, water heaters and baths — all of which, in spite of the fact that they are made from high grade steel, are in their manufactured form of little value for steelmaking because of their high impurity content. The process separates impurities and contaminants (including non-ferrous metals, paints, enamel, wood, glass and plastics) from the steel, creating a clean high quality dense form of scrap that is ideal for steel making.

The process
This is a continuous fully automatic operation. Cars and other forms of scrap are picked up by a crane equipped with a cactus grab and are placed upon an apron conveyor which drops them into the mill — a drop of some 13.3 m. Within 15 seconds, cars are shredded into pieces about the size of a man's hand. (See plates 17 and 22.)

These small pieces travel on an oscillating conveyor to a magnet, which lifts ferrous materials to an upper conveyor while non-ferrous metals and waste, such as upholstery, rubber, glass, wood, etc, continue on a lower conveyor, to be automatically separated into metals and waste.

The ferrous scrap process is completed in a condensing mill which reduces the steel into fist-size pieces. These are conveyed to a hopper which discharges a pre-set tonnage into waiting rail wagons.

The entire process, from the time a car is placed on the conveyor to the time it emerges as clean steel scrap, takes only minutes.

The scrap
This emerges as a homogeneous-type, heavy melting scrap. It is physically dense, weighing about 105 kg/m^3 and can be moved by magnets, grabs or conveyors. It is small enough to be stored in hoppers and can be used in all types of steel making furnaces. It has

fairly constant size and is not prone to bridge in electric furnaces, a frequent cause of damage to the electrodes.

The process returns the sheet steel, used in the motor and consumer goods industries, to its original state of clean, low carbon steel, free from tramp elements, dirt and other contaminants. It removes the 15 to 20 per cent of dirt or other contaminants which would normally be included in low grade scrap bales.

CHECK LIST

Note: Extent of scrap steel recycling industry; scrap steel items which are capable of recycling; process carried out in a scrap fragmentation factory; the condition of the final, recycled steel.

6.8 ELECTROLYTIC RECOVERY SYSTEM

Introduction
In surface finishing operations, rinse baths follow the pickling and plate processes to remove from the items being treated the remnants of the pickling and plating solution. After each wash, the bath becomes further enriched in metal ion, until ultimately it can no longer satisfactorily perform its washing function.

The metal concentration is usually controlled by its continuous removal of contaminated rinse and replacement with clean water. This operation involves a loss of valuable metal and an effluent treatment problem related to regulations on the discharge of toxic metals. Recent legislation in the UK and elsewhere has tightened such regulations on trade effluent discharge, particularly with respect to toxic metals (such as zinc, silver copper, nickel, cadmium and lead) which are commonly used in the plating industry.

The Chemelec cell is an electrolytic recovery system which can remove pickling and plating remnants in such a way that they can be recycled directly to the plating tank at a cost which is ultimately less than that of normal effluent treatment and the value of the replaced metal lost from that system.

Description
The design of the Chemelec cell differs fundamentally from its conventional counterpart in the following respects.

The electrodes are in the form of expanded mesh. The electrolyte is circulated through the cell via a porous distributor located at the bottom of the cell. The cell contains glass beads which are fluidised by the circulation of the electrolyte. Figure 6.13 illustrates the system diagrammatically.

The above characteristics result in higher ion transfer conditions during electrolysis by breaking up the barrier layer at the cathode; this permits the metals to be removed efficiently from dilute solutions and provides a means of increasing the limiting current density and, hence, the current efficiency. In operation, the flow of the electrolyte upwards through the distributor fluidises the glass beads. The upward and downward movement of this fluidised bed produces a polishing effect on the electrode which tends to break

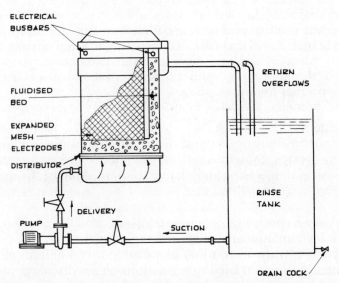

6.13   Diagrammatic arrangement of a Chemelec cell application

up the boundary layer. The fluidised bed of non-conducting particles, in combination with open mesh electrodes, promotes the formation of smooth metal deposits on the cathode. It has been established that the deposition of metal from dilute solutions (less than 1 g/litre) occurs in Chemelec cells at current efficiencies of 90 per cent or more, down to concentration of 0.2 g/l (200 ppm) producing metal plate and not powder. The associated current densities are of the order of 5 mA/cm².

This efficiency is far greater than has been achieved at similar concentration, using cells with fast flowing electrolyte, eg pumped electrolyte or rotating plate cells.

General applications
The Chemelec cell is relatively small and may, therefore, be sited close to the drag-out (static swill) tank of the plating/pickling line.

The contaminated liquor from this tank is pumped through the flow distributor; this fluidises the glass beads contained within the cell to a pre-determined height. It then overflows into a weir and is recirculated through the drag-out tank. The cell can easily and economically maintain the solution in the drag-out tank down to a level of, say 200 ppm, metal, ie sufficient cathode area is available, so that when a current is applied, metal is plated out at a rate equal to that of metal contamination carried over from the process bath.

As the metal is removed at this stage, there is minimum contamination of the running rinses and 99.6 per cent of the metal lost by drag-out from the plating bath is recovered for direct re-use as anode material in that bath. The amount of metal passing to the effluent plant is reduced by the same percentage, drastically reducing the labour, plant and sludge disposal costs associated with a conventional treatment plant.

The Chemelec cell has been used to date to recover copper, zinc, nickel, cadmium, silver, gold and nickel/iron from dilute solution.

Specific applications
Some of the results which have been monitored in specific applications are listed below:

(a) Cadmium (from high cyanide solution).
Bath level maintained at 50 to 200 ppm Cd.
Current density — 40 to 60 amps/m^2.
Cathode area — 1 m^2.
Cathode material — mild steel.
Operation — 160 h/wk.
Amount of cadmium recovered — up to 20 kg/wk.
(b) Nickel (from Nickel Watts solution) — pH maintained at acceptable level.
Bath level maintained at 200 ppm Ni.
Current density — 50 amps/m^2.
Cathode material — titanium.
Current efficiency — 45 per cent.
Total power consumption per tonne of Ni recovered: less than 18,000 kw/tonne.
(c) Nickel (from Nickel Watts solution) — pH maintained at acceptable level.
Bath level maintained at 2000 ppm Ni.
Total power consumption per tonne of Ni recovered less than 18,000 kw/tonne.
(d) Nickel (from Nickel Watts solution) — pH maintained at acceptable level.

Bath level maintained at 2000 ppm Ni.

Total power consumption per tonne of Ni recovered less than 8,000 kw/tonne.

(e) Copper (from copper sulphate solution).

Copper conc — 100 ppm Cu maintained in bath.

Current density — 40 amp/m².

Current efficiency — 60 per cent.

(f) Zinc conc in bath maintained at 250 mg/l.

Cathode material — mild steel.

Current density — 50 amp/m².

Average current efficiency — 45 per cent.

It is considered that, in addition to its electroplating applications, the cell could also be efficiently and effectively used in pickling operations and in all types of electro-winning.

Advantages of the Chemelec cell

The advantages of the Chemelec cell can be summarised:

A reduction of 99.6 per cent in the amount of sludge generated. A consequently similar reduction in the load on the oxide precipitation tank (or on the ion exchange or other treatment equipment), with the corresponding savings in the labour and transport charges associated with its disposal.

A cost saving in the replacement water for the first rinse tank. Because the metal concentration level is maintained at 200 ppm it only has to be replaced when the level of other impurities build up to an unacceptable level.

A major saving in the amount of replacement water required for the second rinse tank, which only receives drag-out of 200 ppm.

The metal recovered can be re-used directly as an anode on the plating bath, and the cost of recovery is only a proportion of the cost of the metal recovered.

The use of the cell does not add to the labour costs of the plating line.

The use of the cell cannot affect the plating tank because it is in a completely isolated, closed circuit.

The size of the cell is such that it can always be placed next to the rinse tank — and so becomes part of the line.

No chemical costs are involved.

The cell costs are comparatively small.

With cyanide solutions up to one-third of the total cyanide passing to effluent may be destroyed at a fraction of the cost of the conventional chemical method of destruction, which is employed at the final effluent stage.

Solution of a specific toxic waste problem

The cadmium plating operations at AB Electronic Components Ltd (South Wales,UK) resulted in 15 to 18 parts per million of cadmium in the effluent discharge from the whole factory, far above the water authority's recently revised standard of 1 ppm maximum content.

The introduction of the Chemelec cell at AB Electronic Components Ltd (UK) has reduced the toxicity of the cadmium solution to between 0.1 and 2 ppm. Without the installation of the Chemelec cell, the plating shop would have been faced with serious problems, as the water authority insisted that the company could not dump the treated sludges on agricultural land because of the cadmium content. There was a distinct possiblity of the plating shop being forced to close, had the toxicity not been greatly reduced.

The Management tried various methods of treating toxic solutions — dilution with water, lime, chlorine treatment and other alkaline treatments — with a degree of success with most metals, but not with cadmium. All the time, the company was faced with three major problems: pressure from the water authority; the growing public awareness that the factory was discharging a poison; valuable cadmium being washed down the drains.

Eventually, the Electricity Council Research Centre at Capenhurst was called in and a prototype Chemelec cell was installed. It has given satisfaction and certain major advantages, including improved security of many jobs at the factory; an average of 2.5 kg of valuable cadmium recovered each week (cadmium costs (1979) about £5000 per tonne); the rinse water is now changed once every six months instead of fornightly; pumping and transport costs have been cut by £5000 a year — payback periods will thus be shorter; the improvement in effluent has proved sufficient reason in itself for the installation, but the recycling is a valuable bonus; the Chemelec cell is also very easy to operate, being checked only first thing in the morning and last thing at night.

AB Electronic Components Ltd have been so impressed with their Chemelec installation that the company is considering installing another cell to recover silver. At present the company employs a conventional plating-out recovery system for its silver work, but it is an expensive process, made even more expensive by contracting out to another company which refines the recovered silver flakes.

Plates 23 and 24 show applications of the Chemelec cell for silver and nickel/iron processes.

REFERENCES

D. Tomlinson, 'Chemelec — the novel electrolytic recovery system', *Product Finishing,* pp 21–22, June 1979.

New process solves factory waste problem, *Circuit News*, p 13, September 1979.

6.9 THE RECOVERY OF PICKLE ACID IN THE STEEL INDUSTRY

Background
The operators of ferrous pickling plants have strong incentives for the recovery of spent pickle liquor on financial grounds.Moreover, current environmental restraints dictate the safe and efficient recovery and re-concentration of the spent acid and plant effluent. The technology and plant are, in fact, now available to enable the operator to reduce waste treatment problems and, at the same time, improve the economic aspects of the process. Nevertheless whilst the economic factors are important, it is becoming clear that the various public authorities will gradually introduce legislation on the control of the pollution caused by the discharge of effluents, irrespective of the possible economic effect on the plant operator.

Ferrous pickling — the problem
The steel industry employs a process called 'ferrous pickling'. Plants are generally operated on a daily basis, though in some cases, on a continuous basis, apart from maintenance. There is therefore an ever-present need to change the pickling acid due to the build-up of iron rendering the acid ineffectual. The operator has to dispose of the spent pickle acid in some way, either by having it removed by a contractor (an expensive method) or by neutralisation and subsequent draining into the nearest river, which in most cases may be fraught with difficulties.

It is best to resolve the problem at the source. In the case of steel pickling with sulphuric acid, a solution is possible, with the added bonus of making the whole operation more profitable.

The acid regeneration process
The Cascade acid regeneration process was first patented by E. Mulcahy. The process is now owned and offered by Chemical Engineering Construction (Pensnett) Ltd (UK). It is an effective process because, by its design and function, the pickle acid is maintained at a level of iron content which allows effective pickling to take place on a continuous basis. There have been many satisfactory installations in the UK and abroad.

The process flow-diagram for such an acid recovery plant is shown in fig 6.14.

The process is the result of much accumulated experience; it has eliminated most of the problems which are inherent in many other designs of similar plant, such as the choking of vessels by crystal settlement, the use of small orifices or jets which cause frequent stoppages, the use of valves for flow control between vessels and the necessity to use tall expensive buildings for gravity flow operation. These changes may be ascribed to the introduction of the choke-proof (KEMEC) air operated crystals pump.

Plant design

In the CEC(P) patented process, all the process vessels are located on one plane, enabling heavy crystal-laden acids to flow freely and continuously from end to end of the plant, with an ultimate separate flow of regenerated acid to the pickle bath and a flow to the filter for the removal of crystals. The plant design keeps the crystals in

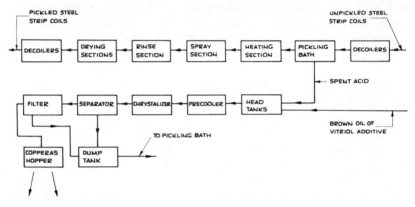

6.14   Pickle acid recovery plant — flow-diagram

suspension, moving them continuously from pre-cooler and crystal-liser to a separation cone where the crystals are conveyed by a Kemec pump to the vacuum filter which is positioned immediately above a storage hopper.

The ferrous sulphate in solution in the spent acid liquor is precipitated by continuous cooling, being carried out in stages. The temperature of the incoming acid is reduced by cooling water, but remains above the crystallisation temperature before being processed in the crystallisating part of the plant. The temperature of the acid is then further reduced in the crystalliser by means of circulating ethylene glycol solution in cooling coils which is continuously circulated from the chiller of a refrigeration plant.

By adequate design of the heat transfer surfaces, the temperature is reduced so that the solubility of $FeSO_4$ in the spent liquor is reduced by about 3 to 3½ per cent (as Fe). In order to assist reduction in the solubility of $FeSO_4$, sufficient concentrated acid, BOV (BOV is brown oil of vitriol — 77 per cent H_3SO_4) is added to the spent acid reception tank, thus decreasing the solubility at the higher acid strength.

The liquor, laden with ferrous sulphate crystals (Copperas), is transferred from the crystalliser to the separator and from there to the tilting pan filter by Kemec air pumps. Surplus acid drains to the regenerated acid tank. The Copperas is then deposited into the hopper to await disposal. The regenerated acid is returned to the pickling plant at temperatures between 80 and 85°C (176 and 185°F), dependent upon where reheating is effected.

The Copperas by-product of the process can be sold to water treatment or horticultural supply companies, for use as flocculants and for lawn sand mixtures, respectively. If such outlets are not available, the disposal of the Copperas either into dumps or at sea does not cause an unacceptable pollution problem.

Plate 25 shows an acid regeneration plant of the type described in this chapter.

Maintenance
The plant is said to require very little operational attention. It is easily accessible from the point of view of cleaning and routine maintenance.

The use of the Kemec pumps ensures that there is no accumulation of deposited crystals in any of the process vessels.

Maintenance is facilitated by the arrangement of the plant, whereby the heating facilities do not take up space in the pickling bath itself, thus leaving the bath clear for the passage of the maximum amount of the steel undergoing pickling.

Economic considerations
As an example, consideration is made of a typical installation where 16.5 tonne/h of steel are pickled. Under prevailing price and cost structures (1979), one such plant could be built at a reasonable capital cost and give an attractive return of at least 20 per cent on a discounted cash flow (DCF) basis. The calculations for the capacity of the plant are shown overleaf. For convenience, the quantities are shown in units per hour and units per tonne of steel pickled.

Cost of operation
Table 6.3 on p 118 shows the cost of operation of the plant at various operating hours per year. The compilation of the operating hours is shown below. The graph fig 6.15 represents graphically the results of table 6.3.

By-product and requirements

		Quantities	
	Units	Per hour	Per tonne of steel pickled
Spent acid	tonne	2.75	0.166
By-product Copperas	tonne	0.537	0.032
Utilities and labour:			
a Electric power	kWh	80.0	4.848
b Water	tonne	1.154	0.069
c Labour	mhr	0.3	0.018
d Make-up acid BOV	tonne	0.244	0.014

Analysis of Copperas and acids

Spent acid $H_2SO_4 = 8.7\%$ w/w
$Fe = 17.65\%$ w/w as $FeSO_4$ (6.5% w/w Fe)

By-product — Copperas $FeSO_4 \, 7H_2O$ (Heptahydrate)

Regenerated acid $H_2SO_4 — 16.4\%$ w/w
$Fe — 9.5\%$ w/w as $FeSO_4$ (-3.5% w/w as Fe)

Note: The Fe content of the acid is normally expressed as a reduction in Fe off the spent acid, equal to 3 to 3.5 per cent w/w as Fe.

Cost data for analysis

Operation see key to table **6.3**
Cost of transporting waste liquor to dump £300/tanker of 25 t ie £12/t
Selling price of Copperas £2.00/t
Turnkey budget cost of plant — excluding cost of land £230,000
Cost of sulphuric acid (H_2SO_4 20% w/w) £5.00/t @ 20% H_2SO_4 W/W
Cost of sulphuric acid BOV (H_2SO_4 77% w/w) £25.00/t

Note: To convert (approximately) to $US, multiply £ sterling by 2.3.

CHECK LIST

Check: scale of acid regeneration requirement; disposal costs; environmental restrictions affecting convenient disposal; suitability of a comprehensive scheme of acid regeneration, as described in this chapter; the space requirements; availability of refrigeration plant and required capacity of same; establishment of process flow line. *Evaluate:* the economic factors in respective of capital costs, operating expenses, maintenance, disposal of by-products to establish economic viability; markets for Copperas by-product.

TABLE 6.3 COST OF OPERATION

Shifts (total hours per year – see key below)

Item	Units	Unit cost	A (5600) Per year	A (5600) Total cost	B (4200) Per year	B (4200) Total cost	C (3800) Per year	C (3800) Total cost	C (2000) Per Year	C (2000) Total cost
Power	KWH	0.012	448.000	5.376	336.000	4.032	304.000	3.648	160.000	1.920
Water	Tonnes	0.035	865	30	649	22	587	20	309	11
Labour	MHR	2.5	1.680	4.200	1.260	3.150	1.140	2.850	600	1.500
O/H				4.200		3.150		2.850		1.500
Make-up acid (BOV)	Tonnes	25.0	1.369	34.225	1.027	25.675	929	23.225	489	12.225
Copperas	Tonnes	2.0	3.009	(6.018)	2.255	(4.510)	2.040	(4.080)	1.074	(2.148)
Maintenance	2% of cap	Cost		4.600		4.600		4.600		4.600
Insurance	1% of cap	Cost		2.300		2.300		2.300		2.300
Depreciation	Over 10	Years		23.000		23.000		23.000		23.000
Cost of dumping				71.913		61.419		58.413		44.908
Spent acid		300.00	15.400	184.800	11.550	138.600	10.450	125.400	5.500	66.000
New pickle acid (20% H_2SO_4)		5.00	15.400	17.000	11.550	57.750	10.450	52.250	5.500	27.500
Dumping total cost				261.800		193.350		177.650		93.500
Nett	Saving/	Income		189.887		131.931		119.237		48.592
Tax	54%			102.538		71.242		64.387		26.240
Net income after tax				87.349		60.689		54.850		22.352
Depreciation				23.000		23.000		23.000		23.000
Gross cash flow				110.349		83.689		77.850		45.352
Payout period	*Capital investment* *Gross cash flow*	Years		2.08		2.74		2.95		5.07
	DCF			49%		35%		32%		14%

Note: Basis for the calculation includes (a) Maintenance 2% of capital investment (b) Insurance 1% of capital investment (c) Depreciation over 10 years on a ... lic basis (d) Corporation tax at 54%.

Key to Table 6.3

	A	B	C	D
Shifts/day	3	2+1	2	1
Hours/shift	8		8	8
Days/week	5	5+1	5	5
Weeks/year	50	50	50	50
Total: hours/year	6000	4400	4000	2000
Maintenance: hours/week	8	4	4	—
Hours/year	400	200	200	—
Grand total: hours/year	5600	4200	3800	2000

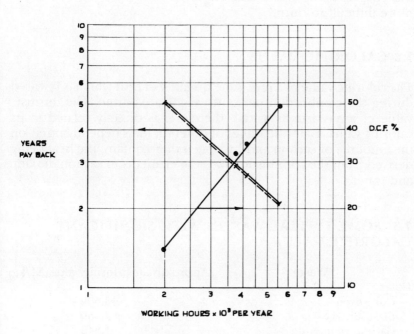

6.15   Graphical presentation of table 6.3 results

7
Waste Combustion for Energy Recovery

7.1 INTRODUCTION

This chapter describes the processes and equipment more suited to wood-wastes, which have, traditionally, been burnt as a fuel for the purpose of energy recovery. The range of the lower calorific value fuels, such as refuse, manures and composts are, in the main, incinerated without energy recovery or discarded. However, most of the principles of combustion and energy recovery described in this chapter apply also to this group of waste products, which are more difficult to burn.

7.2 CALORIFIC VALUE

The calorific value of a fuel is the quantity of heat which is released during the combustion per unit weight or volume. The intrinsic value of any waste as a fuel, therefore, is directly related to its calorific value. Calorific values of different fuels depend largely on the amounts of carbon and hydrogen they contain, the heat being derived from the combustion of these elements to carbon dioxide and water.

7.3 SOME TYPICAL WASTES WITH SIGNIFICANT CALORIFIC VALUE

Waste	Approximate calorific value (KJ/kg)
Gases	
Coke-oven	43,500
Blast furnace	2,650
Carbon monoxide	1,340
Refinery	50,700

Liquids

Industrial sludge	9,000
Black liquor	10,230
Sulfite liquor	9,770
Dirty Solvents	30,000
Spent lubricants	27,500
Paints and resins	18,500
Oily waste and residue	41,870

Solids

Bagasse	11.500
Bark	11,000
General Wood wastes	13,000
Sawdust and shavings	14,000
Coffee grounds	13,500
Nut hulls	17,900
Tice hulls	13,500
Corn cobs	18,900
Paper and cardboard	17,000
Refuse-derived fuel (RDF)	9,000
Chicken litter	12,000
Mushroom compost	8,000

7.4 HIGHER CALORIFIC VALUE

This refers to the gross or upper calorific value, being the quantity of heat liberated per unit mass of fuel burnt when the products of combustion are cooled down to the standard atmospheric temperature.

7.5 LOWER CALORIFIC VALUE

This term refers to the net calorific value, being the higher calorific value, less the latent heat of the steam, which is generated in the combustion of the hydrogen present in the fuel and in the evaporation of the moisture associated with the combustion air.

7.6 COMPLETE COMBUSTION

The complete combustion of a fuel can only take place in the presence of adequate air, which is a mixture of 23 per cent oxygen and 77 per cent nitrogen (by weight), oxygen being the active element. The nitrogen in the air takes no part in the process of combustion. Combustible substances must reach a temperature at least equal to their individual ignition temperatures before they can unite with oxygen.

7.7 IGNITION TEMPERATURES

The ignition temperatures of various elements associated with the combustion of most organic waste forms are:

Carbon	449°C	840°F
Hydrogen	599°C	1110°F
Sulphur	249°C	480°F
Carbon monoxide	649°C	1200°F
Methane	649°C	1200°F

7.8 COMBUSTION AIR REQUIREMENT

This may be theoretically calculated, based upon element molecular weight principles, which yield the following statements:

12 kg of carbon plus 32 kg of oxygen produce 44 kg of carbon dioxide

4 kg of hydrogen plus 32 kg of oxygen produce 36 kg of steam

32 kg of sulphur plus 32 kg of oxygen produce 64 kg of sulphur dioxide.

Since air contains only 23 per cent oxygen, the theoretical air supply quantity for the complete combustion of 1 kg of fuel containing these three combustible elements may be mathematically stated as follows:

$$\frac{1}{0.23}\left(\frac{32}{12}C + 8H + 1S\right) kg$$

where, C, H and S are the carbon, hydrogen and sulphur fractional constituents of 1 kg of the fuel.

7.9 INCOMPLETE COMBUSTION

The incomplete combustion of a fuel is usually associated with inadequate air supply and occurs when carbon is burnt only to carbon monoxide, instead of to carbon dioxide. Considerably less heat is then liberated, since 24 kg of carbon plus 32 kg of oxygen produce 56 kg of carbon monoxide. a sample analysis of carbon monoxide (CO) or of carbon dioxide (CO_2) from the flue gases in a furnace system may be used, together with flue gas temperature measurement, as a practical guide of combustion efficiency.

7.10 EXCESS AIR FOR COMBUSTION

To ensure the thorough mixing of the air with the fuel, excess air for combustion is required. Thorough mixing cannot be achieved by supplying only the theoretical minimum air quantity. The quantity of excess air requirement theoretically varies with variations of calorific value,bulk density, moisture and ash content of the fuel being burnt and with the particular method of incineration.

For example, solid fuel bed type furnaces require some 30 to 50 per cent excess air quantity; cyclone combustion furnaces require as much as 100 per cent. Careful control must be exercised over the exact quantity and distribution of combustion air (including excess air): inadequate air supply causes smoke emission; excessive air supply reduces combustion efficiency.

7.11 PRIMARY AIR

Primary air, when applied to a bed type furnace, is introduced *below* the bed of solid fuel to provide the main or primary air for combustion.

In liquid or gas fuel burning, the primary air is introduced into the combustion chamber with the fuel, often in a pre-mixed fashion. In a cyclone or vortex furnace, the primary air is often the only source of combustion air and is also used to pneumatically convey the solid fuel material into the combustion chamber.

7.12 SECONDARY AIR

Secondary air, when applied to a bed, is introduced *above* the bed of solid fuel to ensure the complete combustion of thick bed fuel layers and (more importantly) fine fuel particles, in suspension above the bed. With certain types of fine-particle fuels (such as sawdust and sander dust), the secondary air supply requires special consideration because as much as 75 per cent of the fuel feed may have to be burnt in suspension above the fuel bed.

In liquid or gas fuel burning, the secondary air is introduced *around* the fuel/primary air mixture to ensure complete fuel combustion and also to assist in the establishment of the flame form or pattern.

7.13 BULK DENSITY

The bulk density of different wastes varies greatly, particularly if the waste is wet. For example, the density of wood-waste may vary from about 80 kg/m^3 to over 160 kg/m^3, depending upon whether it is hard wood or soft wood, whether it is in the form of wood dust, chips or off-cuts and whether it is moist, wet or dry. The variation of bulk density in other forms of waste may be just as great. The variation of waste fuel volume within a combustion chamber has a significant effect on the combustion air requirements.

7.14 MOISTURE CONTENT

A clear understanding of moisture content is most important, since waste is always more difficult to burn wet, rather than dry. Wood-waste is considered to be relatively dry when the moisture content does not exceed 20 per cent (by weight); it can be incinerated, without undue difficulty, in almost any type of furnace.

Certain modern underfeed stoker type furnaces can burn wood-waste with moisture contents of up to about 50 per cent, whereas wood-waste with moisture contents of over 50 per cent, 100 per cent and sometimes 150 per cent are very difficult (if not impossible) to burn in such furnaces. Conventional incinerators cannot success-fully combust very wet material; pre-drying of the waste must be achieved, unless the residence or dwell time of suspended waste matter in a furnace (such as a cyclone) allows drying before ignition *within* the combustion chamber. The burning of wet waste is not as efficient as the burning of dry waste because a proportion of the heat release is expended in converting the water into steam. The calorific value of wet waste/kg is considerably lower than that for dry waste.

Figure 7.1 shows the variation of calorific value with moisture content for some various types of wood. The presence of a high proportion of wet waste will always reduce the furnace output.

7.15 ASH CONTENT

The ash content of a fuel is another important consideration because it affects the calorific value and, in practical terms, determines the required rate of ash removal. For example, wood-waste may have an ash content as low as 2 per cent (by weight) and yet, when combusted continuously in a cyclone furnace, the plant must be shut down every four to six weeks for purposes of ash removal and cleaning. The nature of the ash is also important, ie whether it solidifies and forms clinker or whether it falls freely.

7.16 FLY ASH

Fly ash deposits are sometimes experienced in furnace tubes and flue gas passageways, being the fine particle escape from suspended matter in the combustion chamber, which has not been carried over to the grit arrestors. Fly ash occurs more usually when the flue gases cool; they become more dense and their velocity decreases, encouraging fall-out of ash and grit. A marginal increase of flue gas velocity may avoid the incidence of fly ash if it is possible to effect the appropriate plant adjustment.

7.17 WASTE COMBUSTION

The combustion of waste in an efficient and smoke free manner requires specialist expertise and purpose-made equipment, which often includes oversized combustion chambers, fuel mixing techniques and furnaces external to the heat recovery boiler. Incineration of waste is very punishing to the furnace materials because of the necessary high combustion temperatures and the

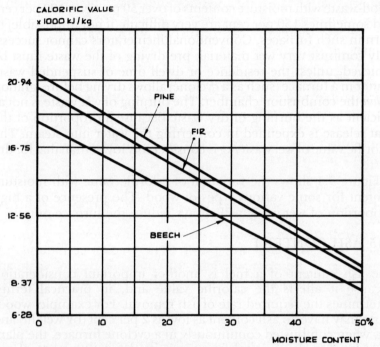

7.1   Moisture content/calorific value variation

nature of the incinerated material. Many problems, not usually encountered in the combustion of conventional solid fuels (such as bituminous coal and anthracite), arise with the incineration of lower grade waste material. Suitable plant must be selected very carefully and always with a view to compliance with the local Clean Air Laws.

The main difficulties associated with the smokeless incineration of waste materials are:

Variation of bulk density
For example, a furnace designed to burn only graded wood-waste

(say small chips) has to be quite different from a furnace designed to burn only wood logs. For this reason, combustion engineers endeavour to minimise the variation in fuel size (by hogging or chopping wood logs into small pieces of about 30 mm cubes), allowing hogged material to be burnt with wood chips, sawdust and other run-of-the-mill waste.

Variation of calorific value
For example, certain hard and soft woods may differ by as much as 30 per cent in terms of heat release capability. For constant furnace heat release input, the rate of fuel should be variable, which is sometimes difficult.

Wetness or moisture content
For example, a bed of wet wood logs is almost impossible to burn without smoke emission. Unless pre-dried, very wet hogged and other wood-waste can only be burnt in suspension, hence oversized combustion chambers and external cyclone furnaces are used mainly for this purpose.

Ash content
For example, refuse-derived fuel, paper and cardboard may have ash contents approaching 20 per cent (by weight) and are almost impossible to burn continuously in conventional equipment, unless there is a large ash pit or some kind of continuous ash removal gear. Equipment which will burn this type of waste and other high ash content wastes successfully must be selected with great care.

Plastic content
For example, refuse in its separated form may, at times, have a high plastic content, which requires higher furnace temperature operation than with organic wastes. The products of combustion are also quite different, possibly producing corrosive chlorine compounds.

Low calorific value
The low heating value of some wastes makes it necessary to burn a minimum amount of alternative supplementary fuel at all times.

Sander dust
Explosive sander dust is a most dangerous waste material, as are many other waste fuels in dust form. In the selection of equipment to burn this waste (although mixed with other waste fuels), great care is necessary.

7.18 FURNACE DESIGN CONSIDERATIONS

To overcome most of the difficulties associated with the incineration of waste material, certain basic design considerations must be adopted in the selection of smokeless incineration plant methods:

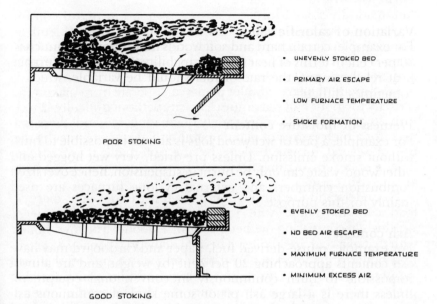

POOR STOKING

- UNEVENLY STOKED BED
- PRIMARY AIR ESCAPE
- LOW FURNACE TEMPERATURE
- SMOKE FORMATION

GOOD STOKING

- EVENLY STOKED BED
- NO BED AIR ESCAPE
- MAXIMUM FURNACE TEMPERATURE
- MINIMUM EXCESS AIR

7.2   Manual bed stoking

Manual stoking

Figure 7.2 shows a manually stoked solid fuel furnace bed with some elementary notes related to poor and good stoking methods. The most common cause of serious efficiency losses in such a furnace is the flow of cold air to the chimney, other than through or over the bed, caused by either allowing air to flow along the ashpit to the back of the bridge or by air leaks in the refractory brickwork. When a furnace bed is overcharged with fuel, though evenly spread, smoke emission will inevitably follow. If a furnace bed is under-charged with fuel, particularly near to the bridge, the air flows straight to the chimney. When a furnace bed is unevenly charged with fuel, the air flows quicker through the thinner parts, with the result that holes or gaps are opened in the bed which cause the primary air to bypass the fuel on its way to the chimney. The furnace must be charged with fuel in an orderly manner to avoid wide fluctuations in combustion conditions and to ensure, as far as possible, that the furnace temperature remains constant. Heavy intermittent charging causes blockage of the primary air supply and accelerates severe cooling off, followed by periods of excessive high temperature, with the likelihood of blow-backs and minor explosions.

Turn-down ratio

Automatically stoked furnaces do not respond to on/off control in the same manner as oil or gas fired boilers. The problems of fluctuating furnace temperature and re-kindling necessitate continuous relatively steady thermal load demands within the variable scope of the plant.

Most modern furnace/boiler plants can operate from maximum capacity to about half maximum capacity without difficulty (2 to 1 turn down ratio). With more widely fluctuating demand, there is a need for a high degree of plant flexibility. This may be met by the use of several furnace/boilers, by the automatic thermal load linking of heat dissipating devices or by supplementary firing with an alternative fuel.

To understand the problem of re-kindling under light thermal load conditions and with limited turn-down capability, it is worthwhile comparing the behaviour of a wood-waste fired boiler with that of a coal fired boiler. Thermal demand is usually detected by a boiler pressure switch or thermostat, which cuts off the heat supply or fuel entry. During this idling condition (which may be prolonged), the furnace temperature may fall below the ignition temperature of the fuel waiting to be admitted. Re-kindling then becomes a problem, which is common to furnaces burning wet fuel and fuel having a relatively low calorific value. Coal fired furnaces are more able (because the residual fire stays bright) to deal with long idling periods. When there is little substance in the fire-bed, the dissipators or supplementary fuel must be used to avoid the need to re-kindle.

As far as possible, the selection of boilers and waste combustion equipment, which can be used with only one specific fuel should be avoided. If a supplementary fuel has to be used, it is best to select equipment, which is suitable for dual-fuel firing to avoid the intermittent use of single-fuel large plant items and consequently higher capital and maintenance costs.

Furnace temperature

In the control of a wood-waste furnace temperature, it is necessary (on one hand) to maintain a high temperature to ensure efficient and smokeless combustion of waste, while (on the other hand) it is necessary to limit the operating furnace temperature to the safe working limits of the refractory brickwork. High quality refractory has a safe upper temperature limit of about 1600°C (2912°F), but at this limiting temperature, the face of the brickwork tends to *run* and become impregnated with wood ash. The resulting chemical combination lowers the slagging temperature of the brickwork face, giving rise to spalling, severe damage, shut-down and costly repairs. A safe furnace operating temperature is in the order of 1000 to 1100°C (1832 to 2012°F), with an upper limit of 1250°C (2282°F). To avoid refractory stress damage, due to temperature fluctuations. a steady combustion operating temperature must be maintained. When shutting down or lighting up, the furnace temperature should be gradually and slowly raised or lowered.

Furnace capacity

The furnace, or combustion chamber, whether external to, or integral with, the boiler, must be of adequate size and capacity for the specified waste throughput. For example, the burning of wood-waste, paper and cardboard causes rapid expansion of the combustion products; it produces intense heat and because of the high volatile content, a considerable propagation of flame. Combustion chambers designed for oil gas and coal burning are not generally suitable for waste incineration.

Explosion risk

The incineration of explosive waste dust demands a high degree of furnace design ability in terms of method and safety. For example, a pocket of sander dust in a wood-waste fuel feed will almost certainly explode as soon as it enters an operating furnace. Such explosions are often referred to as blow-backs and their danger is not generally fully appreciated unless and until there is a major explosion. Clearly, the design of a furnace to burn such material must have sufficient capacity for the instantaneous expansion of the combustion products; the refractories must be able to withstand sudden increases in furnace temperature and pressure and all access apertures must be secure, inspection doors must be interlocked under such circumstances and explosion risk relief panels must be able to relieve such explosions in a controlled fashion. One of the greatest areas of danger is in the fuel feed, where adequate provision must be made to avoid fire spread to outside the furnace.

7.19 DUTCH OVENS

Dutch ovens are oversized adapted combustion chambers and have long been used extensively in the wood-waste burning industry for incineration and energy recovery. The principle is to dig a large hole in the ground, suitably structured and lined with refractory materials, over which is placed a conventional boiler fire-box which communicates with the hole in the ground. The enlarged combustion chamber is then suitably sealed, adopting either a step, or flat grate, arrangement to permit the convenient introduction of waste materials and air supply for combustion. Redundant steam locomotive boilers are admirably suited for this application, having large separate fire-boxes and being excellent steam raisers.

Figure **7.3** shows both the flat and the stepped grate furnace arrangement with locomotive type boiler application. Because of the oversized combustion chamber and ruggedness of design, such a furnace can also burn off-cuts, logs, paper and perhaps some separated refuse. Although this type of incinerator is unsophisticated and not over-efficient and might not altogether satisfy the current Clean Air Laws, there is a lesson to be re-learnt from this equipment in the design of modern flexible incineration plant.

7.20 AUTOMATIC STOKING

The automatic stoking of a boiler is generally more efficient than manual stoking and may be achieved in a number of ways. The most basic original form, the chain grate, is simply a slow moving grate made up of replaceable multiple cast-iron links, which are connected in a continuous belt fashion to rotating cogs driven by an external motor. A close fitting transit waste hopper at the front of the boiler allows the fuel feed to fall gently onto the moving grate, which then conveys the fuel into the combustion chamber. The equipment is so designed that the waste material progresses in defined stages of combustion along the length of the moving grate, from the raw material at the front to completely burnt material at the rear or back end, where the ash is then deposited and collected. The primary air, which is introduced below the bed, serves also to keep the moving parts of the chain grate relatively cool.

A more advanced version of the basic chain grate stoker is shown in fig **7.4**. Ashing is effected by a conveying ash extractor. The stoker is designed to burn a wide range of poor quality fuels and meets the requirements of the UK Clean Air Act. All travelling grate links are cast in a special grade of cast-iron to fine limits. The circular section bright steel link rods, on which the links are mounted, require no special fastenings for location; the links can then be quickly and easily replaced. Fine air spacing between the links reduces the need for riddling, side cooling of the links and maintains even air

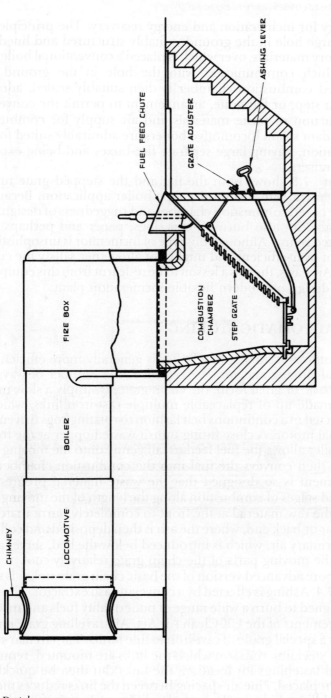

7.3 Dutch ovens

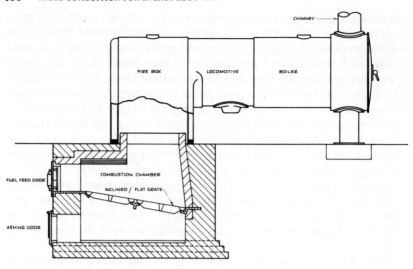

7.3 (contd) Dutch ovens

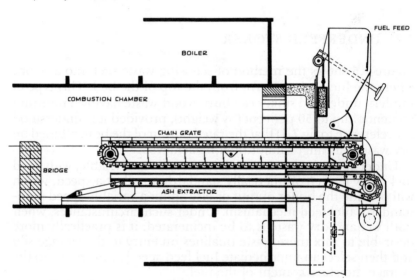

7.4   Chain grate stoker

distribution. Serrated link sides increase total air spacing and improve primary air distribution. Serrated link tops allow the air to pass along the top grate surface under the fuel bridging of serrations. The chain grate provides a minimum surface for the absorption of heat and a maximum cooling surface. Self-cleaning action of the links is effected when the grate revolves, allowing entrained riddlings to be deposited on the ash extractor. The grate is driven by a constant speed, totally enclosed motor through an infinitely variable hydraulic gear and reduction gearing to a main worm and wormwheel driving the stoker front shaft. The grate speed is capable of a fine degree of control from zero to 15m/hr. The grate may be driven in reverse, if necessary. A shear-pin safety device safeguards against overloading; provision is also made for hand operation. The fuel hopper is fitted with a full width shutter, which, when in the open position, acts as a fuel cut-off valve. The depth of the fuel bed is controlled by means of a refractory-lined guillotine door. When the door is raised, sufficient height is provided to give ease of access for inspection or for hand firing.

Similar advanced types of chain grate stokers have been successfully operated with pelletised refuse-derived fuel, when pre-mixed with high quality coal in a not less than 50 per cent (by weight) fuel mixture.

Plate 26 shows pre-mixed fuel, ie coal/RDF burnt in a bed-type furnace at Doncaster.

7.21 UNDERFEED STOKER

Figure 7.5 shows the method of screwing waste fuel into a retort, where the fuel is then burnt from the top of the bed. This type of modern underfeed stoker can burn wood-waste having a moisture content of up to 50 per cent (by weight), provided it is understood (by reference to fig 7.1) that the rated output of the boiler (based on dry waste burning) cannot then be achieved.

Under such circumstances, it is, therefore, advisable, with fixed fuel screw feeds (commercially standard), to select a speed, which will provide the boiler output or else adopt a variable speed (non-standard) fuel feed mechanism. Under such circumstances, when both wet and dry waste is to be incinerated, it is practically more desirable to mix these waste qualities on entry to the storage silo and then select an intermediate fuel feed speed appropriate to the average moisture content of the fuel.

Fan assisted *primary* air is supplied through a distribution manifold below the bed and passes through gaps in the retort fire bars, ash being pushed over the edges of the fire by the new unburnt material which enters from below.Fan-assisted *secondary* air is supplied above the bed and, in this case (under certain conditions when waste is in fine particle form), secondary air supply plays a greater part in the combustion than the primary air.

Figure 7.5 also shows the vertical feed pipe, which discharges into the controlled feed hopper before being dropped into the horizontal furnace screw feed pipe. The primary and secondary air supply fans are clearly shown. With very dry waste, particularly if fine particle fuel (sawdust) is being used, there will most certainly be a need to alter the primary and secondary air quantities to ensure that the secondary air has a larger share of the available supply air quantity to combust the suspended fuel particles above the bed.

A large volume of combustion chamber is generally advantageous in waste burning, but under certain conditions of dry fine particle fuel, it can be a serious disadvantage. The hottest furnace zone is immediately above the fire-bed. Sander dust is immediately ignited and burnt in this zone, but sawdust (being a larger grade fuel) may then escape being incapsulated with a carbon film and fall unburnt into the grit arrestors. Recycling this escaped carbonised fuel back to the retort may be successful; building a reflecting fire-brick arch over the fire-bed may also assist, but it is well known (even with coal burning) that a little wetness assists in the stable combustion of very dry fine waste mixtures.

The equipment shown in fig 7.5 is admirably suited for dual firing with either fuel oil or gas which may be conveniently positioned at the rear or at the side of the boiler, the boiler front being required for waste fuel operating equipment.

In the case of coal being used as an alternative fuel, variable fuel feed is essential since the rate required for waste operation may be three times that required for coal firing. Another important consideration is the slagging of coal, which is different than that for waste and may require an alternative form of fire grate profile and spacing. Yet another important consideration is the primary/secondary combustion air quantity ratio, which will be quite different, requiring alternative damper settings. The combustion chamber size must be adequate for both supplementary and waste fuel. Boiler combustion efficiencies are generally in excess of 80 per cent with this method of waste incineration.

The control and operation of underfeed stoker/boiler systems is fully described in chapter 12.

7.22 FORCED AND INDUCED DRAUGHT BOILERS

Figure 7.6 shows an arrangement of a conventional shell and tube boiler adapted for burning waste in a *pressurised* (forced draught) combustion chamber, which has a full stand-by auxiliary dual firing facility. This method of waste incineration is only suited to automatic/pneumatic fuel feed operation. Manual stoking of the

also the controlled-feed hopper before being dropped into the horizontal furnace screw feed pipe. The primary and secondary air supply fans are clearly shown. With very dry waste, particularly if the particle fuel (saw dust) is being fed, there will most certainly be caused in after the primary, and so secondary air quantities to ensure that the secondary air has a large excess of the available supply, air quantity to combust the suspended fuel particles above the bed.

A large volume of combustion chamber is essential, advantageous in waste burning. Under the certain conditions of dry fine particle fuel, it can be a real problem, where the highest furnace zone is immediately above the screw feed and is immediately ignited and burnt quickly, but saw dust... the larger grade fuel may then escape to central preheated combustion then and tumbling into the grit arrestor, accumulating there and burning and back to the stoker conveyor which... reflecting the brief cold over the burning bed. Under these conditions, well engineered, even with coal burning plant, it is often... in the possible combustion of very fine waste...

A sufficiently large combustion chamber suitably sized for dust firing, waste elimination of waste which may be conveniently positioned at the furnace and indeed the boiler, the boiler being remodelled...

In the case where the wood waste is a native boiler, multiple fuel feed is essential, so the air required for waste operation may be different, unless the waste is a coal firing. Another important consideration is the ignition of coal, which is different than that for waste and may require an additional layer of the grate profile and spigots.

A very important consideration is the primary/secondary combustion quantity ratio, which will be quite different, requiring additional damper settings. The combustion chamber size and temperature for both supplementary and waste fuel boiler combustion furnaces are generally in excess of 80 per cent with this type of waste incineration.

The control arrangement of underfeed stokers systems is fully described...

FORCED AND INDUCED DRAUGHT BOILERS

Figure 7.6 shows an arrangement of a conveyor coal stoker adapted to a furnace fitted to an induced draught combustion chamber, which has an ash stoked by dealer, and ready firing. This method of waste incineration only suited to continuous/pressure fuel techno-operation. Manufacturers of the

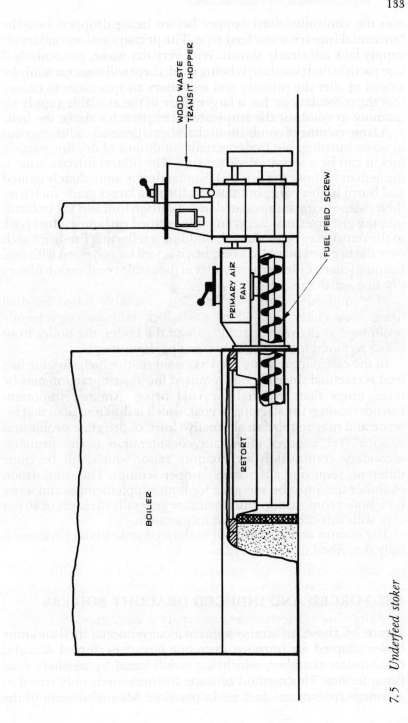

7.5 Underfeed stoker

off-cuts into the furnace is not allowed in a pressurised furnace because of the obvious danger of both fire spread and injury.

Figure **7.7** shows a cross-section of the same boiler when fired only with fuel oil or gas, together with a cross-section showing the required alterations to convert to a multi-fuel waste fired boiler.

Figure **7.8** shows the boiler in figs **7.5** and **7.7** arranged for burning waste in a sub-atmospheric pressure (induced draught) combustion chamber, which allows manual stoking of off-cuts (but

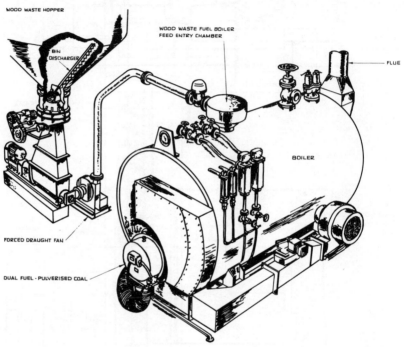

7.6   Forced draught boiler

the stoker must wear protective gear). Manual stoking should be avoided wherever possible, as it lowers combustion efficiency and reduces the life of the refractories.

Many of the wastes derived from wood, leather grindings and off-cuts, cotton seed, sun flower husks, and other (not too troublesome) wastes can be successfully burnt in both forced and induced draught converted waste boilers, provided care is exercised in the variable waste problem matters already discussed.

Most modern packaged oil or gas fired boilers are irrevocably

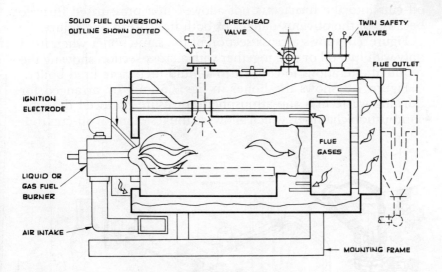

MULTI FUEL BOILER - LIQUID OR GAS FIRED

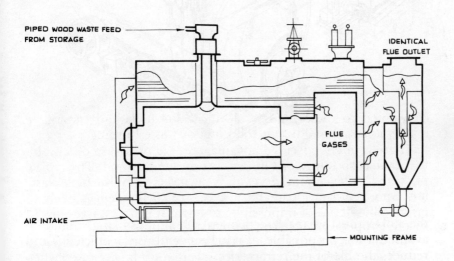

MULTI FUEL BOILER - CONVERTED - SOLID FUEL

7.7 *Multi-fuel boiler*

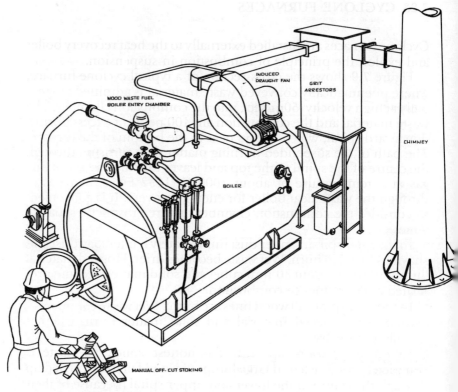

7.8   Induced draught boiler

committed to these higher calorific value fuels and cannot be readily adapted to efficient solid fuel or waste burning.

There is often a decided advantage in the provision of a multi-fuel boiler, so long as its limitations are understood. The typical packaged boiler cannot successfully burn very wet waste fuel. Waste fuel with a moisture content in excess of 30 per cent is likely to prove difficult (if not impossible) to burn. It is necessary to avoid severe temperature stresses, particularly at tube-plates.

Although this type of boiler may be able to burn a wide variety of waste fuels under certain conditions, care must be exercised when burning fuel mixtures, which operate with widely fluctuating heat release properties. Efficiency (when automatically stoked) exceeds 80 per cent; the boiler has a modulating range (turn down ratio of 3 to 1.

The control and operation of forced and induced draught boilers is fully described in chapter12.

7.23 CYCLONE FURNACES

Cyclone furnaces are installed externally to the heat recovery boiler and exploit the principle of combustion in suspension.

Figure **7.9** shows the cross-section of a typical cyclone furnace, where pneumatically conveyed waste material is admitted tangentially at high velocity (50m/sec), into the combustion chamber. The waste material and the combustion air (100 per cent excess) form a downward spiral, which decays near to the bottom of the furnace. The path of the suspended burning matter then turns up through the centre of the spiral to the top and leaves the furnace as hot flue gas at a temperature of about 1000°C (1832°F); it then passes through the waste heat boiler for energy recovery. It is convenient to consider the combustion chamber as three distinctly separate zones:

In the *upper* spiral, sander dust immediately ignites. Sawdust and shavings begin to burn. Wet waste becomes drier. Hogged material (lumps of wood about 30 mm cube) and solid matter become pre-heated and commence combustion.

In the *lower* spiral, all wood fines are burnt. Wet waste commences combustion. Hogged material and solid matter burn, whether initially wet or dry.

In the *lower centre* upsurge (the hottest zone), all waste is completely combusted. If large lumps of wood fail to be carried up through the centre of the lower and upper spiral (because of their weight), they fall onto the hearth of the furnace and there burn completely, their combustible smoke particles being immediately incinerated.

Cyclone furnaces are ideally suited for the incineration of all forms of waste, whether wet or dry, having run-of-the-mill variation of calorific value and of material size. Significantly, this furnace can safely incinerate explosive sander dust. With further development, it may be possible to incinerate lower grade wastes, such as chicken litter, refuse-derived fuels, etc, having relatively high moisture and ash contents, thus offering a possible solution to the farmer and factory owner in the matter of unwanted waste manures, composts and refuse.

The arrangement of a vertical cyclone furnace feeding a three-pass super-economic waste heat boiler is shown in chapter 14. The efficiency of the boiler varies with gas temperature and mass flow, but generally is maintained at about 73 per cent when served with waste heat gases at 1000°C (1832°F). All external combustion chamber plant systems suffer from this lowered efficiency, but offer the advantage of being relatively trouble free.

Some more sophisticated types of cyclone plant embody external combustion wall surface cooling, combustion air pre-heating and secondary combustion chambers.

The control and operation of external cyclone furnace/boiler systems is fully described in chapter 12.

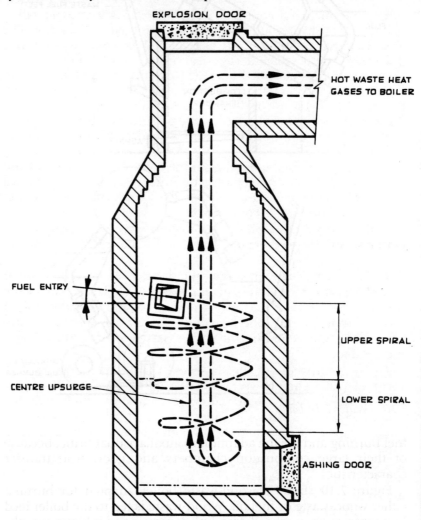

7.9   *Cyclone furnace*

7.24 WATER TUBE AND CORNER TUBE BOILERS

Water tube and corner tube boilers are particularly suited to waste

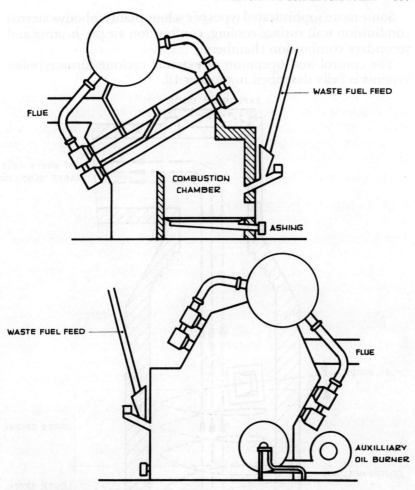

WASTE FUEL FEED

FLUE

COMBUSTION
CHAMBER

ASHING

WASTE FUEL FEED

FLUE

AUXILLIARY
OIL BURNER

7.10   Water tube boiler

fuel burning and for the adaption to auxiliary dual firing, because
of their large combustion chambers and good heat transfer
characteristics.

Figure 7.10 shows a wood-waste boiler adapted for burning
either wood-waste or fuel oil. Wood-waste is fed to the boiler feed
hopper from an overhead drag-link conveyor and is blown into the
furnace. A high pressure forced draught fan, so arranged that it will
not pressurise the furnace bed, permits hand firing of wood off-cuts
and/or coal. The auxiliary oil burner is mounted in the rear of the
boiler side wall behind a refractory bridge wall. Wood-waste and oil
are not fired simultaneously.

The efficiency of this type of boiler (when automatically stoked) is in excess of 80 per cent. Voluminous combustion chambers provide prolonged residence (dwell) times for burning in suspension and endow this type of plant with some of the essential characteristics of external purpose-made cyclone furnaces.

This type of plant can withstand appreciable temperature differences and is, therefore, thoroughly flexible in the type of fuel it can burn. Water and/corner tube boilers must be provided with tailor-made comprehensive water treatment to avoid the formation of scale and the incidence of corrosion in the boiler tubes, which could lead to disastrous and costly tube failure.

7.25 BARK INCINERATION

The Scandinavian countries have only hydro-electric power, wood and peat, and have for many years, out of necessity, burnt bark and wet wood-wastes economically. Two of the most popular types of wood burning furnaces are:

The cyclonic refractory-lined furnace, with an under-feed stoker pushing the fuel up through the bottom of a conical pile with pre-heated combustion air admitted tangentially to provide cyclonic action of the combustion gases.
Water-cooled inclined grates supported on tubes, which are part of the boiler circuit.

In addition, particularly in Finland, the following furnace grates are also employed:

Step grates especially designed for the incineration of sawdust comprising an upper plain grate, an inclined grate and a bottom grate. The shape of the steps is designed to prevent sawdust from baking.
Chain grates onto which bark can be fired directly, the thickness of the fuel layer being about 500 mm. This practice is not, however, very satisfactory and the method of sandwich firing, where bark is fed on top of a coal layer, is preferred.
Mechanical grates used as a continuation of the inclined grate or as a bottom or foot grate.

For the same species of wood, as much as 75 per cent more bark will be obtained from logs cut in the autumn and winter time than from those cut in the early spring, when the sap has begun to flow. While spot samples may show moisture contents in excess of 70 per cent, the general average moisture content of bark (newly scabbed) will be between 62 and 65 per cent.

7.26 THE COMBINED FIRING OF COAL AND WOOD REFUSE

One of the major considerations in designing a furnace and boiler unit for the combined firing of coal and wood refuse is the effect of the fluxing action of the wood ash. The impurities in the wood ash (particularly if logs have been stored in salt water) will reduce the coal ash fusion temperature, with corresponding difficulties from slagging on the grates and flue gas effect on boiler heat transfer surfaces.

One of the first concerted attempts at burning coal and wood refuse simultaneously was in underfeed stoker-fired return-tubular boilers, where the wood was dropped on top of the coal bed through a chute in the furnace front wall. Improvements to the stoker, such as the provision of water-cooled stoker retorts, made it possible to fire wood and coal in combination, without consequent major difficulties. More recently, with improvements to overfeed stokers in burning a wide variety of coals, the combined firing of coal and wood in sandwich fashion with coal as the underlayer, has gained in popularity, particularly, in the use of chain grate stokers with travelling grate continuous ash discharge mechanisms, such as that shown in fig 7.4.

7.27 WASTE GAS INCINERATION

Refinery and coke-oven gases are excellent fuels. Correct combustion of these fuel gases requires only minor changes in the design of conventional natural-gas burners. Refinery gas is produced when crude oil is processed into petrol and similar products. Its heating value is higher than that for natural gas because refinery gas contains a higher percentage of heavier hydro-carbons. For this reason, refinery gas is usually mixed or blended with gases from other plant operations to produce a fuel with a heating value similar to that of natural gas.

Coke-oven gas is produced during the high temperature carbonisation of bituminous coal to make coke. It is usually cleaned and cooled to ambient temperature prior to combustion. The small amounts of solids present in the gas do not demand that restrictions be placed on flue-gas velocity. Thus, in most cases, coke-oven gas can be burnt easily, even in a packaged boiler, once burner modifications have been carried out. Regenerator gas, produced by refinery fluid-catalytic-cracking is typical of most waste gases, in that it has a high inert (non-combustible) gas content and is relatively high in solids. The degree to which the inerts are present and the quantity, size and character of the solids strongly influence boiler design. Regenerator gas has a relatively low combustible content (carbon monoxide) and it is thus necessary to burn a specified minimum amount of supplementary fuel at all times. Blast-furnace gas, a dust laden by-product of the iron-reduction process, derives its value as a waste fuel from its high carbon monoxide content (as much as 30 per cent by volume). Gas can be burned as discharged from the blast furnace, but it generally is cleaned prior to use, because of the high dust content, which tends to foul burners and affects the boiler heat transfer surfaces. Gas burners designed to burn this type of low calorific value waste gas usually incorporate supplementary fuel provision.

Designing a boiler to burn one or more waste gases in conjunction with conventional fossil fuels is not an easy task. For a given rate of boiler output, the quantity of combustion products passing through the boiler may vary considerably as the rate of burning each fuel changes. Variations in the calorific value of the waste gas further complicate the design.

7.28 LIQUID INDUSTRIAL WASTE INCINERATION

Industrial wastes of this kind vary considerably in viscosity, moisture (water) content, heating value and heat release characteristics. Liquid wastes which can be incinerated include solvents, waste oils, oil sludges, oil/water emulsions, polymers, resins, chlorinated hydro-carbons, phenols, cresols, tars, combustible chemicals, grease and fats.

When liquid wastes are relatively homogeneous, burners and boilers may be modified to burn them, but specialist advice is usually necessary to ensure that complete combustion can be achieved to guard against boiler corrosive attack from flue gases and to satisfy the Clean Air Laws.

If large quantities of blended waste are available, one method, worthy of consideration, is to incinerate the entire stream in a cyclone or vortex refractory furnace external to the boiler, the pre-heated waste being sprayed into the combustion chamber through a suitable burner nozzle while secondary combustion air is admitted tangentially along the length of the furnace to create a cyclone effect. Pressure difference between the circular wall and the centre of the furnace causes a portion of the hot gases to re-circulate back to the burner area, liquid waste being then dried in suspension before reaching the wall area.

7.29 SELECTION

In the matter of selection and purchase of waste incineration and energy recovery equipment, specification standards and cost are the major factors. With the usual severe operating conditions, such equipment is bound to be expensive, but with good quality waste and good energy utilisation, the capital investment should show a pay-back period of about three to five years. The specification for such equipment must be correct and entirely suitable for the type of waste being considered, otherwise disastrous results may ensue. It is not easy to alter such complicated equipment if the design specification is incorrect. Assuming that the recovered energy can be effectively utilised, the waste considered being relatively dry (moisture content less than 20 per cent by weight) and the ash content relatively low (not more than 4 per cent by weight), there should be little difficulty in selecting from a number of closely competitive types of plant, such as underfeed stokers, forced and induced draught dual-fuel boilers and conventional manually and automatically stoked grate type incinerators. A golden rule, even with such relatively simple applications, is to examine similar existing operating plant in use where they burn exactly the type of waste being considered. It is also advisable to obtain more than one equipment tender and to examine more than one different existing operating plant before the final selection and purchase.

When the waste is *wet* (moisture content above 20 per cent but not exceeding 50 per cent by weight), the choice of suitable plant is very much more restricted and a more thorough investigation must be carried out into the suitability of the proposed plant (to include written combustion guarantees) before selection and plant purchase. Where the waste has a relatively high ash content (exceeding 4 per cent by weight), similar investigation and caution must be exercised.

When the waste is very wet (moisture content in excess of 50 per cent), sophisticated plant may well be required, such as external cyclone furnaces or water/corner tube boilers with suitable oversized combustion chambers. The cost of such plant is usually greater than that of conventional equipment, but with good quality waste and effective energy utilisation, pay-back should be realised within five years or so.

Extreme caution must be exercised in the selection of suitable plant, if the waste has a relatively high ash content (approaching 20 per cent by weight). Wood-waste is an organic waste and has a low ash and sulphur content. Most of the plants described in this chapter are only suitable for smokeless wood-waste incineration to comply with the Clean Air Laws. Any deviation in the quality of waste, such as plastic content, will most certainly require very specialised plant and, therefore, selection will become difficult. No attempt should be made to burn such wastes in plant not designed for that purpose.

DEFINITIONS

Arrestor
A mechanical device which arrests or separates grit and dirt from flue gases. It is usually in the form of a high efficiency cyclone, working on the principle of a centrifuge.

Ash
a powdery residue left behind after the combustion process — not to be confused with slag or clinker.

Auxiliary
A term which refers to stand-by plant, eg oil or gas burner or any other plant item which is not fully employed in the normal operation of the system.

Chips
A term which describes wood-waste fragments derived from common types of woodworking machinery. Run-of-the-mill wood-waste usually includes wood shavings in the form of chips, sawdust and fine sander dust.

Clinker
Solidified non-combustible fuel residue separated in the fused state, sometimes referred to as slag — not to be confused with ash.

Dew-point
The temperature at which moisture vapour in the air can no longer be held in suspension and is condensed in small water drops.

Dissipator
A mechanical device for discharging excess heat into the atmosphere — usually in the form of a heat exchanger with fan.

Sander dust
The finely powdered wood-waste collected off finishing or sanding machines is highly explosive, being spontaneously ignitible at about 600°C (1112°F). It is usually collected in a separate dust collection system and cannot be safely incinerated in common types of incinerators without risk of dangerous explosion.

Dwell time
The period of time which a suspended waste fuel particle spends in the combustion chamber.

Efficiency (combustion)
The ratio of
$$\frac{\text{Useful heat generated} - \text{minus all system losses}}{\text{fuel heat release when completely burnt.}}$$

Explosion
The rapid instantaneous expansion of air caused by a sudden abnormally high release of energy.

Fines (wood-waste)
Sander dust, sawdust and similar fine particles.

Flame form
The form or shape of a flame, controlled by the air pressure and material feed to induce incineration compatible with the shape and size of the given combustion chamber with the object of avoiding flame impingement.

Heat — latent
Heat energy added during the evaporation stage of water to effect the change of state at constant temperature and pressure.

Heat — sensible
Heat energy which increases the temperature of a fluid (such as water).

Heat — super heat
At any given pressure, there is a specific temperature of saturated steam. Superheat is added at constant steam pressure and raises the steam temperature.

Slag (See Clinker)

Spalling
Defined in chapter 10, Refractories.

CHECK LIST

Check: calorific value of the available fuel, noting differences between higher and lower calorific values; ignition temperatures of fuel;

consequences of incomplete combustion; excess air requirements for combustion; requirements of heat definition and primary and secondary air for combustion; bulk density of fuel; moisture content of fuel; air content of fuel; cause of fly-ash deposits; requirements for efficient combustion of waste fuel; furnace design considerations; function/description of Dutch ovens; advantages of arrangements relating to automatic stoking of furnaces; description and use of underfeed stoker; description of forced and induced boilers; description and function of cyclone furnace; suitability of water tube and corner tube boilers; special aspect of bark incinerators; combined firing of coal and wood refuse; on the incineration of waste gas; on incineration of liquid industrial waste; the recommended method of selecting and purchasing waste incineration and energy recovery equipment; definition of specialist terms employed in the incineration technology.

7.30 FLUIDISED COMBUSTION

Definition
Fluidised combustion is a system of combustion in which waste is burnt continuously in an atmospheric fluidised bed. The latter is an expanded fuel bed where the solids are suspended by the drag forces caused by the gas phase passing at some specific critical velocity through the voids between the particles. The solids and gas phases intermix, acting in the manner of a boiling fluid. See fig 7.11.

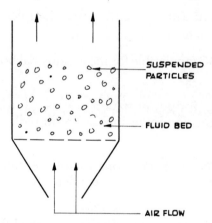

7.11   *The basic principle of fluidised bed combustion*

Principles
Solid particles, when subjected to a current of air, may be either

unaffected if the velocity of the air is below a certain value, or be airborne if the air velocity reaches above a certain higher value. Between these two limiting velocities, a bed of small particles of fairly similar size will not become full airborne, but will have the effective particle density reduced. Under these conditions, the particles move about in the bed as if the bed were fluid; by regulation of the air velocity, the solid particles can be transferred about almost as easily as if they were fluid. Any gas or vapour will achieve the same effect as air, due allowance being made for the relative velocity and density.

Function
The fluidised bed is capable of considerable flexibility in being able to combust a wide range of fuels and wastes with high heat transfer rates to the heat (generally steam) generating system. The fluidised bed is relatively compact and operates at low temperatures; with the addition of limestone, it can desulphurise the fuel (waste or other combustibles) and thereby effect extremely low emission of sulphur dioxide (SO_2) in the products of combustion discharged to atmosphere.

Fluidised combustion terminology

FBC
Fluidised bed combustor.

The combustor
The furnace combustion assembly unit complete.

AFBC
Atmospheric FBC (applicable for most industrial boiler installations).

PFBC
Pressurised FBC (for power station boilers, gas turbines etc where increased combustion intensities are required).

Freeeboard
The dynamic active surface zone established above the working bed, usually about 305mm effective depth.

Bed material
Can be sand, ash from the coal in use, crushed firebrick or other similar inert mineral matter.

Fluidising gas
The primary (fluidising) air supply the velocity of which is dependent

upon the relationship between the bed surface area, volume of gases at operating temperature and the bed particle size.

Shallow beds
Bed depths of less than 456mm can be considered as shallow beds. Deeper beds are referred to as deep bed systems.

Bed temperature
Usually limited to 950°C (1742°F) maximum. At this temperature, clinker formation caused by molten ash in the bed is avoided.

Bed slumping
Cutting off the fluidising air supply after post-purge to drop the bed and to cause dynamic and thermal lock.

Support heat
Required to raise the bed temperature from cold and to provide a trim heat facility during service. Various methods are used, including over-bed firing and an external form of direct fired air heater (oil/gas fired) for trim heating purposes.

Bed zones
FBCs can consist of a number of bed units or zones, without physical sub-division within the main tank and individually controlled.

Bed refinement
The means to control bed ash content and to maintain bed particle size within prescribed limits. Automatically controlled air jetting pumps can be employed for bed material cycling in series with screen separators.

Autothermic balance
The heat release required to maintain the balance within the bed that stabilises the bed temperature at optimum level and equates the heat loss to the submerged transfer surfaces and the gases exhausting from the bed.

Process
In fluidised bed combustion, the fuel, be it coal, oil, gas or refuse, is dispersed and burned in a fluidised bed of inert particles. The temperature of the bed is maintained in the range 750 to 950°C (1382 to 1742°F), so that combustion of the fuel is substantially completed, but particle sintering is prevented. The gaseous com-

bustion products leave the bed at its operating temperature, removing about half of the heat which has been generated. The balance of the heat released is available for direct transmission to heat-transfer surfaces immersed within the bed: in boiler applications these comprise a bank of steam raising tubes. The heat transfer to immersed surfaces is uniformly high as compared to the heat transfer through a conventional combustion chamber. Less heat-transfer surface is required for a given output and a fluidised bed boiler system occupies a smaller volume. The low combustion temperature reduces corrosion and fouling of the heat-transfer surfaces, allows a lower emission of nitrogen oxides and alkalis, and also permits the control of sulphur dioxide emission by the direct addition of limestone or dolomite to the fluidised bed.

The following stages exist generally in the process:

Stage 1
A bed of sand contained in a tank or furnace is subjected to an upward flow of cold air from within the bed until a stage is reached when the sand particles become turbulently suspended in the air stream. At this point, the bed material resembles a bubbling mass of liquid.

Stage 2
The bed is supplied with a heat source until the required operating temperature of 750 to 950°C (1382 to 1742°F) is reached. This heat may be provided from the fluidising air itself, suitably preheated.

Stage 3
The fuel (or waste) is introduced into the bed, which operates as a semi-gasifier, under conditions of starved-air combustion, promoting primary and secondary combustion to continue at a rate of thermal heat release dependent on the fuel supply — this then is fluidised combustion.

Properties of fluidised beds
In fluidised combustion, the fuel is burnt within a fluidised bed of mineral matter, eg coal ash, silica, sand, or limestone for sulphur retention. The passage of the air for combustion through the bed maintains the particles in a violently fluidised state. The turbulent fluidised bed is an ideal environment for combustion because of the rapid heat and mass transfer rates: the fluidising air is heated to bed temperature within a few millimetres of entry; solid fuel is rapidly distributed throughout the bed; the convective-heat-transfer rates to immersed boiler surfaces are high. The pressure drop

across the bed is that required to support the weight of the particles. A typical value is 10Pa (1mm of water gauge) per 1mm of bed depth.

Bed characteristics and material

The size and type of the inert bed material is important. Various materials have been used and tested, including crushed refractory material, types of ash and various types of sand. The size and shape of the material determines the fluidising characteristics of the bed; different applications require different bed characteristics.

Dependent upon particle size, the effect of the air channelling through the bed is to provide vertical stratification to enable the thermal dissociation of the fuel to occur in parallel columns or systems, interfaced by rising columns of air. A considerable proportion of this air will bypass the combustible material, so that mixing will be delayed until the combustion gases pass through the freeboard. The freeboard zone of the fluid bed is a very active dynamic system; within this zone, channelling breaks down completely, thereby achieving final air/fuel mixing, leading to efficient secondary combustion. The degree of which all secondary air can pass through the bed into the freeboard depends upon the thermal rating of the bed. Where highly rated beds are required, as in the case of high performance units, a supplementary secondary air supply system is required. Energy Equipment Co Ltd have designed the primary combustion system for such applications to accommodate complete bypass of a proportion of the combustion air, this being handled by secondary air fans with the added facility for differential cam characterised control.

A basic standard control system of the electro-mechanical relay type with cam characterised control for air/fuel ratio determination is an acceptable arrangement; this type of control is widely used with conventional combustion processes and is well known to engineers and operatives.

The operational safety features related to bed temperature control respond to the in-bed monitoring thermo-couples and are independent of the combustor load control. It is accepted that ideal combustion environment must be maintained, independently of load control, throughout the period of combustor operation.

Combustion in fluidised beds

The amount of fuel that can be burnt in a fluidised bed is determined by the air supply rate, and hence by the fluidising velocity and operating pressure. Velocities of 0.3 to 4m/sec measured at bed temperature have been used, giving heat-release rates of 0.2 to 3MW/m^2 of bed area at atmospheric pressure. The efficiency of combustion is determined by many operating factors, including fuel type, excess-air level, bed temperature, fluidising velocity, bed height, and uniformity of fuel distribution. Volume (bed + freeboard) heat release rates for coal are 2 MW/m³ (5 to 8 pressurised).

Combustion of waste materials

Fluidised beds may be used for incineration of waste materials, with or without heat recovery, eg oil refinery and coal-preparation waste sludges, municipal garbage, and sewage sludge. The usual requirement is the production of a dry inert solid for disposal and high throughput, rather than combustion efficiency, is the most important requirement. Aqueous sludges are best sprayed on to the bed surface in order to obtain some evaporation in the freeboard and to reduce the risk of fusing bed particles together.

Heat transfer in fluidised beds

By convection

The high heat transfer rate to surfaces (eg boiler tubes) immersed within fluidised-combustion beds represents a major advantage of the system. Good convective heat transfer is created by the turbulence of the bed, which constantly replaces the cooled particles against the immersed surfaces with particles at the bulk bed temperature. Since the convective-heat-transfer mechanism is effectively by conduction across a gas film between the hot particles and the heat transfer surface, the heat-transfer coefficient is determined by the thickness of the layer and the mean gas conductivity. It increases with finer particles, owing to the thinner gas film and higher bed and surface temperatures which are attributable to increased gas conductivity. Provided that the bed is maintained in a state of turbulence, fluidising velocity is not important, except in so far as it determines the particle size for the bed. Convective heat transfer coefficients are usually within the range 150 to 400 W/m²K.

Radiation

The importance of radiative heat transfer increases rapidly with increasing bed temperature; it may account for 20 to 50 per cent of the total. The radiation emanates from the particles around the immersed surfaces, and the mean temperature of these particles may be somewhat below that of the bed.

Reduction of sulphur dioxide emissions

A major advantage of fluidised combustion is that sulphur dioxide emission can be reduced simply by adding limestone or dolomite to the bed.

Design and operating considerations

Selection of fluidising velocity

The fluidising velocity is the most important design factor; it must be optimised. Operation at low fluidising velocity gives high heat-transfer rates, good combustion efficiency in shallow beds, good sulphur retention, but a large bed area. Operation at high velocity gives a smaller bed area, but reduces the efficiency of combustion and the sulphur retention. Deeper beds may be needed to pack the heat-transfer surface into the smaller bed area, and additional heat-transfer surface is required because of reduced heat-transfer rates.

Start-up

Coal starts to burn in a fluidised bed at about 500°C (9322F); oil and gas burn in the bed from about 650°C (1202°F). For start-up, the entire bed or a start-up compartment must be heated to the appropriate temperature before the fuel charge is fed to the bed. The simplest heating method is to direct a high intensity oil or gas flame on to the bed surface while it is gently fluidised.

It is desirable to use the minimum air quantity for fluidisation during the start-up stage to reduce heat loss.

An alternative procedure, particularly suitable for gas fired appliances, is to fluidise from cold with an air/gas mixture. The gas initially burns above the bed and then combustion moves back into the bed as it heats above 600°C (1112°F). For large particles, the air flow (which is necessary to promote fluidisation when the bed is cold) may give a hot gas velocity above the bed in excess of the flame velocity. In this situation, or as an alternative method for finer particles, the mixture of air and gas may be adjusted to a velocity at which the bed is static, but would be fluidised if it were hot. The gas burns above the static bed, which is progressively fluidised as it becomes heated throughout its depth.

In some experimental test plants, the bed has been heated by using a hot fluidising gas, but this is not likely to be used commercially because it complicates the design of the air distributor.

Control and turn-down

In order to achieve good combustion efficiency and sulphur retention, it is preferable that the bed temperature should be within the range 750 to 950°C (1382 to 1742°F). For applications in which the bed contains fixed heat-transfer surfaces, particularly boilers, the heat-transfer rate can only be reduced by a reduction in bed temperature. (The heat-transfer coefficient is independent of fluidising velocity.) Depending on the maximum operating temperature, the output from a fluidised combustion boiler unit can only be reduced to 70 or 80 per cent of full load before the temperature becomes too low to support combustion, when the fuel and air feed rates are further reduced. In order to achieve the turn-down ratio of 5 to 1 or more required in most boilers, it is necessary to reduce the area of heat-transfer surface during operation. Two methods are available: divide the bed into cells or compartments and fluidise the appropriate number to meet the load; reduce the effective heat transfer surface area as the output is reduced. This may be achieved automatically, since tubes near the surface of the bed will be progressively uncovered by the contraction of the bed as the fluidising velocity is reduced. Alternatively, particularly for the deeper beds of pressurised combustors, the bed depth may be controlled by withdrawal or replacement of bed material.

Combustors without heat transfer surfaces, eg incinerators and hot gas generators, will usually be operated with excess air to remove the heat generated in the bed, and the excess air level may be used to control bed temperature. The only restriction on turn-down is that a fluidised bed must be maintained.

Applications to incineration
The ability of fluidised combustion to burn variable and low-grade fuels makes it suitable for incineration applications, both with and without heat recovery. Units have been operated to burn sewage sludge, domestic garbage, oil refinery waste and aqueous slurries.

Specific application
A fluidised bed incinerator system is offered by the Energy Equipment Co Ltd (UK). This is particularly suitable for the Incineration of hospital waste, including pathological debris, as well as wet and dry combustible waste — ranging from oily sludges to general industrial waste, such as paper, plastics, sawdust and wood chips.

Bagged hospital waste, loosely packaged into plastic bags and containing a widely variable load including bandages, swabs aerosol containers, plastic cartons, disposable syringes, etc, each load weighing approximately 11.3 kg, are automatically fed to the incinerator at a rate of one bag each minute. The fluid bed, composed of common sand or crushed refractory and operating at 700 to 800°C (1292 to 1472°F), absorbs the burden and consumes the combustibles completely and effectively. The residue of metallic objects are removed sterile and safe, discharged from the combustion chamber by means of the pivoted comb, which sweeps the bed regularly or as required.

Pathological waste is completely combusted, as was demonstrated under test when a complete 20.4 kg animal carcase was burnt, leaving virtually no remains, within a period of ten minutes.

The fluid-bed incinerator provides a controlled and perfect combustion environment, constantly maintained by means of a trim heater unit which preheats the fluidising air. This trim heater exhausts into the fluidising air stream and the mixed hot gases enter the radiant boiling bed,through the multiple sparge distributor.

The trim heater modulates heat output depending upon the variable heat required within the bed, as variable as the nature of the burden of waste fed to the bed.

Bagged waste is accommodated with a monorail feed and stillage system, with automatic discharge into the double-door entry-lock to the incinerator combustion chamber.

An alternative for the continuous feed of pliable waste from hopper storage can be supplied in the form of a conveyor compactor, supplying a submerged feed into the bed through a water-cooled nozzle.

One important feature of the fluid bed incinerator is the capacity to accept variable waste feed rate in accordance to the demands of, for instance, a hospital steam system.

This capacity to respond to a variable heat load is due to the reactivity of combusting materials within the inert bed, and the fact that the combustibles generally do not exceed 5 per cent of the weight of the radiant inert bed.

Separation of incombustibles and ash removal

An essential feature and requirement of every fluidised bed combustor plant is a facility for the continuous refinement of the fluid bed material. A conveyor arrangement recycles the sand continuously and allows the separation of components, such as ash, glass, tins, etc which are incombustible, for separate disposal or recycling.

Support fuel

The consumption of support fuel (oil or gas) is minimised by arranging the level of the autothermic balance to correspond to the heat release requirement for the minimum turn-down condition of the incinerator or fluid bed boiler. The manufacturers' experience indicates that support fuel, after heat raising, is not in excess of 1 per cent of the total heat release required for operation of the fluid combustor bed at full load.

Automatic control

A fluid bed combustor must be automatically controlled. It is essential that the temperature of the bed is constantly monitored and that the control of all trim features, including load control, be completely automatic.

CPU-400

The Combustion Power Company (USA) have adapted the fluid combustion concept to a pollution-free method of economically recovering materials and energy from municipal refuse.

The system is marketed as CPU-400; it is designed to recover energy from solid waste as electrical power.

To recover the energy, the waste is burned in a fluidised bed (or fluid bed combustor); the hot gases from the combustor then pass through a gas turbine to power an electrical generator. Additionally, the system incorporates facilities for the recovery of materials of value through separation and materials-processing sub-systems. The manufacturers project that the plant complex should be capable of supplying about 5 per cent of the electrical power needs of the urban area which generates the waste being processed. In addition, there will be income from the materials being recovered from the waste and possibly also from the sale of ash and clinker. The design of the plant includes facilities for the recovery from solid waste of ferrous metals, aluminium, non-ferrous metals and glass.

Figure 7.12 shows the schematic diagram of the CPU-400 refuse disposal system.

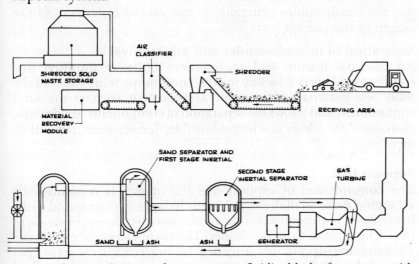

7.12   Schematic diagram of the CPU-400 fluidised bed refuse system with electricity generation

The refuse collection trucks deliver the material to an enclosed receiving area, from where front-end loaders transfer the material onto conveyors. The conveyor belts carry the solid wastes into shredders; the shredded waste then passes into the dry air classifier. In the air classification process (see also p 55) dense materials, such as metals, tins and glass are separated from the general refuse — these dense wastes then go to a material recovery unit for recycling or further processing. The less dense materials, such as shredded paper, pieces of plastics, organic materials and similar substances, are conveyed in the air stream up and away from the air classifier to a storage hopper. This storage facility is designed to process shredded light refuse and to provide a continuous feed of combustible material to the fluid bed combustor.

The shredded waste enters the combustor through high pressure air lock feeders. In the combustor, inert sand-sized particles are maintained in a fluid bed; they are stabilised in position by an upwards flow of air through the combustor unit. This air is delivered from the compressor of the gas turbine. After the solid waste enters the combustor, it is supported on the fluid bed where the process of fluidised combustion produces a relatively constant temperature of about 815°C (1500°F).

The hot gases from the fluid bed combustor progress through a series of inertial separators in which particulate matter is collected and stored for disposal. The cleaned gases then flow to the turbine and through it to the exhaust stack. The CPU-400 is housed in two structures: the receiving building and the turbine building. The former houses the receiving equipment, shredders, air classifier, dense material separation equipment and the storage hopper. The turbine building has three main components: the gas turbine, the fluid bed combustor and the particle collector. Also within this building is the storage and distribution area for the shredded solid waste conveyed there from the receiving building.

It is claimed that the fluid combustion process ensures rapid and complete combustion, whilst minimising greatly the generation and emission into the atmosphere of air pollutants, such as unburnt hydrocarbons (smuts and soot), nitrous and sulphur oxides and acidic gases.

Metals recovery can be achieved with fluidised bed operation. Figure 7.13 indicates one such method.

Fluid bed boilers — recent progress
Industry is coming to realise the potential of fluid bed boilers as extremely efficient replacements for heavy oil burners.

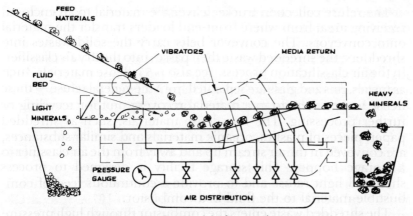

FEED MATERIALS

VIBRATORS

MEDIA RETURN

FLUID BED

LIGHT MINERALS

HEAVY MINERALS

PRESSURE GAUGE

AIR DISTRIBUTION

7.13   Metals recovery with fluidised bed operation

It has been reported that Stone-Platt Fluidfire (England) has unveiled a complete new range of water-tube fluidised bed boilers, and has moved into a new plant for the construction of these units up to capacities of 20,000 kg/h as well as of the company's heat treatment furnaces.

Announcement of the range coincides with the installation of a 5000 kg/h model from it at Hayward Tyler's factory at Keighly in Yorkshire.

Three prototype boilers have been in operation during the past year at the General Motors Technical Centre in Michigan, US, Professor Squire's Coal Workshop at the Virginia Polytechnic, also in the US and at the company's own plant in Kingswinford, Dudley, West Midlands.

The latter unit has demonstrated its ability to operate on wood, refuse-derived fuel and on difficult materials such as rubber and other industrial wastes, without creating polluiton.

Standard and patented boiler equipment derived from this unit will provide steam, or hot water, as required, operating on a very large range of solid fuels from low grade fuel to wastes of various types.

At the Hayward Tyler plant, where submersible pumps are under production, the first boiler will be commissioned during the spring. It will deliver 5000 kg/h of steam at the high efficiency of 82 per cent and is expected to provide a saving of £14,000 ($30,000) a year in fuel and operating costs over the boiler it is replacing.

In general, these patented packaged boilers have been so designed that maximum height and width does not exceed 4.25m and they can be transported in one package by road, with only the screw feeders and certain other auxiliaries to be added at site to complete the installation.

They use a concave bed which draws the fluidised solids down in the centre and returns them to the surface at the sides to achieve high efficiency of combustion. The fuel is screw-fed below the surface in the centre of the bed and there is a lengthy residence time for the fuel particles below the bed surface to give complete carbon burn-out.

Dolomite or limestone feed can be incorporated when high-sulphur coal is being burned; 80 to 90 per cent of the sulphur dioxide is absorbed as it forms.

The company's US associate, Johnston Boilers, currently has eight fluid bed boilers on hand for delivery in 1979. Several UK orders are anticipated in the near future. One of these could be for a unit intended to incinerate tyre waste without smoke.

CHECK LIST

Note: Fluid bed combustors can burn most grades of treated or untreated solid fuels. Due to the tightening energy situation, fluid bed combustors are coming into wider use. Fluid combustors operate under starved air condition, giving high efficiency and low chimney emission. Terms used in the technology of fluid bed combustion are listed and defined. A fluid bed combustor applied to a hospital incineration application is described. The recycling process applied to the bed material of the fluid bed combustor can be utilised for the recovery of valuable waste material.

REFERENCES

The Efficient Use of Energy, pp 59 - 63, IPC Science and Technology Press, 1975.
J.B. Pavoni, J.E. Meer, Jnr, D.J. Hagerty; *Handbook of Solid Waste Disposal*, pp 378-386, Van Nostrand Reinhold Co, 1975.
Financial Times, London, 7 March 1980.

7.31 BIOGAS APPLICATIONS

Introduction

Biogas comprises methane, usually existing in conjunction with carbon dioxide, and carbon monoxide, in the proportions of about 60, 35 and 5 per cent, respectively. The heat (calorific) value of Biogas depends somewhat on the composition of the organic wastes from which it has been generated. For example, the heat value of such gas produced from the digestion of waste water sludge is in the range of 16,280 to 21,000 kJ/kg.

Methane, in the correct proportions, forms an explosive mixture with air. In view of its combustible properties and relatively high calorific value, it is a valuable fuel.

Biogas can be produced out of a wide range of organic materials and wastes. The most commonly available feedstock for the generation of the Biogas is sewage sludge, aerobic sewage treatment processes (ie conducted in the presence of oxygen) or animal wastes, usually available on farms and from animal rearing houses.

Generation of Biogas

Anaerobic fermentation of complex organic materials proceeds in two distinct stages:

Stage 1

Facultative anaerobic acid producers convert complex carbohydrates, proteins and fats into simple organic acids and alcohols.

Stage 2

Anaerobic methane fermenters convert the short-chain organic acids and alcohols into methane and carbon dioxide. The relative proportions of these two gases depend upon the detention time and on the temperature at which the process operates.

Solid organic waste has a similar composition to waste water sludge (these are mainly carbohydrates, proteins and fats), so that such waste can successfully undergo anaerobic digestion for the generation of Biogas.

Decay processes

Figure 7.14 indicates the end-products of organic delay. It will be noted that the end products via the *anaerobic* route are quite different from those obtained by following the *aerobic* processes.

The aerobic path is essentially that followed in the treatment of sewage in either conventional sewage beds or in controlled aerobatic (oxygenated) digestors. The resultant humus and compost, respectively, can be recycled back to the land.

Alternatively, the process can produce a stabilised compost from refuse in 30 to 50 days.

The anaerobic decay process requires a retention time of 10 to 50 days; the process of decay is bacterial. The adoption of the controlled decay procedures speeds up the natural processes of digestion.

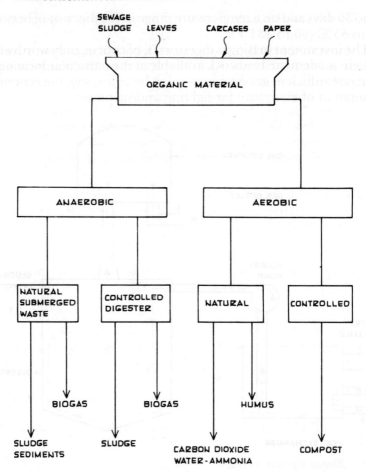

7.14   *Flow diagram of organic decay*

Production of Biogas

The organic material from which the gas is generated is termed the *feedstock*. Apart from sewage sludges, manure is an effective feedstock. The important constituent of the feedstock for the production of Biogas is the content of volatile solids. For example, fresh chicken manure comprises about 75 per cent water, 20 per cent volatile solids and a remainder of fixed solids.

The crucial factor, related to the production of Biogas, is the volume of gas liberated per unit mass of the volatile solids. Depending on the process time and the temperature, this is likely to be in the order of 0.25 to 0.5 m^3 per kg, based on a digestion time of

30 to 50 days and on a temperature range in the digestor of between 32 to 55°C (90 to 131°F).

The investment in Biogas digestors is, of course, only worthwhile if there is adequate feedstock available at the particular location to generate sufficient gas on an on-going basis for, say, the economic generation of electricity for lighting and/or power.

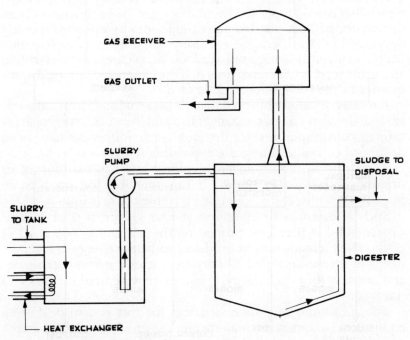

7.15   *Biogas digestor system*

Applications

Figure **7.15** shows the main components of a Biogas digestor system, comprising digestor tank with heating facility, pumped slurry arrangement and gas receiver.

Examples:
1 Farm Gas Ltd of Bishop's Castle, Salop, have developed a range of Biogas digestors from 11,300 to 400,000 l capacity. The retention time is between 10 and 20 days, depending on the available slurries.

The smaller size digestor can be set up as a module in a series of units. It can treat the slurry from 19 to 115 sows with their progeny (taken to bacon weight) or of 12 to 75 dairy cows. The anticipated output per module is 2300 l of gas per day, having a calorific value of 24.2 MJ/m³ (using pig slurry). Slightly lower outputs are obtainable from cow slurry.

The larger digestors operate better when equipped with gas fired heat generators and will produce up to 50 kW of electricity on a continuous basis.

2 It has been reported (Kibbutz Industries Federation of Tel Aviv, Israel) that certain types of agricultural waste (ie cattle manure) can be transformed into methane gas and fodder by a process recently developed in Israel. The system also yields a slurry of high quality which is currently being used as a food supplement in fish farming and cattle feed, where it replaces half the expensive fish meal and a quarter of the conventional cattle feed.

It is categorically confirmed that the bacterial and viral characteristics of the slurry do not endanger fish and livestock or the meat for human consumption, since the pathogenic influences have been destroyed or reduced below any possible danger levels.

The slurry is in a homogeneous form and has lost most of its original objectionable odour; it can therefore be used as an improved fertiliser which can be conveniently distributed.

Such a system is in operation at Kfar Giladi. It is of 200 m³ capacity and is based on processing the manure of 600 head of cattle. The methane output produces sufficient energy to meet the needs of a community of 700 people, including home industries and services (but excluding the energy requirement for cars and tractors).

The minimum recommended size for this system (including equipment to convey the manure and the provision of the digestor system) is 150 head of cattle. The installation is based on 500 cows and will have a capital cost of about US $200,000, depending somewhat on detailed specification. Costs of this system are reduced relative to other systems, as the process does not require the addition of water to the waste and thus permits the use of smaller containers.

The cost of the resultant methane gas is said to be on par with that of industrial fuel oil; the associated animal feed and the fertiliser which are delivered by the process represent a clear profit.

Prospects
Farming tends to be a conservative occupation and its practitioners are reluctant to turn to revolutionary changes in their farming operations. Biogas installations have therefore been accepted only slowly. Widespread publicity and education is required to draw attention to the ease with which Biogas can be produced for use as a

main or supplementary form of energy. There are now clear signs that various equipment manufacturers are taking up this challenge.

CHECK LIST

Check: Availability of organic feed stock (m³/h, m³/d or m³/wk); potential Biogas production from available feedstock; on-going likely demand for Biogas; whether the available supply can match the demand or a worthwhile proportion of it; source of slurry and transport or pumping needs; economic feasibility, ie capital costs, operating costs and cost-effective benefits of generating Biogas; space requirements, compliance with local and government codes, etc; manner of providing the Biogas facility, eg package deal with experienced manufacturers or professional supervision; that the completed plant is handed over with full operating instructions and with essential spares.

REFERENCES

J.B. Pavoni, J.E. Meer, Jnr, J. Hagerty, *Handbook of Solid Waste Recovery,* pp 427-440, Van Nostrand Reinhold Co, 1975.
Andrew Porteous, *Recycling, Resources Refuse*, pp 84-89, Longman *Financial Times*, London, 5 March 1980.

7.32 RECUPERATORS

Introduction
Most gas fired applicances exhaust, at elevated temperatures, 20 per cent or more of the energy they consume. The primary purpose of a recuperator is to save fuel by recovering heat otherwise lost in these exhaust gases.

ICCO Recuperator
The ICCO Recuperator (developed in conjunction with Gaz de France) reclaims 60 to 70 per cent of this wasted energy. It is placed after gas boilers or after any device discharging non-acidic gaseous effluents with high water vapour content into the atmosphere; it does not affect the normal operation of the plant. The recuperator condenses the water vapour of the exhaust gases by washing them by direct contact with water. The gases enter the recuperator at low level, rising through a series of baffles and a counter-current of water, which cools them below their dew-point. During the passage through the recuperator, the gases release much of their heat by the

fall in temperature (sensible heat) and by the condensation of part of the water vapour (latent heat) (see fig **7.16**).

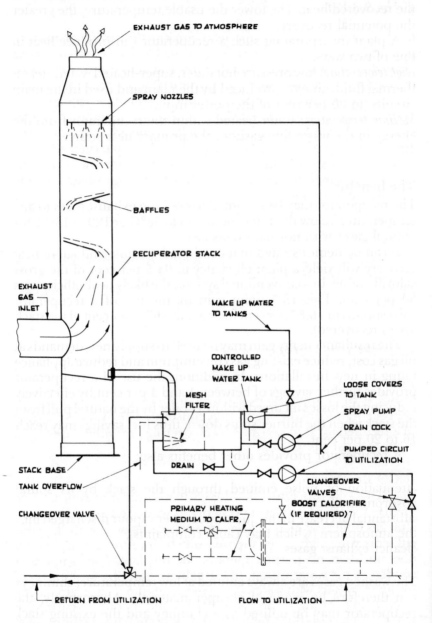

7.16   Basic recuperator system

Heat recovery

The recoverable quantity of heat depends upon the exhaust gas characteristics and the optimum temperature for the utilisation of the recovered heat. The lower the usable temperature, the greater the potential recovery.

A plant incorporating such a recuperator can produce heat in one of two ways:

High temperature: low pressure hot water, super-heated water, steam, thermal fluid, air, etc, produced by the plant and used in the main circuits (to 80 per cent of the power input).

Medium temperature: water heated within the recuperator from the energy in the waste flue gases of the primary heat source.

The benefits

The recuperator may be designed to cool the exhaust gases to any temperature below their dew-point (50 to 58°C or 120 to 136°F for natural gases with normal excess air).

It can be demonstrated that combined sensible and latent heat recovery will yield a plant efficiency to 93.5 per cent of the gross calorific value. In a conventional system, the likely peak efficiency is 80 per cent. This 13.5 point gain by the use of a recuperator corresponds to 16.87 per cent fuel savings (67.5 per cent of the stack losses recovered).

The resultant energy gain may be used to supply new demands at nil gas cost, reduce existing gas consumption and reduce appliance rating in new installations. In addition, the use of a recuperator provides further savings of between 1 and 4 per cent by effectively reducing the losses incurred within a boiler by the natural pull from the stack when the burner shuts down; thus fuel savings may reach 16 to 20 per cent.

A recuperator provides other benefits also:

attenuation of noise emitted through the stack by its sound absorption effect,
substantial decrease in the quantity of water vapour discharged into the atmosphere (which may cause complaints),
cleaner exhaust gases.

The washed gases are always emitted at low temperature; chimneys can therefore be made of cheaper materials. Alternatively, the recuperator may be utilised as a chimney and the existing stack bypassed.

SPUR-ICCO Chimney Recuperator

The SPUR-ICCO Chimney Recuperator is a stainless steel vertical cylinder 3.3 to 9.1m high, having a diameter appropriate to the flow of gases to be processed and to the pressure drop. The ratings of applicances with which the units may be used range from 30 kW to 31,000 kW. The recuperator will create a pressure loss of between 1 and 1.5 mb, which can usually be overcome by increasing the duty of the forced draught fan. On plant not utilising a forced draught fan, it is necessary to provide for an induced draught fan and damper regulation.

Connections from the plant to the recuperator would normally be in heavy steel plate, stainless steel or aluminium, suitably insulated against heat loss. The duct from the recuperator to atmosphere should be of corrosion resistant material, such as stainless steel, asbestos cement or aluminium. Should the duct not be vertical, it must be installed on a continuous slope either towards the unit or towards a low point and provided with a condense drain and trap.

Water pumped to the spray nozzles falls through the recuperator and is collected in a tank, kept at constant level during normal operation by an overflow pipe which drains off the excess water accumulated from condensation. The tank is also equipped with a make-up water valve controlled by a float which only operates under exceptional circumstances, ie at first filling or during vaporisation. The tank is constructed either of two or three compartments (dependent upon utilisation) one of which contains fine mesh stainless steel filters (80 microns) to trap any solids which may be entrained in the combustion air, or from the process work being carried out (dryers etc). The tank has a cover and a quick opening drain valve.

From the filter compartment of the constant level tank, water is taken via a pump to a heat exchanger, or in certain circumstances direct to the utilisation circuit. Where only one recuperator is installed (fig 7.17), a pump provides the circulation. A two-compartment tank is used in this instance. The pump duty will be determined by the required flow and the circuit losses, plus the loss at the spray nozzles (.96 to 1.44 bar).

Should more than one recuperator be installed, the method shown in fig 7.17 is preferable, incorporating a three-compartment tank. The pump provides ciruclation to the utilisation circuit only, water returning from this circuit being piped to the third compartment of the tank. From the bottom of this compartment, water is pumped to the spray nozzles of each recuperator. In this way the circuits are completely independent.

The recuperator has been designed for use with dual fuel burners (gas/oil), but recovering waste energy only when used with gas or indirect fired equipment. Without water circulation, it acts as a simple chimney unit, capable of passing the volume of hotter gases. Because of this structural design, no particular control or safety device is required. When the exhaust gases are cooled below their dew-point, they transfer energy. Should the demand on the utilisation circuit decrease or cease entirely, with the result that the energy produced is not taken up, the temperature of the circulating water will increase, as will the temperature of the final exhaust, until they stabilise between 60 to 70°C (140 to 158°F). Above dew-point, there is vaporising of a certain quantity of water, which is automatically replaced via the ball valve (also used for initial fill).

Indirect system

In *indirect* applications, the heated water produced in the recuperator is passed through the primary side of a heat exchanger, allowing the secondary side of the exchanger to work without contact and at a different condition. The primary circuit may be constructed of non-oxidisable materials, thereby eliminating water treatment.

Direct system

The *direct* application has the advantage of being less costly than installations requiring a heat exchanger, particularly in the case of swimming pools. The heating of the water by contact with the waste products of natural gas combustion does not usually cause harmful pollution of the water, unless the burner is incorrectly adjusted. Any slight oxidisation and carbonic acidification may be treated by introducing an approriate reagent into the water by dosage pump or displacement additive feeder. An alternative method, if the build-up is slight and over an extended period, is to change the small volume of water from time to time.

Use in conjunction with steam boilers

Pre-heat for Hotwell boiler feed tank make-up
Where steam boilers are in use, and the condensate return is such that heat is required to raise the Hotwell temperature, a recuperator can pre-heat the incoming make-up.

Underfloor heating
This type of heating requires low water temperatures which can be provided by this form of recovered energy. Two systems may be used; direct to the underfloor heating element, or via an intermediate exchanger. The main advantage of the latter is to reduce

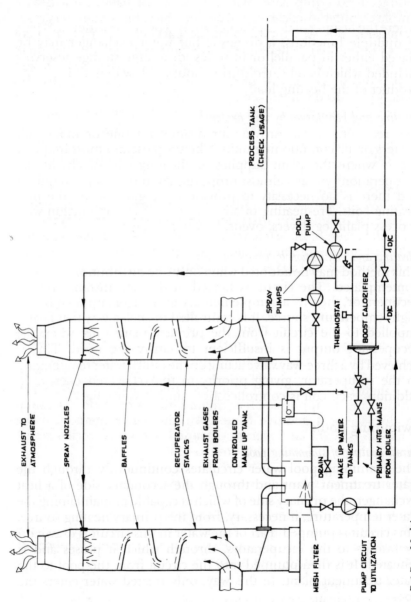

7.17 Multi-recuperator system

EXHAUST TO ATMOSPHERE

SPRAY NOZZLES

BAFFLES

RECUPERATOR STACKS

EXHAUST GASES FROM BOILERS

CONTROLLED MAKE UP TANK

MESH FILTER

PUMP CIRCUIT TO UTILIZATION

DRAIN

MAKE UP WATER TO TANKS

PRIMARY HTG. MAINS FROM BOILER

BOOST CALORIFIER

THERMOSTAT

SPRAY PUMPS

POOL PUMP

PROCESS TANK (CHECK USAGE)

D/C

any risk of corrosion in the heating elements, and to allow supplementary heat to be applied.

Domestic hot water supplies
Where the heating of domestic hot water is being considered as part of multiple functions, a domestic hot water exchanger may be placed either in parallel or in series, or a large storage reservoir included which is reheated during hours of low demand as a by-product of the heating load.

Heating and ventilation by unit heaters
The recuperator can provide air heating for one or more unit heaters or air-conditioning units. The simplest and most frequent use is where the plant supplies air heating exclusively, as the recuperation remains almost proportional to the energy required and there is no necessity to provide for regulation on the pre-heating coils. Pre-heating of air can be used in conjunction with process plant, eg dryers, ovens, and unit heaters.

Heating and ventilation by complementary exchanger
This method may be adopted when only one distribution circuit is contemplated. The circuit is heated in the first instance by the recuperator, then by a complementary exchanger supplied by the high temperature source. It is controlled in such a way that heat is supplied to the circuit from the primary plant only when the recuperator output is insufficient to satisfy the need. This is achieved by a three-way valve acting on the return water temperature to the recuperator, giving priority to the recovered energy. In addition, each coil is controlled by a similar valve, fig 7.18.

Swimming pools

Direct heating of swimming pools
The swimming pool water circulates continuously through the water treatment plant and through the secondary side of a heat exchanger, the primary side of which is capable of maintaining the water temperature, if necessary, from the primary heating source. This circuit is pumped. Part of the water in this circuit is drawn off by pumps to the recuperators, through which it passes and is reheated. It is then pumped into the circuit from the pool to the water treatment plant. In this way, only treated water enters the pool.

The water temperature entering the recuperator would be in the order of 22°C (72°F) and on entering the tank 38°C (100°F). The main heat exchanger is set to give no more heat than is necessary to

170

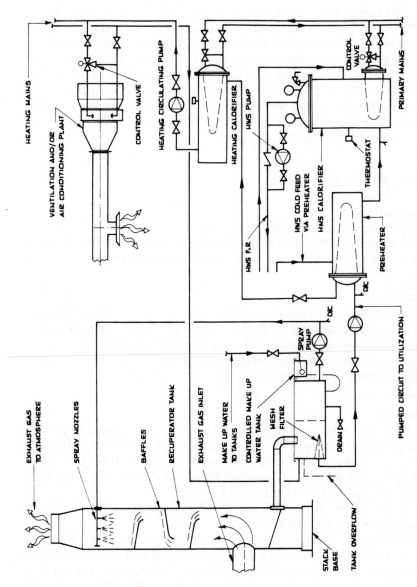

7.18 *Recuperator system connected to heating and ventilation applications*

meet design conditions for the pool. This method cannot be used where the plant room is sited on a lower level than the pool, since leakage or any other malfunction would lead to syphonage.

Indirect heating of swimming pools
Where the plant is situated at a level lower than the pool, it is imperative that the recovered energy is first passed through the primary side of a heat exchanger to prevent syphonage. The pool heating is accomplished by two heat exchangers in parallel. The first, supplied with water from the recuperator(s), provides a varying output dependent upon the loading of the boilers. The second is supplied direct from the boilers through a form of temperature regulator.

7.33 PYROLISIS

Definition
The term *pyrolisis* is applied to a process which involves the physical and chemical decomposition of organic matter under the action of heat in an environment which is deficient in oxygen.

Function
In the process of pyrolisis, organic matter can be readily converted into gases, liquids and inert char. These products constitute about half of the initial volume of the input to the process; these can be convered into useable energy output or be directed to either sustain the process or to produce excess power.

Process
When employed for the recycling of refuse, the pyrolisis process involves the heating of the refuse in a retort in the absence of oxygen and at temperatures ranging between 500 to 1000°C (932 to 1832°F). The actual temperature relates to the specific processing method and to the required end products.

Figure **7.19** shows the plant flow diagram of the Landgard Baltimore Pyrolisis Plant.

The waste can be converted into convenient solid, liquid or gaseous forms to provide a gaseous or liquid fuel which can either be stored or used immediately in an associated process, such as power generation or heat recovery. It thus offers the practicable possiblity of heat storage; this option is not available in the incineration process.

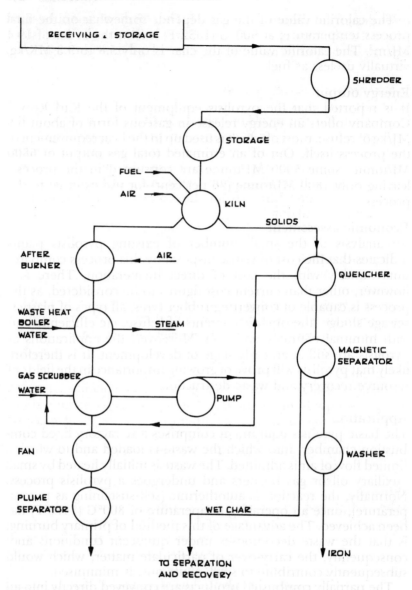

7.19   Diagrammatic arrangement of Langrad Baltimore Pyrolisis Plant

Products

The products of the pyrolisis of refuse are solid, liquid and gaseous fractions; any oil formed in the process is recycled for gasification. The gas output supplies the energy for the pyrolisis process and possibly also a surplus for other uses or for sale.

The calorific value of the gas depends somewhat on the final process temperature; at 900°C (1652°F) it is in the order of 19.4 MJ/m³. The calorific value of the char is only 5.8 to 9.3 MK/kg; virtually useless as fuel.

Energy output
It is reported that the pyrolisis equipment of the Karl Kroyer Company offers an energy release in gaseous form of about 6.8 MJ/kg of refuse, most of which is used up in the heat requirement of the process itself. Out of an estimated total gas output of 6800 MJ/tonne, some 5000 MJ/tonne are consumed in the process, leaving only 1800 MJ/tonne (26 per cent) for use external to the process.

Economic assessment
An analysis of the small number of existing pyrolisis plants indicates that the cost of refuse disposal by this process compares unfavourably with the cost of direct incineration. There are, however, other than current cost figures to be considered, as the process is capable of converting rubber tyres, all types of plastics, sewage sludge, the organic contents of refuse, etc efficiently and with minimal chimney emission. Moreover, the applications of pyrolisis are still at an early stage of development. It is therefore likely that pyrolisis will prove of growing importance in the fields of resource recovery and waste destruction.

Application
The basic pyrolisis equipment comprises a refractory lined combustion chamber, into which the waste is loaded and to which a limited flow of air is admitted. The waste is initially heated by small auxiliary oil or gas burners and undergoes a pyrolisis process. Normally, the reaction is autothermic (self-sustaining as to temperature), once an operating temperature of 800°C (1470°F) has been achieved. The advantage of this method of primary burning, is that the waste decomposes under quiescent conditions and, consequently, the carry-over of particulate matter, which would subsequently contribute to stack emissions, is minimised.

The partially combusted products are conveyed directly into an afterburning chamber, which is mounted immediately above the main combustion chamber. These gases are then admixed with additional air and elevated to a temperature of 1000 to 1200°C (1700 to 2200°F) to ensure the successful burn-out of smoke. Before discharge from the pyrolisis chamber, the gases are cooled to approximately 800°C (1470°F) by entrained ambient air.

The air required for combustion is supplied to the lower and upper chambers by independent centrifugal fans. The rate of air supply to both chambers is adjusted during commissioning to give the correct combustion conditions for each particular application. Temperature control facilities are provided as standard equipment on all pyrolisis incinerators for both the upper and lower chambers, increasing the degree of automation and reducing the amount of personal judgement required from the plant operator. The control fitted to the upper chamber acts primarily as a fuel-saving device and limits the total number of operating hours during which this burner operates. A water spray protection system is incorporated with the lower combustion chamber and prevents the occurrence of excessive temperatures when the pyrolisis wastes of high calorific values are burnt. Pyrolisis equipment is usually safety controlled by a programmed burn-down unit, which automatically shuts down the machine to a safe condition after the last charge of the day has been loaded.

It is claimed, on the basis of working installations, that pyrolisis can achieve a volume reduction of organic waste of 90 per cent, that useable by-products are obtained, that the process can convert many difficult and different wastes, that air pollution is avoided.

Equipment specification

An example of a modern pyrolisis starved air incinerator is the 'Consumat' equipment (see plates 27, 28 and 29). The outline specification of the Consumat is given below:

Range	*Technical data*	
1 The Consumat can cover from the smallest to the largest needs. 15 standard factory prepared models covering from 50 lb/h (22 kg/h) to approximately 1 ton/h. Above this models are placed in parallel. There are a number of installations with eight units working in parallel processing 100 tons/d.	Service requirements: Electricity supply: Fuel supply: Incinerator: Shell:	Voltage, phase or cycle, as required. Gas or oil.
		Hot rolled mild steel plate, painted with heat resistant finish.
	Refractory:	High grade alumina refractory, secured by stainless steel anchors, backed with mineral wool insulation.
2 For each model in the range, permutations are specially designed to destroy the	Chimney:	Mild steel, refractory lined in lower sections, but stainless steel in upper sections if necessitated.
	Ash door:	Refractorised and in-

most difficult wastes and, at the same time, maintain precise control of pollutant emissions.

Loading aperture:	sulated as incinerator. Designed to accept either loading door, air curtain or automatic loader, as designated.
Burners:	One sited in upper chamber. Number in lower chamber according to model, (all linked to automatic burn-down sequencer).
Air ports:	Strategically placed for starved air operation.
Controls:	Automated to supervise combustion with 'start' and 'burn-down' buttons, together with necessary status lights.
Air attemperator:	Fitted to base of chimney to ensure reduction of final gas temperature.

Accessories

Slant charging door:
To assist with hand loading when waste is delivered in small mobile containers.

Pathological configuration:
Upgrading of the design to suit the equipment for the destruction of pathological wastes.

Stack:
Extra stack lengths of free-standing stacks are available to meet special site conditions.

Air modulation:
Design modification to meet the needs of high calorific value wastes.

Additional air plenum
To assist in the programmed burn down for selective wastes.

Weather skirt:
To weatherproof stack exits through a roof in a building.

Plug in optional extras

Loaders and automatic feed devices:
An extensive standard range is available to cover all needs.

Liquid disposal:
A range of liquid adapters to allow liquid waste to be processed at the same time as solid wastes.

Waste heat recovery:
A unique range of heat recovery plant is available to enable the incinerator waste heat to be used to generate either steam or hot water.

Air curtain:
A range of air curtains for hand loaded machines, where the type of waste disposed demands operator protection.

Automatic ash removal:
A range of revolutionary automatic ash removal systems.

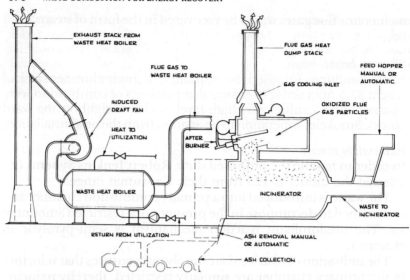

7.20   Diagrammatic arrangement of Consumat pyrolisis unit single module

A case history — Memorial Hospital, Peterborough

Owners and specifiers	East Anglian Regional Health Authority
Design and contract	Robert Jenkins Systems Ltd, Rotherham
Location	Memorial Hospital, Peterborough

Proposed duty
227 kg/h of general hospital waste to be disposed during a 8h period/day. The waste was specified as having an average composition 50 per cent paper, 25 per cent plastic and 25 per cent pathological material, by weight.

Design calorific value
19,470 kj/kg was computed for the mixture.

Automation
The design was to incorporate the maximum of automation, in order to minimise operator decision making.

Space allocation
The complete plant was to be housed in a space of approximate dimensions 12.3 × 5.6 × 3 m.

Heat recovery
The maximum heat that could be realistically abstracted from the

incinerator flue gases was to be recovered in the form of steam at 6.9 bar.

Chimney height
Local conditions imposed the restraint of a single chimney stack of height 33.5 m in order to ensure that products of combustion were discharged at a sufficiently high level to clear neighbouring ward blocks. Smokeless operation to be assured from the new installation.

Incineration concept
In order to handle the proposed duty, Robert Jenkins Systems Ltd selected the model C-125 from their Consumat range.

The waste is introduced into a primary combustion chamber and constrained to decompose in the presence of a restricted amount of air. The predominant reaction mechanism is semi-pyrolytic in character.

The utilisation of restricted air supply rates ensures that velocities in the primary chamber are similarly restricted, thereby reducing the size and hence mass of particles that can be retained in the gas stream.

Waste handling
The hospital waste is predominantly bagged and brought to the incinerator in cages of $2.23m^3$ capacity. To obtain the best utilisation of recovered heat, the incinerator has to be charged at a steady rate. To achieve this, and also to ensure that the highest standard of safety were met, a standard mechanical loader from the Consumat range was provided.

The loader
Comprises a waste reception volume provided with a closure and is isolated from the incinerator by means of a vertically disposed fire door. Waste is displaced into the incinerator by means of a hydraulically driven ram, and the fully inter-locked system, is initiated by a single push button control.

In order to ensure an even charge rate and to prevent overloading of the incinerator, the loading interval is dictated by combustion conditions in the incinerator, and the system is so safeguarded that the operator cannot recharge the machine until the previous charge has been processed.

Electrical interlocks
A system ensures that the operator is never exposed to the fire-bed of the incinerator, thus eliminating any hazard associated with traditional hand-charged incinerators.

To utilise the available space, the mechanical loader was mounted at right angles to the main axis of the primary chamber. This also left a clear route to enable waste to be brought direct to the point of loading.

Waste heat recovery

The available waste, and the proposed loading rate suggested that a maximum heat release rate of 2900 kW could be achieved. After allowing for ductwork and boiler losses, it was estimated that an overall efficiency of 67 per cent could be achieved, or an equivalent steam generation rate of 0.234 kg/sec at a pressure of 6.9 bar.

In designing the boiler, space considerations were of great importance. With an inlet boiler temperature of 1000°C (1832°F) and design outlet temperature of 260°C (500°F) (to fall well above the likely dew-point), a single-pass design would have meant that the boiler length/diameter ratio would have been high, thus intruding overmuch into the available space.

A double-pass firetube arrangement was selected: this offered a compact arrangement and, having inlet and outlet gas connections at the same end, simplified the gas ductwork arrangement. By designing the boiler with a full-width, detachable and-plate, access could be gained to all tubes facilitating boiler cleaning. The boiler was provided with conventional boiler controls including automatic level controls and alarms.

Integration of the steam output from the machine with the existing hospital boiler system was simplified by the fact that the conventional equipment was already arranged so that the firing rate was controlled by pressure-stats impulsed from the boiler output pressure. It was therefore merely necessary to connect the waste heat boiler into the existing steam main and the conventional equipment simply attenuated its output to meet the overall steam demand.

Flue gas control and discharge

To permit the boiler to be taken on and off line, as required, and to guard against any possible emergency conditions, a full bypass was installed on the gas side of the system. A pair of motorised high temperature dampers were located, one on the boiler inlet and the other in a bypass duct, linking the secondary combustion chamber direct to the stack. The dampers were electrically interlocked, so that only one could be open at any one time, thus giving either full steam generating capacity or full boiler bypass.

The damper position is selected from a single switch located on the main control panel. In addition, the dampers are so arranged that the system will divert to bypass in the event that, for any reason, the boiler loses water or the induced draught fan fails to operate.

As the temperature of the gases leaving the incinerator is nominally 1000°C (1837°F), it was necessary to reduce this temperature before discharge into the chimney when the machine is operating on the bypass condition. Available means of attemperating the gases involve the use of either air or water. The use of water offers a reduced gas volume, for a given temperature, and consequently an attemperating spray system was incorporated in the bypass duct, in order to drop the final temperature to 400°C (752°F). The system was arranged to operate automatically in an on/off control mode.

To overcome the gas side resistance of the boiler, an induced draught fan was installed immediately on the outlet, delivering the flue gases into the bypass duct immediately prior to the stack. The operation of the fan was electrically interlocked with the gas dampers, so that it was activated electrically as soon as the boiler inlet damper is proved open.

Operating experience
The plant was put to work in November 1976 and has operated on a daily basis with virtually 100 per cent availability.

Work is in hand to provide continuous monitoring facilities for the steam output, but experience so far suggests that the waste heat boiler is substantially exceeding its rated output. Three conventional boilers currently supply the hospital steam demand and, on one occasion recently, the waste heat equipment was able to support the demand for a three-hour period whilst the conventional plant was out of commission. All the indications are that during the daytime, in the summer months, the hospital could be self-sufficient in steam from the waste heat plant.

The increased output over design is attributed to the fact that the equipment permits lower boiler outlet temperatures to be accommodated than was originally anticipated, without encountering dew-point conditions in the stack.

An inspection of the boiler was undertaken after the first three months of operation. A slight deposition was encountered on the tubes, predominantly in the first pass. There was no evidence of fireside corrosion. Three monthly inspection periods have been adopted as a routine maintenance activity.

Feasibility study
An assessment of the feasibility of incorporating waste heat recovery equipment with a hospital incinerator is a relatively simple exercise. As incineration ie waste destruction is essential in such

circumstances, it is merely necessary to offset capital cost of the additional equipment against the predicted fuel savings. It is illuminating to consider the fuel savings that can result under these circumstances, by comparison with conventional steam generation costs.

Steam production rate: 0.234 kg/sec
Operating hours at full steaming:7 h/day
Operating d/y: 365
Steam production: 2152,900 kg/y at 6.9 bar

Fuel saving
Enthalpy required to generate steam at 6.9 bar from feed water at 76.7°C (170°F): 2.5 MJ/kg.
    Total enthalpy of steam generated: 5275 GJ
    If this amount of energy is released in the form of steam raised in a conventional gas fired boiler having an efficiency of 80 per cent, then:

$$\text{Gas requirement} = \frac{5275}{.8}$$
$$= 6594 \text{ GJ}$$

Annual fuel saving
At unit cost: £1.04/GJ (£0.11/therm)
= £6857/y or about US $ 15,000/y

    (The above fuel cost was applicable to the installation described in July 1975. With the current enhanced fuel costs, greater savings are made.)
    In the above analysis, electricity costs have been neglected as these are roughly equivalent for either conventional or waste heat plant. The waste heat system attracts no additional labour costs and it was assumed that, with comparable conventional firing, a fully automatic system would be selected, attracting no labour costs for operation. It is reasonable to assume that maintenance costs are equivalent for both types of plant.
    The capital cost of a heat recovery plant depends to a significant degree on site conditions. On current figures, a pay-back time of about two years is indicated for the installation described, becoming increasingly more attractive as fuel costs escalate.

The Hoval Pyrolisis System
Plate 29 shows the arrangement of a typical Hoval pyrolisis system. Plate 31 shows an installation.
    The basic modules of a Hoval pyrolytic incinerator are the

pyrolytic chamber and thermo-reactor. A hydraulic loading system can be added to them. Heat exchangers can be provided for any heat recovery to produce warm air, hot water or steam.

The individual modules can be combined systematically within certain limits. The control module co-ordinates the functions.

By suitable selection of the size of the pyrolytic chamber with the thermo-reactor, incineration outputs of between 60 to 600 kg/h can be achieved.

To meet the different applications, the loading system must also be flexible. The Hoval unit can be adapted for either manual, semi-automatic hydraulic or highly sophisticated loading mechanisms, operating with dumpers, conveyors etc.

The heat exchangers are designed for each specific application to provide the specified heat output by warm air, hot water or steam.

Whilst small units are available as indicated above, Hoval multi-pyrolytic incinerators comprising pyrolitic units are suitable for the waste disposal in medium-sized and large centres of population of approximately 10,000 to 20,000 inhabitants.

The manufacturers state that their equipment has proven itself in hundreds of plants throughout the world. Since the engineering content is sophisticated and reliable, it lends itself to the batch production of standardised modules.Special care has been expended in making those parts of the incinerator which are subject to servicing readily accessible to render maintenance economical and easy, so that the plant operator does not require special training and can take over responsibility for the plant and its operation after only a short period of instruction.

CHECK LIST

Consider: advantages of pyrolisis (starved air) incineration. Minimal smoke, smuts and particulate stack emission.
Select: Fuel — gas or oil firing.
Establish: Waste load: also calorific (heat) value of waste mixture. Equipment parameters. Stack height.
Specify: Overall plant performance, including requirement (if any) for waste heat recovery boiler. Approved manufacturer(s). Plant duty. Loading arrangement. Is air curtain required? Safety precautions: personnel, plant, building. Flue gas control system. Ash disposal provision. Optional equipment items relative to specific application.
Obtain: All necessary local authority approvals. Commissioning data. Operators' training scheme. Operating and maintenance instructions and manuals.

REFERENCES

G.S. Coulson and R. Harrison, *The Incineration of Solid and Liquid Wastes Paper*, paper given at the Eurochem Conference, June 1977.
Andrew Porteous, *Recycling Resources Refuse*, pp 77-81, Longmans.
J.L. Pavoni, J.E. Meer Jnr and D.J Hagerty, pp 386-427, *Handbook of Solid Waste Disposal*, Van Nostrand Reinhold Co, 1975.
Robert Jenkins Systems Ltd, Rotherham, South Yorkshire, Consomat details, 1978.
Hoval-Farrar Ltd, Newark, Nottinghamshire, Hoval Pyrolisis System, 1979.

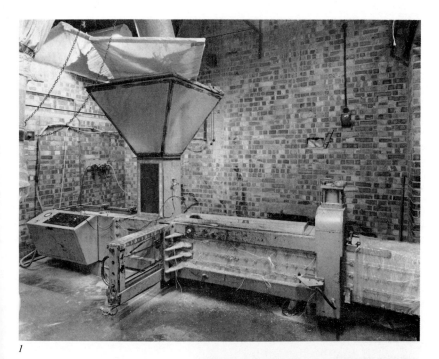

1

1   Industrial baling plant operating

2   Medium size waste compactor

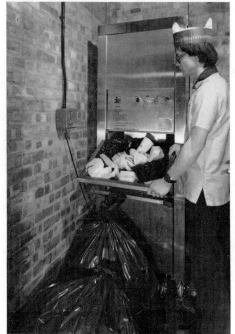

2

3 *Tile lined Borsari underground storage tank under construction*

4 *Tile lined Borsari underground storage tank internal appearance*

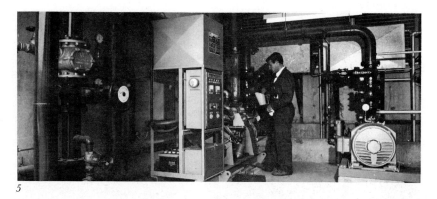

5

5   *Visual display panel of centralised smoke/heat detection installation*

6   *Sprinkler system valve chamber arrangement*

6

7 *External view of furnace plant-room. Note multiple chimneys within an aluminium clad envelope; also adjacent transformer room*

8 *An interesting application of Thorn security lighting to industrial plant at Runcorn*

7

8

9   *External view of large industrial plantroom. Note chimney with access ladder*

10   *External appearance of mechanical sorting and classification recycling centre (Crown copyright reserved)*

11   *Security cubicle and Thorn lighting to industrial complex*

9

10

11

12

12   Rear view of multiple boiler installation, with good example of pipe and flue aluminium clad thermal insulation

13   Plant access landing with guard rails and toe protection

13

14

14   Plant with
supporting structures –
note complexity

15   Horizontal rotary air
classifier installation
(Crown copyright
reserved)

15

16

16   Refuse-derived (RFD) fuel
pellets (Crown copyright reserved)

17   Powerful crane with cactus grab
in operation. Note the compressed
metal blocks leaving by conveyor

18   Monroe County Resource
Recovery Facility

17

18

20

19   *Cars entering the scrapping facility at Willesden*

20   *A sample of recycled steel*

21   *Doncaster Plant – Air Classifier in operation (Crown copyright reserved)*

19

21

22   *Recycled product leaving the Willesden plant by rail trucks*

23   *Chemelec cell plant recovering silver*

24   *Chemelec cell plant recovering nickel*

22

23

24

25   *Pickle acid regeneration plant*

26   *RDF pelletised fuel burning (Crown copyright)*

27 *Consumat single module
equipment*

28 *Consumat pyrolisis
installation – single module*

27

28

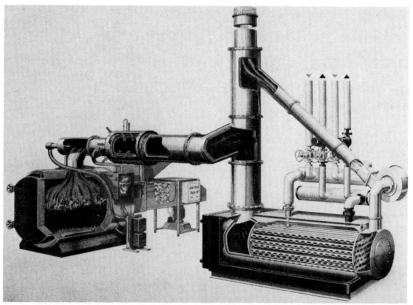

29 Hoval pyrolisis system: general view

30 Consumat pyrolisis twin module installation

31

31   Hoval pyrolisis system: single
module installation

32   Inclined heat dissipator

32

33 *Automatic compacting and baling machine*

34 *Hand baling facility*

35

35 *Coned-bottomed silo*

36 *Rotary valve and standby*

36

37 Bank of 4 high
efficiency grit arresting
cyclones

38 Inside of fabric filter
housing

37

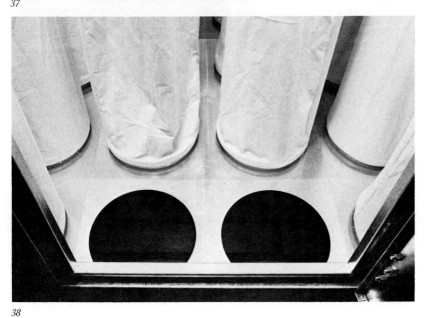

38

39 Cyclone
centrifugal fan

40 Hogger in pit

39

40

41

41 *Fabric filter installation*

42 *Off-cut conveying assembly*

43 *Off-cut conveyor with metal detector*

42

43

44　*Loaded compactor*

45　*In-house compactor*

46

46   Compactor in use

47   Compaction completed

48   Pneumatic refuse conveying
system. View of pipes and plant
house (BRS)

47

48

49

49　*Pneumatic refuse conveying
system. Plant room equipment (BRS)*

50　*Wood waste slag*

50

51 *Cyclone furnace slag adherence*   52 *Cyclone furnace pressure crack*

53 *Refractory installation site conditions*

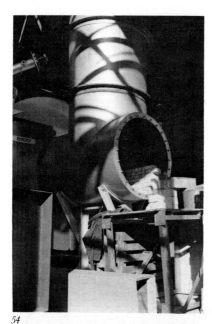

54　*Refractory installation site conditions*

55　*Chimney noise attenuator*

54

55

56

57

58

56 2 no 35 m high × 1800 mm
diameter externally flanged multiflue
chimneys each with 2 no 660 mm
diameter insulated steel liners.
Chimneys fitted with helical
stabilisers and exteriors shot-blasted

57 33.5 m high × 2300 mm
diameter internally flanged multi-
flue chimney with 6 no 450 mm
diameter insulated liners

58 107 m high × 1500 mm
diameter self supporting Insulcore
chimney complete with 1 no 1150
mm diameter insulated steel liner.
Chimney fitted with helical stabilisers

59

60

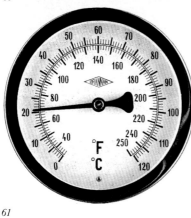

61

59 Lowering windshield section of 40 m high Insulcore chimney into position

60 Steeplejacks applying a final coat of paint after erection of 25 m high multiflue chimney

61 Dial temperature gauge

62 Safety valve

63 Thermocouple

64 Resistance thermometer

62

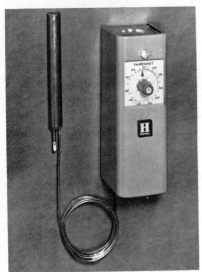

63

64

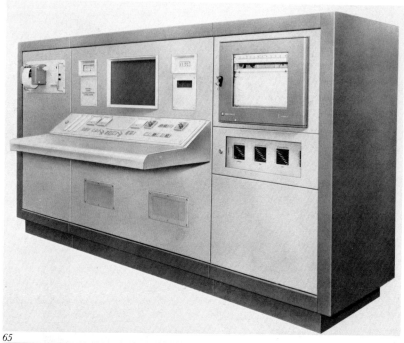

65

66

67

65 Control panel

66 Control and limit sensor

67 Vane anemometer

68 *Thermo-anemometer*

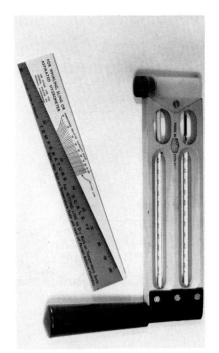

69 *Sling psychrometer*

70 *Recording hygrometer*

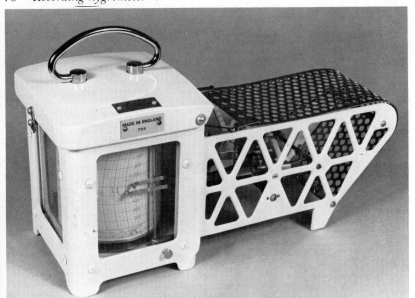

71

71   Neglected water tube boiler

72   Cyclone waste furnace —
overhaul

73   Boiler house louvres

72

73

74

75

74 *Wood-waste arresting cyclones, filters and silo*

75 *Boiler mud hole — inspection*

76

76 *Welding operator —*
maintenance

77 *Refurbishment of boiler firing*
wood-waste

77

8
Waste Handling and Storage

8.1 SUPPLY AND DEMAND

The required quantity of waste to match a known thermal demand involves a number of careful considerations, viz:

Type and quantity of waste
A correct assessment must be made of the varying types and quantities of waste produced. Each woodworking machine operation must be analysed to determine whether sander dust, sawdust, shavings or lumps of waste wood are being produced and their quantities accurately determined. The type of refuse for incineration must be determined, whether it possesses mainly organic waste (paper, wood or other combustible constituents). Without dependable information related to quality and quantity of available waste, it is impossible to match supply and demand.

Evaluation of the calorific value of the waste fuel
A correct calculation of calorific (heat) value for each type of waste must be carried out. For example, if a furniture factory produces 100 tonnes of mixed wood-waste each week, 50 per cent of which is relatively dry and 50 per cent is wet, then it may be seen (by reference to chapter 7) that wet wood-waste may possess only half the calorific value of dry wood-waste. Without this type of detailed analysis, there is a serious danger of overstating the potential waste heat quantity by about one-third.

Variation of thermal load
The variations of thermal load (heat requirement) must be analysed on a daily, weekly, monthly or seasonal basis since such variations can drastically affect the balance of supply and demand and also the required waste storage capacity.

Limited production

In some factories, there is no production of waste at weekends and during holidays though there exists a continuous thermal demand (eg kilning of timber). It is clearly essential in such circumstances to ensure that adequate waste storage capacity is provided to store the fuel when the waste is generated for use during periods when it is not generated.

Operating efficiency

The overall operating efficiency of the incineration plant must be established through accurate measurement, as with many installations there is a tendency to assume unjustified high operating efficiencies. The combustion efficiency of the incinerator may lie between 70 and 80 per cent; yet the overall efficiency of the whole process could be below 50 per cent. The incorrect assessment of the efficiency (ie the available heat output potential) will lead to a mismatch between heat supply and heat load.

Forecasting

Various factors may affect the correct forecast of the future heat supply and demand.

Projected changes in manufacturing methods (eg the increased use of plastic facing materials).

The adoption of conservation methods to improve the utilisation of raw materials.

Changing demands for the final product, etc.

The plant designer should avoid the trap of giving off-the-cuff estimates: he must analyse each case on its own circumstances, but as a preliminary assumption, he may estimate that only two-thirds of the total potential available heat from waste production will, in practice, become available as useful heat.

In assessing the heat potential of the lower grades of waste fuels (such as refuse-derived manures and composts), particular attention must be paid to their moisture and ash content, particularly the latter, which may be ten times that of wood-waste. Such wastes are more likely to be wet and offer also other complications due to the presence of plastic, glass, metal and other mainly incombustible matter which can greatly affect the heat value and combustion properties.

The ideal situation, in which the continuous flow of waste to the incinerators exactly matches the heat demand, very rarely exists. The consequences of serious miscalculations may be disastrous as this will result either in expensive oversized plant with inadequate

low thermal load sensitivity or in undersized plant with unnecessary supplementary fuel devices. Every care must, therefore, be
taken in the feasibility study which should establish the basis of the
design, the capital cost, the successful economic operation of the
chosen plant and the ultimate pay-back period.

Dissipation versus storage

Plate 32 shows an inclined heat dissipator connected to a steam
raising wood-waste fired boiler. Its function is to dissipate the
surplus heat to atmosphere when the heat supply exceeds the heat
demand and when the plant operation (at times of certain light load
conditions) requires an imposed thermal load to maintain the fire-
bed alight.

Seasonal variations of heat demand are likely where the plant
meets space heating requirements, though less pronounced where
there is a substantial continuous process heat load. On the other
hand, the production of waste is usually on a continuous basis,
resulting in unavoidable surpluses (often very large). Such a
situation can be regulated by dissipation of the surplus heat, by
storage, or by a combination of these to match the waste (flow)
supply and the heat demand. Generally, during warm weather,
when there is little space heating demand, vast amounts of useful
heat are dissipated because of the impracticability of providing
adequate summer waste storage capacity. In the great majority of
cases, it is better to condense the steam and return it to the boiler
than to blow-off steam at the boiler safety valve, which is noisy,
unsightly and wastes treated water.

The provision of waste storage facilities is necessary for the
following reasons:

To provide a buffer store between the rate of waste production and
the rate of waste disposal; this also acts as an explosion break
between the factory and the furnaces.

To provide a continuing fuel feed in a situation when the waste heat
boilers operate overnight or at week-ends for continuous kilning or
to give frost protection, at times when the factory is not producing
waste.

To smooth out climatic variations; waste surplus mainly arises
during warm weather spells.

Suitable storage capacity cannot be decided by applying a rule of
thumb. Every application must be individually analysed with a view
to achieving optimum storage, flexibility and adequacy of heat
supply, but it is accepted that one should aim for installing a storage
capacity to hold at least one week's equivalent heat requirement.

8.2 COMPACTING AND STORAGE

The bulk density of combustible waste is generally of a high order, particularly when it is in shredded, chipped, hogged, or in small fragment form suitable for direct firing into a furnace. Numerous problems accompany the accommodation of adequate waste storage and for this reason, compacting, briquetting and other volume reduction methods are sometimes employed to decrease the bulk density of waste and thus reduce the problems of storage. There are, however, a number of major shortcomings which must be considered.

Waste fuel for direct use in any furnace is more suitable when it is dry. The compacting of dry waste is difficult; unless there is a bonding agent, the compacted waste tends to crumble when it is handled.

The smokeless combustion of waste in compacted form can only take place in a furnace designed for that purpose (eg a chain grate stoker); re-shredding of compacted waste will be necessary before it can be admitted into a furnace designed to incinerate only chips or waste fragments.

The pelletising of refuse-derived fuel is often achieved by the addition of waste oil as a bonding agent before compression and extrusion.

Briquetting
In certain circumstances, it is practical to install a briquetting machine, which compresses the surplus wood-waste chips and sawdust into briquettes, which are then placed into store in readiness for excess heat demand. Briquetting presses operate at high pressure and are noisy vibratory machines; thus they must be located and mounted with great care to avoid creating a nuisance. The storage arrangements must allow for the tendency of the briquettes to crumble and to revert to wood fragments. There are successful briquetting installations; this method of burning wood waste is popular in Switzerland and in Scandinavia.

Baling
This well-known method of storage uses a baling machine, which automatically bales the compacted waste with plastic sealed moisture-proof bags. These bags may then be stored without the risk of increased waste moisture content and of waste crumbling.

Plate 33 shows automatically compacted and baled dry run-of-the-mill wood-waste ready for storage or for shipment to a

chipboard manufacturer—an excellent aid to indirect re-cycling.
Plate 34 shows the arrangement of alternative hand baling facility.

8.3 STORAGE HOPPERS OR SILOS

There are two basic types of waste storage hopper: coned-bottomed
and flat-bottomed. Coned-bottomed silos are designed to avoid
bridging of the waste material and to allow the free fall of waste into
a feed regulating rotary valve. Flat-bottomed silos depend upon the
positive displacement of the waste by a rotating worm or screw-
feeder; they possess the obvious advantage of increased storage
capacity for the same silo diameter.

Plate 35 shows a coned-bottomed silo.

Figure 8.1 shows the arrangement of a flat-bottomed silo,
mounted on reinforced concrete supports. The space under the
supports is used to house the boiler plant. Waste is transferred from
the hopper via the screw feed mechanism into a break transit
hopper before delivery into the boiler.

Silo supports may take the form of steel legs, but sufficient space
must be allowed under the silo for accommodation and maintenance of the waste out-feeder. The rotary screw device of the outfeeder is reversible to facilitate the thorough sweeping of the silo
bottom in a clockwise or in an anti-clockwise direction. It is
important with this type of silo to provide access doors for the
cleaning and maintenance of the silo interior and screw-feed. An
access door is also provided in the cone of a coned-bottomed silo
for cleaning and the maintenance of the bin-discharger.

Silo explosion and pressure relief panels are fitted to both types
of storage hopper, usually as part of the top flat section. The
maximum permissible internal pressure within a silo is about 20
mm of water gauge above the atmospheric pressure. Relief panels
are so weighted that they lift at a pre-set pressure which is related to
the nature of the waste being stored and to the silo capacity.

Chemical changes of stored waste, particularly in organic matter,
usually tend to increase the temperature within the silo and consequently the internal pressure. In the event of a fire or explosion,
the silo pressure relief panels open upwards, thereby limiting any
consequent damage. Internal and external access ladders are
required to minimise safety hazards.

Smoke alarm and sprinkler protection should be provided in any
silo which contains combustible waste. Silo level indicators may be
positioned at one-quarter, one-half, three-quarters and full height
positions or at any other desirable measuring positions; all these are

bound to be relatively inaccessible, with the result that the available silo level indicators are many and varied, all being prone to inaccuracy and failure due to lack of maintenance.

Most silo filling methods attempt to deposit the waste in the

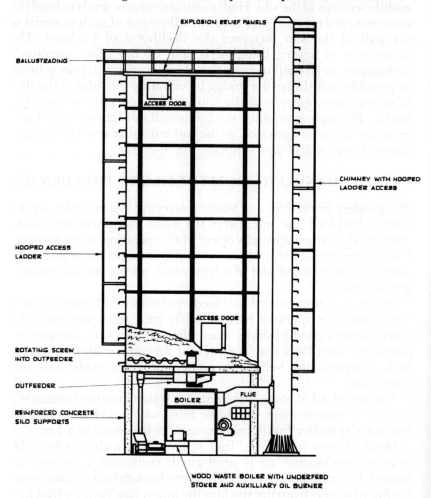

EXPLOSION RELIEF PANELS

BALLUSTRADING

ACCESS DOOR

CHIMNEY WITH HOOPED
LADDER ACCESS

HOOPED ACCESS
LADDER

ACCESS DOOR

ROTATING SCREW
INTO OUTFEEDER

OUTFEEDER

BOILER   FLUE

REINFORCED CONCRETE
SILO SUPPORTS

WOOD WASTE BOILER WITH UNDERFEED
STOKER AND AUXILLIARY OIL BURNER

8.1   Flat-bottomed silo

centre of the silo to provide a pyramid formation with an even spread towards the edges. With graded material (eg grain), the fall to the edges tends to be relatively even; with ungraded waste (eg wood-waste), the lighter fragments tend to fall faster, resulting in an uneven spread. Pneumatic closed loop waste conveying systems are fed tangentially into circular up-stands on the top of the silo; baffles or directing plates underneath are located to ensure centre-of-silo waste deposition.

Bridging of the waste material in a silo can be caused by weight compression and by the packing of the material in the lower and middle sections of the silo. High moisture content tends to bind the waste material together and the firm adherence of such material to the wall of the silo increases the likelihood of bridging. The occurrence of severe bridging is one of the plant operator's nightmares, as all outflow from the silo then ceases. It may at times be possible to dislodge the bridge by vibrating the sides of the silo; in severe cases, entry into the silo will be necessary to clear the bridge. This operation must not be carried out single-handed and great care must be exercised, as the sudden collapse of the bridged material may engulf and suffocate the operator.

8.4 WASTE HANDLING FROM THE SILO TO THE FURNACE

The greatest fire risk in any waste conveying system exists in the furnace fuel feed line and also in the waste transportation system from the silo, which is usually open (when operating) to the furnace. Equipment employed in these conveying systems must always be extra well maintained and of a type which allows fail-safe control and protection.

Pneumatically conveyed fuel feed systems should incorporate a compressed air operated blast or safety gate, must automatically revert to the closed position. Butterfly or non-return dampers in pneumatic feed lines may not prevent fire spread; the use of two such dampers, one behind the other, provides inadequate fire protection.

The screwfeed of an underfeed stoker system into the furnace is a fire critical position and should be fitted with a thermal sensor to activate a sprinkler fire-fighting system in the event of a fire.

Metal objects in furnace fuel systems, particularly when the primary combustion air is pre-heated, constitute a serious fire hazard. In a case known to the authors a broken metal hand wood file found its way from the silo into the pneumatic furnace feed line causing (by spark ignition) an immediate explosion, which split the conveying duct losing all waste conveying pressure. The pressure-stat in the conveying duct sensed this loss of pressure, closed the safety gate, halted the rotary valve silo feed and (in sequence) closed down the plant.

Rotary valves and bin dischargers
Rotary valve mechanisms are usually operated simultaneously with

bin dischargers, which are fitted within the coned section of a coned-bottomed silo to rotate in an angular radial fashion (in either a clockwise or in an anti-clockwise direction), to agitate the waste in the bottom of a silo and to allow the free-flow of waste material into the rotary valve. A manual override is commonly incorporated to permit the operation of the bin discharger, independently of the rotary valve, for use in bridging conditions when fuel starvation is apparent.

Bin dischargers are electrically driven by a direct current motor with infinitely variable speed and non-overloading characteristics.

For the correct and safe operation of an incineration plant, the rate at which the waste (fuel) is fed into the furnace must be strictly controlled. The speed of rotation of a rotary valve provides a suitable method of control which is usually exercised by a direct-current electrically driven motor with non-overloading and infinitely variable speed facilities. The blades of the rotary valve are either frabricated from heavy gauge steel plate with heavy duty rubber or neoprene tips, or from wholly fire resistant heavy duty rubber or neoprene to achieve positive separation between the low pressure stored waste and the higher pressure furnace feed line and to provide a fire-break.

Figure 8.2 shows a rotary valve with neoprene blades.

Plate 36 shows a pair of rotary valves mounted at the bottom of a silo.

One valve is used for automatic fuel metering purposes and the other valve as a standby silo emptying device. Notice the layers of sander dust escape, which probably have been caused by an untidy standby valve bagging operation. Bag attachments should not be greater than 400mm diameter; larger attachments are difficult to secure, unless they are purpose-made.

8.5 PNEUMATIC WASTE AND DUST HANDLING SYSTEMS

Wood-waste (sander and sawdust) chips and similar waste materials are most commonly conveyed from the source of generation to the storage hoppers in ducts, where they are carried in suspension by the conveying air.

Hoods and enclosures
Figures 8.3 and 8.4 show typical galvanised sheet metal hood and duct connections to woodworking machines which generate wood-waste. For optimum extraction efficiency, the dust extraction hoods and enclosures must be fitted close to the dust source to

confine the air suction to the woodworking machine and be engineered to the contours of the relevant machine parts to provide the suction, without interfering unduly with the manufacturing operation.

Air will move in all directions towards openings under suction (negative) pressure. Flow contours (lines of equal velocity in front of

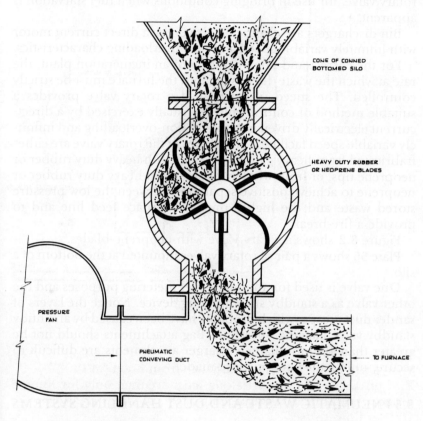

CONE OF CONNED BOTTOMED SILO

HEAVY DUTY RUBBER OR NEOPRENE BLADES

PRESSURE FAN

PNEUMATIC CONVEYING DUCT

TO FURNACE

8.2   Rotary valve function

the hood) should be studied to obtain the greatest degree of streamlining and reduction of energy loss.

The equation of flow before round and rectangular hoods, which are essentially square and unobstructed, is:

$$V = \frac{Q}{10X^2 + A}$$

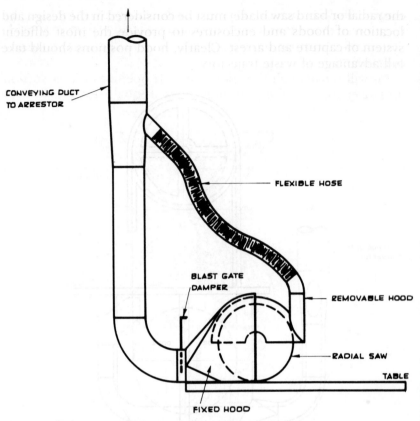

8.3   Radial saw enclosure

Where,
V = centre line velocity at X distance from hood (m/s)
X = distance (m) outward along axis (accurate only for limited distance - up to 1.5 D equivalent)
Q = air flow (m³/sec)
A = area of hood opening (m²)
D = diameter of round hoods or side of essentially square hoods (m).

There is always a rapid velocity decrease with increasing distances from the hood varying almost inversely with the square of the distance, which indicates the importance of tight fitting enclosures, low loss (streamlined) entries and the maximum use of suction effect.

The trajectory of waste dust and particles from the machine (off the radial or band saw blade) must be considered in the design and location of hoods and enclosures to provide the most efficient system of capture and arrest. Clearly, hood positions should take full advantage of waste trajectory.

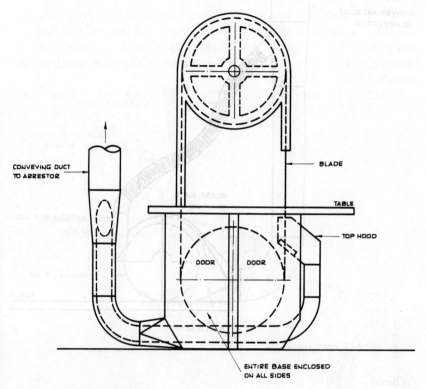

8.4   Band saw enclosure

Effective control of the waste generating process is brought about by first eliminating or minimising all air motion about the process and then capturing the contaminated air by causing it to flow into the exhaust hood. Air flow towards the suction opening must be sufficiently high to maintain the necessary capture velocity to overcome opposing air currents. The capture velocity for sawdust and small fragment arrest is between 15,000 and 30,000 m/sec, depending on the distance of the hood from the blade and depending on the waste fragment size.

Hoods should be flanged wherever possible to reduce the hood entry pressure loss and to avoid suction from adjacent ineffective areas. An important factor in hood design is the reduction of the required suction air volume and the corresponding power consumption; the elimination of external sources of air motion is a first step towards the optimisation of this required air flow.

Conveying ducts and arrestors

Figure **8.5** shows a waste extraction system discharging into an arresting centrifugal cyclone. At the bottom of the cyclone, wood-waste may be collected and conveyed into a storage silo for burning in a wood-waste furnace; at the top of the cyclone, clean air is exhausted to atmosphere.

A cyclone (or similar equipment) must be inserted into any duct

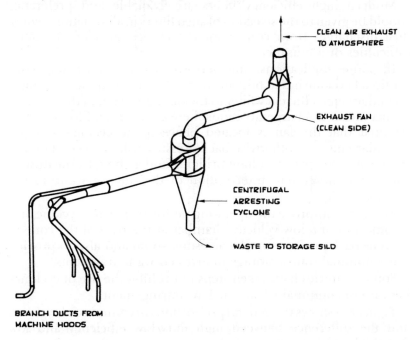

CLEAN AIR EXHAUST
TO ATMOSPHERE

EXHAUST FAN
(CLEAN SIDE)

CENTRIFUGAL
ARRESTING
CYCLONE

WASTE TO STORAGE SILO

BRANCH DUCTS FROM
MACHINE HOODS

8.5   Waste extraction to cyclone arrestor

system which relies on the conveyance of materials by suspending them in air. The cyclone separates the conveyed material from the air, permitting the air to vent to atmosphere or to be recirculated.

The conventional cyclone of the type indicated in fig **8.5** is manufactured of mild steel, usually of minimum thickness 3.5mm. It must be sturdily constructed and must be capable of being located externally to buildings; hence, it must be reasonably weather-proof and watertight. The cyclone supports must be similarly constructed and protected to suit external mounting.

The type of common cyclone which is indicated in fig **8.5** is relatively inefficient in that the air which it exhausts to atmosphere must include light particles of dust which have not settled in the cyclone, with the result that layers of fine dust are spread and deposited around the cyclone locations and usually settle on the roofs and in the gutters of adjacent buildings. Such layers of dust can constitute a grave nuisance and possibly fire and health hazards. In one case, known to the authors, it was found that dust discharged from the cyclone of a furniture factory entered through the construction gaps and windows of a bread bakery and settled on the loaves.

Modern high efficiency filters are available and preference should be given to the selection of such filters in all situations where dust discharges from conventional cyclones are likely to cause difficulties or a nuisance.

In some applications, the performance of an existing conventional cyclone has to be improved. This can be done by fitting a secondary high efficiency filter to the discharge vent of the cyclone, so that the air discharges to atmosphere after further filtration. It is essential that the fan is located between the cyclone and the secondary filter, as otherwise back pressure will be exerted on the storage hopper, with resultant bridging and arching by the dust or chips and subsequent interruption of the flow of waste to the furnace.

To further improve the operating performance of a cyclone, it is common to fit a low velocity chamber at the base of the cone to prevent back pressure on the arresting spiral and also to provide some nominal transit storage of arrested waste fragments.

Some countries have taken steps to prohibit the use of cyclones because of continual Clean Air Law infringement.

Figure **8.6** shows the general proportions of commercial cyclones and the difference between high duty/low efficiency and low duty/high efficiency types.

Consider a dust particle within an arresting cyclone: the centrifugal force exerted on the particle *acting outwards* depends upon the linear velocity of the particle, its mass and the radius of rotation. The resistance of the air *acting inwards,* depends upon the mass and shape of the dust particle and on the properties of the conveying air. The combined effect of these two forces yields a separating force which, with gravitational force *acting downwards,* arrests the particle.

The upper straight section of the cyclone should be of sufficient size to separate the dust particles outwards to the cyclone walls. The

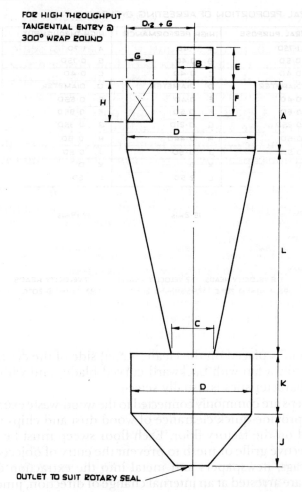

FOR HIGH THROUGHPUT
TANGENTIAL ENTRY @
300° WRAP ROUND

OUTLET TO SUIT ROTARY SEAL

8.6   General proportions of commercial cyclones (see key opposite)

depth of the central internal clean air escape duct should ensure that the heavier dust particles are not admitted; adjustment of the depth of the clean air duct into the upper centre of the cyclone is frequently necessary for optimum performance – the position of a weathering cowl can affect this adjustment. If the diameter of the cyclone is large, it will remove large dust particles; if small, it will be more suitable for the arrest of small particles. Plate 37 shows a bank of four high efficiency grit arresting cyclones.

If the extraction fan is placed on the dirty (inlet) side of the cyclone or fabric arrestor, it must be of the paddle or radial type which is not easily fouled by dusty material handling. If the

GENERAL PROPORTION OF ARRESTING CYCLONE

GENERAL PURPOSE		HIGH PERFORMANCE		HIGH THROUGHPUT	
A	1·75D	A	1·4D	A	1·7D
B	0·5D	B	0·4D	B	0·75D
C	0·4D	C	0·4D	C	0·4D
D	DIAMETER	D	DIAMETER	D	DIAMETER
E	0·4D	E	0·4D	E	0·65D
F	0·6D	F	0·5D	F	0·85D
G	0·25D	G	0·21D	G	0·35D
H	0·5D	H	0·44D	H	0·8D
J	0·5D	J	0·5D	J	0·5D
K	D	K	D	K	D
L	2D	L	2·5D	L	2D

INLET
VELOCITY 14·69m/s   15·2m/s   12·19m/s

THROUGH-
PUT   6·08m³/s   4·5m³/s   11·41m³/s

PRESSURE
DROP   7·6 VELOCITY HEADS   9·2 VELOCITY HEADS   7 VELOCITY HEADS
          996·4 N/m² @ 20°C   1295·3N/m² @ 20°C   622·7 N/m² @ 20°C

extraction fan is placed on the clean (outlet) side of the cyclone or fabric arrestor, a fan with backward curved blades and with non-overload characteristics is usually selected.

Floor sweeps are commonly connected to the wood-waste extraction systems to provide quick clearance of wood dust and chips which have settled on the factory floor. Each floor sweep must be fitted with a protective grille or mesh to prevent the entry of objects such as gloves, rags, newspapers and metal into the extraction ducts, where they are arrested at an internal change of direction, junction, filter or at a projecting screw or lug and cause disruptive blockages causing a possible explosion or a fire hazard.

Figure 8.7 shows a waste extraction system discharging into a series of modular fabric filters which remove all dust particles. Such arrangement allows a clean air discharge to atmosphere and offers the facility of re-circulating the air back to the factory during the heating season to effect an appreciable fuel saving. Arrested material falls into the tapered bottom where it is transported by the motor-chain driven conveyor belts into a separate silo feed conveying system.

Plate 38 shows the inside of a fabric filter (two bags have been removed for illustration)

Plate 41 shows a roof top assembly of modular fabric filters (located in Denmark. This type of fabric arrestor may conveniently be assembled from identical sections which are bolted together. Individual sections may be separated from each other by a sheet metal bulkhead to reduce the risk of fire spread.

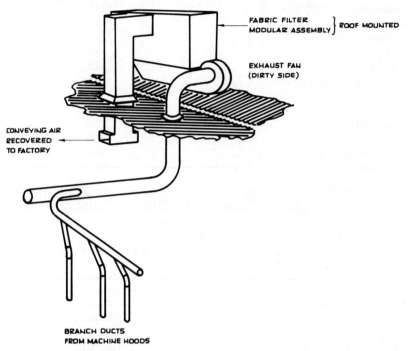

FABRIC FILTER
MODULAR ASSEMBLY } ROOF MOUNTED

EXHAUST FAN
(DIRTY SIDE)

CONVEYING AIR
RECOVERED
TO FACTORY

BRANCH DUCTS
FROM MACHINE HOODS

8.7   Waste extraction to fabric filter

Extraction duct design and construction

The conveying velocities for the efficient transportation of the waste material carried in extraction ducts must relate to the characteristics of the material being conveyed. Table **8.1** lists the recommended minimum conveying velocities for some typical materials which are commonly transported in duct systems.

Figure **8.8** shows detailed recommended methods of constructing waste extraction ducts; these must be designed to minimise the resistance to air flow (to economise in fan power) and to minimise material impact abrasion and shock. Because of the abrasive nature of wood and of some other wastes, conveying ducts for such materials must be of robust construction and of appropriate metal thicknesses. The conveying velocities and the dimensions of the conveying duct must be selected with care and skill.

TABLE 8.1 MINIMUM CARRY-OVER VELOCITIES

Material	Conveying velocity m/sec
Lint	85
Grain and sander dust	115
Jute dust	115
Rubber dust	115
Flour	175
Sawdust	175
Metal dust (grindings)	175
Wood chips and shavings	200
Brass tornings (fine)	230
Fine coal	230
Lead dust	280
Hogged wood-waste	350

The high velocity conveying system is commonly employed for the type of application discussed. Table **8.2** and associated comments relate to a suitable specification for such a system.

TABLE 8.2 SPECIFICATION OF A HIGH VELOCITY CONVEYING SYSTEM

Up to 200mm	0.89mm
Over 200 to 450mm	1.25mm
Over 450 to 900mm	1.65mm
Over 900mm	2.11mm

Construction notes

All externally located straight ductwork should be of not less than 1.65mm thickness.

Elbows and angles should be minimum of two gauges heavier than straight lengths of equal diameter.

Extraction hoods should be a minimum of two gauges heavier than the straight section of the connecting branches.

Where flexible ducting is necessary (and permissible) a non-collapsible type of flexible material should be used; the length should be kept to a minimum.

Longitudinal joints of ducts should be lapped and rivetted or spot welded on 75mm centres, maximum. Lock seams are totally unsuitable to these applications.

Girth joints of ducts should be made with inner lap in the direction of air flow; 25mm lap for diameters up to 450mm and 32mm laps for diameters over 450mm.

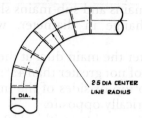

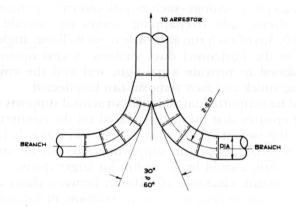

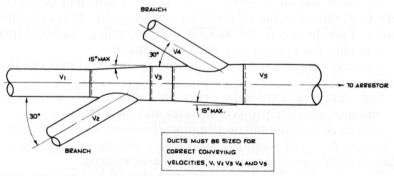

8.8   Methods of duct construction

Elbows and angles should have a centre line radius of 2.5mm pipe diameters.

Construct elbows of 150 mm diameter (or less) of at least five sections; over 150mm diamter, of seven sections. Pre-fabricated elbows of smooth construction may be used to advantage. External hoods must be free of sharp edges and burrs and should be appropriately reinforced to provide adequate stiffness.

Tapered transitions in mains and sub-mains should be 125mm long for each 25mm change in diameter, whenever this is practicable.

All branches should enter the main duct at the large end of the transition and at an angle of not greater than 45°; 30° is preferred. Connect branches only to top or sides of the main, with no two branches entering diametrically opposite.

Dead-end caps should be provided within 150mm from the last branch of all mains and sub-mains.

Access or clean out openings (such as pull-out caps, perimeter slides, hinged doors, split overlapping sleeves etc) should be provided at every 3m of such run and close to each elbow, angle or duct junction in the horizontal duct sections. Access openings should be gasketed to provide a gas-tight seal and the covers arranged so that quick and easy removal can be effected.

Ducts should be supported on adequate structural supports in a manner which ensures that no load is placed on the connecting equipment by the weight of the duct system when this is fully charged with material. Maximum supporting intervals for small ducts (up to 200mm) should be 3.5m; 6m for larger ducts.

Provide a minimum clearance of 150mm between ducts and ceiling, walls, or floors to permit ease of installation, maintenance and cleaning.

Blast gate dampers, where used for the adjustment of system pressure, should be placed at the connection of the branch in to the main. Provide means of locking and recording each damper setting after the adjustments have been made.

Butterfly dampers must not be used in ducted systems of this type.

Fire dampers, explosion vents etc, should be installed in accordance with fire protection codes and local by-laws.

Fans must be mounted on vibration absorbing mountings. Duct connections to fans should be made with heavy-duty non-combustible flexible material, suitably banded and secured.

Fan sets installed in hazardous areas should be spark-resistant and should have non-ferrous impellors and non-ferrous motor shaft bearings.

Electrical earthing should be provided for all fan parts.

Where local codes of practice and/or regulations conflict with the specifications, the more stringent requirements must be met.

Fans

Paddle-bladed or radial fans must incorporate impellors constructed from heavy gauge steel plate to withstand the impact and abrasion of the waste material being handled. The wide spacing of the blades of the impellor for such a fan permits the clearance of large lumps of waste material and serves to avoid blockages. This type of fan is most commonly used for conveying waste-laden air when mounted in the waste material stream (on the dirty side of the filter).

The type of fan most commonly used when installed outside the waste material stream (on the clean side of the filter) is fitted with a backward curved blade impellor. The selection of a backward bladed fan for applications to wood-waste extraction systems is influenced by the risk of blockages within the duct system and a sudden consequent rise in resistance with a fall-off in conveying air displacement. The non-overloading characteristic of the backward bladed fan is of advantage in such circumstances and it is, therefore, preferred to the forward bladed type of fan which does not offer the non-overloading feature. (See plate 39.)

Consider a fan operating under the following condition:

Volume of air handled per minute: Q (m^3)
Total pressure developed: P_t (mb)
Static pressure developed: P_s (mb)
Power absorbed: B (MJ)
Fan static efficiency: e_s (per cent)
Fan total efficiency: e_t (per cent)

then

Power absorbed by fan $= B$ and

$$B = \frac{\text{Volume flow of air } (Q) \times \text{fan total pressure } (P_t)}{2365 \ (6350) \times \text{fan total efficiency } (e_s)}$$

which equals $\dfrac{Q \times P_s \times MJ \ (bhp)}{6350 \times e_s}$

Note: the factor $6350 = \dfrac{33{,}000 \ (1 \ hp = 33{,}000 \ ft \ lb/h)}{5.196 \ (1 \ in \ wg = 5.196 \ lb/ft)}$

the factor $2365 = \dfrac{6350}{2.685}$ (1 hp/h = 2.685 MJ)

Thus $\dfrac{\text{Fan static efficiency}}{\text{Fan total efficiency}} = \dfrac{\text{Fan static pressure}}{\text{Fan total pressure}}$

or $\dfrac{e_s}{e_t} = \dfrac{P_s}{P_t}$

assuming the same volume flow Q.

8.6 SILO WASTE TRANSFER SYSTEMS

There are a number of different methods available for the transfer of waste from arrestors (cyclone or fabric types) and hoggers. The ultimate selection of a particular method depends upon many factors eg whether or not the waste is dust-laden, whether it is wet or dry, whether the silo is close to or at a considerable distance from the waste source or whether the silo can withstand slight pressurisations.

Figure **8.9** shows various methods of waste transfer systems, including the following:

Where the amount of waste is small or of poor quality, a tapered bottom may be fitted to the underside of a fabric filter or a direct connection made to an arresting cyclone to allow the waste to fall through a rotary valve into bags, or into a skip (or other container) for further transportation.

Where there is a considerable distance between the arrestors and the waste source, a non-pressurised silo is preferred: the best system is a silo filter with a rotary valve feed to the main silo. Where the waste includes considerable amounts of dust, this method is also preferred.

Where the distance between the arrestors and the silo is short, a closed re-circulatory system offers a simple solution and entails reduced maintenance requirements.

Another solution offers a pressurised silo and silo filter, where pressurisation of the silo can be accepted. Care must be exercised in the design of such a system to provide and maintain a correct limiting pressure and higher pressure silo relief dampers.

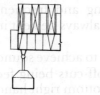

(a) SMALL WASTE TO BAG / CONTAINER

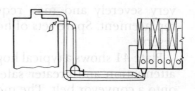

(c) CLOSED RECIRCULATORY SYSTEM

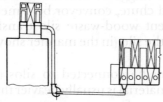

(b) NON PRESSURISED SILO

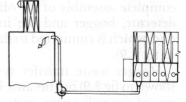

(d) PRESSURISED SILO & FILTER

8.9   Silo waste transfer systems

Silo and fabric (bag or modular) filters are best maintained automatically by bursts of intermittent compressed air blast cleaning.

Hoggers

The manual feeding of furnaces with off-cuts through the open furnace charging door is an undesirable practice for the following reasons:

It results in an unacceptably low boiler efficiency, due to random opening of the charging door when uncontrolled air quantities are admitted.

Resultant uncontrolled combustion can cause smoke emission and consequent infringement of Clean Air Laws.

The manpower employed in hand-firing is increasingly costly and scarce.

Furnace blow-backs are likely to occur.

Refractory life is shortened.

The regulated flow of waste material is best accomplished by feeding fuel of constant and even size or grade. For the automatic operation of an incinerator plant it is, therefore, best practice to hog (reduce in size) the off-cuts in a hogger for transportation into the storage silo.

Hoggers are vibratory, noisy machines; this type of machine is best physically isolated from the factory mill by installation in a pit or in a sound-proofed chamber.

The working lifespan of the hogger knives depends greatly on the type of timber being hogged. Some hard woods punish the knives very severely and may require daily sharpening and frequent replacement. Spare sets of hogger knives should always be kept in reserve.

Plate 41 shows a typical hogger installed in a pit to achieve sound attenuation and greater safety. Plate 43 shows off-cuts being fed onto a conveyor belt. The metal detector in the bottom right hand corner is positioned just ahead of the hogger. Plate 42 shows the complete assembly of the off-cut feed chute, conveyor belt, metal detector, hogger and the independent wood-waste silo transfer duct which is connected to the top of the silo (in the manner shown in fig 8.9).

Hogger waste transfer systems can be connected to silos (as shown in fig 8.9) but because hogged material is usually heavier than run-of-the-mill waste, independent transfer systems are usually employed requiring higher conveying velocities.

Metal detectors

The presence of metal objects in combustible, pneumatically conveyed material is undesirable and dangerous. At the conveying speeds shown in table 8.1, nails, screws, broken files etc, can cause sparks by collision with the inside surfaces of the metal ducts (particularly at bends) which may then ignite the dust.

Metal objects entering the cutting edges of a hogger will become red-hot in a very short time and cause ignition. Within seconds, the fire will spread to the silo or silo filter, causing a major hazard. One such fire occured at the installation shown in plate 43 before the metal detector was installed.

When activated by the detection of a metal object, the metal detector automatically stops the conveyor and sounds an alarm or claxon. The offending metal is then manually removed. Waste conveying systems without metal detectors tend to encourage the deposit of all sorts of incombustible rubbish. Waste conveying systems with metal detectors require periodic attention and are, therefore, usually maintained much better, as the frequent ringing of alarm devices encourages good housekeeping.

8.7 THE HANDLING OF WASTE OF LOW CALORIFIC VALUE

This subject has already been discussed relative to refuse-derived fuel (RDF) and the following comments are supplementary.

The waste from household, factory, and commercial buildings is of low calorific value and seldom justifies the high transportation cost. Therefore, it is usually incinerated locally. Pelletising of RDF reduces the bulk density and permits more economical transport, but it is doubtful whether much fuel will ever be transported over long distances. Large local authority incinerators equipped with energy recovery are now fairly well developed, but smaller incineration plants must be designed for the purpose of burning such fuels before waste handling techniques (other than straightforward collection) are developed. Local authorities may eventually decide to sell container loads of RDF for linking into higher waste grade pneumatic conveying furnace feed lines, so that RDF availability can be fully utilised. Whether shredded or pelletised, the feasibility of RDF incineration for energy recovery in small local communities, factories, commercial buildings and the like, has yet to be technically and economically determined. Develoopments are afoot, particularly in the USA and in Europe, to widen the appeal and consumption of RDF.

The handling of chicken litter is, to a large extent, in the same category as RDF. Poultry production is big business; the floors of breeding houses often contain sufficient waste fuel at the end of one crop to heat the house for the next crop, the fuel being a mixture of fine wood-waste and manure. Small centralised incineration plants (serving usually blocks of eight or ten breeding houses) would appear to be economically feasible, given the availability of suitable incineration plants. Other similar waste sources also exist which would justify well designed automatic handling of the waste and associated energy recovery.

All such lower grade waste handling systems must be automatic; it is inadvisable (for hygienic reasons) to manhandle this type of waste fuel.

8.8 ACCESS AND SAFETY

The provisions of safe and convenient access arrangements to all items of equipment form an essential component of current plant design.

Figure 8.1 and plate 35 show silo top balustrading. Hooped access ladders, which are now compulsory in the UK, are indicated.

Non-slip working and access surfaces are necessary to plant of this type, where frequent inspection is required.

It is good practice to link plant items by protected catwalks wherever this can be done to avoid the use of ladders.

For applications where permanent means of access cannot be conveniently provided (eg to the access covers of a pneumatic conveying system), allowance must be made for the safe placing of ladders and the provision of quick release type fixings to manholes, hand-holes, covers etc.

The temporary storage of waste in and around boiler houses is a common but dangerous practice, particularly where this creates fire and explosion hazards and impedes the means of escape from the plant area.

Recent and now current legislation in the UK related to health and safety at work requires the provision of *safe access* arrangements to all plant items and the provision of substantially made and protected access ladders, catwalks, balustrades, hand-grips, etc and of non-slip surfaces.

CHECK LIST

Check: whether the thermal demand can be matched to the waste production; methods for matching thermal demand and fuel input; requirement of heat dissipation and waste (fuel) storage; suitability of briquetting method; suitability of baling methods; principles and construction of air-borne waste material conveying systems, including process machine exhaust hoods, cyclones, filters, fans and ducting, function and use of rotary valves and bin dischargers; function and use of hoggers; function and use of metal detectors with waste handling systems; function and design of storage hoppers and silos; silo waste transfer systems; adequate plant access and safety.

8.9 COMPACTORS

Definition
A compactor (as described below) is a precision-built item of machinery which incorporates an electrically-operated compaction ram. It is designed to reduce the volume of waste matter by some 80 per cent and to package it into a clean and conveniently handled unit. Plate 45 shows a compactor machine with the associated trolley for the removal of the compacted material.

Function
Compactors of the type shown in plates 45 and 46 have been designed for acceptability in working and public locations, such as kitchens, hotel landings, hospital ward ante-rooms, where the compactor is fed with bulky waste, such as plastic vending cups, discarded packaging material, tins, bottles, carton, paper, foil, wooden boxes. The use of compacting equipment reduces materially the storage space requirement for light compactable wastes and greatly eases the handling and disposal of bulky wastes off site.

Plate 46 shows a compactor which has been loaded and is about to be closed for compation. Plate 47 indicates the manner in which the compacted material has been packaged and is then removed from the machine trolley.

Siting
To obtain optimum benefit from compaction units, these should be located close to, or at, the points where the waste is generated (one example is that of a compactor located immediately adjacent to a vending machine using plastic cups). Such siting results in minimum transport and handling costs of the waste.

Alternatively, the compactor, particularly the larger units, may be located in a special garbage collection and processing space; uncompacted waste is brought there for compaction and storage, pending transport off site. Such an arrangement is especially suited to shopping centres, hospitals, university campuses, etc where there are numerous waste creators and where suitable internal or external transport routes exist. Most types of compactors are available in a weather-proof construction, enabling them to be sited in the open, if required.

Having decided on a centralised location for the compactor equipment, the operation can be assisted by the provision of a number of separate trucks; one truck would be located at the point of waste creation (such as the kitchen) and would be used as a dustbin for the compactable rubbish. When full, the truck is wheeled or transported to the central compactor; an empty truck is left behind to continue the operation.

In all cases, the compactor must be stood upon a section of flat and level floor, about 1m². A further such area must be provided to the front of the unit to permit the entry and withdrawal of the truck.

Installation
The compactor is delivered to site, fully assembled. The castors are fitted with brakes of the foot pedal type and when the machine is in position, the pedal is depressed to tighten the brake band onto the wheel.

The machines are available in two electric motor versions to suit single phase or three phase electric supply. The single phase machine should be connected to a 25 amps fused isolator switch — the three phase unit to be a fused isolator switch rated at 10 amps per phase.

Operation

The waste material is placed into the hopper of the machine, it being best to commence compaction with some cardboard which then forms a solid base in the recovery bag. It is unnecessary to sort the waste material except that it is undesirable to include large amounts of glass with the waste material. There is obviously a limit to the dimensions of the waste article which the machine can accept; material which cannot pass underneath the ram in the top position must not be forced into the machine. The bag should not be over-filled in the compaction operation, as this will make the truck and the bag difficult to remove. The truck has to be lined with a special plastic (or other suitable material) waste bag. With the machine at its top stroke, the truck is removed from the machine by depressing the pedal and pulling on the truck handle. The folded plastic bag is opened out and the bottom of the bag is arranged to cover the base of the truck. The top edges of the bag are then folded over and around the edges of the truck. The truck liners must be in place inside the back before the truck is pushed back into the machine.

When the bag is full, the truck is pulled out of position and the truck liners are withdrawn vertically. The rolled edges over the plastic bag are unfolded and pulled together. The neck of the sack is folded and a wire tied around it, so that the two loops on the tie approach close to each other; the hook of the special tying tool is then inserted into the two loops, the handle is pulled and the tool will twist the wire tight, thereby sealing the bag.

The truck and the tied bag are conveyed to the garbage area, where the toggle clips at the front of the truck are unfastened, the two truck doors then open and the bag with the compacted waste slides out. When handling wet waste, moisture-proof plastic bags should be used.

Under extreme load circumstances, the compactor may over-heat. An integral overload protection device will then come into play and turn off the electricity to prevent damage to the motor. It will automatically reset itself when the machine has cooled sufficiently; it can then be restarted at the press of the start button. If the jammed condition is particularly severe, the ram has to be unloaded by hand.

Compaction

A fully-packaged bag of typical waste weighs about 25 to 30 kg and takes up only one-fifth or less of the space of the uncompacted contents. If the load is a material of light density (eg cartons or vending cups), the compaction gain may be up to 90 per cent.

CHECK LIST

Check: quantity of bulky waste created; whether compactors can be located close to point of waste creation; suitability of a central garbage and compaction area.

Decide: size and type of compactor; siting, transport from compactor to ultimate waste disposal; electric supply requirements; operator training and standing orders.

9
Waste Disposal

9.1 INTRODUCTION

Raw refuse can only be safely stored if it is buried. It is toxic and unhygienic; decomposition commences almost immediately the waste is generated and, therefore, disposal methods are subject to legislation and strict codes of practice in many developed countries.

Until quite recently, it was common practice to gather refuse into trucks and dump it outside town and city limits, where it was left to rot and become a hazard to health, causing pollution of land, air, rivers and streams and a source of permanent contamination and infestation. Such a situation is no longer placidly accepted. For instance, New York has for many years dumped its refuse at the southern end of Staten Island and, even though the City has reduced the volume of refuse by incineration and pulverisation, this particular vast tipping area is now overdumped.

It has become increasingly difficult for densely populated communities to find new refuse tips and, in many cases, it has become a necessity to arrange alternative disposal facilities, some of which are described in this chapter. In these circumstances, environmental and pollution factors often override strictly economical considerations.

Methods for the disposal of difficult wastes require special consideration. Oily sludges have little or no re-sale value; yet their energy recovery potential after processing is considerable. The cost of transport, separation and refining generally outweighs the need for energy recovery. Such sludges are often dumped, as are other difficult chemical wastes, into land-holes, which are becoming ever more scarce. The Thames Conservancy Water Authority (London) has for many years fought against the solid and industrial waste pollution of the river and has, in recent times, achieved major improvements with the result that certain species of fish life have found it possible once more to return to these waters.

A further difficulty is that many lakes and water-courses suffer from the increasing use of artificial farm fertilisers, which, with rainfall, drain into such waterways and there stimulate the growth of parasitic aquatic plants. These eventually decay and deplete the dissolved oxygen of the water, thereby reducing the ability of the water to degrade sewage and sustain healthy aquatic life.

9.2 WASTE GENERATION

Domestic refuse divides into two categories:
- organic, such as plastics, paper, vegetables and foodstuffs,
- inorganic, such as metal, glass and ash.

Organic wastes are generally suited to energy recovery and represent some 60 per cent of the refuse generated; the balance, inorganic waste, is unsuited to energy recovery.

Many industrial wastes in the form of liquids, oils and sludges are inflammable or toxic, these represent more than 10 per cent of the UK national waste production. The energy recovery and recycling potential from such waste is considerable.

The major part of waste production (over 70 per cent in the UK) comes from mining, quarry, power station and like operations and industries, this waste being largely inorganic and non-combustible (ash, clinker, etc). Such waste can often be usefully employed in land reclamation, the building and cement industries and in roadmaking, etc.

Much organic waste is generated in agriculture. The increasing use of intensive farming techniques has upset the natural balance of agricultural recycling to such an extent that manure and associated waste tends to be surplus to requirements. Indeed, a disposal difficulty now exists. The advent of modern methane digestion and sewage sludge incineration techniques will ease this problem and also provide energy recovery.

Figure 9.1 shows the available waste disposal options.

9.3 CONTROLLED TIPPING

Sanitary landfilling of refuse, or controlled tipping, usually has to conform to strict codes of practice and environmental standards.

The disposal site should be free of running or static water and be a natural land depression. Refuse should be tipped in layers of not more than 1.8m in depth, compacted and thoroughly covered with a layer of inert material (such as ash or soil) during the tipping process. The covering layer should never be less than 15cm deep. Refuse must not be left uncovered for a period of more than 24 hours. All exposed surfaces of the final tip should be covered with at least 23 cm of earth with another suitable layer of friable material on all sides, leaving no exposed refuse. Controlled tipping is obviously more expensive than indiscriminate or uncontrolled tipping, so that local authorities must be ever watchful to abort careless and unhygienic, dumping of domestic refuse and industrial wastes.

9.4 WASTE MANAGEMENT

Modern oxygen steel-smelting processes use less scrap iron. In consequence, the derelict automobile is often not worth the cost of collection and haulage to a processing yard. In the past, office users were paid for their waste paper which was then re-pulped. To-day one must pay for the paper to be taken away. Refuse and paper components, as well as being suitable for recycling and energy recovery, may be processed through an accelerated bacterial system, which, within a matter of a few weeks, turns refuse into a

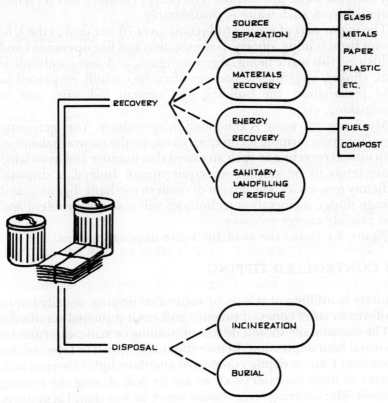

9.1   Disposal options

dark brown, odourless, soil-like material suitable for soil conditioning. The residue from sewage treatment plants could be mixed with such refuse compost to produce a valuable product which can be successfully used, but will require aggressive marketing to achieve a major change of present commercial practices.

The National Academy of Science (USA) has recommended that separated wastes should be banked, so they may easily be recovered at some later date when economics and technology make this attractive.

Good waste management, careful planning and education can achieve co-operation from the local community. The USA is now well ahead of the rest of the world in the provision of modern facilities for the disposal of waste and in environmental improvement, with some 40 or more major mechanical separation and energy recovery plants on-stream. In particular, Los Angeles offers an excellent example of community co-operation, stemming from its need to provide an efficient system of drains to discharge torrential rainfall and to prevent occurrences of severe smog pollution. In 1957, the County banned the use of the thousands of inefficient back-yard incinerators then in operation. The municipal purchase of a large abandoned quarry in Palos Verdes as a refuse tip was bitterly fought by the residents of this prosperous neighbourhood, who were well aware of the smokes, odours, pests and general unsightliness commonly associated with refuse dumps. However, the sanitation department was able to convince the residents that refuse tipping could and would be carried out without nuisance to them and that the unsightly quarry would be converted through controlled tipping into a landscape asset. Today Palos Verdes is a more desirable area than ever, with a landscaped park (previously the quarry).

9.5 THE CONVEYANCE OF SOLID WASTE BY PIPELINE

Major benefits in improved hygiene and convenience can be gained by replacing the conventional manual collection of refuse from buildings and transport of it by road, with a pneumatic suction system which removes refuse from buildings at regular intervals and conveys it in an air stream through underground pipelines to a more distant central collection and disposal complex.

Advantages
A high standard of hygiene is maintained at all times. Unpleasant

odours cannot escape. Relatively little equipment is located at the collection point, freeing space in the building for other purposes. The complete system is efficiently controlled centrally.

Description
Studies at the Building Research Establishment (UK) have indicated that a viable system can be developed in which the refuse is pulverised on site before it enters a pipeline system comprising pipes of between 150 mm and 300 mm bore. Pulverised refuse is of smaller volume than the original material, it can be readily baled (if required), compacted into road transport containers for easy transport to the disposal complex; there, it can be either incinerated, recycled or reclaimed.

Application
The piped refuse transport system is considered currently to be well suited to the following major uses:

new large housing and commercial building complexes,
new city centre developments.

    Waste disposal is a major management function and concern in such major building concentrations. The piped disposal system can be constructed with the development of the project and the control over its operation can be slotted into the management brief. It can also be utilised in existing buildings which already incorporate vertical refuse chutes; these can be adapted to the routing of the refuse collection pipes and connection to a central piped transport system.

    The system can also be adapted to permit the separation from the general refuse of valuable constituents which are suitable for reclamation or recycling; eg paper, glass and metal. These would be stored separately in the local plant room for eventual separate collection and recycling. This aspect has been covered by a UK patent application and would appear to be of particular interest in office buildings, where reclaimable paper can constitute up to 80 per cent of the total refuse.

Costs
Preliminary estimates and experience of a pneumatic refuse system have been gained from a Broads Central Sug System in Lisson Grove (Westminster, London), studied by the Building Research Establishment. In this system, the refuse is not pulverised; it is transported in 500 mm bore pipes.

Preliminary estimates appear to show that pneumatic installation serving areas containing upwards of 1000 dwellings, with about 30 dwellings per refuse chute, can compete economically with the cost of operating a conventional collection system. Capital costwise, it is considered that such systems are likely to break even after 10 to 15 years of use, with pneumatic collection showing tangible cost benefits thereafter.

Plates 48 and 49 indicate the main components of a pneumatic refuse conveying installation.

CHECK LIST

Note: Do not manhandle refuse or fuels derived from refuse – they are toxic; do not dump waste or refuse in an *open* fashion.

Check: local codes of practice, in particular, those related to controlled tipping.

Ensure: there is no river or stream (visible or underground) where controlled tipping intended.

Ensure: (as far as possible) that no controlled tip may drain into any water-course.

Note: do not leave raw refuse exposed for more than 24 hours. If this is a necessity (late collection or strike) ensure that refuse is sealed properly in a good quality plastic bag.

Investigate: every avenue of recycling and energy recovery for difficult industrial wastes and sludges. Do not allow these wastes to accumulate; dispose in relation to waste generation and be aware of the waste nature, which is frequently toxic and inflammable.

Note: disposal of any waste into rivers is not permitted and strict compliance with local water conservancy regulations must be observed.

Investigate: proteinaceous and digestion methods of recycling and energy recovery potential for agricultural wastes; central pneumatic conveyancing of waste in any intended building with more than an equivalent occupancy of 30 dwellings within a 1000-dwelling estate.

Note: do not dispose of any unconventional liquid or solid waste in foul sewers without permission of the local authority. A sample laboratory test is usually required before permission is given. Avoid the burning of rubbish in back-yard or garden incinerators – transport such waste to the local authority dumping yard for proper disposal; if in doubt about problems of waste disposal consult the local authority, a consultant or specialist;always endeavour to recycle, then to incinerate with energy recovery and then to dispose of waste in a safe controlled manner.

REFERENCES

J.T. Smith, 'An appraisal of the pneumatic refuse collection system at Lisson Grove', Westminster Building Research Establishment, Department of the Environment, CP 58/76, August, 1976.
Andrew Porteous, *Recycling Resources Refuse,* Longman, London, 1977.

10
Refractories

10.1 INTRODUCTION

The function of refractories is to protect the various components of any furnace from the high temperatures associated with the process of combustion.

Correct selection, care and maintenance of refractories are major considerations. The aim and endeavour of every furnace operator should be to obtain maximum working life from the furnace under his charge with long uninterrupted service, the required through-put (or rating) and low maintenance cost.

The three prime causes of furnace refractory failure are:

● poor design of combustion chamber,
● poor selection of the type of refractories for a given application,
● a lack of knowledge or a disregard of the rules governing operating conditions.

Poor design alone has been known to be responsible for heavy refractory maintenance costs and, even though many kinds of refractories were tried (including super-grade bricks), no reasonable increase in refractory life was obtained until the design was altered.

It is only by controlled service testing and by following the best possible available advice that optimum brick specification, to ensure maximum economic life, may be obtained. By expressing the refractory brick replacement need or consumption as the weight of bricks used per unit weight of fuel burnt, the fairest assessment can be made of the service life of the particular refractory. First quality refractories should generally be selected in preference to inferior quality to give a lower-brick consumption. Whilst high grade refractories are likely to be more expensive, they generally give longer life; freight and building costs for both grades are the same.

The most likely cause of refractory failure is usually due to one of the following conditions:

● exposure to excessive temperature,
● rapid heating or cooling through spalling temperature ranges,
● corrosive properties of the fuel,
● an adverse furnace atmosphere.

Repeated failure of the refractories is a certain indication that the design, the type of brick used or the operating conditions require examination and modification.

Table 10.1 shows the major factors governing the achievement of maximum economic life.

TABLE 10.1   MAJOR FACTORS FOR ECONOMIC REFRACTORY LIFE

Activity	Related parameters
Design Selection of brick and cement	Furnace bricks (size and shape) Silica Semic-silica Fire-brick (siliceous to high alumina) Special refractories (sillimanite, corundum etc)
Operation	Maximum temperature Temperatures variations Properties of combustion products Nature of furnace atmosphere

Whilst refractories represent the major potential replacement cost in most waste burning plant applications, this area of design and specification is perhaps one of the most vaguely understood (or misunderstood) aspects of plant selection and is generally left to the discretion and expertise of specialists. The authors hope that a discussion of the basic considerations concerning refractories will encourage the reader to appreciate the major impact of correct design and selection of refractories on the performance and life expectancy of furnace plant. The theory of refractories is a complex subject; useful knowledge is to a large extent based on practical experience, one major critical factor being the operational performance of particular bricks.

10.2 THE DEVELOPMENT OF REFRACTORIES

The largest users of refractory materials are the iron and steel, the steam and power plant industries and, to a somewhat lesser extent, the glass, oil, chemical, cement, ceramic and other smaller industries.

Fire-clay used to be the most common refractory material containing about 20 per cent free silica and 5 per cent other non-clay additives. Nowadays fire-clay bricks vary widely in properties and in composition. They are made from a variety of kaolin flint clays, semi-flint clays and plastic bond clays-kaolinite being the clay substance of nearly all fire-clays.

A fire-brick, made from fire-clay, contains 18 to 44 per cent alumina and only a small amount of the fluxes or impurities, which would lower the fusion or softening point of the major constituents. The crystalline phases in a well-fired brick are mullite, cristobalite and tridymite.

As the need became apparent for refractory brickwork capable of withstanding corrosion, ever higher furnace temperatures and load-bearing characteristics, the development of pure chemical refractory compounds followed, with a variety of refractory bricks made to suit the particular specified application. The development of plastic refractory materials began in the 1920s as the need for monolithic furnace linings with fewer joints (to minimise joint corrosion and to give longer refractory life) became apparent.

10.3 SOME TERMS RELATING TO SILICA AND FIRE-CLAY

Alumina
Oxide of aluminium Al_2O_3.
  (Latin 'alumen' meaning salt)

Andalusite
A mineral of the aluminium silicate group, $Al_2O_3SiO_2$, which decomposes when heated, beginning at about 1410 °C (2570°F) to give mullite $3Al_2O_3 2SiO_2$ and siliceous glass.
  (Andalusia, Spain)

Corundum
Crystalline alumina, Al_2O_3.
  (Tamil 'Karumdam' meaning ruby)

Cristobalite

This is the modification of silica, which can be formed at any temperature below $1710°C$ $(3110°F)$. It is the stable form of silica above $1470°C$ $(2678°F)$ and its name is derived from San Cristobal, where it was first discovered.

Cyanite

An aluminium silicate similar to andalusite and sillimanite, Al_2O_3 SiO_2. Decomposition to mullite and siliceous glass begins at about $1100°C$ $(2012°F)$.

(Greek 'Kuanos' meaning blue)

Flux

Any substance which lowers the fusion or softening. point of another material.

Ganister

A particular variety of fine-grained sandstone containing a small amount of clay matter. True Sheffield ganister contains 97 to 98 per cent silica. The term is also applied to other silica-clay mixture containing 70 per cent and more of silica.

Grog

Previously burned clay or bricks which are usually ground and incorporated in the clay batch prior to the actual moulding of the fire-bricks. Grog is mainly used to control the drying and firing behaviour of the bricks.

(French 'gros grain' meaning coarse grain)

Kaolin

This is the general term for china-clay and china-clay rock, the name being derived from Kao-Ling, a high hill in North China from which the Chinese obtained their supplies of clay.

Kaolinite

This is a definite mineral form of china-clay of chemical composition Al_2O_3 $2SiO_2$ $2H_2O$. When heated above $1100°C$ $(2012°F)$, it breaks down to mullite, cristobalite and glass.

Mullite

This is an aluminium silicate mineral $3Al_2O_3$ $2SiO_2$. It is the only compound of alumina and silica, which shows stability at high temperatures. Mullite and glass are the final products obtained by heating andalusite, cyanite and sillimanite. Mullite is one of the principal phases found in the heating of fire-bricks; it is a rare mineral, which occurs in rocks in the Isle of Mull.

Porosity
The amount of pore space in a material is a measure of its porosity. The volume of pore space per unit volume of material usually indicates the percentage porosity. The true porosity is a measure of the total pores, both open and sealed; a measure of open pores is only the apparent porosity.

Quartz
The modification of silica which can be formed at any temperature below 870°C (1598°F).
(Old German mining term, quartz = crystalline).

Silica
This mineral is abundant and constitutes about 12 per cent of the minerals which form the rocks of the earth crust. It can exist in many forms, the most common (related to fire-bricks) is quartz, the modification of silica which may be formed at relatively low temperatures, below 870°C (1598°F).
(Latin 'silex' meaning flint)

Sillimanite
An aluminium silicate mineral, $Al_2O_3 . SiO_2$, which when heated above 1545°C (2813°F) breaks down to mullite and a siliceous glass.
(After Benjamin Silliman)

Spalling
The splintering or cracking of refractories where fragments of the brick are separated and fresh surfaces are exposed.
(German 'spellen' meaning to split)

Texture
This relates to the distribution of individual grains within the material.

Tridymite
The modification of silica which can be formed at any temperature below 1470°C (2678°F). It is the stable form of silica in the range 870 to 1470°C (1598 to 2678°F).
(Greek 'tridymos' meaning three-fold)

Vitrification

The conversion of a material into a glass or a glass-like substance with increased hardness and brittleness. The vitrification, or sintering, characteristics of a brick are of supreme importance in its development of high strength and hardness.

10.4 FIRE-BRICK MANUFACTURE

The burning of a fire-brick takes place at the manufacturers' kilns. The successful completion of this process is as important as the determination of the fire-brick constituents themselves for any given application. Inferior processes may well result in useless products, which, if applied to furnace construction, may lead to refractory failure.

Considerable changes occur when a piece of mouldable clay is transformed into a hard, dense, brittle and useable brick. Clay constituents include hydrated aluminium silicates, such as kaolinite and free quartz, together with small quantities of other minerals, micas, felspars, iron oxides, pyrites, gypsum, calcite, dolomite and carbon.

When a clay is subjected to intense heat for the first time, there occurs a loss of volatile constituents, the oxidisation of carbon and sulphur, permanent changes in volume, colour, specific gravity, porosity and strength and the formation of crystalline and glassy components.

Figure 10.1 shows the major reactions, the percentage expansion and contraction plotted against rising temperature and vertical lines, which separate the stages within which defined changes occur.

From fig 10.1 it will be noted that the following sequence operates:

moisture is expelled from the clay — mechanical dehydration, kaolinite material breaks down, expelling enormous quantities of steam — chemical dehydration.

The oxidisation and removal of carbon and sulphur takes place between 300 to 900°C (572 to 1652°F). During this stage of the process, it is imperative that the removal of carbon is completed while the clay is porous, otherwise at higher temperatures, the porosity of the brick would be decreased and vitrification promoted, trapping the carbon in the heart of the brick. Sulphur associated with pyrites or sulphates is more or less completely expelled in this oxidisation stage after having taken part in several complex reactions with the carbon and oxygen.

During the contraction and vitrification stage, kaolinite matter contracts rapidly and undergoes several changes, resulting finally in the formation of very small crystals of mullite. The free silica present in the clay undergoes conversion to cristobalite and tridymite, the accessory minerals reacting chiefly with the silica-forming viscous glasses, which cement and bond the grains

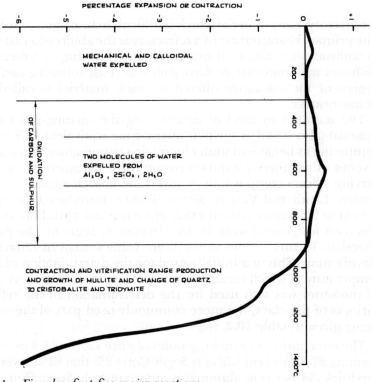

10.1   Fire-clay first-fire major reactions

securely and well together. The ferric oxide loses some oxygen and then acts as a flux which accelerates the growth of mullite crystals.

Thus, there are three major requirements in the manufacture of a well-made and well-burned refractory brick:

● effective removal of steam during chemical dehydration,
● sufficient air to burn out the carbon and sulphur,
● adequate temperature control and soaking of the bricks to ensure (as far as possible) completion of contraction in the kiln.

Clearly, the curing and first firing of mouldable and castable refractories is of paramount importance.

Recommended procedure is outlined in **10.14**, Monolithic refractories, in this chapter.

10.5 REFRACTORINESS

A refractory is any material which is difficult to fuse, melt or soften. The primary characteristic of a refractory is the ability of a material to withstand the action of heat without deforming or softening. Different materials vary in their ability to resist softening and the degree of the resistance offered by each material is called its 'refractoriness'.

The standard method of determining the melting-point of a material (also stated as the pyrometric cone equivalent PCE) is by comparing its behaviour under increasing temperature with that of a series of numbered standard pyramids or pyrometric cones of varying silicate composition, whose softening characteristics are known. Lauth and Vost of Sèvres, France, introduced the cone system of laboratory tests in 1882, but it was not until 1886 that it was used for general work by Dr Herman A. Seger of The Royal Porcelain Factory, Berlin in the Seger Cone system of refractory classification. This was initially used for the determination of kiln temperature at which ceramic products were fired; the upper part of the series was also used for the determination of the refractoriness of fire-clays, the more commonly used part of the series being given in table **10.2**.

The refractoriness or melting-point of pure kaolin (45.9 per cent alumina 54.1 per cent silica) is Seger Cone 35; that of an average fire-brick (35 per cent alumina) is approximately Seger Cone 31. The melting points of fire-clay refractories range from 1600°C (2900°F) to 1750°C (3200°F), the average being nearer the lower figure. The refractoriness of a substance depends on several factors, principally its chemical composition or alumina-silica ratio, the purity of the clay (absence of such fluxes as alkalis and bases) and the grain size of the individual clay particles (the finer the grains, the quicker vitrification and softening commences). Table **10.3** indicates the relative behaviour of some typical fire-clay bricks with differing alumina-silica ratios.

The majority of pure chemical refractory compounds melt sharply at defined temperature, provided that they do not decompose before fusing. Table **10.4** lists the melting-points of the pure

TABLE 10.2   SOFTENING POINTS OF SEGER CONES

Cone no	°C	°F	Cone no	°C	°F	Cone no	°C	°F
05a	1000	1832	10	1300	2372	29	1650	3002
04a	1020	1868	11	1320	2408	30	1670	3038
03a	1040	1904	12	1350	2462	31	1690	3074
02a	1060	1940	13	1380	2516	32	1710	3110
01a	1080	1976	14	1410	2570	33	1730	3146
1a	1100	2012	15	1435	2615	34	1750	3182
2a	1120	2048	16	1460	2660	35	1770	3218
3a	1140	2084	17	1480	2696	36	1790	3254
4a	1160	2120	18	1500	2732	37	1825	3317
5a	1180	2156	19	1520	2768	38	1850	3362
6a	1200	2192	20	1530	2786	39	1880	3416
7	1230	2246	26	1580	2876	40	1920	3488
8	1250	2282	27	1610	2930	41	1960	3560
9	1280	2336	28	1630	2966	42	2000	3632

compounds which form the basis of most of the common refractories

The chemical composition of a fire-brick is not an infallible guide to its value. Pure material can have inadequate physical properties. Knowledge of the composition specifies only one side of the complex character of a refractory brick. Consider the composition of the ideal fire-brick to be derived from kaolinite, which gives a

TABLE 10.3 PROPERTIES OF TYPICAL FIRE-CLAY BRICKS

Brick	Silica SiO_2 per cent	Alumina Al_2O_3 per cent	Other constituents	Melting-point °C	°F
Super duty	49-53	40-44	5-7	1745-1760	3170-3200
High duty	50-80	35-40	5-9	1690-1745	3070-3170
High duty (siliceous)	65-80	18-30	3-8	1620-1680	2940-3060
Intermed-iate	60-70	26-36	5-9	1640-1680	2980-3060
Low duty	60-70	23-33	6-10	1520-1590	2770-2900

TABLE 10.4 MELTING-POINTS OF PURE COMPOUNDS

Pure compound	Formula	°C	°F
Alumina	Al_2O_3	2050	3720
Lime	CaO	2570	4650
Chromite	$FeO. Cr_2O_3$	2180	3955
Chromium oxide	Cr_2O_3	2275	4130
Magnesia	MgO	2800	5070
Silica	SiO_2	1723	3133
Titania	TiO_2	1850	3360

burned analysis of alumina 45.9 per cent and silica 54.1 percent. All fire-bricks fall short of this ideal, since they contain proportions of other oxides. The major accessory constituents are silica, titanium dioxide, iron oxide, lime, magnesia and alkalis (soda and potash); these lower the refractoriness of a brick and are, therefore, classed as fluxes. The presence of fluxes in a brick greatly modifies its properties of thermal expansion, strength, toughness and elasticity. At high temperatures, deformation under load is accelerated and structural spalling tends to be promoted, due to the development of zonal vitrification. The presence of fluxes greatly intensifies corrosion. Table 10.5 lists the lowest melting mixtures of silica and alumina in combination with the principle fluxing oxides. From this table of melting-point temperatures and by comparison with table 10.4, the effect of impurities in the fire-brick may be readily appreciated.

TABLE 10.5 MELTING-POINTS OF COMMON REFRACTORY IMPURITIES

Composition per cent, by weight	Melting-point	
	°C	°F
Silica 94.5, alumina 5.5	1545	2813
Silica 22, ferrous oxide 78	1240	2264
Silica 63, lime 37	1436	2617
Silica 65, magnesia 35	1543	2810
Silica 71.7, potash 28.3	528	982
Silica 73.2, soda 26.8	792	1458
Alumina 50, lime 50	1395	2543
Alumina 98, magnesia 2.	1925	3497
Lime 8, ferric oxide 92	1203	2197
Silica 62, alumina 14.75, lime 23.25	1165	2129
Alumina 13, lime 28, ferric oxide 59	1205	2200

10.6 REFRACTORINESS UNDER LOAD

Fire-bricks deform under modest loads when heated to temperatures over 1300°C (2372°F), some rapidly and others more slowly. This fact emphasises the importance of well-made and well-burned fire-bricks. It also indicates the importance of good furnace design, eg weight limitation compatible with brick type and strength.

With fire-clay materials, there is generally a variable and extended range of temperature between the beginning of subsidence and the point of complete collapse. Usually, the temperature of initial softening falls rapidly with increase in flux content (alkalies and bases). The amount of grading and nature of grog added to fire-clay also affects behaviour under load. Soft lightly burned materials have low resistance to load. Hard firing, on the other hand, produces good bonding and tends to develop a crystalline structure which increases resistance to deformation.

With silica refractories, the under-load resistance largely depends on the degree of conversion of the original silica to cristobalite and tridymite. Thorough burning ensures maximum conversion. A well-made silica brick retains its rigidity almost up to the point of collapse.

A refractory with excellent under-load resistance (found by testing) may not always give the best service for the development of high under-load values, demanding a sacrifice in other properties which may (in some cases) be of greater importance.

In the usual furnace, the temperature through the brick falls rapidly and only a small portion is above the critical temperature at which deformation can become serious. The effect of insulating a wall is to lessen the temperature gradient through the brickwork and thereby increase that portion of the brick which remains above the critical temperature. The insulation of heavy-duty furnaces may, therefore, be neither practical nor economical. Indeed, where temperatures are exceptionally high, it is sometimes necessary to adopt air or water-cooling to materially reduce that portion of brick within the dangerous deformation range. In some large furnaces, the walls are constructed in sections, each independently supported to reduce the load on the brickwork. The same principle is embodied in the flat suspended arch, which has (to a large extent) successfully replaced the sprung arch.

Failure of refractories under load and at high furnace temperatures can occur well below the melting-point in the form of a gradual deformation and collapse or by shearing (breaking clean accross at an angle of 45°). To avoid such failures, the construction methods

must ensure even loading conditions, both structural and thermal.
Figure 10.2 shows some typical refractory under-load curves.

10.7 REVERSIBLE AND IRREVERSIBLE VOLUME CHANGES

Two forms of expansion and contraction arise with furnace
temperature changes: reversible or irreversible. Both must be
considered in the selection of refractories and in the design and
construction of furnaces.

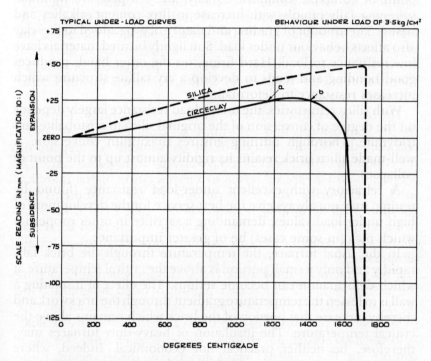

10.2   *Typical under-load refractory curves*

There are three major causes of reversible volume change with
temperature:

All refractories expand with heat and contract with cold,
behaving generally in accordance with known physical laws.

Certain minerals, notably silica, undergo distinct reversible
changes in their crystalline structure at definite temperatures, the
inversion in some cases taking considerable time and being usually
accompanied by a marked change in volume. Greater care is

necessary when heating and cooling through these critical temperatures because the volume change is sudden. For example, if a silica
brick, containing a fairly large proportion of cristobalite, is quickly
heated or cooled in the range 200-300°C (392-572°F) the abrupt
change bursts the brick into fragments.

Internal expansion and contraction may occur due to changes in
the character of the glass-like material which is present in all
refractories; such glasses are not stable. In service at moderately
high temperature (below the melting-point of glass), crystalline
compounds form within the glass and a volume change ac-
companies such separation (termed devitrification of the glass). At
higher temperatures, above the melting-point of the glass, the
process is reversed and the crystalline compounds are re-dissolved.
Irreversible volume changes arise from permanent physical or
chemical changes, which occur in the refractory, mainly for the
following reasons:

The raw material of a refractory changes considerably when fired,
by decomposition and by mineral changes into various
compounds. The distribution of the constituents will depend on
the condition of the bricks as received from the manufacturer. If, in
service, the bricks are subjected to a temperature higher than that
used in kiln-firing, the re-distribution of the constituents will
continue with accompanying volume changes. Even if the kiln-
firing temperatures were higher than those experienced in service,
changes may continue because of longer time exposure at certain
temperatures.

Most refractories show a marked shrinkage when approaching
the melting-point. The increased quantity of fused material and the
decrease in porosity provides a plastic contraction with an increase
of internal gas pressure; this may then cause the refractory to bloat.

Reversible crystalline changes require much time for their
completion. The speed of change depends on the temperature, the
size and nature of the constituent particles and/or the quantity of
impurities present. The density of varying crystalline forms is very
different and this permanent expansion is quite distinct from
conventionally known thermal expansion. If complete conversion
is not achieved in the manufacture of the refractory and some of
these crystalline changes occur for the first time in service, serious
damage to the furnace structure will result. The manufacturer
must, therefore, ensure that complete inversion occurs in the kiln-
firing and that the thoroughness of burning and soaking leaves no
troublesome residuals to safeguard the user against the eventuality
of permanent after expansion or contraction.

10.8 SPALLING

This term refers to the breaking up of a refractory, splintering, cracking and frequent detachment of fragments, caused by the dimensional changes which occur in refractories when they are rapidly heated or cooled and which cause stresses that are sometimes sufficient to induce fractures (the term spalling is sometimes incorrectly used to describe any mechanical failure).

When the co-efficient of thermal expansion of a material is very low, few excessive strains and stresses result and the material will be highly resistant to thermal shock. For example, fused silica and cordierite, with extremely low coefficients, have very high spalling resistance. On the other hand, silica, magnesite, zirconia and thoria with relatively high coefficients, are markedly susceptible to thermal shock.

If a refractory can transmit heat rapidly, regardless of its coefficient of expansion, steep uneven strain and stress temperature gradients across the refractory will be lessened and a high resistance to temperature changes will be shown. Silicon carbide and beryllium oxide, both good heat transmitters, show high resistance to spalling. A material of great strength may remain unfractured when strained by sudden heating or cooling. A material possessing great elasticity and flexibility will be relieved by distortion instead of by rupture.

The factors which favour resistance to sharp temperature changes and to spalling are therefore:

- low coefficient of expansion
- high rate of heat transmission
- high strength
- high flexibility.

Figure 10.3 shows the typical expansion of a good quality fire-brick. Most of the expansion is complete at 800°C (1472°F); it follows that the main danger of refractory spalling lies below red-heat where both expansion and rigidity are significant. The longer fire-bricks have been employed at furnace operating temperatures, the more sensitive they become to temperature changes because of further vitrification and reduced elasticity.

The risk of spalling can be minimised by the following recommended practices:

Lighting up of the furnace should be with coal fires, as wool and oily waste release too much flame for the surface of cold brickwork.

Better still is the use of a controllable fuel, such as gas or oil auxiliary firing.

The slowest practical period of heating and cooling below 800°C (1472°F) should be adopted.

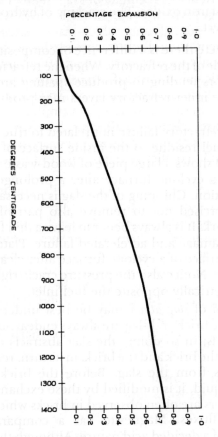

PERCENTAGE EXPANSION

10.3   Expansion of fire-brick

Bricks of standard sizes should be used (where possible), in preference to special shapes which may suffer severe changes in mass and section.

Bricks should be used where rapid heating and/or cooling cannot be avoided.

10.9 REFRACTORY FAILURE

Certain types of refractory failure which have some of the characteristics of true thermal spalling are:

Pressure cracks due to uneven refractory expansion or contraction, usually attributable to poor design, selection or bricklaying.

Carbon transfers in a true reducing atmosphere, containing carbon monoxide, where particles of iron may be formed in the refractory by the reduction of iron oxides. The cracking of hydrocarbons may have a similar effect.

Slag penetration, where there is a difference of composition from the inside to the outside of the refractory. When the refractory is cooled, many of the factors tending to produce spalling are intensified. Vitrification of the inner refractory layers may produce the same effect.

Some types of refractory failure not related to true spalling are: *Slag adherence* of fuel residue to the inside surface of a furnace is common. Plate 50 shows a large piece of wood-waste slag chipped from the wall of a cyclone furnace after a prolonged period of continuous operation. Chipping of the slag is necessary, but great care must be exercised not to remove also part of the face of refractory brickwork. It is always better to leave a thin film of slag to avoid refractory damage and accelerated failure. Plates 51 and 52 show the inside surface of a cyclone furnace after cleaning. Notice the slag adherence. Notice also the pressure crack (right-hand side of plate 52) diametrically opposite the fuel inlet.

The mechanism of *slag attack* may be best understood if it is considered that the brick and slag are always endeavouring to form low melting liquids; in so doing, the slag abstracts one or more constituents from the brick and the brick, in its turn, receives one or more constituents from the slag. Before the brick completely disappears into liquid, it is modified by these exchanges and thin white or black layers are often observed in bricks which have been in contact with fluxes. Magnesite has a comparatively high resistance to slag of a decided acid nature. Although the first action of dissolved magnesia on acid slag is to lower the melting point of the slag film, the final result is a film of extremely high melting - point and viscosity. The upper layers of the refractory brickwork in open hearth regenerators are usually made of silica, rather then fire-clay, as even the best fire-clay brick, although less acid in nature and often having a higher melting-point, in practice erodes much more rapidly than silica brick under the action of the basic slag and dust carried over with the hot gases.

Refractory bricks of *high porosity* tend to soak slag by capillary attraction. This may prove to be serious if the slag is not particularly active on the refractory. The saturation of a refractory with relatively harmless slag deposits is common in the consolidation of new furnace hearths.

In a furnace which is operated intermittently, the soaking of the slag into the refractory is likely to have an extremely serious effect by causing spalling due to uneven composition and texture of the brick. Even in a continuously operated furnace, absorbed slag may be harmful. Bricks of limited porosity last longer, as they contain a greater weight of pure refractory material.

Cracks and poorly made joints permit slag penetration, with likely subsequent breaking up and brick dislodgement; the jointing material is then eaten away faster then the brick itself.

In addition to the refractories which are in constant contact with liquid slag, joints and cracks may be subjected to splashing or to the action of gas-borne slag particles. The action or such slag particles may be severe due to the high temperature and velocity of the gases.

Fire-clay and high alumina bricks have moderate resistance to acid slags; silica bricks have good resistance. High alumina bricks and silica bricks are commonly used when there is contact with alkaline fumes at high temperature. Fosterite bricks also have good alkaline resistance.

It is worth noting that a relatively small increase in the furnace operating temperature can greatly increase the effect of slag attack and may destroy the furnace lining in a very short time. Thus, slag and brick reaction should govern the maximum furnace operating temperature in such circumstances.

Gas attack may occur through chemical action. Reducing gas, in particular, may considerably lower the melting-point of the refractory, especially when they contain free oxides of iron.
Carbon transfer (mentioned earlier) has a true spalling effect.

Dolomite and, to a lesser extent, magnesite are susceptible to hydration; even the moisture in the air can cause rapid disintegration of such refractories. Clearly, refractories which are susceptible to hydration should be used in a moist furnace atmosphere, such as that which prevails in the combustion of wet fuels.

10.10 REFRACTORY BRICK MATERIALS

These should be selected very carefully and always with the aid of the manufacturers or of an experienced consultant. The following list of comments are intended as a general guide to the behaviour of various materials (not to be used for selection purpose).

Fire-clay

Bricks vary widely in both properties and in composition. The suitability of this material for any particular application will be determined by the purity of the clay, the absence of fluxes, the alumina-silica ratio and the grain size. Fire-clay bricks are not generally suitable for high temperature furnace applications.

High alumina

Bricks are used for high furnace temperature applications. The alumina content may vary from 50 to 99 per cent, oxides from 1 to 8 per cent and silica from 1 to 46 per cent. The silica inversions decrease with decreased amounts of free silica; 99 per cent alumina brick behaves as a pure compound. High alumina bricks will undergo slow plastic deformation when subject to pressure at high temperatures.

This group of refractories is probably the most important in waste combustion furnace lining applications.

Bauxite forms the basis of the most highly aluminous refractories; sillimanite and kaolinite are also used as a principal mineral. The different minerals are frequently mixed to provide the desired alumina content; the more expensive varieties are made from unmixed minerals, sintered to remove shrinkage and bonded.

Electrically fused bauxite, crushed, bonded and re-fired avoids the high shrinkage shown by very high alumina refractories. Fused alumina has been widely used in laboratory work and for electric furnace crowns, being characterised by a high melting-point, good resistance to load at high temperatures and excellent resistance to abrasion. The resistance to spalling is, however, not good and thermal conductivity is high.

Both bauxite and fused alumina bricks show good resistance to the action of basic slags.

Silica

The sensitivity of silica to abrupt changes in temperature restricts its use as a refractory. It contains glass of high melting-point and retains its stiffness under load to within a few degrees of the melting-point and is, therefore, suitable for high furnace temperatures. It has a strong spalling tendency at low temperatures (below dull redness).

Magnesite

Bricks show very high reversible expansion, independent of crystalline change and high resistance to slag attack of a decided acid nature. Magnesite, although an impure refractory, is suitable for high furnace temperature, except when under load and when large amounts of steam are present. It shows poor resistance to spalling, unless it is pure electrically sintered magnesite, crushed, bonded with a magnesia salt and fired. Fused magnesite shows fair resistance to spalling and may be used when subjected to high temperature and the action of basic slags.

Dolomite
This refractory can carry a high percentage of impurities without serious lowering of its melting-point, but, in contrast to magnesite, dolomite is an energetic flux-forming viscous silicate. It is susceptible to hydration. The lime content of any brick should always be low.

Chrome
The pure mineral, chromite, shows good resistance to slag attack. It is an impure and complex refractory whose properties depend to a large extent on the nature of the glass. It contains a certain amount of low-melting slag and fails under load test at about the same temperature as magnesite.

Chrome magnesite and magnesite-chrome
When a mixture of chrome ore and dead-burnt magnesite is formed into bricks, chemically bonded or fired, a chrome-magnesite brick results if the chrome predominates; a magnesite-chrome brick results if the magnesite predominates. Good resistance to spalling and superior strength have prompted wider use of this type of refractory.

Fosterite
This is another important type of basic brick, which is commonly employed where there is exposure to high temperature, alkaline dust and fumes. It is used in walls, checkers, roofs, uptakes and ports of high temperature furnaces. It shows a high reversible expansion rate.

Modified silica
By the addition of ferrous slag (plus carbon to retain the iron in the ferrous condition), it is possible to lower the temperature at which quartz inverts to tridymite and thus produce a brick relatively free of unfavourable expansion characteristics. In spite of their slightly lower melting-point, these black silica bricks give better results than ordinary silica bricks.

Semi-silica

This refractory has a limited application, being made from fire-clay and a large proportion of silica grog. It has a low melting-point and poor resistance to slag attack. Its resistance to spalling is good and it is resistant to load at moderate furnace temperatures. The usual tendency of the clay to shrink is offset by the corresponding tendency of the silica to expand to tridymite. The result is a material which shows a constancy of volume in service and is suitable for use in furnaces where the temperature is not too high and where there can be no slag attack.

Firestone

Quartzite sometimes occurs as a laminated rock, which can easily be split and made into blocks having much the same chemical properties as silica. It shows considerable expansion when partially converted to cristobalite and tridymite, and for this reason the blocks are usually laid up with thick raw fire-clay joints, which, because of clay shrinkage, permit free expansion of the blocks. They are sometimes used for lining cupolas etc.

Spinel

The refractory is made from a mixture of good grades of magnesite and bauxite to provide a high melting-point compound. It shows better resistance to load at high temperatures with less expansion and heat conductivity. Its resistance to spalling is poor, but it is more resistant than magnesite to slag attack.

Graphite

Fire-clay bricks are sometimes made with graphite addition, but the principle use of graphite as a refractory is in the manufacture of crucibles.

Silicon carbide

This refractory (SiC) is used extensively in high temperature and abrasive applications, such as in cyclone wood-waste incineration plants. It is a carborundum (proprietary name) refractory made in an electric furnace, sorted, crushed, mixed with a clay binder, shaped and fired. It does not fuse even at temperature as high as 2700°C (4892°F), but it decomposes slowly at temperatures in excess of 2200°C (3992°F). Silicon carbide is very strong, hard and resistant to abrasion, its coefficient of expansion is low and uniform, it has good resistance to spalling and to the action of most slags.

High cost restricts the application of silicon carbide; it is usually employed in a cyclone furnace only as the inner skin, the cheaper alumina bricks being used as the intermediate and outer linings.

Zircon and zirconia

$(Zr\ SiO_4)\ (Zr\ O_2)$, these are highly refractory compounds with low expansion characteristics and resistance to slag attack. Their cost which is higher than silicon carbide, restricts their use; laboratory crucibles are made from purer grades of zirconia.

Corundum (alpha alumina)

This is the naturally occurring form of alumina, or alpha alumina, chiefly known by its value as a gas stone ruby (red) and sapphire (blue). Artificial corundum is extremely hard, highly refractory and retains its rigidity and load-bearing capacity up to high temperature. It has a uniform expansion, which enables it to resist thermal shock and it resists the action of reducing gases, such as H_2 and CO at high temperatures.

10.11 FIRE-BRICK BONDING

The provision of well-designed expansion joints and the correct bonding of the bricks or sections of refractory are most important to facilitate and guide the movements of thermal expansion and contraction.

As a general guide, 1 per cent expansion approximates to 1 cm/m of brickwork. Common allowance to be made for the thermal movement of refractories are shown in table 10.6.

TABLE 10.6 ALLOWANCE FOR THERMAL MOVEMENT

Refractory	Allowance (cm/m of brickwork)
Silica	1.6
Fireclay	0.53
High alumina	
80 per cent	0.8
90 per cent	1.08
Magnesite	1.6
Magnesite-chrome	1.6
Chrome	1.08
Chrome-magnesite	1.08-2.16
Fosterite	1.6

The bonding cement must truly bond the bricks, not too rigidly and without local fluxing of the bricks, the joints showing reasonable strength over a wide temperature range. The ideal bonding cement retains much of its initial strength, right up to the vitrification point, so that the cool outer parts of the brick continue to be held together by the cement, rather than the bricks being separated by a powdered filler which is held imperfectly in place by the weight of the bricks.

A simple fire-clay bond possessess only limited strength from the time it dries right up to vitrification point.

The ideal of providing similar expansion coefficients of bond and brick is unlikely to be achieved, but the shrinkage of the bond should be as small as possible. With slag penetration and gas leak susceptibility, the thinner these joints, the better. Poured and dipped joints are preferred at not more than 1.6mm in thickness.

Most cements are prepared with a plastic preparation, but with enough parent brick and fire-clay to give a thin slip with water. With silica cement, a small quantity of Portland cement is occasionally used instead of clay. Chrome cement may be used for laying almost any type of brick; it has a low shrinkage characteristic and is also particularly useful as a substitute for cements which contain a high percentage of raw clay and in situations where thick joints are unavoidable.

Cements for special application are commercially available for use with most types of bricks. Of these, the air-setting cements are generally superior to the home-made hot-setting cements.

Different types of bricks may be inter-bonded with a suitable cement, provided that the two materials do not exert mutual slagging action and provided that their coefficients of expansion do not differ too widely. In a silica brick wall, chrome brick panels are frequently inter-bonded to prevent heavy local erosion of the silica brick by basic slags.

Practically all cements may be used as protective washes to be brushed over the surface of the wall after laying.

Although the basic principles of furnace bricklaying are similar to conventional bricklaying, such work should only be carried out by bricklayers who understand the behaviour of brickwork under furnace operating conditions.

For non-specialised work, standard brick sizes of dimensions 228.6 x 114.3 x76.2mm (9 x 4½ x 3 in) are used.

The various tried methods of bonding standard bricks are shown in fig 10.4.

The *stretcher bond* is mainly used in small furnace construction.

Header bonds provide the best arrangement for high temperature furnaces.

English bond comprises alternative courses of headers and stretchers,

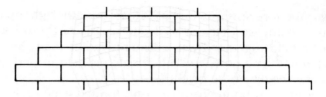

1. STRETCHER BOND

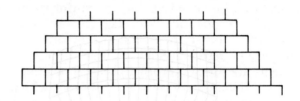

2. HEADER BOND

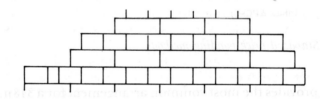

3. ENGLISH BOND

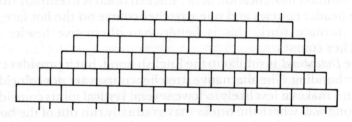

4. MODIFIED ENGLISH BOND

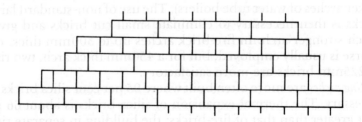

5. DUTCH BOND

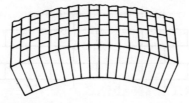

6. BONDED ARCH

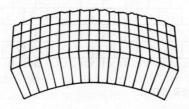

7. RING ARCH

10.4   Standard brick bonding methods

which provides the most common arrangement for a 348 mm (13½ in) wall and for thicker walls.

A common modification of the English bond is to employ two or three header courses and one stretcher course on the hot face; for most furnace work, this is better than alternative header and stretcher courses.

The *Dutch bond* is similar to the English bond, but it provides even better bonding. The alternative stretcher courses are not coincident and this makes it less likely to have several vertical joints coinciding in a long wall where the bricks may gradually run out of the bond.

Standard fire-brick *bonded arches* are usual, except where the conditions are severe and the end of the arch is exposed (as in the stoker arches of water tube boilers). The use of non-standard larger bricks is then necessary to eliminate small cut bricks and give a much stronger arch. In fire-brick arches up to 300 mm thick, one course is usually employed, but for a 450 mm thick arch, two rings of 225 mm bricks are more satisfactory.

Ring arches are more often built where 95 per cent silica bricks are necessary. The thermal expansion of silica bricks is about 66 per cent greater than that of fire-bricks; the building in separate rings provides greater flexibility for thermal movement. Silica arches are often built dry because most cements are unsatisfactory; in that case, it is essential to adopt the ring construction to ensure the closest contact between the bricks.

10.12 FIRE-BRICK SHAPING

The moulding and shaping of a refractory material may be carried out in various ways. Hand moulding is still largely used, especially for special shapes and sizes, whereas machine pressing is preferred and employed for standard shapes and sizes. To obtain uniform, homogeneous bodies and the elimination of entrapped air, it is best to reduce plasticity as much as possible and to employ machine pressing, which also reduces flaws to a minimum and provides better accuracy of size and low porosity. Machine pressing is, however, prohibitively expensive where the number of bricks is small and the fitting up of a press is uneconomical. The simple time-honoured method of hand moulding is, therefore, still a chief method of fire-brick shaping.

Certain plastic refractory bodies can be made thin and fluid by the addition of less than ½ per cent of certain inorganic salts (such as sodium carbonate) and the formation of a fluid mass enables it to be cast into moulds made of plaster of Paris. Slip casting is only used for special refractories where low contraction, accuracy of shape and homogeneity of structure are desired. Large blocks, of up to 0.5 tonnes and small laboratory articles, can be successfully made by this process.

Fusion casting was developed chiefly in the USA. A refractory mixture is melted in an electric furnace and the liquid is cast into moulds and then cooled under controlled conditions. Re-fired fusion cast refractories are characterised by their denseness and absence of porosity.

TABLE 10.7 METHODS OF SHAPING

Method	Consistency of body
Hand moulding	Plastics
Machine pressing	Plastic, stiff-plastic semi-dry
Machine extrusion	Plastic
Slip casting	Liquid
Fusion casting	Liquid

Figure 10.5 shows some standard available brick shapes.

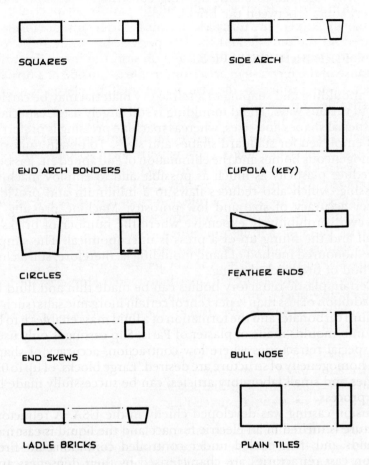

SQUARES   SIDE ARCH

END ARCH BONDERS   CUPOLA (KEY)

CIRCLES   FEATHER ENDS

END SKEWS   BULL NOSE

LADLE BRICKS   PLAIN TILES

10.5   Some standard brick shapes

10.13 INSULATING MATERIAL

The function of insulating materials is to reduce heat losses from the hearths, walls and roofs of furnaces.

The more recent development of the light-weight insulating bricks has substantially changed the methods of insulating furnaces. Insulating bricks may be of materials having inherent high porosity, eg diatomaceous earth and expanded vermiculite. Alternatively, insulating bricks may be manufactured from relatively non-porous materials, such as clay or quartzite containing some combustibles such as coke or sawdust, which are burnt out during firing, leaving small insulating voids (air pockets).

In high temperature furnaces, the most efficient furnace insulator is used on the outside and the less perfect, but more refractory, insulator between the outer insulation and the inner fire-brick. Because of the increase in area from inside to outside of a furnace, for optimum insulation, the insulation should be placed as near as practicable to the inside.

All insulating materials are highly porous; thus, if the furnace operating temperature is exceeded, major permanent shrinkage of the insulating layer is likely, causing permanent serious damage to the insulation. Insulating bricks are mechanically weak and are not suitable for exposure to slag or dirty gases, since they spall readily. Insulating walls are not, as a rule, joined to refractory layers; they are completely and independently supported to allow for the differing rates of thermal movement.

Insulating fire-bricks are light in weight and are excellent insulators. In that capacity, the low temperature bricks are from seven to eight times more effective than standard fire-clay; the high temperature bricks, three to four times as effective.

Insulating materials are usually classified according to their application as follows:

- insulated brick and insulating fire-brick
- insulating block or sheeting
- insulating cements and plastics
- powdered or granular material.

The use of efficient insulating materials is essential in some furnace construction, which have reduced heat storage capacity in the furnace walls as well as smaller, lighter and often cheaper structures. On the other hand, in the design of some furnaces, it is necessary to create a refractory thermal store (or fly-wheel effect) to enable the temperature in the combustion chamber of the furnace to remain above the ignition temperature of the fuel and thereby avoid hunting.

Great care has to be exercised in designing a furnace which requires separate insulating layers. See fig 10.6 where the cyclone furnace is a composite structure incorporating an inner layer of silicon carbide refractory, which has to withstand severe fuel feed abrasion. Insulating fire-bricks are used to reduce the heat losses from the furnace and to provide a predetermined refractory thermal capacity. Figure 10.7 shows the cyclone furnace hearth brick construction. Plates 53 and 54 illustrate usual site installation conditions.

10.14 MONOLITHIC REFRACTORIES

Refractory plastics, mixed with water or another suitable fluid agent, become sufficiently adherent to ram into a furnace structure where they can then burn-in, forming a monolithic lining. Such refractories can be installed *in situ* in casting, gunning, trowelling, hand or mechanical ramming. Sections of furnace linings may also be prefabricated and fitted into place. The full advantages arising from the use of monolithic refractories can only be realised if the application is properly planned.

Simple plastic mixtures for the filling in of holes and general furnace brickwork patching have long been made and used by furnace men. Probably one of the earliest mixtures consisted of crushed ganister rock with the addition of fire-clay and enough water to give a plastic consistency. The proportion of clay did not exceed one to six parts of ganister, depending on the degree of plasticity shown by the fire-clay. A mixture of Portland cement and water glass is now more popular for such purposes, lime acting as a bond when heated. These fluxes must, however, be used with caution since they lower the melting-point of the refractory.

If the repair is made to a silica lining while the furnace is hot, it is better to make a concrete of old silica brick in a suitable mortar.

In the preparation of a *fire-clay plastic,* it is important to use a mixture which will not shrink unduly and fall away. Fire-clay and water are usually mixed with crushed fire-clay bricks. A variety of commercially prepared fire-clay plastics are available, including high-alumina ramming mixtures.

Open-hearth bottoms are often made from dead-burnt magnesite. To form a *magnesite plastic,* it is mixed with basic open-hearth slag and spread in layers on the bottom, each layer being burned-in at high temperature and allowed to cool before the next layer is applied. Plasticity and cold setting strength may be obtained by mixing with a magnesium chloride (or magnesium sulphate) solution instead of with water.

Dolomite plastic is best formed with hot boiled tar which, for patching purposes, sets much more quickly than dead-burnt magnesite.

Chrome is probably the most valuable of the non-siliceous plastics. Since crushed chrome ore has low shrinkage properties and is usually self-bond and neutral, it is possible to make plastics of such materials as magnesite by the addition of crushed chrome ore and water. With some commercially prepared chrome mixtures, it is also possible to patch in one operation without the need to burn-in.

Prepared plastics are mixed, under careful supervision, with fluxes to give the best results for a given purpose. They are more expensive

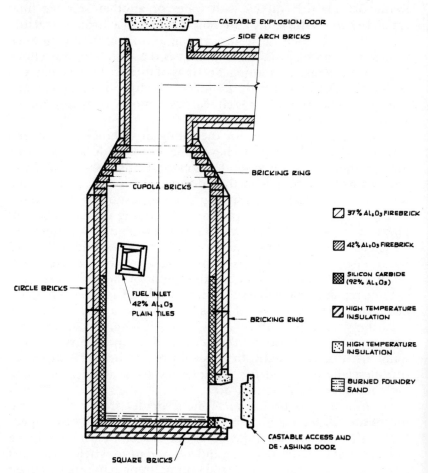

10.6   Cyclone refractory composition

than home-made mixtures, but they usually give longer economical life. Many special refractories may also be obtained in plastic form, such as firesand, a granular variety of silicon carbide.

Refractory castables or refractory concrete may be employed in the formation of complete furnace linings.

The majority of monolithic refractories fall into two categories, those containing hydraulic cement (castables) and those containing a heat setting binder, such as clay (mouldables). Materials especially developed for application by gunning can be similar to either castables or mouldables. Ramming materials are usually very similar to mouldables, but they are usually less plastic and require much higher pressure for consolidation.

Some advantages of monolithic refractories are:

- simple construction of complex linings,
- elimination of costly pre-fired shapes,
- speedy installation,
- usually lower cost than brickwork,

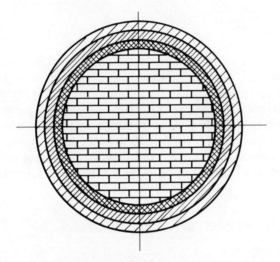

CYCLONE FURNACE HEARTH

10.7   Cyclone hearth brick construction

- freedom from joints,
- excellent resistance to thermal shock,
- lower thermal conductivity,
- simplified furnace maintenance.

Failure of such monolithic refractory linings is usually caused by one or more of the following factors:
- incorrect selection,
- poor application
- inadequate care during installation,
- incorrect commissioning procedure,
- operation outside the design limitation.

The following text does not represent an infallible guide: it is suggested that specialist advice should always be sought.

Preparation

Select the refractory castable best suited to meet the particular service and operating needs. Thus account will need to be taken of operating furnace temperature; upper and lower operating temperature limitations; strength required; suitable thermal conductivity; resistance to abrasion; suitability to combustion product properties and nature of furnace atmosphere consideration.

Decide the best method of installation, pouring gunning, trowelling, extruding or cast vibrating. The quantity of refractory material required should then be correctly calculated with an over-allowance of not more than 10 per cent.

Mixing

Equipment and tools must be clean and free from old mortar, cement, lime and dirt. Clean fresh water should be added to the mix in strict accordance with the manufacturers' instructions; less water will be required for internal vibrating applications. Excess water should be avoided, as it reduces structural strength and increases shrinkage and setting time. Mixing temperatures are generally between 10 to 20°C (50 to 68°F). Water should be pre-heated to mixing temperature. Avoid mixing in freezing conditions.

Placing

The four main methods of castable installation are:

- casting in forms,
- tramping and ramming into position,
- pneumatic emplacement,
- trowelling.

Forms and other surfaces should be coated, covered or water-soaked to avoid moisture loss from the refractory. Forms should be tight-fitting to avoid leakages. Internal vibrating (heavy castables only) will eliminate voids, free entrapped air and increase the strength of the refractory. The quantity of mixed materials should be limited to the amount that can be placed in 20 minutes after water addition. The after-addition of water to the mix decreases strength and increases shrinkage.

The amount of water, the feed rate and the air pressure for pneumatic application must be closely controlled to prevent rebound and slumping. Pre-dampening in dry gunning is extremely important to achieve lower rebound, less dusting and more uniform lining. Planes of weakness must be avoided, regardless of the chosen placement method; the refractory will only be as good as its weakest section.

Curing

The 24 hour period following placement is the most important curing time. Fast hard-setting castables will cure after six hours, but forms should not be removed until a 24 hour period has elapsed. Curing may be aided by the application of a fine water spray to keep exposed surfaces moistened, but not soaked. Curing water should be applied if, by rubbing the surface with a moistened finger, finger soiling does not take place. By repeating the same test, when a moistened finger does become soiled by rubbing, air curing should then continue.

Firing

Under no circumstances should heat be applied within 24 hours of placement. After curing, moisture in the refractories will remain. Only slow and gradual heat-up will satisfactorily evaporate this moisture. Too rapid heat-up can cause bond disruption, spalling and cracking. Generally, the initial heat curing schedule will not permit a faster heat-up rate than that which gives 149°C (268 °F) in six hours. The furnace temperature should then not be allowed to increase by more than 10°C (18°F) each hour until 538°C (1000°F) is reached. This temperature should then be held for a further six hours.

Some high-purity castables require more curing and firing time; the manufacturers' instructions should be carefully carried out. Once a castable has been taken through the prescribed initial heat-up cycle, normal operating furnace temperature may then be applied. Heating and cooling, below dull-redness, should always be a slow process. Initial cooling must, however, be carried out with even more care. Furnace thermal shock is undesirable; it may be disastrous in the early life of a monolithic refractory lining.

Figure 10.8 shows how cyclone furnace refractory bricks might be replaced by monolithic linings. Silicon carbide bricks are, however, preferred for their high abrasion resistance.

10.15 REFRACTORY ANCHORS

Figure 10.8 also shows nickel chrome anchors, which hold the mouldable and castable linings in position. Most of this anchor type is standard.

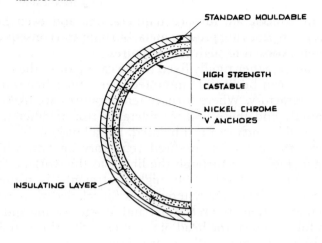

10.8   Cyclone refractory monolithic linings

Figure **10.9** shows the supporting structure necessary to anchor a suspended arch and roof of a furnace. Clearly, most of the supporting steelwork has to be purpose-made.

Prevention against high temperature exposure of refractory support and anchor is vital to the continual satisfactory operation of any furnace. For this reason, many support components are manufactured from ceramic materials. Ordinary mild steel cannot

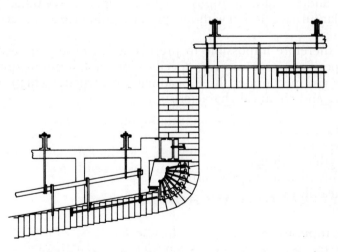

10.9   Suspended arch and roof anchors

withstand even moderate furnace temperatures and even heat resistant treatment does not prevent metal burning and consequent collapse when exposed to high temperature.

Anchors can be either rigidly fixed to the casing or to the main support or they can be flexibly mounted, permitting free movement of the refractory. Where furnace temperatures are likely to fluctuate rapidly and there is a considerable risk of differential expansion, flexible anchors must be used. For all monolithic roof constructions, the use of a pre-fired refractory anchor, which provides anchorage right through the lining to the working face where the refractory develops its highest strength, is strongly recommended. Some anchor systems allow for relative movement in any direction between the refractory and furnace casing and by providing a fulcrum near the head of the anchor tile, shear strains are greatly reduced. Large wall constructions are often provided with special anchor supports and lintels designed for the purpose. The position of expansion joints and cuts must not coincide with the position of anchors.

10.16 REFRACTORY SELECTION AND SPECIFICATION

The selection of refractory bricks for a given furnace application (as has already been stated) must not be a haphazard affair; neither the layman nor the non-specialist engineer should select critical refractories and insulators without specialist advice. Refractory failures most commonly arise from a combination of circumstances, and it is almost impossible to anticipate every pitfall in a particular furnace design without specialist guidance and practical expertise.

It is, therefore impossible to prepare a universally applicable rigid specification. However, specification of minimum quality may be grouped under three headings: construction, high temperature and chemical characteristics.

Construction
  Shape and size
  Strength (crushing)
  Porosity (true and apparent)
  Permeability
* Texture

High temperature
  Refractoriness
  Refractoriness under load

After-contraction
Thermal expansion
* Spalling resistance
* Thermal properties
* Slagging resistance

* *Properties not capable of straightforward measurement and which cannot be expressed quantitatively.*

Chemical characteristics
Composition including major and minor constituents

The designer should refer to his experience or consult a specialist with reference to the purpose for which the refractory is required. If one property of the material is overstressed, then some weakness may appear in another direction. For example, it is well known that maximum load and slag resistance often accompany minimum spalling resistance and (in some cases) a brick, which is highly refractory, may give less satisfactory service than a listed second or third quality brick. Experience and judgement must be called upon at all times in order that specifications may be constructed with some degree of success.

CHECK LIST

Check: on the function of refractories; on the function of insulation to furnaces; the major factors to be considered to provide economic refractory life; the basic properties and applications to the different refractory materials; on the method of manufacture of refactories; on the refractory characteristics of different refractory materials; the properties of typical fire-clay bricks; the melting-points of pure (refractory) compounds; on reversible and irreversible volume changes of refractories; on the definition of spalling and on the circumstances which promote this; on the causes of refractory failures; on the available refractory brick materials; the most suitable methods of bonding the fire-bricks; the required allowance for thermal movement of refractories; the available methods of shaping fire-brick forms; the properties of insulating materials used in conjunction with refractories; the definition, purposes, uses of monolithic refractories and application; the construction and use of refractory anchors; on the general guidance for the selection and specification of refractory materials.

TABLE 15.3 SELECTION OF REFRACTORIES

Temperature	Spalling conditions	Load conditions	Slagging conditions		
			None	Acid	Basic
High [over 1400° C (2550°F)]	Severe	Heavy	High alumina, silicon carbide	High alumina, silicon carbide	High alumina
		Light	Also, high grade fire-clay; Insulating fire-brick		Fused magnesite
	Light	Heavy	Silica, high alumina, silicon carbide	Silica, high alumina, silicon carbide	Magnesite, chrome-magnesite chromite, magnesite-chrome dolomite, forsterite
		Light	Also, high grade fire-clay; Insulating fire-brick		
Medium [1100°–1400° C (2000°–2550°F)]	Severe	Heavy	High-grade fire-clay; Semi-silica	High-grade fire-clay	High alumina
		Light	Fire-clay, high temp insulator; Insulating fire-brick	High alumina	
	Light	Heavy	High-grade fire-clay; Semi-silica	Silica, high alumina; Dense fire-clay; Silicon carbide	Magnesite; Chrome-magnesite; Chromite
		Light	Fire-clay, high temp insulator; Insulating fire-brick	Silica, dense fire-clay	Magnesite-chrome; Dolomite; Forsterite
Low [under 1100° C (2000° F)]	Light		Low-grade fire-clay; High temp insulator; Insulating fire-brick		Low-grade or medium grade fire-clay
	All other conditions				

REFERENCES

Modern Furnace Technology, Etherington and Etherington, London, 1961.

Technical Information, Plibrico, Luton, Bedford UK.

John G. Stein, *Refractory Bulletins,* Bonnybridge, Scotland.

Refractoric: Production and Properties, Metals Society, London, 1973.

Monolithic Refractories, Kaiser Refractories, Leeds 12, England.

F. H. Norton, *Refractories,* 3rd edition, McGraw-Hill, New York, 1949.

A. B. Searle, *Refractory Materials, their Manufacture and Uses,* 2nd edition, Griffin, London, 1950.

J. Spotts, *Modern Refractory Practice,* McDowell Caton and Co, Cleveland, Ohio, 1950.

Technical Bulletins, Morgan Refractories, Cheshire, England.

11
Chimneys

11.1 THE CHIMNEY SYSTEM – GENERAL PRINCIPLES

The chimney must satisfy certain essential conditions. It must:
- assist the combustion process by providing adequate draught for this purpose,
- ensure that the combustion gases are swept well clear of the stack and that temperature inversions do not take place in the chimney,
- be suitably constructed and insulated to withstand the operating temperature,
- be adequately supported to retain stability in all likely wind and weather conditions,
- be protected to resist both internal and external corrosion.

11.2 CHIMNEY DRAUGHT – DEFINITIONS

The term draught as applied to boilers, furnaces and chimneys, refers to the differential gas pressures obtaining in different parts of the equipment and chimney system. These differences are small, and are measured in milibar mb (or in inches of water gauge). Chimneys operate under one of the following draught conditions:

Natural draught
The hot flue gases from a furnace are drawn upwards through a vertical chimney by the buoyancy effect of the chimney height and the flue gas temperature. The higher the chimney and the hotter the gases, the greater this draught.

Basically, the chimney, boiler and the outer air constitute a U-tube; the chimney is one limb of this tube and a column of cool atmospheric air of similar height is the other limb.

An elementary understanding of the basic principles of natural draught is desirable.

Example:
Assume that the chimney is 30 m high and 0.28 m² in area. The weight of a column of air at 15.6°C (60°F) and 30 m high is 3.4 kg. The weight of a column of flue gases of the same height and at 15.6°C (60°F) is 3.58 kg.

As the temperature in the chimney rises, the weight of the column of flue gases reduces, since the density of a gas is inversely proportional to its absolute temperature.

Assuming a mean temperature for the flue gases of 204°C (400°F), the new weight of the column of gas is 2.3 kg.

Therefore, an imbalance is set up inside the imaginary U-tube of 1.25 mb and this static pressure differential causes the cool atmospheric air column to descend towards the boiler near the base of the chimney, displacing the lighter flue gases upwards towards the chimney terminal.

In theory, a knowledge of the static pressure differential, ie of the available natural draught, should enable one to compute the required chimney dimensions. In practice, the natural draught actually available will be reduced by the pressure loss in the chimney due to friction and by the loss of energy at the chimney entry and terminal. In smaller diameter chimneys of say up to 300 mm there may also be a noticeable loss due to fouling between cleaning periods. In larger diameter chimneys, such loss is likely to be insignificant. A chimney designed on the basis of theoretical draught alone would not function well at times when the furnace is started up when the chimney is cold and the flue gas movement is therefore sluggish.

The height of a chimney serving an *incinerator* is, in most cases, dictated by environmental and statutory considerations to avoid localised pollution (see chimney height later in this chapter).

The draught losses through the incinerator plant depend on the choice of the plant components. Thus, whilst one can establish a theoretical basis for the sizing of a chimney which serves a conventional boiler system, chimneys for incinerator plant are designed on a one-off basis, taking due account of the local and plant design aspects relating to the specific incinerator installation.

A natural-draught chimney offers these advantages:

absence of fan noise,
saving in fan energy input,
reduced maintenance.

However, chimneys relying solely on natural draught are expensive in capital cost, as they must be of relatively great height and cross-section. They are expensive in operating cost also, as effective natural draught requires a high flue gas temperature, with consequent heat wastage. Engineers therefore turn to mechanically created draught (mechanical draught) for the great majority of medium and large size furnace installations.

Large-scale incinerator plants seldom operate with natural chimney draught for the reasons set out below.

Mechanical draught

The insertion of a fan (or fans) into the chimney circuit enables the engineer to precisely design and control the draught conditions under which the incinerator is to operate. This is particularly important with plant of this kind to control and restrict the chimney emission. Chimneys operating with mechanical draught equipment are generally more economical to construct, permitting higher gas velocities and smaller chimney cross-section.

Definitions

The term draught, as applied to boilers, furnaces and chimneys, refers to the differential gas pressures obtaining in different parts of the equipment and chimney system. These differences are small, and are measured in millibar mb (or in inches of water gauge). Mechanical draught using equipment operates under one of the following draught conditions.

Induced draught:

A fan is inserted between the equipment flue outlet and the chimney (fig 11.1). Usually, the fan is located in a bypass to the main flue connection, the latter being fitted with a damper which is closed when the induced draught fan operates. The discharge pressure of the fan must be sufficient to discharge the flue gases against the resistance of the chimney circuit and to provide the required efflux velocity. The fan suction pressure must be adequate to overcome the friction through the incinerator, the boiler and the firing equipment.

Forced draught:

Using forced draught, the fan supplies the air for combustion, overcomes the resistance of the boiler and chimney system and provides the required efflux velocity (fig 11.1). In some plants, the fan pressure is calculated to overcome the resistance of the boiler system only, the chimney draught providing the necessary pull for removal of the flue gases to the atmosphere.

Balanced draught:

Two fans are employed: one to supply air for combustion and the other to induce draught, the arrangement is referred to as a

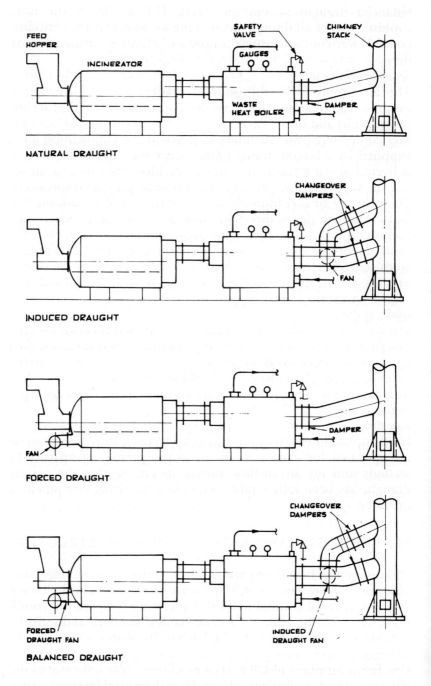

11.1   Alternative arrangements for furnace draught provision

balanced draught system (fig 11.1). This is clearly the most sophisticated of all draught arrangements, as it permits very close control over combustion air supply and chimney draught conditions.

Secondary draught:
The air supply for combustion is made up of the theoretical minimum air quantity calculated to give combustion of the fuel (the primary air) and of the excess air required in practice to burn the fuel completely (the secondary air). When the combustion air is supplied by a forced draught fan, then either all the air may be delivered in one stream, or it may be divided into two separate air circuits supplying the primary and the secondary air respectively. The primary air is commonly delivered from underneath the fuel bed via the ash pit, or directly around the oil or gas jet when such fuel is employed. The secondary air would be delivered *above* the solid fuel bed or around the outside of the cone of primary air and atomised oil. The adoption of such a split system of air supply permits good control over the final stages of combustion and over smoke emission.

Choice of draught:
The particular choice of a draught system depends entirely on the design and construction of the particular incinerator and associated equipment, as well as on the intended method of operation. On the other hand, the plant assembly should be designed to minimise loss of draught and pressure to economise in the electrical energy input to the fan(s).

Fan time delay:
In all applications of fans for draught purposes, provision must be incorporated for a time delay (or purge period) of at least 15 seconds and for an air-flow switch, to ensure that the correct draught has been fully established before the firing equipment is operated.

11.3 BRICK AND CONCRETE CHIMNEY CONSTRUCTION

Chimneys may be constructed of brick, concrete, steel, fibreglass, asbestos or plastic material. Care must be taken to check that the selected material is suitable for the operating temperature conditions. It should be of adequate mechanical strength and must be capable of withstanding the higher temperatures which can be brought about by wrongful operation of the plant. It is known that significant numbers of GRP (glass reinforced plastics) constructed chimneys have caught fire and have been destroyed by overheating.

Brick and concrete are common materials which have been used extensively in chimney construction. They can be neatly integrated with the building to which the chimney is connected and should be long-lasting.

Concrete construction may be carried out either by casting the chimney *in situ* or by use of pre-cast sections assembled in position at site.

Internal insulation of brick and concrete chimneys is necessary to protect the primary building material from the corrosive effects and high temperature of the flue gases and to prevent excessive cooling of the flue gases. The precise specification for the internal insulation must relate to the nature of the material being incinerated, relative to corrosive or otherwise damaging flue gas constituents.

Typical brick and concrete flue constructions are shown in figs 11.2, 11.3, 11.4 and 11.5.

11.4 STEEL CHIMNEY CONSTRUCTION

Steel chimneys are nearly always cheaper than brick or concrete. The break-even height is currently in the region of about 137 m. Steel chimneys generally cost less below this height; concrete ones are cheaper for the greater heights.

Steel chimneys occupy less space, require smaller foundations, are more speedily erected and may be cheaper.

The use of oil or waste burning in plants served by steel chimneys has sometimes led to cases of low-temperature corrosion of the boilers and chimneys and, in some instances, to the emission of smuts. In the case of oil firing, corrosion of the mild steel occurs freely when the temperature of the flue gases drops below around 132°C (270°F), the acid dew-point of the flue gases, when condensation of sulphuric acid takes place inside the chimney.

When burning waste, rubbish or refuse-derived fuel the acid dew-point of the flue gases depends on the properties of the material being incinerated.

With regard to steel chimneys, internal insulation is used to protect the steel from temperatures over 500°C (900°F) with the object of preventing heat impingement upon the steel, or on low temperature chimneys with gases at temperatures below 132°C (270°F), to act as a barrier against acid attack.

11.5 CHIMNEY INSULATION

Since the temperature of the flue gases entering a chimney is seldom below 204°C (400°F), one might reasonably assume that

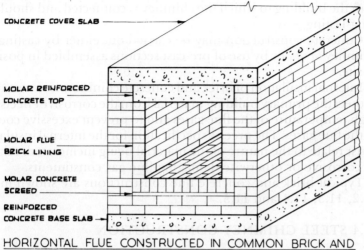

CONCRETE COVER SLAB

MOLAR REINFORCED
CONCRETE TOP

MOLAR FLUE
BRICK LINING

MOLAR CONCRETE
SCREED

REINFORCED
CONCRETE BASE SLAB

HORIZONTAL FLUE CONSTRUCTED IN COMMON BRICK AND
REINFORCED CONCRETE LINED WITH MOLAR FLUE BRICKS AND
MOLAR CONCRETE TOP COVER

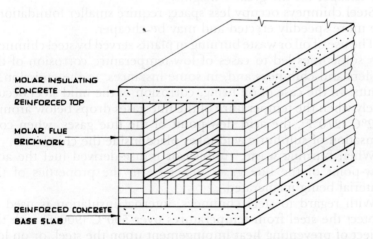

MOLAR INSULATING
CONCRETE
REINFORCED TOP

MOLAR FLUE
BRICKWORK

REINFORCED CONCRETE
BASE SLAB

HORIZONTAL FLUE CONSTRUCTED OF MOLAR BRICKWORK
ON REINFORCED CONCRETE SLAB

11.2   Horizontal flue construction — brick and reinforced concrete

sufficient heat can be retained in the flue gases travelling through the chimney by thermal insulation applied to the chimney. Such insulation can be incorporated with relative ease to chimneys

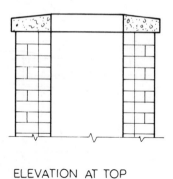

ELEVATION AT TOP

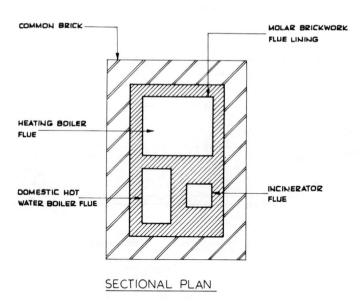

SECTIONAL PLAN

11.3   Multiple compartment chimney construction

constructed of masonry. In practice, insulation may be applied to such chimneys by a process of internal molar refractory lining, by constructing the chimney of two mild steel skins, leaving an annular air space or insulated space between them, or by cladding externally with aluminium. The double skin steel chimney is rarely adopted nowadays and for most chimneys, all-aluminium cladding is placed over mineral wool insulation. Air gap cladding is not often

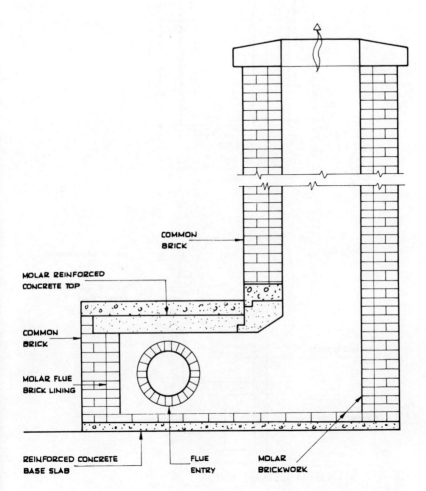

COMMON BRICK

MOLAR REINFORCED CONCRETE TOP

COMMON BRICK

MOLAR FLUE BRICK LINING

REINFORCED CONCRETE BASE SLAB

FLUE ENTRY

MOLAR BRICKWORK

11.4   A view of flue connection from furnace entering a brick chimney

used. Chimneys carrying high temperature flue gases, such as from wood-waste incinerators, generally must be protected with internal refractory lining. Chimneys serving efficient plants operating with low flue gas exit temperature may be insulated with aluminium cladding or by the double mild steel skin arrangement.

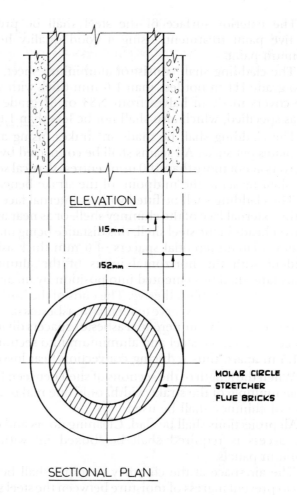

ELEVATION

115mm

152mm

MOLAR CIRCLE
STRETCHER
FLUE BRICKS

SECTIONAL PLAN

11.5   Circular chimney — typical construction detail

11.6 ALUMINIUM CLADDING

In the typical system of cladding mild steel chimneys with aluminium sheeting, the application is so arranged that the chimney after completion presents a completely smooth appearance, the flanged joints of the mild steel chimney being entirely contained within the cladding. The method of applying the insulation, as generally laid down in British Standard Specification BS 4076: 1978 is as follows:

(a) The exterior surface of the steel shall be prepared with protective paint treatment, using a good quality heat resisting aluminium paint.

(b) The cladding shall consist of aluminium sheet, from grade NS3 to grade H4 in not less than 1.6 mm thick with symmetrical flange covers made in halves from NS3 or S1 grade aluminium sheet as specified, which also shall not be less than 1.6 mm thick.

(c) The cladding shall be made in strakes, using a number of equal plates per stake. All seams shall be connected by aluminium alloy rivets at not more than 100 mm centres. Vertical seams of each strake shall be set at the midpoint of the strake beneath.

(d) The cladding shall be fitted with its internal face 6 mm away from the external face of the chimney shell, or as near as possible to clear rivet heads in the steel shell, this distance being maintained by continuous circumferential spacers of 6 mm thick asbestos tape, coincident with the horizontal joints of the aluminium. The asbestos tape shall be cemented into position by means of sodium silicate or other suitable adhesive. The ends of the horizontal rivets in the aluminium sheets serve to retain the asbestos tape in position after erection. The circumferential asbestos spacers divide the 6 mm air space between the steel and aluminium into sections not more than 1.5 m apart, thus reducing convection heat losses.

(e) When the length of the sections of shell between flanges is not a whole multiple of the strake width, only one make-up strake per section of chimney shall be used.

(f) 'All projections shall be clad. Cleaning doors and other points where access is required shall be 'boxed in' with removable aluminium panels.

(g) The air space at the chimney terminal shall be completely sealed to prevent ingress of moisture between the steel shell and the cladding.

(h) Each upper strake of aluminium shall lap over the lower strake by a minimum of 25 mm. The vertical seams similarly shall have a minium lap of 25 mm.

(j) To permit examination of the steel shell of the chimney without removing the cladding, 150 mm² openings, located at carefully selected points and covered by removable panels approximately 230 mm², shall be provided. Suitable positions are:
diametrically opposite any inlet,
approximately 1.25 m from the top of the chimney.

(k) After erection, the cladding may be degreased and painted with a clear lacquer. The top 650 mm of the cladding can be roughened and painted with two coats of heat resisting black bitumastic paint, giving a neat appearance of the chimney under operating conditions when some soot darkness of the chimney terminal is likely.

(m) The aluminium cladding may be applied on site either before or after the chimney is erected, or at the manufacturer's works. If the aluminium is applied at works or on site before erection, great care shall be taken not to damage the aluminium sheets. If a sheet becomes damaged, it shall be removed and replaced with a new sheet. Riveting a patch of aluminium over the damaged area is not acceptable.

(n) Great care shall be taken to ensure that dissimilar metals do not come into contact with each other. If it is essential in the design that two dissimilar metals have to be connected, a suitable non-conductive and water-impervious film or agent shall be placed between them.

(o) Self-tapping screws should be avoided, as they fall out after a short time. Pop rivets are recommended for general use.

11.7 MINERAL WOOL INSULATION

Wrapping the steel shell with a suitable grade of mineral wool fibre insulating material of sufficient thickness provides more effective insulation than aluminium cladding with the usual 6 mm air gap. Thicknesses of over 50 mm are applied in two separate layers, the outer layer being fitted so that the vertical and horizontal joints are staggered from the joints of the inner layer. If the angle jointing flange of the chimney section projects past the outer face of the mineral wool, it shall be wrapped with an additional layer of mineral wool of the same thickness for at least 75 mm on each side of the flange joint. As mineral wool has to be protected from the weather, a convenient way of doing this is to cover it with an aluminium cladding without an air gap.

Double-skin chimney

The space between the outer shell and the liner of the double-skin chimney can be filled with mineral wool, expanded mineral, or other suitable insulator. Unless a special heat-resisting steel is used for the liner, the temperature should not exceed 480°C (896°F).

It is essential that there shall be no metal contact between the liner and the outer shell, otherwise 'cold spots' occur on the liner, thus reducing local areas to below the acid dew-point level and facilitating acidic condensation and corrosion.

11.8 MULTI-FLUE CHIMNEY

The multi-flue chimney is an effective method of maintaining the velocity of the flue gases at various operating levels and of providing adequate insulation.

The liners in a multi-flue chimney may be contained in a structural shell of steel, brick or reinforced concrete, in a shaft within the structure of a building or in an open structural load-bearing frame built from steel sections or reinforced concrete. Normally, each liner is connected to one combustion unit so that the optimum gas velocity can be achieved in all operating conditions

The temperature of the inner surface of the liner can be maintained either by wrapping the exterior of the liner with a mineral wool mattress or by filling the space between the liners and the structural shell with an expanded mineral, or both.

When granular insulating material is used, a gate valve must be provided for its removal and a notice be affixed adjacent to the gate valve warning of the dangers of operation by unauthorised personnel.

If the liners are supported by an open structural frame, they must be adequately insulated and protected from the weather.

In view of the improved results obtained with aluminium-clad insulated chimneys, it is becoming increasingly common practice to protect mild steel chimneys against corrosion and smutting by the application of such procedures rather than by adopting double-skin construction.

11.9 LIMITATIONS OF INSULATED CHIMNEYS

User experience with tall aluminium-clad or double-skin chimneys has shown that these methods of insulation are not always sufficient to avoid the nuisance of smut emission. Furthermore, certain field investigations have highlighted the following three particular difficulties which cause smut emission:

The connection of a number of boilers or furnaces to one chimney: trouble is likely to be experienced through smut emission when only *some* of these are in operation.

The use of firing equipment with a high turn-down ratio. The problem is similar to that of a number of boilers connected to one common chimney compartment.

Temperature inversion due to outside air being drawn from the top of the chimney around its periphery, whilst the hot gases rise in the centre, causing smut deposition local to the top of the chimney.

Inversion can occur at gas speeds below about 5 m/sec; much higher gas discharge velocities are therefore necessary to avoid inversion.

Heat losses from tall chimneys insulated with an air gap and aluminium cladding or double-skin can be sufficiently great to cause the internal metal temperature to fall below the acid dew-point. A moderate thickness (about 50 mm) of a common insulating material, such as mineral wool, is sufficient to ensure the maintenance of an adequate working temperature above the dew-point, even when working at below half the connected load. Both with insulated and uninsulated chimneys, conditions are such that smuts can be formed during the warming-up period of the furnace; such conditions cannot be avoided by insulation.

11.10 DOUBLE-SKIN CHIMNEY

In the design of a double-skin insulated chimney, the inner and outer steel casings are of similar thickness, the space between being filled with low-density mineral wool, 25 to 50 mm thick, depending on the minimum temperature of the gases entering the chimney, to allow for the differential expansion arising from the difference in temperature between the inner and outer casings. The inner skin expands due to the heat of the flue gases and must be designed to permit movement of the outer sheath without stress.

Double-skin chimneys are rarely made or used these days; they are a very expensive and not very effective form of construction.

11.11 AIR LEAKAGE

Air leakage into the ductwork between furnace and chimney must be avoided as the ingress of relatively cool air into the chimney system will reduce the natural buoyancy of the flue gases and may encourage condensation in the chimney, with damaging results. Such leakage can be efficiently sealed with flexible rubber-impregnated asbestos cloth, capable of withstanding temperatures in excess of the maximum likely flue gas temperature.

11.12 BLANKING PLATE

The provision of a blanking plate below the entry of the flue pipe into the chimney is desirable to prevent loss of heat at the base of the chimney which would otherwise form a dead leg (fig **11.6**). The presence of a deep chimney pocket below the entry point may cause unstable gas flow in the chimney and/or vibration.

When burning wastes and/or supplementary fuels which result in wet combustion products, adequate drains must be provided in the blanking plate and these must incorporate a trap to isolate the chimney draught from the drain termination.

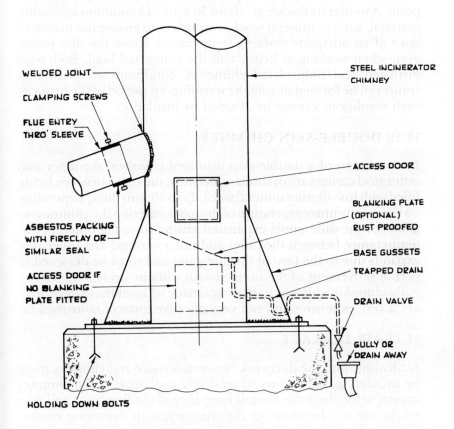

11.6   Arrangements near bottom of chimney

11.13 TERMINAL

Temperature inversion at the top of the chimney can be overcome by fitting a truncated cone to the chimney terminal, designed to increase the flue gas exit velocity to a minimum of 3.3 m/sec. Such cone should have sides at an angle of 15° to the vertical and be insulated with 37 mm thickness of rock wool below the cladding (fig 11.7).

11.14 NOISE ATTENUATION

At times, objectional noise can be generated at the chimney entry connections. Attenuators are available to reduce noise levels (see plate 55).

At the cheapest end of the scale, it is not unknown for essentially standard cylindrical attenuators to be employed, constructed to a marine quality specification. This usually entails an all-welded construction and all materials are galvanised after machining and welding, giving a very high degree of protection, more especially so if the flue gases have been diluted.

However, a more professional approach employs a specification in which improved mechanical strength and corrosion resistance is incorporated by the use of 10g steel in conjunction with stainless steel. The particular format is that the cylindrical casing is formed from 10g black steel, all-welded construction, galvanised after manufacture. The perforated metal facing, which takes the brunt of the attack from the flue gas, is from perforated stainless steel of fairly thin gauge and has to be retained in such a way as to allow for differential expansion, as the hot flue gas and the outer casing are not always at the same temperature. The acoustic infill is selected to stand up to temperature as high as 800°C (1472°F) and is suitably retained behind this stainless steel facing. Some manufacturers increase the thickness of this infill to ensure a reasonable degree of low frequency attenuation.

This basic attenuator is simply a lined duct and contains no pod. Generally, a pod is not included, as it obviously produces an obstruction to the flue gas flow and the resultant back pressures are very sensitive features of combustion. If a requirement for improved low frequency attenuation *does* demand the inclusion of a pod, then a transformation piece is employed to bring the open area of the free annular airway equal to the main flue area, essentially eliminating any extra back pressure.

11.15 MULTI-FLUE CHIMNEY–REDUCTION IN SMUT EMISSION

One of the most efficient ways of overcoming low chimney temperatures, and the consequent smut emission, is the provision of a multi-flue insulated chimney assembly as shown in (fig 11.3) where each furnace is provided with its own correctly sized flue.

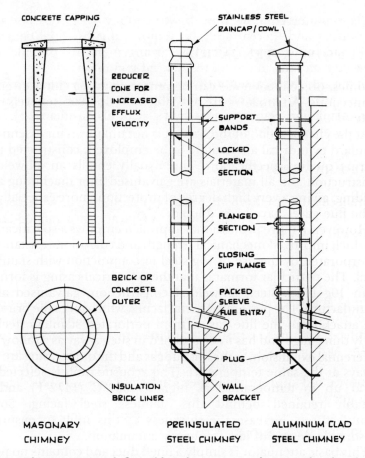

CONCRETE CAPPING

STAINLESS STEEL
RAINCAP / COWL

REDUCER
CONE FOR
INCREASED
EFFLUX
VELOCITY

SUPPORT
BANDS

LOCKED
SCREW
SECTION

FLANGED
SECTION

CLOSING
SLIP FLANGE

BRICK OR
CONCRETE
OUTER

PACKED
SLEEVE

FLUE ENTRY

PLUG

INSULATION
BRICK LINER

WALL
BRACKET

MASONARY
CHIMNEY

PREINSULATED
STEEL CHIMNEY

ALUMINIUM CLAD
STEEL CHIMNEY

11.7   Chimney terminals for mild steel, masonry and pre-insulated packaged chimneys

11.16 SUPPORTS

Mild steel chimneys may be supported by brackets attached to the building, by guys secured with straining screws and wire rope to secure anchor points or they may be entirely self-supporting and free-standing. The latter type of chimney is becoming increasingly popular, particularly for chimneys which are taller than the building served by the chimney. Figure 11.8 illustrates different types of chimney supports

11.17 FREE-STANDING CHIMNEY

A free-standing chimney must be structurally designed to be self-supporting and therefore always requires a substantial concrete base and mild steel base-plate arrangement to provide the necessary stability under all likely wind conditions.

In the UK, the local authority engineers generally require a copy of the structural design calculations for their approval. It is usual for such calculations to be provided by a structural consultant or by the manufacturers of the chimney.

11.18 DRAIN POINT

A drain point, with drain-cock and trap should be provided at the base of each chimney compartment. A typical such arrangement is shown in fig 11.6.

11.19 APPROVALS

Formal approval must be obtained from the appropriate local authorities in respect of the construction and stability of all new chimneys. Chimneys constructed of masonry are usually regarded by the authorities as *permanent* structures; mild steel chimneys as *temporary* structures, subject to periodic licensing by the local authority and appropriate inspection before renewal of the licence is granted.

11.20 ENTRY SLEEVE

Care must be taken in the design of the final connection between the furnace flue pipe and the chimney to obviate the transmission of vibration from the furnace and firing equipment to the chimney.

It is therefore good practice to build an over-size sleeve into the chimney to receive each individual flue pipe, the space between the sleeve and the flue pipe being caulked with a suitable flexible heat resistant filling, such as asbestos rope (fig 11.6).

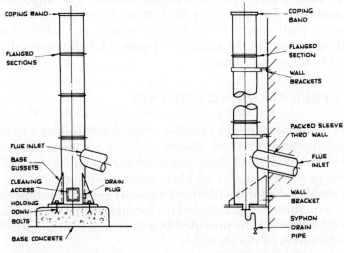

(a) FREE STANDING CHIMNEY

COPING BAND
FLANGED SECTIONS
FLUE INLET
BASE GUSSETS
CLEANING ACCESS
DRAIN PLUG
HOLDING DOWN BOLTS
BASE CONCRETE

(b) WALL BRACKETTED CHIMNEY

COPING BAND
FLANGED SECTION
WALL BRACKETS
PACKED SLEEVE THRO' WALL
FLUE INLET
WALL BRACKET
SYPHON DRAIN PIPE

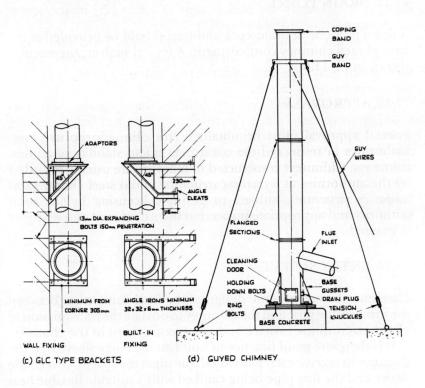

(c) GLC TYPE BRACKETS

ADAPTORS
45°
45°
230mm
ANGLE CLEATS
6
13mm DIA.EXPANDING BOLTS 150mm PENETRATION
MINIMUM FROM CORNER 305mm
ANGLE IRONS MINIMUM 32 x 32 x 6mm THICKNESS
WALL FIXING
BUILT-IN FIXING

(d) GUYED CHIMNEY

COPING BAND
GUY BAND
GUY WIRES
FLANGED SECTIONS
FLUE INLET
CLEANING DOOR
HOLDING DOWN BOLTS
RING BOLTS
BASE CONCRETE
BASE GUSSETS
DRAIN PLUG
TENSION KNUCKLES

11.8   Various types of chimney supports

11.21 THERMAL INSULATION OF FLUE PIPES AND CHIMNEY CONNECTIONS

These are best insulated with 50 mm thick canvas-backed glass wool slabs, fitted to allow a 25 mm air space between the flue duct and the insulation materials. At all inspection doors, dampers, shaft exits and instrument tappings, the insulation should be neatly chamfered down and be protected overall with metal cladding. The air space may be formed by the provision of mild steel spacing stools welded to the ducting at suitable intervals; the stools are then overlaid with expanded metal and held in position by binding wire.

11.22 SIZING OF CHIMNEYS FOR INCINERATORS

The cross-sectional area of the chimney is sized to suit the quantity of combustion products and the available chimney draught. The velocity of the flue gases, just above their point of entry into the chimney, should be in the range of 4.5 to 7.5 m/sec for natural draught flue systems and in the range of 7.5 to 12.5 m/sec where mechanical draught is employed.

The volume of the products of combustion which enter the chimney stack depends on the properties of the material being incinerated, on the control over the combustion air supply and on the temperature of the flue gases.

When a waste heat recovery boiler is incorporated with the incinerator, the exit temperature of the flue gases will be in the order of 200 to 260°C (392 to 500°F). The volume of the 'average' flue gas will be in the order of 1.3 m³/MJ at the lower temperature, and in the order of 1.4 m³/MJ, at the higher temperature.

When the incinerator operates without heat recovery, very much higher flue gas temperatures apply. The volume of the flue gases varies relative to pressure and temperature in accordance with the relationship

$$\frac{P_1 V_1}{T_1} = \frac{P_2 V_2}{T_2}$$

which, at constant pressure $(P_1 = P_2)$

becomes $\dfrac{V_1}{V_2} = \dfrac{T_1}{T_2}$

V_1 and V_2 are the respective specific volumes of the flue gas at absolute temperatures T_1 and T_2, respectively.

11.23 CHIMNEY HEIGHT

This is determined in some countries by government or local authority codes. In the UK, it is governed by the provisions of the Clean Air Act 1956 - Memorandum of Chimney Heights - which offers a relatively simple method of calculating the approximate chimney height (for conventional boilers) commonly desirable in normal circumstances, and acceptable to the local authorities, for boiler and furnaces having a rating in excess of 180 kW.

The minimum permissible height of an *incinerator* chimney is, in many countries, governed by local government regulations or codes, relative to the output of the incinerator, the nature of product being incinerated, the likely pollution from grit, smuts, sparks, smoke and on the nature of the environment in which the incinerator is to be located.

For example, in the UK, the Memorandum on Chimney Heights, which forms part of the Clean Air Act, differentiates between different chimney locations in the following way:

An underdeveloped area where development is unlikely, where background pollution is low, and where there is no development within half a mile of the new chimney;

A partially developed area with scattered houses, low background pollution and no other comparable industrial emissions within a quarter of a mile of the new chimney;

A built-up residential area with only moderate background pollution and without other comparable industrial emissions;

An urban area of mixed industrial and residential development, with considerable background pollution and with other comparable industrial emissions within a quarter of a mile of the new chimney;

A large city, or an urban area, of mixed heavy industrial and dense residential development, with severe background pollution,.

The method of calculation, outlined in the Memorandum, is based on the quantity of flue gas which the chimney is expected to discharge, as a function of the maximum rate of emission of sulphur dioxide. In the case of incinerators, difficulty with grit and dust cannot be avoided solely by increasing the height of the chimney; the provision of dust and grit-arresting equipment is generally necessary.

The Memorandum is available from HMSO. It will assist

engineers practising in the UK and will provide guidance for the selection of chimney heights in other countries where there are no similar local authority requirements.

Technically, the minimum height of a natural-draught chimney is determined by the difference in pressure which the chimney must develop to overcome the pressure losses of the system when conveying the flue gases. Theoretically, there exists a limiting chimney height beyond which no increase in draught can be achieved, due to increasing friction loss and reduction in gas temperature. In practice, the chimney losses tend to be much smaller than the other pressure losses in the flue system; hence, any increase in chimney height will almost invariably increase the available draught. However one should always be cost conscious and compare the cost of raising a natural-draught chimney above the minimum accepted height for the application, to the alternative of adopting mechanical draught with the minimum acceptable chimney height.

11.24 CHIMNEY EFFLUX VELOCITY (EXIT VELOCITY)

This is increased by the specific design for minimum cross-sectional area of the flue gases. If the efflux velocity is too low, then the plume of gas leaving the chimney terminal tends to flow down the outside of the stack on the leeward side; the effective chimney height is thereby effectively reduced. The maintenance of a high efflux velocity will avoid this downwash. This velocity should be about 6 m/sec for natural-draught operation and between 7.5 to 15 m/sec for mechanical-draught systems. Incinerators equipped with forced-draught fans only, should have a chimney efflux velocity of not less than 6 m/sec when operating at full output. Incinerators equipped with induced-draught fans should have a chimney efflux velocity of not less than 7.5 m/sec at full load for outputs up to 9000 kW, increasing to a maximum of 15 m/sec at full load for outputs of 135,000 kW.

11.25 MULTIPLE FLUES

When two, or more, incinerators discharge into one common chimney, this would have to be sized for the quantity of flue gases flowing when all the connected units are operating at full load. At times, when there is below-capacity operation, the cross-section of the common chimney will be too large for the gas flow and a high efflux velocity can then not be achieved, even when a high-velocity discharge terminal is fitted to the top of the chimney. Wherever possible, each flue should be connected to a separate chimney or chimney compartment.

11.26 EXCESS AIR

Complete and efficient combustion of fuel or waste cannot be attained in practice without supplying a quantity of air greater than that theoretically required; the difference between the air actually supplied for combustion and the theoretical air requirement is termed the 'excess air'.

11.27 COMPUTATION OF CHIMNEY CROSS-SECTION

To determine the cross-section of any particular chimney, the following information must be available:

a furnace/incinerator outlet flue gas temperatures,
b quantity of flue gases arising from combustion,
c available chimney draught.

Information under item a is generally obtainable from the equipment designers or suppliers.

To arrive at the quantity of flue gases, the following subsidiary information is required:

1 output rating,
2 combustion efficiency,
3 by calculation, from 1 and 2, total fuel input,
4 theoretical quantity of flue gas per unit connected to chimney, when at full load,
5 excess air required for combustion,
6 by addition of 4 and 5, total flow of flue gases through chimney.

Chimney sizing

Technical procedures
1 Decide whether chimney is to operate with natural draught or with mechanical draught.
2 Select the design velocity for the flue gases being.conveyed in the chimney.
3 Determine the area and/or diameter of the chimney, using the chart in fig 11.11.

4 Determine the loss of pressure (draught loss) in the chimney of the selected diameter (3 above), using the chart in fig **11.9**.
5 Establish or assess the height of the chimney (note text). Consult the chart in fig **11.9** for the draught loss in the chimney.

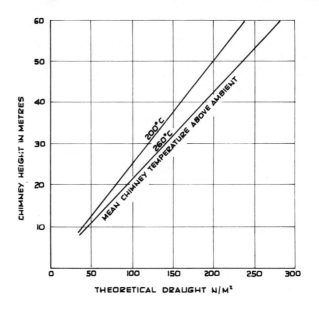

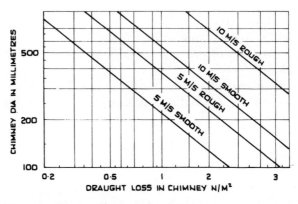

11.9   Charts indicating chimney draught losses

6 Ascertain (usually, by inquiry of the plant manufacturers or by independent calculations) the draught loss of each item connected to the chimney system (eg waste heat boiler, grit arrestor, flue connection into the chimney, efflux terminal). Add together.

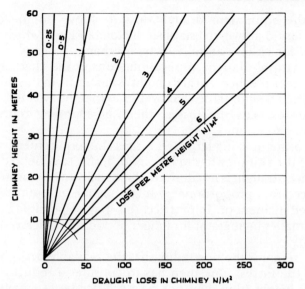

11.10   Chart indicating draught loss within natural draught chimneys

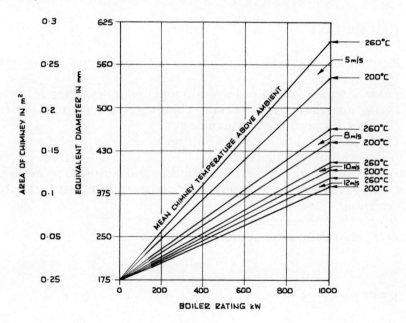

11.11   Chart indicating relationship between boiler rating, flue gas velocity and chimney area

7 Add the equipment draught loss (6 above) to the chimney draught loss (5 above) to establish the total draught which must be provided for either naturally or by mechanical means.

8 For a natural-draught application, consult the chart fig **11.10**. This provides the theoretical draught available from the chimney of the specified height. If the chart indicates that the available draught equals or exceeds the losses, then the chimney represents a satisfactory solution.

If the draught is inadequate to meet the requirement, then the height of the chimney has to be raised. If this cannot be done and mechanical draught is not desired, the velocity in the chimney must be reduced by a proportional reduction in the output rating of the connected incinerator. In practice, this may be possible by operating the smaller incinerator for longer periods to burn an equivalent quantity.

There remains the possibility that the available draught greatly exceeds the losses. One then has to consider a reduction in the chimney height (this may not be permissible), a smaller cross-section of the fitting of draught control damper(s). Plates 56 to 60 show some interesting applications.

CHECK LIST

Ascertain: local bylaws or regulations relating to chimney design and specification.
Check: whether natural or forced-draught chimney design.
Decide: materials of construction, chimney system (eg multi-flue); chimney supports (eg free-standing).
Check: connected furnace and flue gas load.
Design: chimney dimensions.
Specify: construction, insulation, cladding and corrosion protective.
Check: gas velocity at exit terminal; design to avoid temperature inversion.
Design: chimney supports and foundations.
Approvals: obtain local authority approvals.

REFERENCES

H. A. Blum, B. Lees and L. K. Rendle. The prevention of steel stack corrosion and smut emission with oil-fired boilers, *Journal Institute of Fuel,* April, 1959. BS 4076: 1968.

B. G. Gills and B. Lees, Specification for steel chimneys, Design and operation of an insulated steel chimney, *Journal Institute of Fuel*, March, 1966.

Faber and Kell, *Heating and Air Conditioning of Buildings*, pp 81-3, The Architectural Press, 1971.

D. Kut, Boiler chimneys, *The Architectural Review*, p 382, no 837 November, 1966.

R. P. Ravenscroft, Field investigation and design of insulated chimneys, *Journal Institute of Fuel*, March, 1966.

12
Control and Instrumentation

12.1 INTRODUCTION

The control and instrumentation of a waste incineration plant (with or without energy recovery) must be designed, executed and operated in a manner which provides complete safety and achieves efficient and smokeless combustion. An automatically stoked incinerator is usually safer and more efficient than a manually stoked plant.

Control systems should not be over-specified or be excessively elaborate. The most effective control system is usually the simplest one, provided that each plant function is adequately controlled and sequenced. Certain control malfunctions cannot be readily detected without an appropriate instrument indication or recording.

12.2 MANUAL STOKING

Manual stoking of a boiler necessitates the provision of a thermometer and/or a steam pressure gauge and a boiler safety valve. A steam boiler also requires a water level gauge. These indicators guide the stoker in the stoking and pressure/temperature control which is essential for safe and reasonably efficient boiler usage.

The boiler damper-regulator which controls the primary combustion air (admitted below the fire-bed) requires frequent adjustment to suit the heat load and firing conditions when this damper is manually operated; the boiler is then inevitably often fired below the design output capacity, with consequent risk of internal boiler condensation.

Variations of boiler temperature encourage internal boiler condensation, particularly with gas, oil and wet waste combustion; it is, therefore, desirable to operate boilers at reasonably constant temperature. This can only be effectively achieved by automatic means.

12.3 GAUGES

It is desirable to fit all pressure vessels with instruments which clearly indicate their operating pressure and/or temperature.

Temperature gauge

Plate 61 shows a dial type bi-metal temperature gauge; this is more easily read than a plain mercury-in-glass thermometer and hence is more reliable. The dial thermometer is usually (and best) immersed into a thermometer well which is screwed into a boiler tapping to allow repair or replacement of the instrument without the need to drain the boiler. Hot water boilers are usually controlled by relating the fuel input to the boiler operating temperature.

Altitude gauge

A continuous indication of the static head which is imposed on the system at the gauge point is provided by a simple (dial-type) low pressure altitude gauge. An adjustable red index hand is set to the correct system pressure at commissioning and provides an immediate indication of a deviation or of a loss of water from the system.

Water gauge

Each steam or vapour boiler must be provided with an approved set of water gauge glasses which indicate the water level in the boiler. These must be fitted with gauge glass protectors and water sampling points.

Pressure gauge

Steam or vapour boilers can only be output controlled by relating the fuel input to the boiler pressure. Each pressure gauge for such boilers is screwed into the top of a U-tube which is fitted with an isolating cock. The U-tube prevents direct contact between the steam and the gauge mechanism. Pressure gauges (with shut-off valves) should be fitted at the suction and delivery port of each main pump to continually indicate the pump performance.

Manometer (low pressure) gauges are required to indicate the difference of pressure across an air filter to indicate the filter condition and the need for cleaning.

Draught gauges must be provided to indicate boiler flue and chimney conditions.

It is a false economy to omit the provision of indicating gauges at key positions throughout the plant; such omission can contribute towards unsafe working conditions. Generally, the factory inspectorate and the relevant insurance company lay down rules for the minimum acceptable standards of instrumentation.

12.4 SAFETY VALVES

Plate 62 shows a spring-loaded safety valve applied to a hot water boiler; the object of such a valve is to automatically relieve any excessive pressure by overflow of water through a discharge pipe connection. This discharge must be carried to the outside of the boiler chamber and terminate with a chamfered end at a suitable visible drain location (usually over the nearest gulley).

Safety valves are sometimes fitted with dead weights, rather than with springs. Both types of safety valves are dependable when matched to the boiler pressure or head condition; they must be insurance company approved.

All hot water boilers and pressure vessels must (by law) be fitted with an approved type of safety valve. All steam boilers must be fitted with duplicate blow-off safety valves, which must be set marginally above the boiler working pressure, so that any increase in pressure is immediately relieved.

Steam pressure reducing valve sets in pipelines must be provided with related safety valves and pressure gauges.

12.5 BLOW-DOWN

Steam boilers must be fitted with manual or automatic blow-down arrangements to control the total dissolved solids (TDS) content within the boiler water. The quantity of blow-down water required each day is usually calculated accurately by regular water sampling and analysis.

If this operation is carried out manually, great care must be exercised to ensure that the blow-down pit covers are correctly in position, that blow-down pipe trenches are covered and that no person is standing near to any crack or crevice from which live steam may issue. In one case known to the authors, the blow-down valve was opened and allowed live steam to escape into the boilerhouse through an uncovered fracture in the blow-down pipe; the boiler-man (overcome by steam) fell into the pipe trench and was fatally injured.

12.6 AUTOMATIC STOKING

The principle of the automatic control of a waste burning plant is the measurement and corresponding matching of the rate at which heat is drawn (thermal demand) to the heat release from the fuel over a given period. Automatic stoking measures the boiler temperature or pressure by the use of sensors immersed in the boiler and relays this information through a central control panel to the fuel feed mechanism, with the object of maintaining the specified temperature or pressure by adjusting the fuel feed. All this is carried out at optimum efficiency.

This simple principle is the basis of all furnace/boiler automatic control systems; refined sophistication is only required to improve the quality of control and to improve safety.

12.7 CONTROLLERS

Limit control

If the operating temperature of a boiler is 85° C (185° F) and the automatic fuel feed controller is maintaining this constant boiler temperature (by varying the rate of fuel feed with variations of thermal demand), then there must be another boiler temperature sensor, set at a higher control limit level (say, 90°C (194°F)) which (when activated through some malfunction) prevents the fuel feed mechanism from operating until the fault has been noted and cleared. Such a sensor is called a *limit sensor* and the action it takes, a *lock-out*. Once locked-out, the controls *must be* manually re-set to re-start the plant. This should only be attempted after the cause of the fault has been diagnosed and the appropriate remedial action completed.

Temperature sensors

These are resistance thermometers or electric resistors which are manufactured from a material whose resistance varies with temperature in a known and stable manner. By connecting the resistance element into a bridge circuit, any variation in temperature will result in an out-of-balance electro-motive force (emf) in the circuit which will then actuate the control(s). The most suitable resistance material for this purpose is pure platinum.

Plate 64 shows a typical resistance thermometer suitable for immersion-sensing of a fluid (water) temperature.

Pressure sensors

Pressure sensors use the principle of contraction and expansion of a fluid container under varying pressure to operate an electrical circuit.

Thermocouples

Thermocouples, consisting of two wires of dissimilar metals joined together at both ends, are used to measure and relay temperature readings. The junction placed at the point where the hot temperature is to be measured is called the *hot junction*, the other, the *cold junction*, is located so that a difference in temperature exists between both junctions; an emf is generated in the loop and a suitable measuring instrument is included in the circuit, which may then be accurately calibrated in terms of temperature sensing. Plate 63 shows a thermocouple assembly.

Direct acting controller

This comprises a sensing element which, by liquid or vapour pressure expansion through a capillary tube, transmits power directly to a bellows or diaphragm, which then actuates the controlled device. This may be used to control a water or steam heating medium (eg to a herater battery, air system damper, etc.) Direct acting controllers have modulating characteristics, but their application is usually limited to small independent units; they are not suitable for multiple central control.

Transistors, thermistors

The use of transistors and thermistors has eliminated many mechanical control parts and by their use with improved electronics, control systems have become much more compact and reliable. The advent of micro-processing (silicon chip) and the improved ability to sequence many functions has greatly simplified a hitherto exacting science.

Central control panels

These are commonly employed with the larger installations; it is good practice to locate the whole of the major control system components within, and on, such a central control facility. Factory-assembled and pre-wired, these panels may accommodate boiler auxillaries, time switches, pump starters, contactors, relays, temperature and pressure indicating and recording dials, draught gauges, CO_2/O_2 indicators, various metering devices (steam and water consumption), mimic operating diagrams and pilot indicator lights to achieve central indication and supervision of operation and maintenance.

Plate 65 shows a typical central control panel for a large plant installation.

Compressed air

Compressed air is widely used as a pneumatic control medium for the activation of valves, dampers, etc. The main advantage in the use of compressed air for the driving of the heavy machinery associated with certain plant items of an incineration plant is the dependability of such a power source under extreme conditions (high temperature). In the case of a blast gate damper (furnace fuel feed), the response of the gate to a signal is immediate and positive — the air pressure being always available at the ram-cylinder ports to drive the gate into the closed position. Pneumatic/electric control is often preferred to pure electronic control because of the versatile adaptability of an air pressure stream to modulation, particularly, in the case of valve and damper movement requirements to intermediate positions dictated by electronic signals (temperature or pressure). Pneumatic/electric control can eliminate a multiplicity of electric motors and thus increase dependability and reduce maintenance need.

For every major control application, the relative advantages of pneumatic control or electric/electronic control should be evaluated to achieve the best results.

12.8 BOILERS

Steam

In addition to pressure indication and safety valve relief, the following boiler controls and indicators are usually incorporated in a packaged steam boiler.

Boiler water level controls — duplicated because of the danger inherent in low boiler water conditions. The boiler water level is maintained by float type controllers which are linked to the start and stop controls of the boiler feed pump. In the event of a dangerous low water condition, an alarm is sounded and the fuel feed is locked-out, necessitating manual re-start, but retaining the operation of the boiler feed pumps. Condensate return starvation and surge conditions are not uncommonly encountered and usually indicate inadequate condensate storage tank or system condensate return pumping facility.

Duplicate water-in-glass or sight glasses are fitted to each boiler to permit observation of the actual boiler water level at all times.

Pressure sensing automatically varies the fuel feed and locks out the plant if the boiler pressure rises sufficiently to activate the pressure limit sensor, which is usually duplicated.

Automatic steam blow-down is usually an optional feature of most modern steam packaged boilers, but is essential for large plants where the protection afforded by correct blow-down procedures is critical. The amount of blow-down is related to the boiler water condition and the device is usually operated on a timing mechanism. Indiscriminate blow-down procedures can waste much heat energy.

Water

The following operational boiler controls are usually incorporated for packaged water boilers:

Boiler operating control thermostat or sensor.

Boiler limit thermostat, which cuts off the feed when the plant locks out in an emergency or due to a malfunction associated with a compulsory manual re-start.

Plate 66 shows a combined operating and limit sensing controller (differential) suitable for the smaller output type of packaged boiler.

In the case of open or non-pressurised hot water system boilers, altitude gauges are fitted to continuously indicate the static head of the system.

The pressurisation unit of closed or pressurised hot water systems is separately controlled; loss of pressure triggers the boiler fuel feed controller to lock-out the plant. Pressure gauges are used and sensors provide an audible alarm if the design operating pressure is not maintained at all times during operation.

Steam and water

General to water, steam, vapour and oil fired packaged boilers, additional control features are usually incorporated.

Supplementary oil or gas burners have individual controls and control boxes, but they are usually integrated into the main packaged boiler control panel. When coal is used as a supplementary fuel, particularly in underfeed stoker fashion, complete automatic integration and change-over may not be possible, unless a separate supplementary fuel stoker is used. All such supplementary fuel devices must have complete lock-out plant integration when employed in sequence. Great care must be exercised when manually firing out-of-sequence supplementary fuel devices to ensure that the main waste firing plant is locked out and vice-versa.

Chimney draught regulating dampers are heavily constructed, and may be manually lever or automatically operated; the advantages of providing automatic damper control are particularly useful in multi-boiler applications and where alternative damper settings are frequently required (eg supplementary fuel ignition burner for a waste cyclone furnace).

A smoke indicating/recording instrument system is usually required (often by the local authority) in situations where maladjustment of the plant can cause offensive smoke.

Waste fuel moisture content control

The forced-draught wood-waste burning packaged boiler shown in chapter 7 is separately controlled for low and high moisture content waste fuel when fitted with an oil burning auxiliary as illustrated in fig 12.1. A pneumatic fuel metering device is available, as is an automatic pneumatic ash removal system for high ash content waste fuels.

12.9 UNDERFEED STOKERS

Figure 12.2 shows the essential control element positions for an automatic underfeed wood-waste hot water boiler stoker plant. The control components are:

a Silo out feeder (screw type) with electro-mechanical safety damper, which closes on the sensing of excess temperature.
b Level controller in break-hopper which regulates the amount of wood-waste being admitted to the boiler screw feed and is also linked to a.
c Primary combustion air fan.
d Secondary combustion air fan.
e Constant speed fuel screw feed into boiler.
f Boiler control thermostat.
g Boiler limit thermostat.
h Induced draught fan.
j Inspection door interlocks.
k Viewing port cooling fan.
l Sprinkler safety control in boiler fuel feed.
m Sprinkler safety control in silo fuel feed.
n Auxiliary burner.
o Control panel.

The boiler control thermostat, f, operates the boiler within a specified band of hot water temperature differential. Below the lower temperature setting, the thermostat calls for full boiler fuel input; at the higher level, it prevents further fuel feed until the

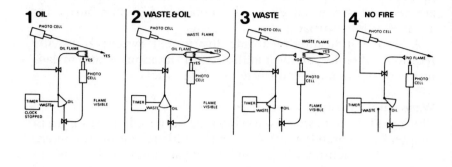

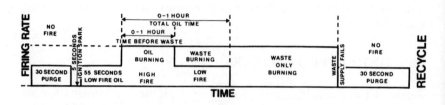

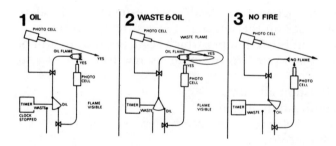

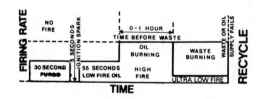

12.1   Photo cell control for low moisture content (above) and high moisture content (below)

boiler temperature has fallen back to below the lower level. Thus, this differential boiler thermostat (when correctly set) prevents rapid on and off fuel input (hunting). The boiler limit thermostat (set at a specified level above the boiler control thermostat setting) will lock-out the plant if activated by temperature overrun.

The starting sequence *(from cold)* is:

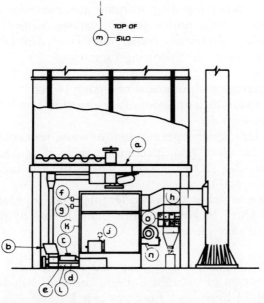

12.2   Underfeed stoker controls

Manual lighting of wood-waste pilot sample through the access door—close door and activate the inter-lock circuit when the flame has been established.

Switch on:
viewing port cooling fan, k
primary combustion air fan, c
secondary combustion air fan, d
induced draught fan, h.
Switch to automatic operation at control panel c. The boiler control thermostat, f, will then activate the fuel screw feeder which will match the boiler heat demand with the fuel input until the heat demand has been satisfied.

The silo outfeeder safety device closes the plant down when activated, as also will the sprinkler safety controls (1 and m).

When change-over to auxiliary burner operation is required, a main control panel switch will lock-out the wood-waste fuel feed mechanism and the boiler will then function as a conventional boiler.

12.10 EXTERNAL CYCLONE FURNACES

Figure **12.3** shows the diagrammatic arrangement of a cyclone furnace plant with the positions of the various controls indicated by letter; these are electrically connected to the plant central control panel and perform the following functions:

(a) Bin discharger with optional reversing switch.
(b) Rotary valve, which operates when waste fuel is to be admitted (in conjunction with a).
(c) Primary fan, which operates before waste fuel admittance.
(d) Primary fan duct relay pressure switch; if not activated in a certain time, this shuts the safety gate, stops the fuel supply and locks-out the plant.
(e) Safety gate, which is always under pneumatic operating pressure and slams shut, locking out the plant if any of the following malfunctions take place:

> non-activation of primary air pressure switch d,
> non-activation of induced draught pressure switch t,
> activation of blow-back pressure switch f,
> activation of micro-switch (explosion door) j,
> activation of boiler high pressure limit switches p,
> activation of low level water switches q,
> activation of back boiler limit temperature sensor r,
> activation of furnace door micro-switches l and m.
> failure of viewing port cooling fan,
> activation of sprinkler in silo,
> non-establishment of any specified control function within a specified time.

In the event of the loss of compressed air to operate the safety gate, the plant locks-out automatically.
(f) Furnace inlet pressure switch, which senses any reverse air flow or blow-back into the fuel feed line.
(g) Furnace temperature control sensor, usually set at 800°C (1472°F), being the lower level of furnace temperature control.
h Furnace temperature control sensor, usually set at 1000°C

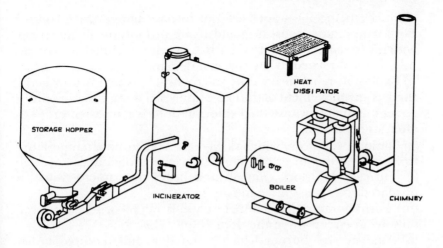

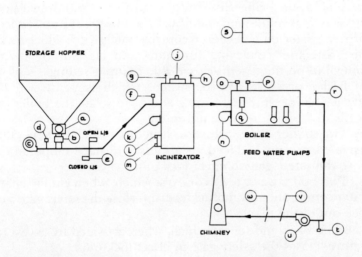

a	BIN DISCHARGER (VARIABLE SPEED)	n	MAIN OIL BURNER
b	ROTARY VALVE (" ")	o	BOILER LIMIT PRESSURE SWITCH
c	PRIMARY AIR FAN	p	" CONTROL " "
d	PRIMARY AIR PRESSURE SWITCH	q	BOILER WATER LEVEL ALARMS
e	SAFETY GATE (WITH OPEN & CLOSED LIMIT SWITCHES)	r	BOILER BACK TEMP.
f	FURNACE INLET PRESSURE SWITCH	s	HEAT DISSIPATOR
g	FURNACE TEMP (T,)	t	I.D. SUCTION SWITCH
h	" " (T₂)	u	I.D. FAN
j	EXPLOSION RELIEF LIMIT SWITCH	v	I.D. PRIMARY DAMPER
k	IGNITION OIL BURNER	w	I.D. SECONDARY "
L	FURNACE DOOR LOCK CONTROL LIMIT SWITCH		
m	" " CLOSED LIMIT SWITCH		

12.3   Cyclone furnace controls

(1832°F), being the upper level of furnace temperature control. Both temperature sensors, g and h, are proportionally integrated with the speed of the rotary valve b to provide a refined level of fuel inlet control related to the thermal demand.

(j) Explosion relief heavy-duty micro-switch, which is activated if there is any movement of the explosion relief door; this can only be re-set manually (in case the explosion door is not seated properly after an explosion).

(k) Ignition oil burner which slowly raises the furnace temperature from cold to the lower operating furnace temperature.

(l) Furnace door-lock control limit heavy duty micro-switch; if displaced, this must be manually re-set.

(m) Furnace-door-closed limit heavy duty micro-switch, which can only be in circuit when the door is fully closed.

(n) Auxiliary oil burner which is rated at full required boiler thermal input, being electrically dead in the withdrawn position and acting as a full-load standby. When brought into service, this burner is selected by a central control panel switch which locks-out the waste fuel conveying functions and amends the sequence control to permit a semi-closed flue damper setting.

(o) Boiler pressure control switch, which is connected to the furnace temperature sensors, g and h, to relate the boiler output needs to the fuel input requirement.

(p) Two boiler limit pressure switches, which, when either is activated, prevent fuel feed, regardless of furnace temperature, and close the safety gate to effect lock-out.

(q) Two boiler water level controls, which, when either senses low water condition, prevent fuel feed and close the safety gate to effect lock-out of the plant.

(r) Boiler back-end sensor which, when activated by excess temperature, closes the safety gate to effect lock-out.

(s) Heat dissipators which, when activated automatically, dump the excess boiler heat output (usually to the atmosphere).

(t) Induced draught pressure (suction) switch which, if not satisfied within a specified time period, locks-out the plant.

(u) Induced draft fan which operates in sequence before waste fuel admittance.

(v) Induced draught primary damper which is automatically set fully open for waste fuel input and is set into a semi-closed position for full stand-by auxiliary oil burner operation.

(w) Induced draught fan secondary damper which is automatically moved to a semi-closed position when the ignition oil burner operates in sequence and moves to full open position just before waste fuel admittance when the minimum specified furnace temperature has been reached.

The cyclone plant logic sequence controller, housed in the central control panel, dictates the following sequence of operation functions. (If any function is not established in strict order, the controller recycles to the start of the sequence (plant shut down) with eventual lock-out if non-establishment of any one function persists.)

From cold
Induced draught fan ON, u
Induced draught secondary damper moved to semi-closed position, w
Ignition oil burner ON, k
When lower furnace temperature control sensor is satisfied g, then
Ignition oil burner OFF
Induced draught primary and secondary dampers move to fully-open positions, v and w
Safety gate is opened, e
Primary fan ON, c
Bin discharger and rotary valve ON
Waste fuel admitted to furnace.

When the plant is closed down automatically or when there is a change over to the stand-by oil burner, the logic sequence controller must allow the establishment of each plant function and initiate the immediate plant lock-out when any of the overriding safety features are activated. The sequence controller cannot be altered, except by the insertion of a different programme.

12.11 MEASURING AND METERING DEVICES

In addition to the essential controls, gauges and instruments, there are available a number of desirable measuring devices which assist greatly in the correct operation of the plant and in the accurate assessment of the plant efficiency. In the employment of such devices, it is essential that the manufacturers' installation structions are obtained and are strictly obeyed.

Temperature
Temperature indicators are designed to display the operating conditions received from the resistance thermometer or thermocouple elements. An indicator may be arranged to function in conjunction with an external cold junction, but standard indicators have electronic cold junction compensation. Where multi-point installations are required, it is possible to obtain a multi-point

control-panel-mounted switch box. Provisions may also be incorporated for clearly stated service legends, so that each individual measuring point is identified.

Compact multi-channel potentiometric temperature recorders provide simultaneous continuous recording; three pens overlapping across a full width chart (100 mm) provide easy identification when using different coloured inks. Modular construction provides additional recording channel facility; a multi-speed electronic gear box may be fitted to the chart synchronous motor drive system to give the required rate of multi-channel recording.

High temperature thermometers (pyrometers) are used to measure the flue gas temperature. These instruments may be of either the nitrogen filled, mercury-in-steel or electrical type.

Fluid flow

Compressible fluid (air, steam, etc) may be measured by the insertion of either an orifice plate, Dall tube, Venturi, or pitot tube in a pipeline. The primary element may be operated through the differential pressures (dp) achieved by the insertion of such a device. This dp moves a liquid filled differential bellows unit and (in turn) transfers the movement through a torque tube to a linkage assembly. For differing gases, the shape of the orifice plate or primary element is selected in relation to the relevant Reynolds number, the wetness, dirtiness, specific gravity and the corrosive properties of the gas.

Care must be exercised in the location of such instrument primary elements, as smooth, even laminar flow of fluid is necessary for accurate flow measurement. Installation instructions should be carefully followed to avoid the proximity of the primary element to pipe changes of direction (eg bends, elbows, junctions) and turbulent flow conditions.

Non-compressible fluid or liquid flow meters may be simple vane or piston displacement types, the specification and choice depending on viscosity, specific gravity, dirtiness and the corrosive properties of the liquid.

Liquid level recorders include the pressure bulb type which senses the pressure of liquid at the bottom of a tank and correctly proportions this pressure to the height of the liquid above the bulb. Float type recorders are primarily used in open or vented vessels, where the vertical motion of the float and of the counterweight is transmitted to the pulley and then, via gears and linkage, to the recording pen. Bubbler type recorders use the principle of air bleed through a pipe to the liquid; the air pressure required to displace the liquid in the pipe is proportional to the liquid head above the pipe opening. A pressure recorder, calibrated in terms of depth, measures the bleed air pressure and records the depth of liquid on a chart.

Pressure

Absolute pressure recorders may consist of a single evacuated capsular element mounted inside a pressure-tight housing. The pressure medium being measured acts against the exterior surface of the capsular element, causing it to contract in direct proportion to the applied pressure. The resulting motion is transmitted from the housing through a bellows-sealed lever arm to the recording pen.

Special helical elements are used for high pressure measurement; virtually every industrial application can be subjected to the use of helical and capsular elements for the recording of pressure, vacuum and compound pressure and vacuum.

Smoke density

The measurement of the smoke density of the flue gas discharged is achieved by the projection of a parallel beam of light across the chimney or flue duct to a photo-sensitive cell to produce a photo-electric signal which is fed to a remotely situated indicator unit and gives a Ringleman scales reading which is proportional to the intensity of the received light beam (ie to the extent by which the light transmission is obscured by the flue gas).

Provision is usually made for a visual and/or audible alarm signal to indicate whenever the smoke concentration in the chimney exceeds a (variable) predetermined level. A time delay (five seconds) of alarm condition is required to activate alarms; an alarm-mute with a timer ensures automatic reinstatement of the alarm after approximately three minutes until the fault is corrected. There must be an arrangement for keeping the viewing system clean (air purge). A continuous recording device may be integrated into the assembly as shown in fig 12.4.

Carbon dioxide (CO_2)

Measurement of the carbon dioxide (CO_2) content of the flue gases is an esential item in the establishment of the furnace boiler efficiency; correctly interpreted, this specifies the proportion of excess air in the flue gas. Various CO_2 measuring instruments are available, some based on the relative electrical or thermal conductivity of the flue gases, some on relative mass and some on chemical reaction, such as the Orsat apparatus. In chemical sampling a sample of the flue gas is dried to remove the water vapour and then absorbed by caustic soda to remove CO_2, by pyrogallol to remove O_2 (oxygen) and then by acid (cuprous chloride) to remove CO (carbon monoxide).

Each proportion of the absorbed gas is measured and then subjected to volumetric analysis. For an acceptable optimum furnace combustion efficiency, the CO must be minimised and the CO_2 content maximised.

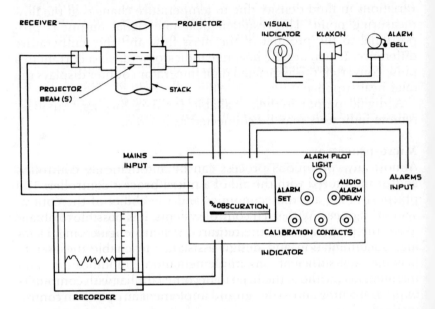

12.4   Smoke density measurement

Oxygen analysers assist in determining the amount of excess air in the flue gases and in the optimisation of the flue gas operating conditions.

Pneumatic
Pneumatic controllers are used to automatically record and control temperature, pressure, absolute pressure, differential pressure, vacuum, flow and liquid level conditions, providing fast response and optimum control stability. Indicating and recording units of this type are particularly suitable for furnace plant operation because of their ruggedness, simplicity and dependability.

Heat meters
Heat meters are used to measure the boiler thermal onput. The rate

of fluid flow is determined by a transmitter which senses the differential pressure across a primary element located in the pipeline and transmits this to a square root extractor within the computer unit of the heat meter. The output from this extractor acts as the input to a bridge network.

Resistance thermometers, which sense the temperature difference across the load, constitute two arms of the bridge which is so arranged that the computer unit compensates automatically for variations in fluid density due to temperature changes at the flow measuring point. The resultant heat rate signal output is proportional to the product of the mass flow and the temperature difference. It actuates the heat rate indicator and, via a current to a pulse converter, the associated digit integrator counter displays the total heat supplied.

A digital output is then available for data logging. Auxiliary remote indicators may be connected as desired.

Micro-processors

Almost any continuous process can be automatically controlled and/or monitored with the aid of a micro-process controller. The practical limits are the economics and the ability of the control system engineer. With such control systems, it is possible to obtain (from the manufacturer) the required systems engineering, training, documentation and design assistance to enable the user to become self-sufficient in implementation, modification and maintenance, without the need to become familiar with computers or programming and to design and implement an optimum control method.

The process operator panel allows operators (with access rights) to modify or completely change the control scheme, change set points, read signals, determine values and completely re-wire all points in the control system. Micro-processors are programmed to perform operations which are identical to those accomplished by components such as timers, counters, integrators, programmable controllers, calculators, etc. The user requires only sufficient knowledge to prepare a block diagram of his specific control scheme.

12.12 SWITCH GEAR

Central control panels or cubicles are usually designed for the accommodation and interconnection of the switch gear components, such as main isolator bus-bars electrical starting equipment, transformers, etc. The centralisation of this equipment is convenient and conducive to safety; the access doors must be interlocked with the main isolator to render the panel electrically dead when the doors are opened. A mains override facility is usually provided within the panel for authorised attendance and maintenance, usually operated by a key-switch. Alternatively, the panel doors can be opened only by authorised personnel with suitable security key-operated locks.

Many switch gear components are generally not flame-proof. Electric spark ignition is a common cause of fire and explosion; switch gear housed in dust-proof enclosures is obviously safer.

Flame-proof control components are available, but in the case of a high fire-risk, it is essential that all switch gear is mounted outside the high risk areas. Provided a boiler house is kept clean, it is not usually considered to be of high fire risk. In the event of electrical mains interruption (maintenance or power cut), it is essential to ensure that no hazard is caused by such interruption. Time switches should therefore be fitted with spring reserve mechanisms, controls must be of the fail-safe type and the emergency lighting system should protect strategic maintenance positions.

12.13 PORTABLE MEASURING INSTRUMENTS

Many different portable instruments are available to assist in the efficient day-to-day operation of a plant. Some of these are described below.

The simple vane anemometer, shown in plate 67, will assist in the determination of draught conditions surrounding a dust extract hood. It may also be used to check the entry and exit velocities at grilles and has many other practical uses.

The instrument shown in plate 68 which operates on a thermal principle, provides an instant reading of air velocities.

The sling psychrometer shown in plate 69 is a most useful, inexpensive aid to the determination of ambient temperatures. It indicates the wet and the dry bulb temperatures.

The relative humidity is then obtained from a prepared reference chart or table. Plate 70 shows a recording hygrometer which measures and records the temperature and humidity conditions in a space. This is useful for areas where waste is bulk-stored and where the waste moisture gain is critical and must be monitored.

A portable temperature sensing device is an invaluable aid in the checking of pipe temperatures for balancing purposes.

Other portable test equipment, such as water sampling devices, flue gas analysers, etc, should be stored with the portable measuring instruments in a safe lockable (but readily accessible) cupboard.

The instruments must be maintained in good working order. Preferably, one person should be in charge of the instrument inventory.

12.14 HEAT BALANCE AND EFFICIENCY TESTS

The correct evaluation of the efficiency of a waste burning plant with energy recovery is not an easy task. The combustion efficiency may be represented by:

$$\frac{\text{The useful heat regenerated - minus all system losses}}{\text{The heat release in the fuel when completely burnt.}}$$

To establish the amount of useful generated heat, an instrument such as a heat meter (for hot water) or a steam flow meter is used and the result should be fairly dependable, given reliable meters.

The major energy losses are:

Heat losses from the boiler. These are usually assessed relative to boiler size and insulation quality.

The heat content of the flue gases and excess air are determined by measurement. The sensible and latent heat content of the steam caused by the combustion of hydrogen must also be accounted in this loss. Mass flow is proportional to excess combustion air quantity, which may be assessed from the CO_2 and/or the O_2 flue gas analysis.

The heat release from waste (fuel) when completely burnt, is not capable of exact measurement, such as fuel oil or gas which can be accurately metered and which are fairly consistent in terms of calorific value. Waste quality varies considerably over any given period, the variables being bulk density, moisture content, ash content and calorific value. It is only possible to assess the heat release of a typical sample and, by fuel feed measurement, the potential continuous heat release may then be approximated. Grit, ash, carbon and sulphur tests on samples taken from grit arrestors indicate the losses due to unburnt fuel.

The construction of an accurate heat balance for a major sophisticated plant is a technical exercise which is best carried out by a fuel technologist.

CHECK LIST

Check: that reliable temperature and/or pressure gauges are fitted to all presure vessels; the operation of safety valves regularly; by simulation, each possible control malfunction, particularly limit and safety switches, to ensure correct operation in the event of an emergency; the correct operation of control and safety devices after each plant closure; the validity of gauges, indicating and recording instruments at regular intervals; any abnormal control indication trend, even though lock-out has not been effected; that essential spares are always at hand; the operational readiness of all fire extinguishing equipment, particularly that adjacent to switch gear; all inter-locks and do not disconnect for maintenance convenience (such malpractice is common and is dangerous); that all manu-facturers' instructions and wiring diagrams are at hand and take good care of controls and instruments on a planned maintenance basis.

13
Operation and Safety

13.1 INTRODUCTION

There are numerous dangers and risks to lives and property in the operating and maintenance of waste recycling plants related particularly to explosive dust, noxious materials, environmental pollution, the handling of unhygienic matter and unsafe, mechanical and electrical practices.

3.2 THE LAW

Many laws, regulations and codes (eg The Health and Safety at Work Act in the UK) endeavour to provide a legal framework within which all unskilled and skilled activity should be conducted. Every manager should be familiar with legislation and possess all relevant codes of practice. He must ensure the provision of appropriate procedures, adequate protection equipment and clothing as well as their correct practice and use, or run the risk of being held responsible for injury and damage. The law usually penalises a negligent employer.

13.3 SAFETY

The key to safety lies in education and in the compulsory implementation of safe and comprehensive servicing procedures and related standing orders. Where strict compliance with procedures and orders inconveniences the operator or work processes, it is frequently the case that ignorance or deliberate non-compliance jeopardises continued safety. For example it is not uncommon to observe an experienced boilerman examining a white-hot furnace bed at close quarters without wearing protection gear though this is at hand. A pocket of sander dust admitted through the feed line at the moment might cause a damaging blow-back or minor explosion.

13.4 OPERATING MANAGEMENT

When equipment does not receive adequate maintenance and attention, the result is not only inevitable break-down, but also a threat to safety. The preparation and adoption of well planned maintenance schedules goes hand-in-hand with safe operation.

Plate 71 shows a badly neglected, fouled and unsafe water tube boiler combustion chamber open for inspection and overhaul.

13.5 GUIDE-LINES

The following checklist is intended as a guide. It should be interpreted sensibly and in a practical manner, with an overriding consideration for safety.

Furnaces

Do not open furnace doors or inspection ports by disconnecting inter-locks which prevent such opening. Always protect eyes and face and wear protection gear.

Do not, under any circumstances, open the ash door of an operating cyclone furnace; inter-locks to prevent such opening must be provided.

Allow adequate time to elapse for furnace refractories to cool before opening furnace doors or ports when shutting down furnaces for overhaul or maintenance.

Be aware of the furnace design pressure (whether positive, negative or neutral) and the related likelihood of injury or fire, which might be caused by the opening of furnace doors or ports.

Periodically check the primary and secondary fuel feed air settings to ensure complete and smokeless combustion.

Ensure that the incoming air supply to the boiler house is sufficient for combustion purposes and that additional adequate input and exhaust air is available for comfort and operating needs (particularly in respect of the electrical equipment). Plate 73 shows permanent input ventilation louvres at low level to ensure adequate air for combustion purposes.

Periodically check slag, clinker and ash to ensure that there is no carbon or other combustible matter, which has passed unburnt through the combustion chamber. The presence of such material, when present in large quantities, indicates poor combustion efficiency and is not acceptable.

Check for satisfactory clinker collapse and ash removal from the fuel bed during furnace operation. Excessive build-up of clinker or ash interferes with the adequate circulation of combustion air.

Periodically, view the top of the chimney for signs of excess smoke, even though an automatic smoke detector and alarm may exist. If there is excess smoke, take immediate remedial action to avoid contravention of Clean Air Laws and fouling of the heat exchanger/waste heat boiler. Carry out furnace combustion efficiency tests at regular intervals to ensure clean continuous plant operation; observe and record instrument readings in a prepared log book on an appropriate time basis (eg hourly, daily, weekly).

Check furnace explosion relief doors and panels to ensure their working. They may not work correctly in an emergency, unless they are kept in good order.

Check furnace dampers and linkages to ensure free and easy movement; dampers which are subject to high temperature tend to stick in position and when least expected.

Check all fail-safe devices and controls. Carry out routine fail-safe checks and simulate emergencies to ensure that these devices will definitely function when called upon to do so.

Check the refractories during shut-down periods for signs of spalling, corrosion, splitting, bond deterioration, damage and general signs of wear and tear. Instruct urgent corrective measures; do not permit prolonged exposure of the insulating brick or metal surface to excessive and damaging heat.

Check all furnace seals, such as the asbestos rope packing at doors and inspection ports.

Ensure that slag deposits are removed from the surfaces of refractories, but take care not to damage the surfaces of the brickwork during such operations. When in doubt, it is better to leave a thin film of slag on the brick.

Unnecessary damage to the refractories must be avoided.

Check that all fire detection and extinguishing devices in near proximity to furnaces are in working order.

Check that all quick-release mechanisms operate correctly.

Check that the access spaces for routine operation and maintenance to, from, around and on top of the furnaces are kept clear and unobstructed. Under no circumstances must solid waste fuel and/or associated dust be stored close to a furnace.

Ensure that all operators are made familiar with the type of furnace being operated by reference to the manufacturers' catalogues, the maintenance schedules, the system charts, the wiring diagram, and by carefully thought out and documented training methods. Under no circumstances must an operator be allowed to be in charge if he does not fully understand the plant, the equipment, the mode or sequence of operation, the controls, all safety devices and the emergency procedures.

Ensure that the correct tools for operating and maintenance are always at hand and that these are maintained in good condition. In addition to the cleaning and fire-bed tools such as rakes, flue brushes, long chisels, etc, other hand tools such as levers, keys, hand spanners, hammers, screw drivers, etc, should be readily accessible at all times. Valve keys and other essential operating implements should be duplicated.

Keep essential spares in stock, in particular items prone to frequent failure, rapid deterioration or extended delivery periods. Maintain an updated record of such spares, if appropriate incorporate with the computerised stock control.

Maintain and stock comprehensive and clearly labelled first aid medical supplies. Ensure that all operators know how to deal with likely emergencies such as burns and electric shock.

Flues, grit arrestors and chimneys

Maintain in good condition the internal and external surfaces of all flue gas exhaust equipment. The peeling and flaking of paint is common with high temperature surfaces; keep a record of special paint requirement and hold suitable stocks.

Plate 72 shows a cyclone wood-waste furnace and boiler down for overhaul. Notice paint flaking on the furnace shell. If paint flaking is confined to cooler parts of a refractory lined flue gas system, this usually indicates flue gas leakage through the refractories to the outer steel shell and should be investigated immediately.

Watch for signs of internal corrosion and pitting of metal surfaces. This may indicate a defect in a plant item or operation and should be evaluated for appropriate remedial action.

Remove accumulated grit from grit arrestors at regular intervals. Observe whether unburnt combustible matter is deposited with the grit; and if so, check the plant operation for defects. Periodically weigh the amount of grit collected from grit arrestors over a period of time related to furnace fuel feed to ensure no excess emission of grit and dust.

Observe and maintain instruments, such as smoke meters, monitoring thermometers, pressure switches, gauges, etc, and keep same clean and in operating condition, paying special attention to the continued cleanliness of viewing lenses (eg of smoke density detector).

Attend to damper settings. At flue gas temperatures, these tend to 'stick'; if incorrectly set, the efficiency of the furnace operation will be reduced and a dangerous condition may arise in consequence.

The induced draught fan bearings must be checked and lubricated at regular intervals. The development of unusual noises, such as screeching or knocking, may indicate lack of lubrication, out-of-balance, a worn bearing or loosened holding down bolt.

Boiler bypass furnace systems or wet flue gas washing processes require regular inspection of the washing system to ensure free and unobstructed water spray and sludge-free water sump. Frequent instrument checks should be carried out; failure of the gas cooling or cleaning facilities (by pump malfunction, for example) must lock-out the fuel feed system. Regular maintenance should be carried out and particular attention paid to the prevention of corrosion within flue gas tubes and passageways.

Examine the external flue cladding and chimney surfaces for signs of damage in high wind condition. Excessive staining of the chimney and/or gas streaking marks at the chimney joints indicates flue gas leakage, which must be investigated and rectified.

Examine the condition of the chimney interior above the furnace flue entry where surfaces should be free of corrosion. If internal condensation is evident, check the flue gas temperature at the top of the stack. The gas efflux must be above the dew-point temperature.

Ensure that chimneys and flue passage-ways are kept clean.

Periodically examine the chimney supports, access ladders, guy ropes, strainers and fixings for damage, loosening or deterioration.

Excessively high temperatures in boiler houses are usually caused by the heat emission from exposed high temperature surfaces from pipes, flues, grit arrestors, induced draught fans, chimney connections and the like. Check that all possible thermal insulation has been provided and that this remains in good order. The boiler house ventilation provisions must be adequate to limit the ambient air temperature.

Ensure that electrical wiring is not in contact with, or in close proximity to, high temperature surfaces.

Ensure that access platforms, ladders, gantries, etc, are maintained with care and that operating and maintenance personnel do not undertake dangerous tasks single-handed.

Boilers and furnace fuel feed lines

Check that standby/auxiliary gas or oil burners are not live (electrically) when in the withdrawn position.

Check that standby/auxiliary burners can neither discharge gas nor spray oil into a solid fuel combustion chamber as this type of operational malfunction constitutes a major explosion hazard. Whether the furnace is hot or cold no attempt should be made to ignite either the solid or auxiliary fuel until the furnace has been purged in the correct sequence and the defect has been rectified.

The excess air requirement for standby/auxiliary or ignition burners is usually less than that required for solid fuel burnt in the same furnace. When changing over from one fuel to another, check that the correct damper positions have been set and that combustion is satisfactory.

Ensure the protection from exposure to high temperature (by fan cooling or other means) of standby auxiliary and ignition burners. Following only momentary unprotected exposure to an operating furnace, do not attempt to re-use the auxiliary burner without a close inspection or overhaul, since it may be damaged and its use dangerous.

Check periodically whether there are deposits of fly ash and grit in the boiler tubes and flue gas ways. The presence of excessive fly ash usually indicates inadequate draught. Keep all flue-side heat exchanger surfaces clean.

Check regularly that all boiler fail-safe devices and alarm systems operate as intended. Boiler pressure switches, thermostats, relays and magnetic valves, etc, may fail if not regularly checked in the fail-safe mode.

The practice of installing only one non-return damper in pneumatic furnace feed lines is unsafe.

At least two such non-return dampers should be fitted in the absence of a recommended fail-safe, tight-closing safety gate. Such dampers must be carefully maintained, since damper failure can expose the waste material feed line to furnace temperature and the consequent risk of fire spread and explosion.

Periodically, check and lift all boiler safety valves for correct pressure relief and seating. The safety valve discharge pipes must terminate externally to the boiler house. A continuous discharge or dripping from the drain termination indicates a safety valve defect.

Steam boiler high pressure and low water alarm system, water gauges, feed and water level controls require close attention during all operating periods.

Correct operation of the steam boiler blow-down system is essential to control the specified operating water condition within the boiler and to avoid energy losses. Great care must be exercised during blow-down procedures, particularly if the pipe conveying trench and the blow-down pit are not totally enclosed and are not fitted with adequate vent pipe for discharge of the flash steam to a safe place. Uncontrolled discharge of live steam, even at low pressure, can be very dangerous and damaging.

Blow-down operation should be closely monitored and be followed by sample checking of the boiler water condition until the correct blow-down quantities have been accurately established. Periodic sample checks should be carried out to ensure that there is no deviation or malfunction of the automatic blow-down devices.

Routine sampling of the boiler feed water should be carried out with regular checks of the water treatment equipment and its correct operation. Do not allow raw untreated water to be introduced into a steam boiler system which requires continuous make-up water.

Steam traps, dirt pockets, strainers and sight glasses require frequent routine inspection and servicing to ensure their correct function, as high grade energy will be wasted if these are not well maintained.

Check the interior of the condensate and treated water storage tanks for signs of corrosion; ensure that ball valves operate freely and that there are no wasteful overflow discharges.

Frequently check the correct operation of valves. Re-pack seals if necessary, remove encrustation and always ensure easy unrestricted operation. Particularly check the standby valves, which may only seldom be operated.

Ensure that all gauges function correctly by testing, particularly those indicating conditions within pressure vessels.

Do not allow raw untreated water to be introduced into any hot water boiler, even though there may be only nominal water losses from the system. Occasional sampling is necessary to ensure that the circulating water is not corrosive and is of acceptable condition.

Water pressurisation systems and alarms require routine observation.

Check all boiler feed, sump and lift pumps at regular intervals. Ensure that all non-return and foot valves and strainers are free from sludge and debris which may collect in pits and sumps. Water level trip connections should also be thoroughly checked at the same time.

Provide routine attention to feed and water circulating pumps, particularly if the bearings are water-cooled. Ensure optimum flow of cooling water and always visually inspect the tundishes and drains for unrestricted discharge.

Daily routine checking of the boiler feed water controls is essential, with special attention to needle and test valves.

Check all electric switch gear, isolators, contactors, relays, fuses etc, at least once each year or more frequently if the environment is dusty or hot. Examine cable terminals for correct fit and signs of wear. Renew any suspect wiring and electrical components.

Check and maintain the light fittings and systems. Ensure that there are adequate hand lamps for 'dark corner' inspection and for internal examination of boilers, heat exchangers, furnaces, etc.

Ensure that the correct tools are available and readily to hand for operational maintenance and safety of boilers and fuel feed systems. Follow the various manufacturers' recommendations. Stack the operating tools, valve keys, and the like separately from cleaning tools where possible. Provide well arranged tool racks and boxes. Maintain an adequate stock of essential spares. Record and replace this stock at regular intervals. Fuses, pressure switches, relays, high temperature controls and other regularly needed spares should be at hand at all times.

Observe all requirements of the insurance companies and particularly prepare the plant for required insurance inspection.

Plate 75 shows a shell-type steam boiler mud hole open for inspection.

Extraction conveying and storage systems

The factory or workshop in which the waste originates should be kept neat, tidy and well swept.

Floor suction sweep positions should be left unobstructed by equipment and kept free of material which is likely to cause blockages in the extraction system.

Flexible connections to the extraction ducts and hoods are susceptible to external damage, which is then likely to allow the escape of waste material and dust. The connections must be inspected frequently and kept in good repair

Dust creating machinery should be totally enclosed with minimum interference to the operator. Check that all such machines remain suitably enclosed; do not allow unnecessary escape of dust.

Avoid the entrainment of metal objects in the extraction system, unless the system is specifically designed for that purpose. Spark-producing abrasive objects, travelling at high speed with explosive dust within a metal duct, are likely to cause fire or explosion. The most common cause of such metal object entrainment and hazard is from floor sweepings, such as nails and screws carelessly dropped and then swept into the extraction system.

The clean-out doors in the extraction system should be regularly inspected and test operated. Extraction systems should be kept continuously clean for efficient operation.

Check that the explosion relief panels are maintained in working order and that they comply with relevant safety regulations.

Dry-type centrifugal collectors, such as arresting cyclones, do not, as a rule, require close attention. Once set, they should continue to operate efficiently. If dust is escaping from the top of a cyclone, adjustment is required to the cyclone or to the process. Cyclones are not very good dust arrestors, unless they are of a special high efficiency type.

Plate 74 shows a waste collection cyclone in need of maintenance (extensive paint deterioration); note also a badly stained uninsulated chimney.

Fabric type dust collectors require frequent maintenance, since filters and filter bags must be kept clean at all times to operate efficiently. The provision of automatic compressed air cleaning and shaking reduces maintenance. Such cleaners and shakers (whether in readily accessible positions or fitted to the tops of silos) must be well maintained at all times.

An adequate quantity of spare filter fabric or filter bags must be kept in store.

All equipment with moving parts, such as fans, pumps and compressors must be kept free from dust and moisture. Adequate lubrication and physical protection is essential.

Check fan belt alignment and belt tightening at regular intervals and carry spare belts in stock.

Ensure that hogger or chipper knives, blades and cutting edges are always maintained in good sharp working condition; arrange sharpening facilities and procedures. Knives working on very hard woods require very frequent sharpening. Keep a stock of spare knives. Do not allow this type of high horsepower machinery to operate inefficiently. Maintain the drive mechanism alignment, etc, on a regular basis.

Metal detectors, separators, alarm systems and other specialised equipment must be maintained in accordance with the manufacturers' written instructions and to standing orders, which must include an orderly shut-down of feed line in the event of failure.

Conveyor belts tend to fail, usually because of oversized material (such as large lumps of wood) being fed into the system. Carry out frequent checks on feed methods and systems and regularly maintain chain drives, linkages, belts and motors.

Silo maintenance is straightforward and simple, if the stored material is neither oversized nor wet and if the screw feeders, bin dischargers and rotary valves are continuously maintained in good working order.

Be aware of the quantity of waste in store at any one time. Maintain and observe the level indicators.

Level gauges or indicators fitted to silos tend to be troublesome because waste levels at the perimeters are seldom consistent and because level indicators (whether electrical or mechanical) are difficult to maintain in what are often almost inaccessible locations. Visual transparent panels are sometimes preferred and considerably reduce maintenance; however, these must be kept clean.

The explosion relief panels should be checked periodically. It is essential that there is no excess pressure within the silo.

Bridging of waste material is not uncommon in storage silos and is usually caused by clogging due to oversized or moist material. Provide safe means of access to the silo interior, otherwise breaking the bridge becomes a hazardous affair. With or without proper access, great care should be exercised and such operations must not be carried out single-handed.

Periodic routine checks should be carried out on silo, sprinkler, smoke detector and lighting systems.

Compressed air systems should be maintained free from dirt and collected moisture to allow efficient operation. Water separators and filters should be regularly checked.

Each silo must be fitted with top perimeter balustrading. Access ladders should be hooped with top hold-bars. Non-slip surfaces must be maintained in good condition.

The spontaneous combustion of stored industrial waste is rare, but may be caused by a build-up of heat within the silo and by the inability of the store to dissipate such heat. If the ignition temperature of dust within the silo is exceeded, there may be a fire or an explosion. Particular care should be exercised when storing organic substances. Adequate silo vents must be provided and kept clear.

Provide and maintain communication links with the emergency services especially when dust, the material most vulnerable to hazards, is being handled and stored.

General
Good housekeeping is essential. Clean and tidy waste handling and burning equipment and their enclosures are definitely safer and more accessible when well kept and well maintained.

At all times keep dust and waste debris away from hot surfaces. A clean and tidy boiler house may exist even when manual stoking methods are employed.

Means of escape in the event of fire or explosion must be left uncluttered and unobstructed.

Check that the fire-fighting (automatic or otherwise) equipment is always in working condition. Hand devices and quick release mechanisms should be regularly checked for position and operation. Periodically inspect and check the sprinkler valve, hose reels and foam fire extinguishing devices.

All gas detection, system foam protection and special risk equipment such as CO_2 and non-toxic extinguishing gas assemblies must be periodically inspected and insurance-tested.

Information concerning all items of plant and equipment should be displayed in diagramatic form in the main plant room, with the function of each item clearly illustrated. All valves should be numbered and their function indicated. Pipes and ducts should be colour-coded for quick and easy recognition.

Record drawings, manufacturers' maintenance instructions, wiring diagrams, etc, should be kept in a fire-resistant chest or suitable place, but readily accessible for inspection.

All flammable materials, such as paints and solvents should be stored in a safe independent store in accordance with relevant regulations.

The plant room floors and finishes should be carefully maintained , particularly in respect of non-slip surfaces and access equipment.

Keys to transformers and switch gear housings, control panels and other equipment, requiring access by authorised persons only, should be in the keeping of a responsible and trained operator, but readily accessible in case of emergency.

Protective clothing

Protective clothing for operators should be available and worn in all situations demanding protection. For example:

Helmets of an approved type should be worn whenever an operator (or visitor) is touring the plant.

Ear-muffs should be worn when entering a hogger chamber or other high noise level environment.

Protective gloves and safety glasses should be worn by all furnace operators, together with some robust protective shield when manually stoking.

All operators should wear approved boots with steel or non-crushable toe-caps.

Clean overalls should be provided for all operators.

High temperature furnace viewing screens should be provided for close up furnace bed examination.

Portable steel radiant shields should be available to protect operators engaged in maintenance work close to furnaces.

Mouth filters or dust masks should be provided for operators working in contaminated atmospheres.

Protective gloves should be worn when removing explosion panels, flanges, or any metal parts, which are likely to have sharp edges or be too heavy to hold when removed. Well maintained lifting gear is also essential in such operations.

Adequate local wash and sanitary facilities should be provided for operators, so that they remain close to the plant.

Hazardous maintenance

Hazardous maintenance operations should be planned and carried out with great care. For example, operators should be paired in such circumstances when:

Inspecting tops of silos or other high climbing requirement.
Bagging-off from the bottom of a cyclone to avoid dust spillage.
Welding in any area where dust is being handled (welding must not be permitted in the direct presence of dust).
Hot ash and clinker removal.
Cleaning of flammable liquid vessels and containers, such as auxiliary oil tanks.
Boiler chemical cleaning.
Maintenance work within any boiler smoke box, silo, cyclone furnace, lift or other item of plant where a man might become trapped.
Manual blow-down operation.

Plate 76 shows the welding repair of an induced draught fan duct flanged connection to a chimney.

As a further general principle take pride in maintaining plant, even to the extent of polishing copper and brassware; a clean and pleasant environment is compatible with safety.

CHECK LIST

Check: the risks and dangers associated with the operation of the particular plant; the incidence of the national and local laws and codes on the design and operation of the complex; the training programmes and demonstrations in respect of personnel and equipment safety; the schemes and planning of routine maintenance schedules and activities; the special requirements relating to furnaces; the special requirements relating to flues, grit arrestors and chimneys; the special requirements relating to boilers and furnace feed lines; the special requirements relating to extraction conveying and storage systems; on matters relating to good housekeeping procedures; on the inventory of protective clothing related to the particular project; on the precautions necessary when carrying out hazardous maintenance operations.

14
The Future

What of the future?

During the latter part of the 16th century, firewood grew very scarce in England and the price escalated rapidly and painfully. In direct consequence, the population turned to an alternative fuel-coal. From small beginnings, King Coal reigned supreme for nearly 400 years, fuelling the industrial revolution, the great railways, the fast steam ships across the oceans and the ever rising standards of living in the industrialised world.

In the final years of the 20th century, the consumers of energy are again faced with the realisation that their favourite convenience fuels – oil and gas – are indeed exhaustible. Many prophets of gloom forecast damaging shortages, industrial recession, falling standards of living and worldwide disaster as the diminishing supplies of gas and oil command ever higher prices.

The authors point to the lesson of the 16th century and rely on the great upsurge in the massive technology, which has been developed and accumulated in modern times, to confound the pessimists. They are optimistic as regards the longer term prospects for the supply of abundant energy (30 to 50 years in the future) which must surely come from gasified coal, nuclear fission, solar power and from other marvels of science which may be hitherto unpublicised or unknown. The immediate challenge which faces the present generation is the construction of an energy bridge between current procedures and the eventual availability of cheap and abundant energy; it is hoped that this book will make a major contribution to this effect.

In the field of waste recycling, certain predictable developments are likely.

The encouragement at the highest government levels of waste recycling in the national interest by fiscal measures and exhortation.

The maximum energy recovery from all types of furnaces to

achieve the highest possible utilisation of the energy potential in the fuel.

The recovery of metals and raw materials from plant effluents before these are irrevocably discharged to waste.

The disciplined, orderly collection of municipal waste and the separation of it for the recovery of valuable useful materials. The production and efficient use of densified waste-derived fuels.

The adaptation of power stations and boilers to the combustion of waste-derived fuels and, in suitable locations, of shredded refuse, on a large scale.

The wide application of combined power and heat schemes (CPH) to provide district heating and hot water to industrial, commercial and residential consumers, accompanied by the development of effective and efficient methods of metering such heat supply.

The adoption of the heat pump by which low grade energy can be upgraded at a thermal and cost advantage.

The exploitation of solar energy for the heat supply to swimming pools, industrial, commercial and residential applications.

Co-operation between manufacturers and consumers to establish recycling procedures relating to containers and packaging. The incorporation of recycled materials within the manufacturing flow-sheet.

A major drive towards energy self-sufficiency in small communities, such as farms, animal breeders, universities and prisons, by the production of heat and power from waste, using Biogas.

The recycling of animal waste products to animal feed and fertiliser.

The growing of energy efficient plants, such as trees, to provide a renewable source of energy; the utilisation of such energy without waste.

The widespread adoption of in-house waste recycling to replace conventional fuel, by pyrolisis and incineration.

The above list cannot be exhaustive, as new ideas and applications for the recycling of waste will undoubtedly accompany growing shortages of energy and of certain raw materials. The totality of such measures is likely to form an important component of any overall policy for the conservation of energy and resources.

Index

Page numbers in italics indicate figures or tables in the text. Plate numbers are printed in bold type.

AVOIDING FAILURE OF LEACHATE COLLECTION AND CAP DRAINAGE SYSTEMS

AVOIDING FAILURE OF LEACHATE COLLECTION AND CAP DRAINAGE SYSTEMS

by

Jeffrey Bass

Arthur D. Little, Inc.
Cambridge, Massachusetts

NOYES DATA CORPORATION

Park Ridge, New Jersey, U.S.A

1986

$$\overset{)}{628 \cdot 445}$$
$$BAS$$

Library of Congress Cataloging-in-Publication Data

Bass, Jeffrey.
    Avoiding failure of leachate collection and cap
drainage systems.

    (Pollution technology review, ISSN 0090-516X ;
no. 138)
    Bibliography: p.
    Includes index.
    1. Hazardous waste sites--United States--Leaching.
2. Sanitary landfills--United States--Leaching.
3. Leachate. 4. Drainage. I. Title. II. Series.
TD811.5.B36   1986   628.4'45   86-18191
ISBN 0-8155-1106-X

Foreword

Avoiding failure in leachate collection systems is the subject of this study, which covers design, construction, inspection, maintenance, and repair aspects of these systems. Today's rapidly developing and changing technologies and industrial products and practices frequently carry with them the increased generation of solid and hazardous wastes. These materials, if improperly dealt with, can threaten both public health and the environment. Abandoned waste sites and accidental releases of toxic and hazardous substances to the environment also have important environmental and public health implications.

Failure, caused by a variety of mechanisms, is common to drainage systems of all kinds. Leachate collection and cap drainage systems, which remove excess liquid from hazardous waste land disposal facilities, are no exception. Failure of these systems, however, may be a greater cause for concern than failure, for example, of agricultural drainage systems. This is especially true for leachate collection systems at hazardous waste disposal facilities. Undetected failures may cause leachate to build up on top of the liner. This can lead to failure of the liner system and contamination of groundwater. Furthermore, failures which are detected may be difficult to repair, and replacement is no longer a simple last resort since excavation of hazardous wastes would be required.

This book summarizes current knowledge and experience regarding potential failure mechanisms and presents information on factors to consider in design, construction, inspection, maintenance and repair of leachate collection and cap drainage systems. It was written to provide general guidance to design engineers, facility operators, and others involved in regulating waste facilities. It will be an important guide for those involved in the review of new and existing hazardous waste facilities.

The information in the book is from *Avoiding Failure of Leachate Collection and Cap Drainage Systems,* prepared by Jeffrey Bass of Arthur D. Little, Inc. for the U.S. Environmental Protection Agency, June 1986.

The table of contents is organized in such a way as to serve as a subject index and provides easy access to the information contained in the book.

ACKNOWLEDGEMENTS

Arthur D. Little, Inc. (ADL) prepared this document for EPA's Hazardous Waste Engineering Research Laboratory. Jonathan Herrmann was the EPA Project Officer. Input to Sections 3 and 4 of the document was provided by the E.C. Jordan Company of Portland, MA, under subcontract to ADL. Principal technical contributors to the report were Jeffrey Bass (Project Manager), Patricia Deese, John Ehrenfeld, Mildred Broome and Kate Findland for ADL, and Douglas Allen, Dirk Brunner, Guy Cote, Mark Larochelle, Matthew Muzzy and Kenneth Whittaker for E.C. Jordan.

Peer review comments on the draft report were provided by Peter Kmet of the Washington Department of Ecology, Jean-Pierre Giroud of Geoservices, Inc., and Fred Erdmann of Soil & Material Engineers, Inc. Their comments, along with those of the Project Officer, were extremely useful in preparing the final report.

NOTICE

Contents and Subject Index

1. Introduction

This document summarizes current knowledge and experience regarding potential failure mechanisms and presents information on factors to consider in design, construction, inspection, maintenance and repair of leachate collection and cap drainage systems. It was written to provide general guidance to design engineers, facility operators, and state and Federal regulatory officials. It should not be considered as a comprehensive design and operation manual for leachate collection and cap drainage systems. Detailed design and operation plans for leachate collection and cap drainage systems at a specific facility should be prepared by a qualified design engineer based on site-specific conditions.

Emphasis is placed throughout the document on avoiding failure of leachate collection systems at hazardous waste facilities. Most of the information presented for leachate collection systems can also be applied to cap drainage systems, since the basic components of the two systems are similar. Failure of cap drainage systems, however, is less critical than failure of leachate collection systems since the cap drainage system is accessible and therefore can be more readily maintained or repaired. Cap drainage systems are discussed separately in this document only when the information presented is significantly different from the discussion of leachate collection systems. The mechanisms by which drainage systems can fail and experience with these mechanisms in leachate collection systems are discussed in Section 2. Sections 3 through 6 describes the design, construction, inspection and maintenance of these systems to avoid failure. Repair of failed systems is discussed in Section 7.

A schematic of a closed landfill cell, showing the leachate collection system and the cap drainage system, is presented in Figure 1. The basic components of the leachate collection system shown are the drainage layer, the collection pipe and the filter layer. Other important components include manholes, cleanout risers, sumps, monitoring equipment and pumps. The function of these components is described in Section 3. The basic components of a cap drainage system are the drainage layer, filter layer and perimeter collection pipes. The cap drainage system collects liquid from over the cap liner which is designed to prevent liquid from infiltrating the waste.

1.1 LEACHATE GENERATION AND CONTROL

Leachate is defined as "any liquid, including any suspended components in the liquid, that has percolated through or drained from hazardous waste" (40 CFR 260.10). Leachate results from the seepage of liquid wastes (or liquids contained in primarily solid wastes) placed in the facility. Leachate is also

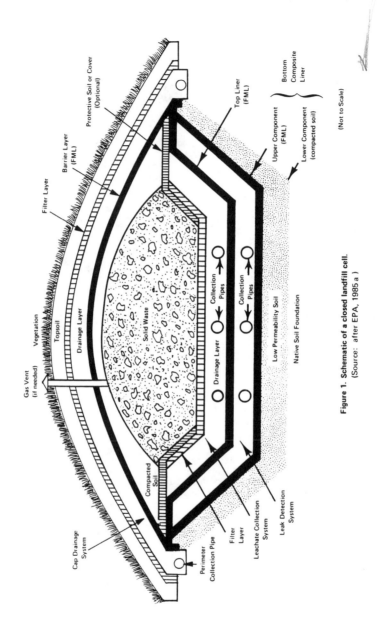

Figure 1. Schematic of a closed landfill cell.
(Source: after EPA, 1985 a)

generated when water contacts the waste mass and becomes contaminated with waste constituents.

Leachate quality depends on the amount of precipitation, type of leachate collection system, types of wastes, time and location of waste placement, and site operating methods. In general, leachate quality is difficult to predict, and may vary considerably from site to site and among different locations in the same facility. Factors affecting leachate quality are discussed in Shuckrow et al. (1982), and information on leachate quality from a number of facilities is presented in Ghassemi et al.(1983).

The quantity of leachate generated at a facility is determined by the water (or liquid) balance at the site. Liquid inputs include liquids in the deposited waste and precipitation. Groundwater flow may also contribute to leachate quantity in facilities constructed in the saturated zone (depending on liner design). Liquid outputs include evaporation, transpiration, and seepage out of the facility. Water storage in the waste mass is also important; the leachate quantity increases as the waste mass reaches saturation. Leachate generation can be minimized by controlling the various parameters in the water balance. The water balance for a facility is discussed in detail in Lutton et al. (1979), and techniques for estimating leachate volume are discussed in Perrier and Gibson (1982).

Low permeability soil and flexible membrane liners are installed to contain waste and leachate and to prevent the contamination of groundwater and surface water near the disposal facility. High leachate levels increase the potential for seepage through a liner system. Leachate collection systems are used to control leachate levels over the liner and thereby reduce the potential for leachate migration. Leachate collection systems that meet current regulatory requirements are designed to maintain liquid levels over the liner at less than 30 cm (1 ft). The system is intended to function effectively through the facility's active life and closure period and until leachate generation has ceased.

Experience with leachate collection systems is limited. The first leachate collection systems were installed in landfills in the early 1970s. Since then, design and operating practices have changed significantly. As a result, experience with "modern" leachate collection system design performance is even more limited. According to the WESTAT data base (EPA, 1983a), approximately 40 percent of the 200 landfills which accept hazardous waste have leachate collection systems. A summary of the WESTAT data pertaining to leachate collection systems is given in Table 1.

1.2 APPLICABLE FEDERAL REGULATIONS

Regulations promulgated under the Resource Conservation and Recovery Act (RCRA) require the use of leachate collection systems for new landfills and waste piles which dispose of hazardous wastes. Regulations which apply to leachate collection and cap drainage systems, or directly apply to the water balance at the site, include (40 CFR 264.301-.310):

TABLE 1

SUMMARY OF WESTAT DATA FOR LEACHATE COLLECTION SYSTEMS

	Surveyed Landfills		Estimate of all Landfills
Question	Number	Percent	Number
Active Landfill	79	100	199
Leachate Collection System (LCS)			
-yes	31	39.2	78
-no	48	60.8	121
LCS has gravel	23	74.2	58
LCS has sand	12	38.7	30
LCS has geotextile	5	16.1	12
LCS has pipe	27	87.1	67
LCS has sumps	25	80.6	62
one	14	58.3	36
two	4	16.7	10
three	1	4.2	3
four	2	8.3	5
six	2	8.3	5
seven	1	4.2	3
LCS has sump pumps	20	64.5	50
LCS has intermediate storage	21	67.7	54
in tanks	8	38.1	20
in surface impoundments	10	47.6	25
in containers	1	4.8	2
other method	3	14.3	8
Onsite leachate treatment	20	66.7	48

(continued)

TABLE 1 (continued)

Question	Surveyed Landfills Number	Surveyed Landfills Percent	Estimate of all Landfills Number
Year LCS Installed			
1973	1	3.3	2
1975	2	6.7	5
1976	3	10.0	7
1977	2	6.7	5
1978	3	10.0	7
1979	3	10.0	7
1980	6	20.0	15
1981	5	16.7	12
1982	5	16.7	12
Total Cost of Materials per LCS			
maximum	$1,470,000		
median	$ 200,000		
minimum	$ 15,000		
Quantity Leachate Collection in 1981			
maximum	5,550,000 gal		
median	22,500 gal		
minimum	0 gal		

Source: EPA, 1983a

264.301   Design and operating requirements.

(a) A landfill (except for an existing portion of a landfill) must have:

(1) A liner that is designed, constructed, and installed to prevent any migration of wastes out of the landfill to the adjacent subsurface soil or groundwater or surface water at any time during the active life (including the closure period) of the landfill. The liner must be constructed of materials that prevent wastes from passing into the liner during the active life of the facility.

(2) A leachate collection and removal system immediately above the liner that is designed, constructed, maintained, and operated to collect and remove leachate from the landfill. The Regional Administrator will specify design and operating conditions in the permit to ensure that the leachate depth over the liner does not exceed 30 cm (one foot). The leachate collection and removal system must be:

(i) Constructed of materials that are:

(A) Chemically resistant to the waste managed in the landfill and the leachate expected to be generated; and

(B) Of sufficient strength and thickness to prevent collapse under the pressures exerted by overlying wastes, waste cover materials, and by any equipment used at the landfill; and

(ii) Designed and operated to function without clogging through the scheduled closure of the landfill.

(c) The owner or operator must design, construct, operate, and maintain a runon control system capable of preventing flow onto the active portion of the landfill during peak discharge from at least a 25-year storm.

(e) Collection and holding facilities (e.g., tanks or basins) associated with runon and runoff control systems must be emptied or otherwise managed expeditiously after storms to maintain design capacity of the system.

264.302   Double-lined landfills.

(3) A leak detection system must be designed, constructed, maintained, and operated between the liners to detect any migration of liquid into the space between the liners.

264.303   Monitoring and inspection.

(b) While a landfill is in operation, it must be inspected weekly and after storms to detect evidence of any of the following:

    (1) Deterioration, malfunctions, or improper operation of runon and runoff control systems;

    (2) The presence of liquids in leak detection systems, where installed to comply with 264.302;

    (4) The presence of leachate in and proper functioning of leachate collection and removal systems, where present.

264.310   Closure and post-closure care.

(a) At final closure of the landfill or upon closure of any cell, the owner or operator must cover the landfill or cell with a final cover designed and constructed to:

    (1) Provide long-term minimization of migration of liquids through the closed landfill;

    (3) Promote drainage and minimize erosion or abrasion of the cover;

(b) After final closure, the owner must:

    (1) Maintain the integrity and effectiveness of the final cover, including making repairs to the cap as necessary to correct the effects of settling, subsidence, erosion, or other events.;

    (2) Maintain and monitor the leak detection system in accordance with 264.302, where such a system is present between double liner systems;

    (3) Continue to operate the leachate collection and removal system until leachate is no longer detected;

    (4) Maintain and monitor the groundwater monitoring system.

1.3 MINIMUM TECHNOLOGY GUIDANCE

EPA (1985a) provides technical guidance on how to meet the double liner standards set forth in the Hazardous and Solid Waste Amendments of 1984.

Specific guidance on leachate collection system design includes:

• A granular drainage layer should be at least 30 cm (12 in.) thick with a minimum hydraulic conductivity of 1×10^{-2} cm/s and a minimum bottom slope of 2 percent.

- Synthetic drainage layers may be used if they are equivalent to the granular design, including chemical compatibility, flow under load, and protection of the FML.

- The drainage layer should include a pipe network which is designed to efficiently collect leachate. The pipe and drainage layer materials should be chemically resistant to the waste and leachate. The pipe should also be strong enough to withstand expected loading.

- A filter layer (granular or synthetic) should be used above the drainage layer to prevent clogging.

- The leachate collection system should cover the bottom and sidewalls of the unit.

Specific guidance on leachate collection system construction includes:

- Granular drainage and filter material should be washed prior to installation to remove fines.

- A written construction quality assurance plan should be followed during construction of the leachate collection system.

- Construction documentation should be kept onsite.

Specific guidance on leachate collection system operation includes:

- The leachate removal system should be capable of continuous and automatic functioning, and should operate automatically whenever leachate is present in the sump. The sump should remove accumulated leachate at the earliest practicable time to minimize leachate head on the liner.

- The system should be inspected weekly and after major storms, and records should be kept to provide sufficient information that the system is functional and operated properly. Weekly recording of the quantity of leachate collected is recommended.

- Collection pipes in the drainage layer should be cleaned out periodically.

In addition, the guidance for flexible membrane liners (FMLs) states:

FMLs in landfill units, and in units with the minimum recommended thickness, should be protected from damage from above and below the membrane by at least 30 centimeters (12 inches) nominal, 25 centimeters (10 inches) minimum, bedding material (no coarser than Unified Soil Classification System (SCS) sand (SP) with 100 percent of the washed, rounded sand passing the 1/4-inch sieve) that is free of rock, fractured stone, debris, cobbles, rubbish, and roots, unless it is known that the FML material is not physically impaired by the material under load (EPA, 1985a).

This guidance may affect leachate collection system design since a maximum particle size over a liner is specified. A geotextile between the liner and drainage layer which is demonstrated to provide adequate protection to the liner would be needed if larger particle sizes are used for the drainage layer.

2. Failure Mechanisms

Leachate collection and cap drainage systems can fail or clog due to a variety of physical, chemical, biological, and biochemical mechanisms (Table 2). These mechanisms are discussed in detail in Young, et al. (1982) and Bass et al. (1984). Some of the most common failure mechanisms are those which lead to system clogging. Clogging is defined as the physical buildup of material in the collection pipe, drainage layer, or filter layer to the extent that leachate flow is significantly restricted. Other failure mechanisms which do not involve clogging include differential settling and deterioration of the collection pipe because of chemical attack or corrosion. Failure may also occur because the design capacity is exceeded. In this case liquid is not adequately removed from the system, even though system components may not be physically blocked.

2.1 DISCUSSION OF POTENTIAL MECHANISMS

2.1.1   Clogging Mechanisms

Clogging can be caused by the buildup of soil, biological organisms, chemical (and biochemical) precipitates, or combinations of the three. This buildup can occur either in the collection pipe or in the surrounding drainage or filter layers. Soil clogging (sedimentation or siltation) requires both a source of soils and a mechanism by which they can settle out. Surrounding soils can enter the drainage or filter layers if the particle size in these layers is too large. Alternatively, soil from the drainage and filter layers will enter the collection pipe if the particle-size distribution is too small, or the pipe slot-size is too large. After soils have entered the pipe they can settle out if the flow is insufficient to keep them suspended. Low flow rates can occur throughout the pipe if the slope is too small, or locally in areas of hydraulic perturbations such as poorly designed or installed pipe joints, turns, or intersections. Sedimentation of soils in the collection pipe is one of the most widely recognized clogging mechanisms.

Biological clogging occurs when organism growth fills the collection pipe or interstices of the drainage or filter layers and interferes with normal system flow. Biological growth is dependent on the presence of micro-organisms together with the appropriate nutrients, growth conditions and energy sources. In particular, Vitreoscilla, a filamentous slime-forming organism, and Pseudomonas, a common soil bacteria, are known clogging agents when iron is not present. Enterobacter is also known to contribute to clogging of the area abutting the drain in agricultural systems (Young et al., 1982). Factors thought to influence biological clogging include carbon-to-nitrogen ratio in the leachate, rate of nutrient supply, the concentration

TABLE 2

FAILURE MECHANISMS

Mechanism	Description
Sedimentation	build-up of solid materials in pipe, drain layer or filter layer. Also, siltation or soil clogging.
Biological growth	build-up of biological materials in the pipe, drain layer or filter layer.
Chemical Precipitation	build-up of chemical materials in the pipe, drain layer or filter layer due to chemical reactions.
Biochemical Precipitation	build-up of chemical or chemical and biological material in the pipe, drain layer or filter layer due to biological activity.
Pipe Breakage	collapse of pipe due to overburden or equipment loading which allows entrance of surrounding materials.
Pipe Separation	two adjacent sections of pipe are pulled apart because of overburden or equipment loading or problems with the joint.
Pipe Deterioration	pipe material is weakened or destroyed by chemical attack, oxidation or corrosion, causing failure as with pipe breakage, above.
Other non-clogging problems	includes failure of system components, such as pumps or tanks, and exceeding system or component design capacity.

of polyuronides, temperature, and soil moisture (Avnimelech and Nevo, 1964; Kristiansen, 1981).

Chemical precipitation can occur as the result of simple chemical processes or more complex biochemical processes. Chemical processes include the precipitation of calcium carbonate, manganese carbonate (rhodochrosite) and other insoluble forms (such as sulfides and silicates). Chemical precipitates can form when the pH exceeds 5, and are also dependent on the hardness and total alkalinity of the leachate. Precipitation can be caused by the presence of oxygen, changes in pH, changes in pressure or partial pressure of CO_2, or evaporation of residual liquid.

The principal biochemical precipitates are $Fe(OH)_3$ and FeS, although manganese compounds may also be involved. The biochemical process for iron depends primarily on the availability of dissolved (free) ions (influenced by redox potential, pH, and complexing agents) and on the presence of iron-reducing bacteria. The precipitate is generally mixed with a biological slime, creating a product which is quite adherent and which can very rapidly block flow through a drainage system. The precipitates produced as a result of biochemical activity are generally quite different in form or structure from those resulting from chemical processes alone, and may be more effective in leading to clogging. Chemically precipitated iron, for example, does not adhere to plastic pipe as readily and is more porous than biochemically precipitated iron (Ford, 1980).

2.1.2   Non-Clogging Mechanisms

Design capacity can be exceeded if the system or a component of the system is so undersized that the amount of liquid to be removed is greater than the amount which can be handled by the system. Underestimation of maximum design flow can be the result of a design error, an unanticipated event which causes flows in excess of design limits (such as failure of run-on diversion structures), or a condition which was inadequately accounted for in the original design (such as groundwater inflow). Differential settling can cause insufficient or inconsistent slope and displacement or crushing of collection pipes and can result in the buildup of leachate in localized areas. Problems with slope or pipe displacement and crushing can also be a result of errors in design or construction. Finally, deterioration of construction materials can be caused by chemical attack (acids, solvents, oxidizing agents) or corrosion.

2.2   CONFIRMATION OF MECHANISMS

Much of the above discussion is based on experiences with agricultural drainage systems which do not handle hazardous leachates. Confirmation testing was therefore conducted to verify that the failure mechanisms described above are indeed possible for hazardous waste leachate collection systems. Cap drainage systems are not addressed because they do not handle hazardous leachate.

A three-step approach was utilized to confirm the failure mechanisms:

Step 1:   Confirmation by experience;
Step 2:   Confirmation by first principles;
Step 3:   Confirmation by laboratory investigation.

The first step, confirmation by experience, is the preferred method since it gives positive proof that the mechanism can occur. For example, disposal of waste in the wrong cell caused collection pipe deterioration in a leachate collection system at a hazardous waste landfill. The mechanism, collection pipe deterioration, is confirmed by the fact that it has already happened.

The second step, confirmation by first principles, confirms by mathematical and scientific principles, and by common sense rationale, those failure mechanisms which have not yet been experienced. For example, a bulldozer driving over a weak collection pipe is likely to crush the pipe, whether experience with pipe crushing can be found at a land disposal facility or not. Design, construction, and operation of leachate collection systems must address the possibility of pipe crushing based on an understanding of mechanical principles. In addition, first principles are used to determine whether experience with leachate collection systems at facilities which do not dispose of hazardous wastes is applicable to hazardous waste facilities. Mechanisms which can be demonstrated to be obviously possible independent of actual experience at a hazardous waste facility are considered to be confirmed by first principles.

Finally, mechanisms which were not adequately confirmed by experience or first principles were considered candidates for laboratory investigation. Conclusions from laboratory testing of biochemical precipitation, however, were inconclusive and did not affect the confirmation testing results.

The conclusions made from the three-step confirmation testing process conducted as part of this study are summarized in Table 3. These results indicate that all the failure mechanisms must be considered in the design, construction and operation of leachate collection systems. Special attention should be given to the seven mechanisms which are confirmed or strongly suspected. Consideration must also be given to the prevention of biochemical precipitation since the mechanism is still considered a possibility. The confirmation testing process is described in more detail below.

2.2.1   Confirmation by Experience

Experience with leachate collection system failure mechanisms is summarized in Tables 4, 5 and 6. These tables are based on interviews conducted by Arthur D. Little in late 1983 and on a review of the literature. The interviews included 16 individuals from companies or agencies which design, construct, operate, and/or regulate landfills which have leachate collection systems.

The purpose of the interviews was to determine whether the failure mechanisms discussed above have indeed occurred in the field, not to provide a statistical basis for determining service life or quantifying the potential for failure of leachate collection systems. Information was based on the

TABLE 3

CONFIRMATION OF FAILURE MECHANISMS

Mechanism	Experience	First Principles	Laboratory	Conclusion*
Sedimentation	strong	strong	-	Confirmed
Biological precipitation	moderate	moderate	-	Strongly suspected
Chemical precipitation	weak-moderate	moderate-strong	-	Strongly suspected
Biochemical precipitation	weak	moderate	weak	Suspected
Pipe breakage	moderate	strong	-	Confirmed
Pipe separation	moderate	strong	-	Confirmed
Pipe deterioration	confirmed	-	-	Confirmed
Other non-clogging problems	confirmed	-	-	Confirmed

*A mechanism is

- confirmed if it has occurred at a hazardous waste facility, or if experience at other facilities is considered to be directly applicable, based on first principles.

- strongly suspected if experience at other facilities is not directly applicable, but first principles indicate the mechanism can occur in hazardous waste facilities.

- suspected if experience and first principles are inconclusive, but the mechanism cannot be ruled out at hazardous waste facilities.

TABLE 4

EXPERIENCE WITH LEACHATE COLLECTION SYSTEM

Failure Mechanism	Facility Type	Cause	Comments
Sedimentation	NS	C	no filter installed
Sedimentation	NS	U	general experience
Sedimentation	co-disposal	U	in 1 year old system
Sedimentation	co-disposal	U	of gravel layer and pipe
Sedimentation	municipal	U	general experience
Sedimentation	NS	C	general experience
Biological growth	industrial	D	100 ft. long biological growth flushed out under high pressure
Biological growth	municipal	U	reduction in flow every 2 years; flushed out
Biological growth	municipal	U	of filter fabric
Biological growth	co-disposal	U	on 3/4 inch stone, not clogged
Chemical precipitation	municipal	O	EPA test cell, not clogged
Chemical precipitation	co-disposal	U	iron oxide, not clogged
Chemical precipitation	co-disposal	O	attributed to waste characteristics
Biochemical precipitation	co-disposal	U	in leachate collection wells
Pipe breakage	NS	O	by clean-out equipment if bends greater than 22°, general experience
Pipe breakage	municipal	D	differential settling, improper bedding
Pipe separation	municipal	C	joints not glued
Pipe deterioration	NS	D	problems with ABS pipe, general experience
Pipe deterioration	hazardous	O	from acid or solvent disposed of in wrong cell
Tank failure	co-disposal	D	leachate holding tank
Capacity exceeded	co-disposal	D	under-design, other problems noted
Capacity exceeded	hazardous	O	periodic rather than automatic pumping of sump
Outlet inadequate	co-disposal	D	caused leachate buildup

NS = not specified; O = operation related; D = design related;
C = construction related; U = undetermined.

TABLE 5

SUMMARY BY FACILITY TYPE

Mechanism	Facility Type				
	Municipal	Co-disposal/ Industrial	Hazardous	Not Specified	Total
Sedimentation	1	2	-	3	6
Biological growth	2	2	-	-	4
Chemical precipitation	1	2	-	-	3
Biochemical precipitation	-	1	-	-	1
Pipe breakage	1	-	-	1	2
Pipe separation	1	-	-	-	1
Pipe deterioration	-	-	1	1	2
Other non-clogging problems	-	3	1	-	4
TOTAL	6	10	2	5	23

TABLE 6

SUMMARY BY CAUSE

Design related	6
Construction related	3
Operation related	5
Unknown	9

experience of the individuals interviewed. Information which is based on general experience is noted in the comments of Table 4.

Based on an analysis of Tables 4, 5, and 6 the following preliminary conclusions and observations can be made regarding the failure mechanisms:

- Exceeding design capacity was confirmed by experience at a hazardous waste landfill. Failure occurred when an operator failed to activate the sump pump, allowing leachate to back up in the facility. This type of failure would not occur if an automatic sump pump were used, provided the pump was turned on and properly maintained.

- Collection-pipe deterioration was confirmed by experience at a hazardous waste landfill. Failure occurred when an operator disposed of a waste which was incompatible with the materials of construction of the leachate collection system. This type of failure could occur with any type of leachate collection system, regardless of design.

- There is strong evidence that sedimentation is a problem at all types of leachate collection systems. Two of the six sedimentation mechanisms noted in Table 4 were based on general experience where the facility type was not specified. This experience may include hazardous waste leachate collection systems.

- In addition to the problem of exceeding design capacity, other non-clogging problems noted include tank failure and inadequate outlet design capacity. These problems are independent of the type of waste handled by the facility and independent of operational practices.

- Biological growth was a problem at four sites which did not exclusively dispose of hazardous waste. Three of the four sites handled municipal waste (one as co-disposal). Confirmation by first principles is needed to demonstrate that biological growth may be a problem in sites which exclusively dispose of hazardous wastes.

- While chemical precipitation was noted at three sites, two of these did not involve system clogging. As with biological growth, the potential for chemical precipitation in a hazardous waste environment should be demonstrated.

- Biochemical precipitation was noted in only one site where leachate collection wells rather than a more conventional leachate collection system were utilized.

2.2.2   Confirmation by First Principles

Confirmation by first principles is based on the analysis conducted by Bass et al. (1984). The conclusions of this analysis are summarized in Table 7. Bass et al. (1984) utilized failure mode analysis to examine drainage-system failure mechanisms and to determine the conditions needed for the mechanisms to occur. The conditions expected to be present at agricultural drainage systems, sanitary landfill leachate collection systems, and hazardous

TABLE 7

POTENTIAL FOR CLOGGING OF LEACHATE COLLECTION SYSTEMS
RELATIVE TO AGRICULTURAL DRAINS

Mechanism	Agricultural Drains	Sanitary Landfills	Hazardous Waste Landfills	Significant Differences
Sedimentation	*	-	-	More careful design and construction expected
Chemical ($CaCO_3$)	*	*	-	Lower pH expected
Biochemical (Ochre, Fe)	*	*	-	Toxicity to indigenous bacteria, lower pH
Biological	*	*	-	Toxicity to indigenous bacteria, lower pH
Differential Settling, Crushing	*	+	+	Compaction, greater equipment loading
Deterioration	*	*	+	Chemicals, solvents, lower pH
Exceed Design Capacity	*	-	-	Daily cover restricts leachate flow to system

- = less likely
+ = more likely
* = same likelihood as agricultural drains

Source: Bass et al., 1984.

waste landfill leachate collection systems were then compared to estimate the relative potential for system failure.

A similar approach is used in the present study to relate experience at municipal, co-disposal and industrial facilities, as well as experience which is not facility specific, to expected conditions at hazardous waste facilities. Mechanisms which were found to be active in other facilities, due to design, construction or operational conditions that may also be found at hazardous waste facilities, are considered to be possible at hazardous waste facilities.

Table 4 gives six examples of sedimentation problems at leachate collection systems, two of which are based on general experience. The cause of sedimentation is generally difficult to determine, although in two cases construction problems were cited. The construction problems were of the type that could occur at any facility; sedimentation in one case was due to a construction error and in the other case related to construction techniques which allow surface sediments to wash into open excavations. Any leachate collection system will need to be designed, constructed and operated to avoid clogging with sediments.

Biological growth was noted at four sites--two municipal, one co-disposal and one industrial facility. The industrial site was a paper mill sludge disposal facility with a leachate collection system designed with a 0% slope. The lack of flushing action in the pipe may have been a factor in the formation of the 30 m (100 ft) long biological mass which packed the leachate collection pipe. This case is particularly interesting because of the degree of clogging experienced, and because it is the only one of the four cases of biological clogging noted where municipal refuse was not present. Research conducted by Kobayashi and Rittmann (1982) indicates that micro-organisms can be used to biodegrade a wide variety of hazardous organic compounds. Furthermore, Ghassemi et al. (1983) found that organic and inorganic constituents identified in 30 different leachates from eleven hazardous waste landfills fall within the reported ranges for municipal landfill leachates. While data on microbiological populations in actual hazardous waste leachates are limited, the above observations indicate that micro-organisms are expected to be active in hazardous waste leachate collection systems. Given the range of micro-organisms found in the environment and in waste materials, and given the range of conditions which can be expected in various leachate collection systems, it would be difficult to rule out biological clogging as a failure mechanism based on first principles.

Chemical precipitation was found at one municipal and two co-disposal sites. In two of these cases, the chemical precipitate coated only portions of the drainage layer, causing the gravel to be cemented together in one case, but in neither case was leachate flow significantly restricted. Chemical precipitation involves relatively simple chemical reactions. Since chemicals which can form precipitates, including Ca, Fe, Mn and Mg, are relatively common leachate constituents (Ghassemi et al., 1983), chemical precipitation would be expected to occur in some hazardous waste leachate collection systems just as it has occurred at municipal and co-disposal facilities. However, the ability of the precipitates to actually clog a leachate collection pipe, drainage layer or filter layer has not been demonstrated.

Experience with biochemical precipitation in leachate collection systems is extremely limited. In addition, the conditions needed for biochemical precipitation to occur are more complex than those needed for chemical precipitation or biological growth alone. Biochemical precipitation of iron, however, is a common and serious problem in certain agricultural drainage systems (Ford, 1980), and the range of conditions expected in hazardous waste leachate collection systems does not rule out this mechanism in every case.

Breakage of collection pipe (due to operational problems (improper use of clean-out equipment) and design problems (differential settling, improper bedding, pipe bends)), was noted in two cases in Table 4. Collection pipes can also be damaged by equipment loading during construction and during placement of the first lift of waste. To avoid damaging collection pipes, leachate collection system design and operation may include:

- placement of collection pipes in trenches;

- careful attention to pipe bedding and material selection; and

- establishment of specific traffic patterns to keep heavy equipment off all collection pipes.

In addition, collection pipes may be physically inspected after construction and after the first lift of waste is placed to make sure that the pipe has not been damaged or broken.

Experience found with separation of collection pipe is limited to a single instance at a municipal landfill. In this case, a contractor neglected to glue the pipe joints as specified in the design. The problem was discovered during a preliminary inspection and was corrected prior to placement of the first lift of waste. Construction errors are independent of facility type, and are a function of the level of construction quality assurance used.

Deterioration of collection pipe and exceeding of design capacity were confirmed by experience at hazardous waste landfills. Experience with other non-clogging mechanisms includes failure of a leachate holding tank because of inadequate design, and high leachate levels due to insufficient outlet capacity. Both of these mechanisms, as well as a second case of exceeded capacity, occurred at co-disposal facilities which accept municipal, industrial and/or hazardous wastes. The failure mechanism in each case, however, is independent of waste type, and could have occurred at a hazardous waste facility.

3. Design

3.1 INTRODUCTION

Beginning July 26, 1982, RCRA regulations for hazardous waste treatment, storage, and disposal facilities (40 CFR Part 264) required the use of leachate collection systems in new, or new portions of, waste piles and landfills. The leachate collection system is designed to collect and remove leachate above the primary liner throughout the lifetime of the facility. In addition, Lutton (1979) recommends the use of drainage layers in cap or final cover systems for disposal units to collect and remove infiltrating precipitation. This eliminates additional liquid inputs to the waste mass during the facility's closure and post-closure care period.

Regulatory requirements for leachate collection and cap drainage systems in hazardous waste disposal facilities are presented in Section 1.2. Design guidance for leachate collection systems based on the Hazardous and Solid Waste Amendments of 1984 is summarized in Section 1.3.

The basic component of a leachate collection or cap drainage system is the drainage layer. The drainage layer generally consists of 30 cm (1 ft) or more of granular soil containing a network of perforated pipe, but may also be made of synthetic materials (i.e., geotextile). The Minimum Technology Guidance (EPA, 1985a) recommends that the drainage layer cover the entire liner, have a hydraulic conductivity of 10^{-2} cm/s or more, and have a minimum slope of 2 percent. A granular or synthetic (geotextile) filter layer is generally placed between the drainage layer and the waste (or topsoil for a cap) to keep small particle-size soils and other materials from clogging the drainage layer. Other components of these systems include sumps, pumps, access structures, and monitoring and control devices.

This Section addresses the design considerations important in preventing failure of leachate collection and cap drainage systems. General guidance on leachate collection system design can be found in EPA (1983b).

3.2 SYSTEM LAYOUT

Layout or configuration of leachate collection and cap drainage systems varies from site to site depending on factors such as the type of waste material being deposited, site topography, facility size, climatic conditions, design preference and regulatory requirements.

3.2.1 Leachate Collection System

The leachate collection system is designed to facilitate leachate flow over the liner and out of the system. Leachate flows out of the waste and through the drainage layer to a collection point (sump) where it is pumped out

21

of the containment area for treatment. Layout of the system should provide alternative paths for leachate to flow to the collection point, should allow for access to the drainage layer and collection sump for inspection and maintenance, and should allow for minor subsidence of the drainage layer.

3.2.1.1   Alternative Paths of Leachate Flow

Figure 2 is an example of a leachate collection system which provides alternative paths of leachate flow. The system is designed to maintain leachate levels at less than 30 cm (1 ft) even if clogging decreases the hydraulic conductivity of the drainage layer or one or more of the collection pipes clogs. Table 8 gives the estimated maximum leachate level over the liner at different drainage-layer permeabilities and collection-pipe spacings. A 6 m (20 ft) pipe spacing is effective in maintaining leachate levels at less than 30 cm even if the hydraulic conductivity of the drainage layer decreases nearly two orders of magnitude (Cases 1, 2 and 3), or if a pipe clogs (effectively increasing the spacing between pipes, as in Cases 4 and 5). However, if Case 5 were the initial design (collection pipes at a 24 m (79 ft) spacing), an order of magnitude decrease in hydraulic conductivity would result in leachate levels in excess of the 30 cm standard (Case 6).

3.2.1.2   Access

Layout of the leachate collection system should also allow for access to the entire collection pipe network, including the sump, for inspection and cleaning. This is important for two reasons. First, since access to the granular or synthetic drainage material is not possible, access to the pipe network is needed in case the capacity of both components is reduced by clogging (as in Case 6 in Table 8). The pipe network can be unclogged and maintained to maximize system capacity if access is provided. Second, the collection pipe network is sensitive to damage, especially during construction and during placement of the first lift of waste. Access is needed to allow for inspection of the pipe network to ensure that the network was constructed as designed, and was not damaged in the initial placement of waste. If problems are found, the pipe network can be repaired before leachate collection problems occur, and before the damaged area is buried in several layers of hazardous waste.

Access to the collection pipe network is provided by installing a manhole or a riser pipe at each end of every pipe. Two possible designs are shown in Figure 3. Access at both ends of the collection pipe is needed for most inspection and maintenance procedures (Sections 5 and 6). In addition, bends or branches in collection pipes at angles greater than 45 degrees and pipe lengths greater than 300 m (1000 ft) between access points should be avoided. The designs in Figure 3 are intended to minimize the number of manholes required in order to minimize stress on the liner, reduce construction costs and simplify waste placement.

Optimum spacing of the collection pipe, manholes and riser pipes to maintain leachate levels less than 30 cm (1 ft) and allow for access to the system may be determined using site-specific information such as topography, climate, waste characteristics (e.g., expected leachate generation, propensity

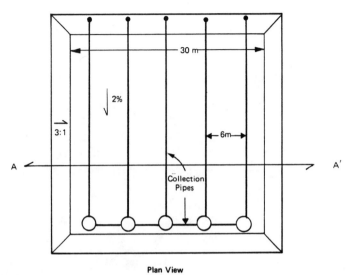

Plan View

—— Collection Pipe

◯ Manhole

● Riser

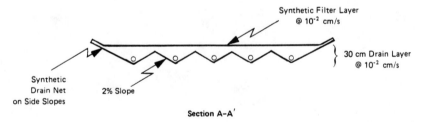

Section A-A′

Figure 2. Leachate collection system layout providing alternative paths of leachate flow.

TABLE 8

MAXIMUM LEACHATE LEVELS GIVEN VARIOUS DESIGN ASSUMPTIONS

Parameter	Unit	Case 1	Case 2	Case 3	Case 4	Case 5	Case 6
Maximum Leachate Level*	cm	5	17	29	11	21	67
Permeability	cm/s	10^{-2}	10^{-3}	3.5×10^{-4}	10^{-2}	10^{-2}	10^{-3}
Pipe Spacing	m	6	6	6	12	24	24
Leachate Production Rate	cm/year	100	100	100	100	100	100
Slope	--	.02	.02	.02	.02	.02	.02

*Approximate level based on Figure 2; calculated using the equation in Moore (1980) (see Section 3.4).

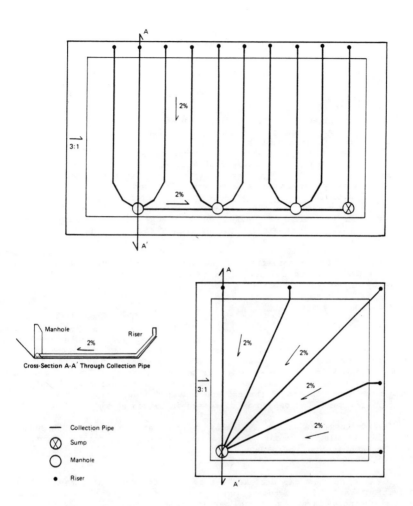

Figure 3. Leachate collection system layouts providing access to collection pipes.

for clogging), and facility size including future expansion needs. (See Sections 3.4 and 3.5.)

3.2.1.3 Minor Subsidence

Subsidence of the waste or sublayers may result in a final grade which does not allow flow of leachate through the drainage layer to the sump. Uneven settling in localized areas of the disposal cell may result in low spots in the drainage layer and lead to pooling of the leachate and eventual clogging. Settlement may also result in the buckling of collection pipes, the breaking of joints, and eventual failure of the drainage system. Subsidence may be controlled by preloading the waste disposal area during construction to allow the sublayers to come to final grade before the drainage system is installed and the wastes are placed. A more commonly used approach in controlling subsidence is to factor in the effects of subsidence on final grade slopes in the design calculations. The expected consolidation of the wastes and sublayers can be calculated based on knowledge of the sublayer material properties (e.g., density, composition, compatibility) and waste characteristics (e.g., void fraction, density). An allowance or safety factor may then be incorporated into the design to ensure that the final slope after settlement will be as specified in the design. In addition, flexible joints should be used between collection pipes which may be subjected to stresses created by uneven waste subsidence.

3.2.2 Cap Drainage System

The primary purpose of the cap is to minimize infiltration of precipitation into the waste mass after closure by increasing runoff and evapotranspiration. The cap is generally constructed in several layers, including a low permeability barrier layer, a drainage layer, a filter layer, and a vegetated topsoil layer which is graded to increase runoff and reduce erosion (Figure 4). The drainage layer removes precipitation which infiltrates through the upper layers of the cap and prevents liquid from accumulating over the barrier layer. Cap design is discussed in Lutton et al. (1979).

The drainage layer is typically a granular soil, although geotextile materials may also be used. The U.S. Environmental Protection Agency (EPA, 1982) recommends that a drainage layer be at least 30 cm (1 ft) thick (if soil is used) and have a permeability of at least 10^{-3} cm/s.

The layout of a cap drainage system is less complicated than a leachate collection system since a collection pipe network is generally not incorporated in the drainage layer (although perforated or slotted pipe located at the perimeter of the cap is used to convey water from the drainage layer to surface drainage facilities). A major concern is that the cap drainage system be able to function with minimum maintenance (pursuant to 40 CFR 264.310), even with minor subsidence of the cap. As a result, steeper slopes than would be necessary for drainage alone are used so that flow through the drainage system is maintained. The optimal slope will be shallow enough to minimize erosion of the topsoil layer from surface runoff, and steep enough to avoid ponding of water over the barrier layer if minor subsidence occurs.

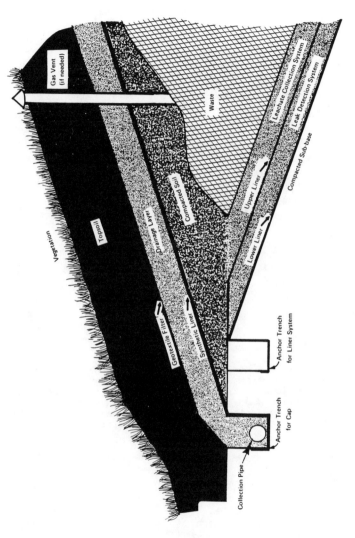

Gas Vent
(if needed)

Vegetation

Topsoil

Drainage Layer

Geotextile Filter

Synthetic Liner

Compacted Soil

Upper Liner

Lower Liner

Waste

Leachate Collection System

Leak Detection System

Compacted Sub-base

Anchor Trench
for Liner System

Anchor Trench
for Cap

Collection Pipe

Figure 4. Schematic of a landfill cap.

3.3   GENERAL DESIGN CONSIDERATIONS

Leachate collection system design is affected by the characteristics of both the expected waste to be disposed of and the expected leachate to be generated from that waste. The liquid content of the waste contributes to the volume of leachate expected, and the particle size of the waste influences design of the filter layer. Hydraulic conductivity of the waste also affects the ability of the leachate to reach the collection system.

Leachate characteristics which influence design include the volume expected, suspended solids, pH, redox potential, and chemical constituents such as organics, calcium, iron, manganese and nutrients. These characteristics are considered in sizing system components, selecting construction materials, and designing individual components to avoid failure by the mechanisms discussed in Section 2.

This section discusses material selection for chemical compatibility and the ability to influence leachate characteristics once the facility is in operation. The application of this information is limited to leachate collection systems since cap drainage systems are not exposed to waste. Specific design considerations for each component are discussed in subsequent sections.

3.3.1   Material Selection

Each component of a leachate collection system must be constructed of materials which are chemically resistant to the waste managed and leachate expected at the facility (40 CFR 264.301a). In assessing chemical/material compatibility, the designer should recognize that the resistance of any given material to chemical attack is a function of several elements including the specific chemical, the concentration of the chemical, temperature, and duration of contact. Examples of organic and inorganic constituents that may be present in leachate are given in Table 9.

In general, data regarding the resistance of various construction materials to specific chemicals are limited. The data that are available originate from sources such as manufacturers' product testing information, reference texts and engineering handbooks, reports from private or academic research and testing institutions and government-sponsored studies. These data are typically reported for pure compounds, with limited information on dilute solutions.

Little information is available on the chemical resistance of granular materials that would be used in filter or drainage layers. A number of studies have shown that strong bases will partially solubilize silica - containing soil constituents (Nutting, 1984; Grim, 1953). Since sand is predominantly silica in composition, drainage or filter layers constructed of sand which come in contact with alkaline wastes may be susceptible to structural damage. Silica dissolution may cause the formation of large voids and channels and may ultimately lead to collapse of the filter or drainage layers.

Geotextiles are made from various single or multi-component petroleum-based polymers such as polypropylene, polyester, and polyethylene. The

TABLE 9

ORGANICS AND INORGANICS WHICH MAY BE PRESENT IN WASTE LEACHATES

Type	Group	Class	Examples
Organic	Acids		acetic, propionic, butyric, lactic
	Bases		aniline
	Neutral Polar	Alcohols & Phenols	methanol, isobutanol, phenol, pentachlorophenol
		Acid Anhydrides	acetic anhydride benzoic anhydride
		Glycols	ethylene glycol
		Aldehydes	formaldehyde butyraldehyde
		Esters	bis(2-ethyl hexyl) phthalate di-n-butylphthalate
		Ethers	methyl ethyl ether diethylether
		Ketones	acetone, methylethylketone 2-hexanone
		Halogenated	vinyl chloride, chlorinated ethanes, ethylenes, methylene chloride, chloroform
	Neutral Non-Polar	Aliphatic Hydrocarbons	propane, butane, methane
		Aromatic Hydrocarbons	benzene, toluene, xylene naphthalene
Inorganic	Acids		hydrochloric, hydrofluoric, nitric, sulfuric

(continued)

TABLE 9 (continued)

Type	Group	Class	Examples
	Bases (Alkalies)		soda ash (NaOH) potash (KOH) magnesium hydroxide
	Salt	Acid	ammonium chloride
		Base	sodium acetate sodium carbonate
		Neutral	sodium chloride potassium sulfate
	Metals		lead, chromium, mercury

Source: From Haxo, 1983

majority of all geotextile fabrics are composed of either polyester or polypropylene. As shown in Table 10, geotextiles made from polypropylene are, in general, more resistant to chemicals than are geotextiles made from polyester.

The most commonly used materials for leachate collection pipe are thermoplastics, although vitrified clay, asbestos cement and concrete, ductile iron and fiberglass may also be used. With the exceptions of fiberglass and thermoplastics, data regarding resistance of these materials to specific chemicals are limited. Data regarding the resistance of fiberglass and thermoplastic materials to specific chemicals are often supplied in manufacturers' product literature. Since there are many formulations for thermoplastics (e.g., polyvinyl chloride (PVC), chlorinated polyethylene (CPE)) and fiberglass (using various polyethylene and polyester resins) care must be taken to select the proper formulation of piping material for a specific waste application.

Sump materials must be compatible with the physical and chemical properties of the leachate. Materials which may be used include:

- concrete;
- concrete with fiberglass, plastic, or brushed-on epoxy liner material; and
- PVC, ABS or fiberglass reinforced vessels.

Pump materials should be resistant to the corrosive or chemically-active environment. Normally pumps are constructed of cast iron with stainless steel or bronze shafts, gates and seals. Table 11 presents general information on the chemical resistance of these materials. Pumps may also be constructed of stainless steel and PVC, and may be coated with Teflon liners, aliphatic urethane coatings, or epoxy coatings. Valves are available in fiberglass, PVC, CPE, polyethylene, stainless steel, and metal fabricated with a variety of chemically resistant coatings.

Chemical resistance data for many chemical/material combinations either are not available or are limited in scope. Empirical methods or laboratory testing may be necessary to estimate the chemical resistance of certain materials to chemicals.

In general, two types of testing can be performed: exposure testing, and material property testing. Exposure testing attempts to simulate expected in-service conditions to which a material in direct contact with chemicals will be subjected. Testing conditions such as temperature, duration of exposure and chemical concentration may be varied to provide information on the short- and long-term resistance of the material. The most widely used exposure test method is the immersion test. Procedures for conducting immersion tests can be found in ASTM D471-79 (Rubber Property - Effect of Liquids) or ASTM D543 (Resistance of Plastics to Chemical Reagents). Similar procedures could be adopted for immersion testing of other construction materials. For example, EPA requires waste-liner compatibility testing for flexible membrane liners. Two methods, EPA 9090 and NSF Standard No. 54, are generally recommended. These and other test method are evaluated in Tratnyek et al. (1984).

TABLE 10

CHEMICAL RESISTANCE OF POLYPROPYLENE VERSUS POLYESTER

	Polypropylene	Polyester
Mineral Acids, weak	Excellent	Good
Mineral Acids, strong	Excellent	Poor
Oxidizing Acids, conc.	Good to Poor	Poor
Alkalies, weak	Excellent to Good	Good
Alkalies, strong	Excellent to Good	Poor
Alcohols	Excellent to Good	Good
Ketones	Excellent to Good	Poor
Esters	Excellent to Good	Good
Hydrocarbons, aliphatic	Good to Fair	Good
Hydrocarbons, aromatic	Good to Fair	Poor to Fair
Oils, vegetable, animal, mineral	Good	Good

Source: Bolz and Tuve, 1976.

TABLE 11

CHEMICAL RESISTANCE OF CAST IRON
STAINLESS STEEL, BRONZE AND MONEL

Metal	Subject to Corrosion by	Resistant to
Cast Iron	all water solutions; moist gases, dilute acids, acid-salt solutions	concentrated acids (nitric, sulfuric, phosphoric), weak or strong alkalies, organic acids
Stainless Steel	inorganic acids, ammonia, mercury, oxidizing salts (Fe, Cu, Hg)	water, caustic and mild alkalies, organic acids, neutral and alkaline organic compounds, dry gases
Bronze	mercury and its salts, aqueous ammonia, saturated halogen vapors, sulfur and sulfides, oxidizing acids (nitric, concentrated sulfuric), oxidizing salts (Hg Ag, Cr, Fe, Cu), cyanides	water, sulfate and carbonate solutions, dry halogens alkaline solutions, petrochemicals, non-oxidizing acids (acetic, hydrochloric, sulfuric)
Monel	inorganic acids, sulfur, chlorine, acid solutions of ferric, stannic or mecuric salts	food acids, neutral and alkaline salt solutions, dry gases, most alkalies, ammonia

Source: Bolz and Tuve, 1976.

Material property testing is usually performed before and after exposure tests to provide a comparative basis for establishing changes in properties after the material has been exposed to a chemical or leachate. Commonly measured properties include:

- weight change;
- swelling or shrinking;
- tensile strength; and
- hardness.

Visual inspections, optically aided or unaided, may also be useful for assessing changes not necessarily detectable in any of the above property tests. Surface cracks, inclusions and other material defects may be uncovered in materials such as vitrified clay, ductile iron, and concrete or cement. Visual inspection may uncover reactivity of leachate with a plastic material as manifested by discoloration, delamination or bubbling of the material.

Numerous methods are available for conducting exposure and material properties tests. The selection of the most appropriate technique depends on the particular material and property to be tested.

3.3.2   Control of Leachate Characteristics

Controlling the wastes placed in a landfill may provide a means to prevent or mitigate the potential for failure of leachate collection systems. In many cases, the failure of a leachate collection system is attributed at least in part to the wastes disposed of at the facility. For example, at a site in California which experienced chemical deposition and solidification, clogging was attributed to "the variations in the type of waste handled and hence .... the leachate characteristics" (MEESA, 1984). Attention must be given both to the chemical and physical characteristics of the waste, as well as the manner in which the waste is placed.

The first step in controlling leachate characteristics to minimize failure of a leachate collection system is to not dispose of wastes which may adversely affect the functioning of the system. This would include not accepting any liquid wastes or any wastes which are incompatible with system components. Not accepting bulk liquid wastes, which is required under the Hazardous and Solid Waste Amendments of 1984, significantly reduces leachate generation. In the California facility mentioned above, about 30% of the wastes were liquid industrial wastes. Not accepting incompatible wastes is necessary since the system is constructed of materials which are resistant only to certain types of waste. Disposal of incompatible wastes can result in failure of a component due to material degradation. In one case discussed in Section 2, for example, failure of a hazardous waste leachate collection system was attributed to disposal of a solvent or acid in a cell which was not designed for such wastes. Segregating wastes with different chemical characteristics into different cells may also be useful in avoiding leachate collection system failure, since construction materials can be selected for a narrower range of waste characteristics.

The second step for controlling leachate characteristics to avoid failure involves careful selection of wastes placed in the first lift. These wastes should be high-permeability wastes and may have special chemical characteristics. High-permeability wastes are placed in the first lift to facilitate the flow of leachate to the collection system. Special waste characteristics may include wastes of relatively low pH, wastes which inhibit biological activity, and wastes which do not contain high iron, calcium, magnesium, nutrient, or sediment content. The chemical characteristics desirable in the first lift of waste vary with the leachate characteristics expected at the facility, and the failure mechanisms which are expected to be active.

Proper placement of the first lift of waste is also critical in maintaining leachate collection system performance since wastes are deposited directly on top of the exposed leachate collection system. The movement of equipment and careless dumping of the waste on top of a granular filter layer may result in ruts and/or compaction of a granular filter layer beyond design specifications for proper filtration. Filter layers of geotextiles may be ripped or punctured during careless waste placement activity. The underlying leachate collection piping may also be damaged (e.g., pipe buckling, breaking of joints) during waste placement. Initial placement of wastes should be performed using equipment properly sized for the job. Sizing of equipment should consider the ability of the underlying drainage and filter layers to withstand vertical loading, which is a function of the characteristics of the drainage or filter materials and the maximum allowable loading stresses for the collection pipes. Waste placement should proceed ahead of the placement equipment, and wastes should be dumped as close to ground level as possible. Equipment movement on the waste placement area should be limited to the portion covered with the initial or subsequent layers of wastes.

Controlling waste characteristics in later lifts may be difficult because of restrictions on storing wastes onsite and the difficulty in controlling the wastes which come through the gate. This may also be a problem during the first lift of waste. Where possible, however, waste should be placed to reduce the possibility of clogging. For example, placing iron-containing waste in portions of the landfill where the leachate pH is low and/or the redox potential is low (i.e., oxidizing) should maintain any iron leached out at the higher ferric oxidization state and reduce the possibility of iron deposition since ferrous ions are oxidized rapidly in acidic conditions. This approach, however, will have limited applicability in large landfills which accept a variety of wastes, and where leachate from several parts of the cell drains into a common leachate collection system. In this case leachate characteristics in the collection system itself would be very difficult to control.

In general, the effects of waste characteristics on the leachate collection system should be considered in the placement of wastes in the landfill. This is especially important during placement of the first lift of waste. While waste placement may be difficult to control at some facilities, waste characteristics do influence the function of the leachate collection system. This correlation should be understood by the facility operator and waste placement should be controlled where possible to avoid potential problems with the leachate collection system.

3.4   DRAINAGE LAYER

3.4.1   <u>Material Selection</u>

Drainage layers generally consist of granular soils such as coarse sands which provide the required hydraulic conductivity (10^{-2} cm/s) and protect the underlying flexible membrane liner.   The particle-size distribution of the drainage layer must be selected to allow liquid transport, prevent puncture of the underlying synthetic liner, and minimize migration of filter-layer materials into the drainage layer.

Geotextiles may be used as a substitute for granular material in portions or all of the drainage layer.   Geotextile materials include needlepunched, non-woven polypropylene or polyester fabric and polyethylene grids. Combinations of the two may also be used; for example, placing a grid between two layers of geotextile fabric.   Properties of typical geotextile drainage materials are given in Table 12.

The primary advantages of using a geotextile drainage layer are:

- geotextiles may be more accessible or less expensive than granular material in a given location;

- geotextiles are thin compared with granular drainage layers and therefore allow for larger disposal capacity; and

- geotextiles can be placed on steeper side slopes than granular materials, again allowing for larger disposal capacity.

The primary disadvantages of using a geotextile drainage layer are:

- geotextiles are thin and may be more susceptible to clogging than granular materials;

- the hydraulic conductivity of some geotextiles may decrease up to two orders of magnitude under loading conditions (Giroud, 1981); and

- experience with geotextiles in land-disposal applications is limited and their ability to perform on a long-term basis is unproven.

3.4.2   <u>Design Considerations</u>

The design of the drainage layer will be based primarily upon the system hydraulics necessary to maintain a leachate level over the liner of less than 30 cm (1 ft).   Protection requirements for the synthetic liner should also be addressed as well as the physical properties of the materials (e.g., ability to place granular materials on side slopes, physical strength of geotextiles). The design for the filter layer (Section 3.6) will usually follow drainage layer design.   Design of the collection pipe network (Section 3.5) will occur concurrently.

TABLE 12

PROPERTIES OF TYPICAL GEOTEXTILE DRAINAGE MATERIALS*

Product Name	Manufacturer	Material Type	Weight, oz/yd² (ASTM D1910)	Thickness, mils (ASTM D1777)	Permeability, cm/s	Equivalent Opening Size, U.S. Std. Seive Size (COE CW-02215)
Typar Spunbonded, 3601	DuPont	non-woven, polypropylene	6	18	1.4×10^{-2}	140 - 170
GTF-125D	Exxon	non-woven, polypropylene	4	45	1×10^{-1}	50 - 100 (ASTM .03.81.08)
Fibretex, 400	Crown Zellerbach	non-woven, polypropylene	no data	110	3×10^{-1}	80 - 100
Bidim, U34	Quline Corp.	non-woven, polyester	8	100	3×10^{-1}	70 - 100
Trevira Type 1120	American Hoest Corp.	non-woven, polyester	6	100	no data	50 - 70
Tensar DN-3	Tensar Corp.	polyethylene grid	20.6	160	5×10^{-4} m²/s**	7mm x 7mm
Conwed Geo-Net XB8200	Conwed	polyethylene grid	20.2	160	5×10^{-4} m²/s**	no data

*1 oz/yd² = 33.9 gm/m²
1 mil = 1.0254mm
1 lb = .45 kg

**Transmissivity under pressure. For comparison, a 30 cm (1 ft) thick granular layer with a permeability of 1×10^{-1} cm/s has a transmissivity of 3×10^{-4} m²/s

Source: Vendor product information.

The movement of leachate through the drainage layer is primarily a function of the liner slope, collection-pipe size and spacing, the number and size of perforations in the collection pipe, hydraulic conductivity of the drainage material, and rate of leachate generation. A variation in any one of these parameters may affect the requirements of the other parameters if a maximum head of 30 cm (1 ft) is to be maintained.

The anticipated volume of leachate within the drainage system must be determined so that the components of the drainage layer can be sized appropriately. Leachate within the landfill can come from the liquid in the waste, precipitation and, in some cases, groundwater flow. The amount of liquid generated from the waste may be determined if the moisture content of the waste is known. As a conservative estimate, it can be assumed that the quantity of leachate generated from a waste is equal to the moisture content of the waste times the volume of waste deposited. In reality, however, the amount of leachate generated from the waste will be less than this value since the waste will retain and store a certain volume of liquid (called the "field capacity"). In some cases, liquid in the waste may not make any contribution to leachate quantity, but may reduce the time required for leachate to appear in the leachate collection system (i.e., the field capacity of the waste will be reached more quickly).

Leachate produced from infiltrating precipitation may be estimated using a computer model. Two examples of computer models are:

1.   HELP (Schroeder et al., 1984); and

2.   HSSWDS (Perrier and Gibson, 1982).

HELP and HSSWDS are very similar, and both give output on water movement through the system including percolation, drainage, evapotranspiration, runoff and soil water storage. These results are based on a variety of climatologic and soil data for each layer of soil or waste. The function of each layer is considered, as is the distance between collection piping, the slope of the drainage layer, and an anticipated percentage of leachate that leaks through the liner. Other equations that model water movement through soil and waste are available, and many can be easily adapted to a computer program.

An important consideration in drainage-layer design is the maximum height to which leachate rises in the drainage layer. Leachate tends to mound up in granular drainage layers due to viscous resistance to horizontal flow. The maximum height of this mounding must not exceed 30 cm (1 ft), as stipulated by RCRA regulations. For a particular drainage-layer configuration, drainage-layer permeability, and liquid infiltration rate, the maximum height of leachate mounding in the drainage layer can be calculated by the following formula (Moore, 1980):

$$h_{max} = \left(\frac{L^2 e}{4k}\right)^{\frac{1}{2}} \left(\frac{k\tan^2 s}{e} + 1 - \frac{k\tan s}{e}\left(\tan^2 s + \frac{e}{k}\right)^{\frac{1}{2}}\right)$$

where: h_{max} - maximum height of leachate over the liner (cm)
         L - length of spacing between drainage pipes (cm)
         e - quantity of leachate seeping into drainage layer (cm/sec)
         k - permeability of drainage layer (cm/sec)
         s - slope of liner

Figure 5 illustrates a drainage layer geometry for this formula and identifies formula variables. Given a value for e (representing infiltrating precipitation and liquid generated by the waste itself), this equation may be used to select combinations of values for L, s, and k which will maintain an h_{max} of 30 cm (1 ft) or less.

It should be noted that the above equation for h_{max} gives only an approximate value. A more rigorous, non-linear equation can be found in McBean et al. (1982). It should also be noted that the second term of the equation goes to one if the slope equals zero. This gives a simplified equation which slightly overestimates h_{max}, but which can be more easily solved.

The designer should consult additional references for a more detailed explanation of this design calculation using other drainage-layer geometries and associated design equations (EPA, 1983b; Harr, 1962; Bear, 1972).

Although EPA (1982) recommends a drainage-layer thickness of 30 cm (1 ft), thicker layers should be considered to increase drainage efficiency (EPA, 1985a). The drainage-layer design should include a safety factor to account for possible clogging because of solids infiltration or other clogging mechanisms. A safety factor can be achieved by increasing liner slope, decreasing pipe spacing, or increasing drainage-layer permeability or thickness.

3.5 COLLECTION PIPE NETWORK

The collection pipe network of a leachate collection system drains, collects and transports leachate through the drainage layer to a collection sump where it is removed for treatment or disposal. The pipes also serve as drains within the drainage layer to minimize mounding of leachate in the layer. In a cap drainage system, pipes are used to collect and transport water from the drainage layer to surface drainage facilities. Specific information on design of drainage pipes which may also be applicable to collection pipe design is given in USBR (1978).

3.5.1 Capacity

Pipes must be sized and spaced to remove liquid from the drainage layer without causing any significant back-up. In a leachate collection system, the collection pipes must be designed to carry the leachate without allowing more than 30 cm (1 ft) of leachate buildup within the drainage layer.

Many factors must be considered in designing the collection pipe network. The slope of the cell bottom and the distance between collection pipes are parameters used in the HELP Computer Model. Other factors include the flow through the pipe perforations, the slope of the pipe, the layout of the pipe network, and the maximum amount of liquid expected to be carried by the pipe.

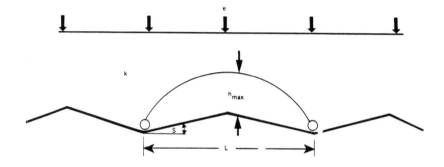

Figure 5. Landfill geometry assumed for calculating maximum height of leachate over liner.

Darcy's Formula or flow net calculations can be used to determine the design capacity of collection pipe. These techniques are discussed in detail in Cedergren (1977). Typically, based on flow considerations, 10 cm (4 in.) diameter pipe is considered adequate for drainage system laterals while 15 cm (6 in.) diameter pipe is used for collection headers in most landfill applications. Increasing the lateral pipe diameter to 15 cm (6 in.) and the collection header diameter to 20 cm (8 in.) would allow easier access for inspection and maintenance equipment, provide a greater cross-sectional area for leachate flow, and reduce blockage of leachate flow from partial clogging within the pipe.

3.5.2   Structural Stability

Pipes used to collect and convey leachate from leachate collection systems must be structurally stable to withstand the loading of the overlying filter and drainage layers, wastes, cap materials, and vehicular traffic that may move over the disposal cell. Collection pipes in landfill drainage systems may be rigid (e.g., concrete and cast iron) or flexible (e.g., plastic and fiberglass), and may be placed in trenches (Figure 6) or above-grade (i.e., positive projection, Figure 7). Since many landfills experience some uneven settling, flexible pipe with fittings designed to withstand this settlement is recommended, especially for the cap drainage system.

Factors which must be considered in determining the required structural stability of the collection pipe include, but are not limited to:

- vertical loading;
- perforations;
- deflection;
- buckling;
- compressive strength;
- backfill compaction; and
- loadings during construction.

Design equations for calculating the vertical loads acting on flexible pipe because of overlying materials are summarized in Table 13. The equations can be used to calculate the vertical loading stress acting on perforated collection pipe installed in trenches or above grade, and to calculate flexible pipe deflection. A complete explanation on the use of these equations may be found in Haxo (1983). A problem in using these equations with respect to landfill sites is that it may be difficult to determine the average unit weight of fill since dense waste (high unit weight) may be placed in a single area, rather than spread evenly over the site. The designer should include a safety factor to account for these uncertainties. The selection, for example, of the next greater standard wall thickness would provide an extra measure of protection against excessive loading on the pipe.

Most pipe standards assume flexible pipe failure at a deflection of 5 to 7.5 percent, although pipe deflected beyond this point may still conduct fluid (Personal Interview, P. Kmet). A severely deflected collection pipe may develop bottlenecks that could restrict flow. Pipe deflection depends greatly on the bedding compaction. Compaction is often difficult to achieve at a site with soft clays. Although sand and gravel are acceptable bedding materials,

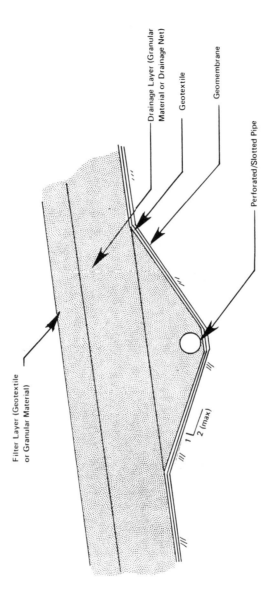

Drainage Layer (Granular Material or Drainage Net)

Geotextile

Geomembrane

Perforated/Slotted Pipe

Filter Layer (Geotextile or Granular Material)

1

2 (max.)

Figure 6. Collection pipe installation in trench.

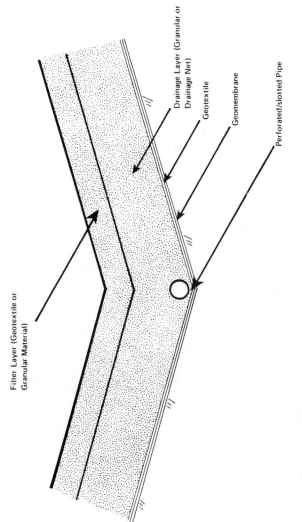

Filter Layer (Geotextile or Granular Material)

Drainage Layer (Granular or Drainage Net)

Geotextile

Geomembrane

Perforated/slotted Pipe

Figure 7. Collection pipe installation above liner.

TABLE 13

DESIGN EQUATIONS FOR CALCULATING
VERTICLE LOADING STRESSES
ON FLEXIBLE PIPE USED IN
LANDFILL DRAINAGE SYSTEMS

Description	Equations

Vertical loading stress acting on
pipe installed in:

   - Trench

$$\sigma_v = B_d w C_D + q_f C_{\mu s}$$

Where:

$$C_D = [\frac{1-e^{-2K\mu(Z/B_d)}}{2K\mu}]$$

$$C_{\mu s} = e^{-2K\mu(Z/B_d)}$$

   - Above Grade

$$\sigma_v = (\omega_f)(H_f) + \omega Z_1$$

Increased vertical stress for
perforated pipe:

$$(\sigma_v)_{design} = \frac{12}{12-Ip}(\sigma_v)_{actual}$$

Flexible pipe deflections under
vertical loading:

$$\Delta y = D_e \frac{kWr^3}{EI + 0.061E^1 r^3}$$

(continued)

TABLE 13 (continued)

Definitions:

σ_v = vertical pressure at the top of the pipe (psi)

B_d = width of trench (ft)

w = unit weight of backfill (lb)

K = lateral pressure coefficient of backfill (psi)

μ = coefficient of friction between backfill and the walls

Z = height of backfill above pipe (ft)

q_f = vertical pressure at the bottom of the waste fill (psi)

H_f = height of waste fill (ft)

lp = cumulative length (in inches) of perforations per foot of pipe

Δy = horizontal and vertical deflection of the pipe (inches)

D_e = a factor, generally taken at a conservative value of 1.5, compensating for the lag or time dependent behavior of the soil pipe system

W = vertical load action on the pipe per unit of pipe length (lb/in.)

r = mean radius of the pipe (inches)

E = modulus of elasticity of the pipe materials (psi)

E^1 = modulus of passive soil resistance (psi), (normally estimated to be 300 psi for soils of proper density of 65% and 700 psi for soils of proper density of at least 90%)

k = bedding constant, reflecting the support of the pipe receives from the bottom of the trench (dimensionless) (a conservative value generally taken 0.107)

I = moment of inertia of pipe wall per unit of length $(in^4/in.)$; for any round pipe, $J = t^3/r$ where t is the average thickness (inches)

Source: Haxo, 1983.

crushed stone is easier to compact and offers greater strength to the pipe. Crushed stone, however, should not be placed directly over the liner. The Minimum Technology Guidance (EPA, 1985a) states that granular materials coarser than fine sand should not be in contact with the liner.

The pipe manufacturer should be consulted for information on buckling and compressive strength which are specific to each kind of pipe. The strength of plastic pipe may be reduced with age and warmer temperatures (greater than $21^{\circ}C$). Plasticizers may be broken down with time, reducing pipe strength. Some compounds in pipes are broken down by ultraviolet rays. This can be minimized by covering pipes during storage prior to use, covering installed pipe with a layer of soil, and protecting risers from exposure with a steel outer casing or similar device. As with all components in a leachate collection system, the collection pipe should be compatible with the leachate.

3.5.3   Perforations

Design of collection pipe must consider the size, spacing and orientation of holes or slots used to perforate the pipe. Perforations must allow free passage of leachate but prevent the migration of drainage media into the collection pipe. The size or diameter of these perforations therefore depends on media particle size and the volume of leachate that must be removed from the drainage system. For slotted pipe, Cedergren (1977) suggests:

$$\frac{D_{85} \text{ of the filter}}{\text{Slot Width}} > 1.2$$

and for pipes with circular holes:

$$\frac{D_{85} \text{ of the filter}}{\text{Hole diameter}} > 1.0$$

where D_{85} is the particle size which 85 percent of the soil particles are smaller than (on a dry-weight basis, as determined by ASTM D421 and D422).

Alternately, USBR (1977) recommends:

$$\frac{D_{85} \text{ of the filter}}{\text{Maximum pipe opening}} \geq 2$$

Cedergren (1977) concludes that all three equations represent a reasonable range over which satisfactory performance can be expected.

Spacing of perforations depends on flow as well as pipe strength considerations. The U.S. Soil Conservation Service and the U.S. Bureau of Reclamation require a minimum open area of 21 cm^2/m (1 $in.^2$/ft) for drainage pipe (Mohammad and Skaggs, 1983). The number of perforations per length of pipe affects the effective radius of the pipe used in design calculations. Use of effective radius in pipe design is discussed in Mohammad and Skaggs (1983) and in Skaggs (1978). The number of perforations per length of pipe also affects pipe strength, as shown in Table 13. Both factors should be taken into account in the design of perforated collection pipe.

Orientation of perforations on the pipe depends on flow and clogging considerations. Mohammad and Skaggs (1983) found that orientation of the perforations did not affect the rate of flow when the pipe was full of water. However, Luthin and Haig (1972) found that the rate of flow in a pipe which was not full was greater when perforations were at the bottom of the pipe due to the increased head difference between the water level and the entry points. Since collection pipes will not always be full of liquid, these studies suggest that placing perforations near the bottom of the pipe will increase collection efficiency. This also minimizes the depth over the liner required for leachate to enter the pipe. However, placing additional perforations in the upper portion of the pipe will increase the ability of the pipe to collect leachate and will be just as effective as other perforations when the pipe is running full.

To prevent the perforations from plugging with sediment, the perforations should not be placed straight down but should be offset at an angle (eg. 30 degrees) from the straightdown position. In addition, holes should not be drilled along the pipe seam as this weakens the pipe.

3.6 FILTER LAYER

Two types of filters are typically used in engineering practice: granular filters and geotextile filters (Figure 8). Granular filters were first introduced in the 1920's (Terzaghi and Peck, 1967) and consist of a soil layer or combination of soil layers having a coarser gradation in the direction of seepage than the soil to be protected (i.e., the material above the filter layer). Geotextiles, first introduced in the 1970's (Hoare, 1982), are cloth-like sheets made of synthetic fibers and are sometimes referred to as filter fabrics or geofabrics. Geotextiles are manufactured in two varieties -- woven and non-woven. Woven geotextiles are similar to screens which have uniform sized openings whereas the non-woven variety consists of fibers placed in a random orientation. Both types can be made with high permeability relative to most soils while having an opening or mesh size sufficiently small to prevent soil particle movement.

The filter layer is used above the drainage layer in both leachate collection and cap drainage systems to trap fines and prevent waste and other solid materials from entering the drainage layer while allowing the passage of liquid. Information regarding physical characteristics of the fines and the anticipated loading rates is needed to formulate design criteria for constructing a filter that will continue to function through the design life of the drainage system. Information on the selection and sizing of the filter medium is presented in this section.

Some designers argue that a filter layer is not necessary when the quantity and loading rate of fines introduced to a drainage layer are small enough to allow infiltration into or transport through the drainage layer without adversely affecting the performance of the drainage layer. Physical characteristics of fines such as the particle size and shape may dictate

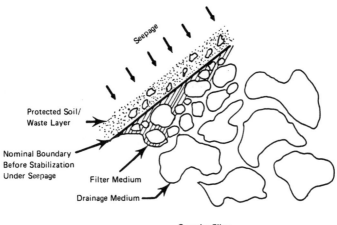

Granular Filter

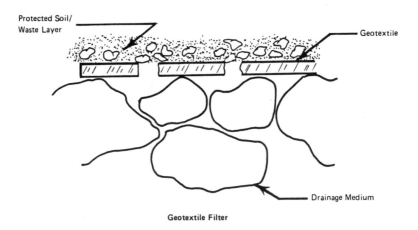

Geotextile Filter

Figure 8. Schematic of granular and geotextile filters.

whether it is practical to design a filter layer to trap fines or a drainage layer to allow transport of fines. Information on physical characteristics of the fines, such as the particle mass and density, coupled with anticipated flow velocity of liquid through the drainage system, will aid in determining whether transport of fines will be possible.

The factors that influence the decision to include a filter layer in a drainage system will also influence the decision whether or not to wrap collection piping or the pipe trench with geotextile. It is generally considered unwise to wrap a pipe since the geotextile may clog with fines. However, where it can be conclusively demonstrated that fines will not be a problem, wrapping the pipe with a compatible geotextile would be effective in preventing migration of drainage media into the pipe and may allow for larger perforations in the pipe.

The designer of a leachate collection system will need to balance the presence of fines in the deposited waste against the advantages (i.e., meeting the design goals) and the disadvantages (i.e., potential causes of sedimentation) of using a filter layer and/or wrapping collection piping or the trench the pipe is in with geotextile. Figure 9 presents design goals which need to be addressed in considering the use of a filter layer or geotextile-wrapped pipe. In most cases, a filter layer will be needed to prevent migration of overlying materials into the drainage layer. EPA (1985) recommends the use of a granular or synthetic filter layer above the drainage layer to prevent clogging.

3.6.1   Granular Filters

Various design criteria are available for granular filters (Peck et al., 1974; Cedergren, 1977; U.S. Bureau of Reclamation, 1977; U.S. Army Corp of Engineers, 1955; Canada Centre for Mineral and Energy Technology, 1977; and Sherard et al., 1984a and b). Review of these publications shows that the variations among design criteria are minimal.

Generally, filter design is based on the particle-size distribution of the overlying soils. For a leachate collection system the overlying soil would most likely be the waste, and for a cap drainage system the overlying soil would most likely be the topsoil. Particle-size distribution or gradation of soil is the relative proportion of each particle size on a dry-weight basis. Determination of a soil's gradation is defined in ASTM Specifications D421 and D422 (1982). A soil's gradation is commonly shown graphically in the form of a particle-size (or grain-size) distribution curve (Figure 10).

Peck et al. (1974) present design criteria for granular filters based on the concept of filter ratios (Table 14). Peck et al. (1974) also recommend that the particle-size curve representing the filter material should have a smooth shape without pronounced breaks and should be roughly parallel to that of the soil being protected.

Cedergren (1977) suggests the following two criteria for granular filters:

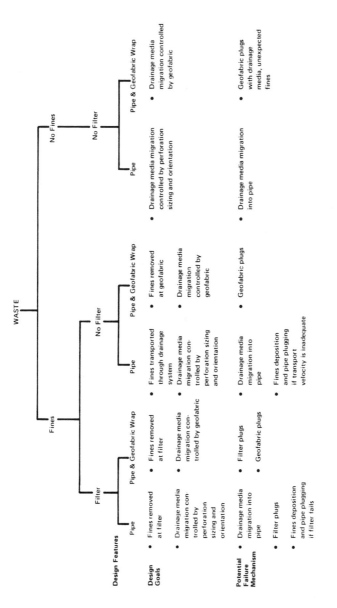

Figure 9. Potential design options for collection or transport of fines.

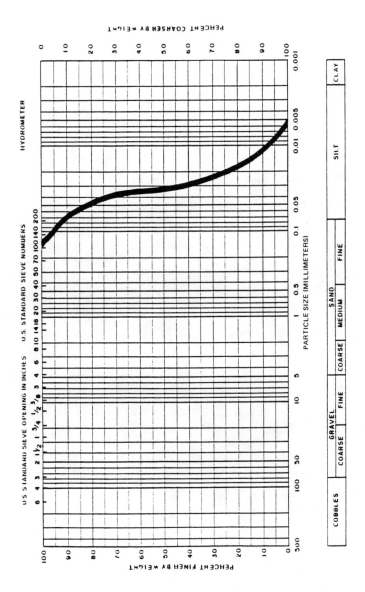

Figure 10. Particle-size (or grain-size) distribution curve.

TABLE 14

PARTICLE-SIZE REQUIREMENTS FOR FILTERS[*]

Grading of Filter Material	R_{50}	R_{15}
Uniform	5 to 10	No requirements
Nonuniform[**], subrounded particles	12 to 58	12 to 40
Nonuniform[**], angular particles	9 to 30	6 to 18

[*] R_n = the filter ratio for the n percent size = $\dfrac{D_n \text{ of Filter}}{D_n \text{ of overlying soil}}$

D_n = particle size which n percent of the soil particles are smaller than (on a dry-weight basis, as determined by ASTM D421 and D422).

[**] The filter material is considered nonuniform if D_{60}/D_{10} (coefficient of uniformity) is greater than 4.

Source: Peck et al., 1974

Criterion 1:

$$\frac{D_{15} \text{ of the filter}}{D_{85} \text{ of the overlying soil}} < 4 \text{ to } 5$$

Criterion 2:

$$\frac{D_{15} \text{ of the filter}}{D_{15} \text{ of the overlying soil}} > 4 \text{ to } 5$$

where D_n is defined in Table 14.

The first criterion is intended to prevent migration of overlying soils into the filter layer, and the second to allow sufficient hydraulic conductivity to prevent buildup of liquid above the filter.

Where the particle-size difference between the overlying soil and the underlying soil is great, a single filter layer which meets the design criteria may not be possible. In this case, several filter layers may be necessary (e.g., the "overlying soil" for one filter layer may be a second filter layer). In addition, the above criteria must be satisfied between the drainage layer and the filter layer to prevent migration of filter soils into the drainage layer and to ensure sufficient hydraulic conductivity between the two layers.

3.6.2   Geotextile Filters

Filter design criteria are not as well established for geotextiles as they are for granular materials. This is mainly due to the short time geotextiles have been available for engineering use. Discussions of design criteria for geotextiles are presented in publications by Cedergren (1977), Koerner and Welsh (1980), Chen et al. (1981), Giroud (1982), Lawson (1982), Carrol (1983) and Horz (1984).

Chen et al. (1981) suggest the following criteria:

Criterion 1:

$$\frac{P_{95} \text{ of the geotextile}}{D_{85} \text{ of the overlying soil}} \leq 2$$

Criterion 2:

$$\frac{P_{95} \text{ of the geotextile}}{D_{15} \text{ of the overlying soil}} \geq 2$$

where: P_{95} = pore diameter of the geotextile which 95% of the pores are
            smaller than (also called the equivalent opening size or
            EOS)

D_n is defined in Table 14.

The first criterion is intended to prevent overlying soils from passing through
the filter, and the second to prevent clogging of the geotextile with fines.
Procedures for determining P_{95} are found in Carrol (1983).

In addition, Carrol (1983) recommends that the hydraulic conductivity of
the geotextile be greater than ten times the hydraulic conductivity of the
overlying soil, and that the gradient ratio be less than or equal to 3.   The
gradient ratio is a laboratory parameter determined by comparing head losses
across the geotextile and the immediately adjacent protected soil to head
losses across the undisturbed protected soil.   Procedures for determining the
hydraulic conductivity of a geotextile can be found in Celanese Fibers
Marketing Company (1981).   Procedures for determining the gradient ratio for a
geotextile are presented by Haliburton and Wood (1982).

Giroud (1982) provides a critique of conventional geotextile filter
criteria, claiming they are overly restrictive.   He suggests alternative
criteria based on a theoretical analysis of the governing equations.

3.7   OTHER COMPONENTS

3.7.1   Sumps

Collection pipes typically convey the leachate by gravity to one or more
sumps depending upon the size of the area drained.   Leachate collected in the
sump is removed by pumping directly to a vehicle, to a holding facility for
subsequent vehicle pickup, or to an on-site treatment facility.

Sump dimensions are governed by the amount of leachate to be stored, pump
capacity and minimum pump drawdown.   Two possible sump designs are given in
Figure 11.   Manholes may also be used as sumps (see Section 3.7.4).

The volume of the sump must be sufficient to hold the maximum amount of
leachate anticipated between pump cycles, plus an additional volume equal to
the minimum pump drawdown volume (i.e., liquid reservoir to keep pump from
running dry).   Sump size should also consider dimensional requirements for
conducting maintenance and inspection activities, including equipment and
personnel access.   Sump pumps may operate with preset cycling times (e.g., 15
minutes) or, if leachate flow is less predictable, the pumps may be
automatically switched on when leachate reaches a certain level.   The Minimum
Technology Guidance (EPA, 1985a) states that sumps should have the capability
of continuous and automatic operation.   This avoids the problem of leachate
buildup when an operator fails to activate the pump when the sump is full.
This problem was noted in the interview results in Section 2.

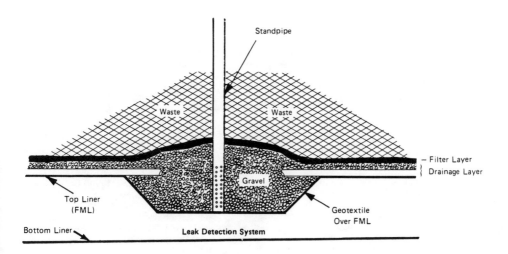

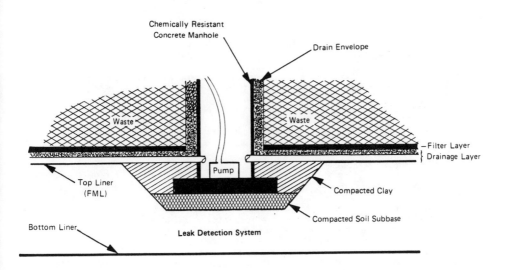

Figure 11. Typical sump designs.

3.7.2   Pumps

Sump pumps should be designed to provide adequate head and volume to discharge leachate from the collection sump to either a collection vehicle or holding facility. Sizing pumps for pumping capacity greater than the anticipated design capacity will ensure that unpredicted surges in leachate flow may be accommodated without causing a buildup in leachate within the facility. Where multiple pumps are used, it may be advantageous to size pumps for a capacity equal to the total flow rate of the leachate collection. In the event that one or more pumps fail to operate, the remaining pump(s) could accommodate the increased load.

When the pump is discharging directly to a collection vehicle, the pump capacity should be large enough to empty the sump contents in an efficient manner. An alternative to pumping directly from the sump is to use a diaphragm pump or vacuum pump system mounted directly on the collection vehicle, much like septic tank scavenger vehicles. These vehicles typically hold several thousand gallons.

Pump types which may be used to pump leachate include submersible, centrifugal-type pumps, which offer economical capital and operating costs. Shaft-driven centrifugal pumps are also applicable in leachate pumping because the motors are mounted above the sump and out of the liquid. End suction centrifugal pumps may be used if suction lifts are limited to 4.5 m (15 ft). Diaphragm pumps are not recommended because of high maintenance and low reliability resulting from loss of prime.

In cold weather climates, provisions may be needed to heat enclosures for exposed pumps and motors. Pump controls for pumps that discharge to collection vehicles should be equipped with a lockable on-off switch. A low-level float may be used to turn off the pump to prevent motor overheating or loss of prime.

Pumps discharging to holding tanks or surface impoundments should include float or liquid-level control devices to perform the following functions:

- low-level cutoff;
- pump start;
- high-water alarm in storage tank and sump; and
- second pump start if two pumps are used.

3.7.3   Discharge Lines

The discharge lines should feed through a valve pit that contains a suitable valve (gate, butterfly or ball type). A check valve should also be installed after the main control valve to prevent back-siphonage. The volume of leachate should be monitored by inserting a flow meter into the discharge line and recording the amount pumped and visually indicating the rate of flow. The flow meter and recorder can also be placed in the valve pit. The meter may be a differential head type consisting of a venturi tube, a magnetic meter, or a Doppler meter. A flow totalizer may also be installed to document system operation.

3.7.4   Manholes

Manholes may be placed at the junction of leachate collection pipes to allow access to the collection system for inspection and maintenance. They should be placed within the containment area so the leachate collection pipe does not penetrate the liner. Manholes should be designed to minimize stresses on the liner and to maintain structural integrity over the lifetime of the facility.

Manholes normally are fabricated concrete structures. The normal entrance should be at least 60 cm (24 in.) in diameter to allow for personnel and equipment entry. Larger diameter openings may be necessary to accommodate bulky inspection equipment, or workers using self-contained air supplies. The manhole should be 1.2 m (4 ft) in diameter with an eccentric conical section to make the transition to the diameter of the entrance section. The channel of the manhole should be shaped with a channel of the same diameter as the entering pipe with the channel depth equal to the pipe radius. This channel should be lined with appropriate material to prevent deterioration. A wide base should be used to increase stability and minimize stresses on the liner. In addition, pipe couplings to manholes should be made with flexible, chemically-resistant boots.

3.7.5   Liquid-Level Monitors

Liquid-level monitoring provides information on the level of the leachate at selected points within the site. Level monitoring coupled with high level alarms will ensure that leachate levels above the liner will not exceed 30 cm (1 ft) or that leachate in storage tanks will not overflow before being transported to a treatment facility. Liquid-level monitoring devices are discussed in Section 5.2.2.

4. Construction

4.1 INTRODUCTION

Following the design of a leachate collection or cap drainage system, construction documents are prepared. These documents provide the necessary information in the form of graphical plans, specifications and a construction quality assurance plan to describe and control construction of the system. The construction documents also include estimated costs to construct the system and provide quality assurance. These documents may also address the prevention of drainage system failure during and after the construction phase. The term "drainage system" is used to refer to both leachate collection and cap drainage systems.

4.2 PLANS AND SPECIFICATIONS

Plans are working drawings which describe in graphic form the dimensions, location, size, arrangement, layout, and spatial relationships of the drainage system to be installed. Specifications are written documents that specify the amount, type and quality of materials required, details of work to be performed, quality control requirements, and construction schedules.

4.2.1 Detail

The detail contained in the plans and specifications should be complete enough to provide a high degree of confidence that the constructed drainage system will perform as designed. Recommended methods of component installation, aimed at preventing failure of the drainage system, should be clearly presented in graphic and written form. Particular attention should be given to ensure that dimensions are correct and consistent, and that step-by-step written procedures for installation of components are concise, accurate, and follow a logical sequence. For example, plans and specifications for collection pipes should contain detailed drawings and written descriptions of:

- placement of bedding material around pipes;

- spacing, size, and circumferential location of holes or slots in collection laterals;

- orientation of collection laterals with respect to grade, and orientation of holes or slots; and

- joining of pipe sections and alignment of pipe to manholes.

58

Strict adherence to detail contained in the plans and specifications will help ensure that the installed drainage system will function as designed according to the criteria established to prevent failure.

The contract drawings should contain details of all components of the project such as:

- typical sections of the liner, filter layer, and drainage layer;

- collection pipe trenches;

- manholes and sumps; and

- specific details for variances from these typical sections.

4.2.2   Specific Plans

Plans and specifications should include a layout of the existing facility or site, a geometric plan of drainage system components, and a grading plan.

A layout of the site should be prepared showing, at a minimum, the following details:

- location of all physical features within the proposed limit of work;

- survey baseline;

- all utility locations and elevations;

- north arrow;

- graphic scale;

- contours of drainage system layers; and

- horizontal and vertical orientation and type and quantity of all drainage system components.

A geometric plan should show elevation and location of all major components of the project such as excavation limit, the horizontal and vertical limits of the filter and drainage layers, liner, utilities, and leachate removal structures. The plan should also show orientation of the collection pipe network including spacing between laterals, and vertical and horizontal positioning of the pipe within the drainage layer and with respect to established baselines and benchmarks. Before construction starts, installation location data given on the plans should be verified to determine whether the control points are as stated and undisturbed. This verification will determine whether these points can be maintained during construction. If not, the plans and specifications should provide for alternative working baselines and benchmarks. The essential element is to establish points that are sure to remain undisturbed or that can be replaced from secure reference points.

The grading plan is a graphic representation of the finished elevation of the various components of the work relative to the existing conditions. The grading plan should contain enough data to allow the contractor to compute the cut-and-fill requirements of the project, and establish heights of surface-water-control structures needed. Of primary importance is the illustration of run-on and runoff control structures and conformance with locations for surface-water interception or control facilities.

4.2.3   Phased Development

For landfills, common practice is to deposit wastes in functional units called cells. Each cell is sized to handle an estimated volume of waste within a specified time frame. Typically, cells are constructed to final dimensions even though the cell may be filled with waste over a period of time. During the active life of the cell, the filter and drainage layers (including the collection pipe) not covered by wastes will be exposed and subject to potential damage. Climatic events such as rain storms may cause serious erosion of the filter and drainage layers and result in loss of structural integrity. High ambient air temperatures may cause thermal expansion of plastic collection-pipe within the drainage layer that permanently displaces the pipe and breaks pipe joints. Photo-oxidation of plastic materials may cause embrittlement or failure of components such as geotextiles and pipes.

Phased development of individual disposal cells is an alternative construction technique to alleviate the problems mentioned above. Using this approach, only that area of the cell which would soon be covered with wastes is constructed. This minimizes the time these components are subject to potential damage from exposure. However, wastes should not be placed in the cell until all components are installed and certified as functional.

Another alternative would be to construct the entire cell but cover unutilized portions with a temporary synthetic or natural (i.e., soil) protective cover. A disadvantage of this alternative is the potential difficulties in applying and removing the temporary cover without damaging the underlying drainage-system components.

The plans and specifications should consider operational procedures and schedules to reduce the potential for these factors to clog and affect drainage-system performance.

4.2.4   Material

The quantity, size, type and quality of all construction materials must be identified in the plans and specifications. Reference to established material specifications such as state highway specifications for soils, the National Sanitation Foundation or American Water Works Association for pipe and fittings and the Underwriters Laboratory for electrical equipment are appropriate. Additional specification of the quality of material may be required, particularly for drainage-system components that require special materials or where chemical resistance of construction materials is important in preventing failure.

Material specifications should also identify how drainage-system components will be placed or joined together. For example, the method for connecting multiple lengths of perforated pipe should be specified, as should the connection of collection pipe to manholes. Compaction requirements of soil or granular components should also be specified.

Material specifications should include all installed pumping, monitoring, inspection and maintenance equipment. Sizes of materials and equipment should be checked to verify that specifications for different materials are compatible with each other. Specifications of materials should also include climatic conditions that will influence proper placement. For example, the placement of plastic materials in extremely cold temperatures may cause cracking or other thermal defects. Curing of concrete or special coatings may require a minimum temperature to assure proper performance.

All materials used in the construction of the drainage system should be verified for conformance to design criteria as specified in the plans and specifications. This verification should be performed in accordance with the Construction Quality Assurance (CQA) plan discussed in detail in Section 4.3.

4.2.5   Installation Procedures

4.2.5.1   Drainage Layer and Collection Pipe

Plans and specifications for the installation of the drainage layer (including collection pipe) should provide detailed information concerning material placement, construction sequence, phased or staged construction, and testing and inspection.

The drainage-layer material should be placed using equipment and techniques that accomplish the task without damaging the materials or the structural integrity of the finished drainage layer or the underlying liner. Materials used in the construction of the drainage layer include the drainage medium, collection pipe, bedding material for the pipe, and geotextile for wrapping the bedding material (when used). Granular material should be washed prior to placement to eliminate fines and should be placed directly on top of the liner system in a manner that avoids dumping of materials or operation of equipment directly on the liner. Equipment used to place aggregate material should operate only on the placed granular material and should be compatible with the selected allowable design loads on the liner system. A small front-end loader generically referred to as a "Bobcat" may be a suitable piece of equipment to place granular material even though its daily output might be substantially lower than that of a heavy-duty front-end loader. All construction equipment, including Bobcats, should avoid sharp turns that may create tearing or shearing stresses in the liner.

Procedures for testing and inspection of the drainage layer should be detailed in the plans and specifications and performed in accordance with the construction quality assurance (CQA) plan discussed in Section 4.3. Specific items which should be addressed include:

- grade (slopes) of finished drainage layer;

- drainage-layer thickness;

- correct horizontal and vertical alignment of collection pipe;

- correct orientation, size and spacing of slots or holes in collection pipe;

- proper construction of pipe section joints;

- construction sequence; and

- control of fines during construction.

4.2.5.2   Filter Layer

Plans and specifications for the installation of the filter layer should provide detailed information on material placement, and on testing and inspection procedures.

The filter-layer will consist of either a specified granular or geotextile material. Granular filter-layer material should be placed with care to minimize potential damage to the underlying drainage layer. Equipment should be selected to minimize vertical loadings and care should be taken during equipment operation to avoid quick turns (causing ruts which could damage the underlying drainage layer). The granular material should be spread uniformly to grade and depth in accordance with the plans and specifications. A geotextile filter fabric should be placed with care to avoid ripping or puncturing the fabric. Adjacent runs of fabric should overlap as specified in manufacturer's recommendations to prevent short-circuiting of leachate.

The installed filter layer should be tested and inspected in accordance with the CQA plan discussed in Section 4.3. Specific items which should be addressed include:

- final grade slope;

- thickness;

- particle-size analysis (or geotextile properties); and

- hydraulic conductivity.

4.2.5.3   Other Components

Installation procedures for manholes and sumps detailed in the plans and specifications should address procedures for verification of vertical and horizontal positioning of manholes and their foundations. Proper orientation of the manholes is important with respect to collection-pipe connections. Flexible joints should be used to connect manholes and collection pipes.

Manhole installation procedures should also include details on access doors, interior steps or ladders, ventilation ports and locking devices to limit access to the manhole. Installation of monitoring equipment installed in the manholes, such as flow meters or level alarms, should also be detailed in the plans and specifications.

In some instances, it may be necessary to apply chemically-resistant and leak-proofing coatings to manholes or sumps in the field. Details of application procedures and coating thicknesses should be provided in the plans and specifications.

The installation details of pumps and discharge piping should address locations and should reference appropriate benchmarks for the piping and, in the case of pumps, any special installation and testing cited by the manufacturer.

The removal system should be tested and inspected in accordance with the CQA plan and should focus on the following items:

- testing for alignment of manholes and collection headers;

- inspecting integrity and thickness of any coatings; and

- inspecting and circuit testing all electrical connections, control devices, and monitoring and pumping equipment.

4.3   CONSTRUCTION QUALITY ASSURANCE PLAN

Construction quality assurance (CQA) for a leachate collection and cap drainage system is needed to assure, with a reasonable degree of certainty, that the completed system meets or exceeds the specified design. This involves monitoring and documenting the quality of materials used and the conditions and manner of their placement. CQA serves to detect variations from design, whether as a result of error or negligence on the part of the construction contractor, and to provide for suitable corrective measure before wastes are accepted at the facility. Without proper CQA, problems with the leachate collection or cap drainage system that are due to construction may not be discovered until the system fails during operation.

4.3.1   Elements of a CQA Plan

The Construction Quality Assurance Plan is the written document describing the specific approach to be followed in attaining and maintaining consistently high quality in the construction of a hazardous waste disposal facility so that the completed facility meets or exceeds the specified design. While the overall content of the CQA plan will depend on the site-specific nature of the proposed facility, specific elements that should be included in the plan are (EPA, 1985b):

- Responsibility and Authority--The responsibility and authority of all organizations and key personnel involved in permitting, designing, and constructing the hazardous waste land disposal facility should be described fully in the CQA plan.

- CQA Personnel Qualifications--The qualifications of the CQA officer and supporting inspection personnel should be presented in the CQA plan to demonstrate that they possess the training and experience necessary to fulfill their identified responsibilities.

- Inspection Activities--The observations and tests that will be used to monitor the installation of the leachate collection system should be summarized in the CQA plan.

- Sampling Requirements--The sampling activities, sample size, sample locations, frequency of testing, acceptance and rejection criteria, and plans for implementing corrective measures as addressed in the project specifications should be presented in the CQA plan.

- Documentation--Reporting requirements for CQA activities should be described in detail in the CQA plan. This should include such items as daily summary repots, inspection data sheets, problem identification and corrective measures reports, block evaluation reports, design acceptance reports, and final documentation. Provisions for the final storage of all records also should be presented in the CQA plan.

Each of these elements is described in detail in EPA (1985b). In addition, inspection activities for leachate collection systems are discussed below.

4.3.2   Inspection Activities

Observations and tests are performed by CQA inspectors to verify that the materials and procedures used during construction are in conformance with the plans and specifications. Observation and testing is conducted throughout the construction process, beginning with the materials selected for use and continuing through verification that the entire system has been constructed as designed.

4.3.2.1   Types of Testing

The three types of testing generally used by CQA inspectors are:

- visual inspection (observation);

- non-destructive testing; and

- destructive testing.

Visual inspection is used to evaluate and document the overall quality of materials and procedures used during construction, including:

- construction materials (storage conditions, conformance with specifications, material quality, defects);

- installation procedures (overall quality, methods used);

- work conditions (temperature, precipitation, wind);

- personnel and equipment utilization (vehicle routing, crew assignments); and

- construction sequence.

Experience and training of the inspector are particularly important in controlling quality by visual inspection.

Non-destructive testing is used to evaluate installed components of the drainage system. It has the advantage that the component being tested is not damaged by the test. Non-destructive testing is used to verify dimensional, physical or mechanical characteristics to locate defects. Tests to determine dimensional, physical and mechanical characteristics may include permeability analysis of soil layers, or physical measurement of elevation, grade or location of placement of system components. Defects may be located by methods such as cleaning out lengths of collection pipe to verify continuity of the pipe network (see Section 5).

Destructive testing often involves preparation of specimens taken from the installed component which are tested to either partial or complete destruction. Destructive testing is often performed to determine the tensile, compressive or ultimate strength of installed materials, and usually requires repair or replacement of a portion of the component from which the specimen was taken.

4.3.2.2   Test Methods

Testing performed as part of a CQA program should be conducted in accordance with standard procedures. Applicable procedures that are well-established and generally accepted by professional consensus should be selected. Typical sources of consensus standards include the American Society of Testing and Materials (ASTM), the American Association for State Highway and Transportation Officials (AASHTO), and the American Water Works Association (AWWA). Non-standard test procedures should be avoided. When non-standard procedures are used, they should be described in detail to assure consistent application of measurement throughout the CQA program. Commonly used testing procedures that are applicable for drainage system quality assurance are listed in Table 15.

TABLE 15
CQA TEST PROCEDURES

Component	Factors to be Inspected	Inspection Methods	Test Method Reference
Granular drainage and filter layers	Thickness	Surveying; measurement	NA
	Coverage	Observation	NA
	Soil type	Visual-manual procedure	ASTM D2488-84
		Particle-size analysis	ASTM D422-63
		Soil classification	ASTM D2487-83
	Density	Nuclear methods	ASTM D2922-81
		Sand cone	ASTM D1556-82
		Rubber balloon	ASTM D2167-84
	Permeability (laboratory)	Constant head	ASTM D2434-38
Synthetic drainage and filter layers	Material type	Manufacturer's certification	NA
	Handling and storage	Observation	NA
	Coverage	Observation	NA
	Overlap	Observation	NA
	Temporary anchoring	Observation	NA
	Folds and wrinkles	Observation	NA
	Geotextile properties	Tensile strength	Horz (1984)
		Puncture or burst resistance	Horz (1984)
		Tear resistance	Horz (1984)
		Flexibility	Horz (1984)
		Outdoor weatherability	Horz (1984)

(continued)

TABLE 15 (continued)

Component	Factors to be Inspected	Inspection Methods	Test Method Reference
Pipes		Short-term chemical resistance	Horz (1984)
		Fabric permeability	Horz (1984)
		Percent open area	Horz (1984)
	Material type	Manufacturer's certification	NA
	Handling and storage	Observation	NA
	Location	Surveying	NA
	Layout	Surveying	NA
	Orientation of perforations	Observation	NA
	Jointing		
	• Solid pressure pipe	Hydrostatic pressure test	Section 4, AWWA C600-82
	• Perforated pipe	Observation	NA
Cast-in-place concrete structures	Sampling	Sampling fresh concrete	ASTM C172
	Consistency	Slump of portland cement concrete	ASTM C143
	Compressive strength	Making, curing, and testing concrete specimens	ASTM C31
	Air content	Pressure method	ASTM C231
	Unit weight, yield, and air content	Gravimetric method	ASTM C138

(continued)

TABLE 15 (continued)

Component	Factors to be Inspected	Inspection Methods	Test Method Reference
	Form work inspection	Observation	NA
Electrical and mechanical equipment	Equipment type	Manufacturer's certification	NA
	Material type	Manufacturer's certification	NA
	Operation	As per manufacturer's instruction	NA
	Electrical connections	As per manufacturer's instruction	NA
	Insulation	As per manufacturer's instruction	NA
	Grounding	As per manufacturer's certification	NA

Source: EPA, 1985b.

5. Inspection

5.1 INTRODUCTION

Leachate collection and cap drainage systems must be inspected to ensure that the constructed system continues to operate according to design specifications. Undetected failure of drainage-system components can lead to buildup of excess liquid over the liner, liner failure, and/or contamination of groundwater. Inspections serve to discover failed components of the system as well as to determine where failure mechanisms are active. In addition, inspection of the drainage system can be useful in discovering problems with other components of the disposal facility, especially the liner. Reduced outflow from the drainage system, for example, may indicate a variety of problems with the drainage system or a leaky liner.

Federal regulations under the Resource Conservation and Recovery Act require the leachate collection systems to be inspected. While in operation, a landfill, for example, "must be inspected weekly and after storms to detect evidence of the presence of leachate in and proper functioning of leachate collection and removal systems, where present" (40 CFR 264.303(b)). The Minimum Technology Guidance (EPA, 1985a) also recommends that records be kept "to provide sufficient information that the primary leachate collection system is functional and operated properly" and that "the amount of leachate collected be recorded in the facility operating record for each unit on a weekly basis." A plan for inspecting the leachate collection system should be included in a Part B permit application as part of the overall Facility Inspection Plan under 40 CFR 270.14(b)(5).

There are no similar Federal requirements for inspection of cap drainage systems at closed facilities, although the "integrity and effectiveness of the final cover" must be maintained (40 CFR 264.117). This implies the need for inspection to make sure that the cap drainage system is functioning as intended.

State regulatory agencies may make requirements for inspecting leachate collection or cap drainage systems in addition to the Federal requirements. Requirements vary from state to state, and often from facility to facility within a state. The Wisconsin Department of Natural Resources (WIDNR), for example, does not have a standard set of requirements for the inspection of leachate collection systems. Typical requirements, based on WIDNR permit approvals and conversations with WIDNR staff (Personal Interview, P. Kmet), include:

- cleaning the collection pipe after construction and after the first lift of waste is placed to verify continuity of the lines (conducted with Department representative present);

- field-checking collection pipe for clogging at least annually;

69

- daily recording of leachate levels in leachate collection tanks;

- quarterly recording of levels in leachate-level wells installed at site closure.

Inspections required at the Federal and state levels are intended to provide enough information to the regulatory agencies to ensure that the leachate collection or cap drainage system is performing adequately. They also provide the owner/operator with performance data. Guidance on how to conduct the required inspections, however, is generally not given; it is left up to the facility owner to specify in the permit application how the requirements will be met. This section presents information on inspection procedures which can be used to meet state or Federal regulations or the requirements of the facility owner.

Two types of inspection procedures may be used. The first, Regular or Periodic Inspections, includes visual inspection, monitoring leachate level over the liner, indicators of system failure or clogging, and direct inspection methods. The second section, Special Inspections, includes cleaning to verify the continuity of system after construction and after the first lift of waste is placed, and methods to locate and diagnose leachate collection system problems. A summary of the inspection methods addressed is given in Table 16.

Inspection can most easily be accomplished by using a checklist which summarizes the inspection protocol and provides an example record. Example checklists provided herein can be used as a reference while the procedure is conducted or as a guide in making data sheets to record test results for a specific facility.

5.2 REGULAR OR PERIODIC INSPECTIONS

Regular (weekly and after storm) inspections may include visual inspection, monitoring the leachate level over the liner, correlating amount of precipitation and site parameters with leachate quantity and correlating leachate quality with clogging indicators. The regulations do not specify the type of inspection which must be performed weekly and after storms, so selection of the appropriate methods is left up to the owner/operator (with the approval of the permitting agency).

Periodic inspections may include procedures which are conducted on a monthly, quarterly or yearly basis. These longer frequency inspections may be required by the state or performed as part of the facility owner or operator's own inspection and maintenance plan. These inspections are more involved and more costly than the methods used on a weekly basis, but provide a direct evaluation of the condition of the drainage system. Methods include television and photographic inspection and maintenance related techniques such as checking system continuity by passing sewer-cleaning equipment through the collection lines.

The first four inspection procedures discussed below (visual, leachate level, leachate quantity, leachate quality) provide primarily indirect

TABLE 16

SUMMARY OF INSPECTION METHODS

Method	Recommended Frequency	Purpose	Comments
Visual	weekly and after storms	verify presence of leachate in and proper functioning of leachate collection system	required by RCRA; does not determine cause of problem; not useful for prevention
Leachate Level Measurement	quarterly or when problems suspected	locate areas where leachate level over liner is greater than one foot	can locate general area of problem but does not determine cause
Leachate Quantity Analysis	quarterly	evaluate overall performance of system in removing leachate from over liner	does not determine cause of problem; should be verified by other techniques
Leachate Quality Analysis	as needed	evaluate potential for failure mechanisms to occur	additional research needed to determine usefulness of this method
Television and Photographic	annually	observe condition of pipe network, determine cause and location of problem	requires adequate access to pipe network
Maintenance Related	annually, after construction, after placement of first lift of waste	verify continuity of pipe network, determine cause and location of problem	requires adequate access to pipe network
Excavation	as needed	determine cause of problem	used when problem is already located; used in conjunction with repair - See Section 7

evidence of clogging or system failure. Problems are discovered by analyzing leachate characteristics and flow through the system. Direct inspection methods (television and photographic, inspection during pipe maintenance) find the problem itself (e.g., a clogged pipe) and do not depend on the effects of the problem (e.g., restricted flow). The direct methods discussed below are applicable only to collection pipe which is accessible to the equipment used. No direct methods exist for the periodic inspection of buried granular drainage and filter layers, or, of course, for collection pipe without adequate access.

5.2.1   Visual Inspection

Discussion

Visual inspection is the simplest inspection procedure. It requires the inspector to use no more than his or her senses and perhaps some basic equipment such as a flashlight or liquid level measuring device. Visual inspection is limited because most of the system is buried and not accessible to the inspector. Access is provided primarily by manholes and riser pipes; visual inspection therefore focuses on the information obtained via these two features. Components of the system which are not buried can also be inspected.

The purpose of visual inspection is to verify qualitatively that the leachate collection system is functioning as intended. The inspection required by RCRA, referred to in Section 5.1 above, would likely be a visual inspection. The purpose of that inspection is to detect whether leachate is in the system and determine whether any problems are apparent.

Visual inspection is relatively inexpensive and can be performed as part of the regular routine of facility operation. It also can provide the first evidence that problems exist in the drainage system. An example of this would be finding no flow in a manhole where flow is expected. Visual inspection, however, is qualitative and does not reflect failure mechanisms which are in progress but are not readily evident. There may be flow in a manhole, for example, even when the drainage layer is partially clogged. More quantitative techniques are needed to discover a reduction rather than a stoppage of flow. Visual inspection is therefore less useful in preventing problems since it primarily indicates when maintenance or repair is required.

Protocol

The protocol for visual inspection at a given facility will depend on the site-specific layout of the leachate collection or cap drainage system. In particular, it will depend on the number, type and location of access points to the buried system, and on the parts of the system which are not buried. Access points to the system may include:

- manholes;
- riser or clean-out pipes;
- risers for collection sumps or tanks;
- system outflows; and

• leachate level wells.

Each of these access points should be checked for the presence of leachate and the overall condition of the access structure. Leachate flow rate and level of standing leachate should be measured, where possible. Methods for measuring leachate level are discussed in Section 5.2.2.

Components which may be accessible above ground include:

• mechanical equipment and controls;
• system outflows; and
• leachate storage tanks or surface impoundments.

The inspector should make sure that all mechanical equipment (monitors, meters, pumps) is functioning properly, and should check leachate flow (presence and rate) at system outflows and leachate level in tanks or surface impoundments. The overall condition of each component should also be evaluated.

All observations made during a visual inspection should be recorded. A generic checklist for visual inspections is provided in Figure 12. The checklist provides an example of the type of information to be recorded for each component mentioned above. The facility operator should design a checklist for a specific facility based on the layout of the leachate collection or cap drainage system at that facility.

Inspection results which indicate potential problems with the leachate collection or cap drainage system include:

• irregular flow patterns;
• no flow when expected;
• significantly higher or lower flow than expected;
• high leachate levels over the liner;
• full collection tank or sump;
• declining level in tank or sump which has not been pumped;
• inoperable equipment; and
• mechanical or structural problems, including seepage, cracks, and broken parts.

Leachate levels, flow rates, and location where leachate was noted or measured can be plotted on a diagram of the leachate collection system. Preparing such a diagram weekly facilitates the analysis of visual inspection data in assessing the performance of a leachate collection system over time. The status of facility operations (e.g., operating areas, number of lift(s) in place, waste types disposed of) on the day of inspection should also be recorded on the diagram.

Basic Data

Name:_____

Time:_____ a.m. p.m.

Date:_____ / _____ / _____

Weather Conditions:

Precipitation since previous inspection:

Depth of snow pack:

Type of Inspection

Daily _____

Weekly _____

After
Storm _____

Other:

Storm Data

Date(s) of storm_____

Duration _____ hrs.*

Amount Rain _____ in.

Comments:

Manhole*

1. Location or ID: _____

2. Flow observed? _yes/no_

   a If yes, rate ____cfm

   b Meas. techn: _____

3. Pump on ___ or off ___

4. Standing leachate? ____yes/no

   a If yes, level: _____ft

   b Meas. techn: _____

5. Problems noted:

6. Comments

Sump/Tank*

1. Location or ID: _____

2. a Leachate level _____ft

   b Meas. techn: _____

3. Flow observed? _____yes/no_____

   a If yes, rate _____cfm

   b Meas. techn: _____

4. Pump on ___ or off ___

5. Problems noted:

6. Comments:

Riser*

1. Location or ID: _____

2. Leachate present _yes/no_____

   a If yes, level: _____ft

   b Meas. techn: _____

3. Problems noted:

4. Comments:

Outflow*

1. Location or ID: _____

2. a Flow rate _____cfm

   b Meas. Techn. _____

3. Problems Comments:

*Attach diagram of entire leachate collection
system with results recorded.

Mechanical Equipment*

1. Location or ID: _____

2. a Operating: _yes/no_ b operable: _yes/no_

3. Problems:

4. Comments:

Inspector:		Approved by: _____ (print)
Signature:	Date:	Signed: _____ Date: _____

Figure 12. Checklist for visual and leachate level inspections.

5.2.2   <u>Leachate Level Over Liner</u>

<u>Discussion</u>

While visual inspection of leachate collection systems will indicate
whether leachate is being generated, it will not address the basic questions
of whether all the leachate generated is being collected. Observing the
leachate level above the liner provides a direct measurement of leachate
collection system performance. Since the leachate collection system is
designed to maintain leachate levels over the liner at less than 30 cm (1 ft),
higher levels may indicate problems with the leachate collection system. This
is especially true if levels are significantly higher or occur over prolonged
periods. Therefore, observation of the leachate level above the liner should
be an integral part of an inspection program.

The preferred method for observing and measuring leachate level above the
liner is through the use of observation wells installed specifically for this
purpose. Design of observation wells is similar to that of groundwater
monitoring wells, which are discussed in detail in Fenn <u>et</u> <u>al</u>. (1977). The
observation-well casing pipe is extended down to a point in the drainage layer
below the desired maximum liquid level. The bottom meter (or more) of the
pipe is packed in gravel and the pipe screened to allow free movement of the
liquid through the pipe.

When observation wells are not available, some insights into the probable
leachate level above the liner can be derived by analyzing measurements of the
leachate level at key points in the leachate collection system. This analysis
is recommended even in cases where observation wells are available in order to
give a more complete picture of leachate conditions.

Figure 13 summarizes the probable leachate levels in observation wells
and leachate collection system measurement points under different leachate and
system performance conditions. This figure demonstrates that leachate levels
in a sump or riser pipe may not give an accurate indication of leachate levels
over the liner. This is due to drawdown of leachate levels in the vicinity of
leachate collection pipe, and abrupt changes in leachate level which may be
caused by clogged pipe or drainage material. Only a properly installed
observation well gives a reliable measurement of leachate level over the liner
at a given point. While measurement points in the collection system will
provide some information on leachate level above the liner in landfills with
no observation wells, these results must be used cautiously and in conjunction
with other data. Ideally it will be possible to measure leachate levels in
observation wells and the collection system. In such cases, the data can be
used not only to identify situations of high leachate level but also as a
diagnostic tool to determine the type and location of the collection system
failure.

<u>Protocol</u>

During the design and initial start-up phase of a facility, the operator
should work closely with the design engineer to establish a site-specific

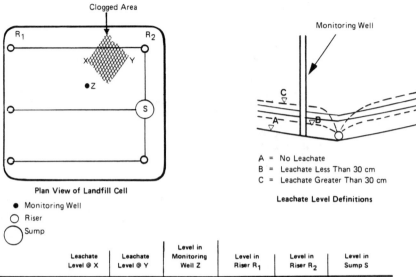

A = No Leachate
B = Leachate Less Than 30 cm
C = Leachate Greater Than 30 cm

Leachate Level Definitions

Plan View of Landfill Cell

● Monitoring Well
○ Riser
⬭ Sump

	Leachate Level @ X	Leachate Level @ Y	Level in Monitoring Well Z	Level in Riser R_1	Level in Riser R_2	Level in Sump S
Before Clog						
	A	A	A	A	A	A
	B	B	B	B	B	B
	C	C	C	B	B	B
After Clog						
	A	A	A	A	A	A
	B	A	B	B or A	B or A	B or A
	C	A	C	C or B	B or A	B

Assumes uniform leachate production across cell.

Figure 13. Probable leachate levels at observation points before and after clogging under varying flow conditions.

protocol for collecting, recording, and analyzing leachate level data. At an existing facility, the operator should complete the following preparation steps prior to initiating a comprehensive leachate level measurement program:

Step 1 - Identify Measurement Points: All points where leachate level can be measured should be identified and labeled. In addition to observation wells, points in the leachate collection system such as manholes, risers, and sumps should be included. Factors should be developed for converting the anticipated field measurement (e.g., distance from top of observation well to leachate level) to the leachate level above the liner for analysis.

Step 2 - Map Measurement Points: All identified measurement points should be plotted on a site map.

Step 3 - Develop Conceptual Leachate Flow Model: An expected leachate flow pattern, expressed in terms of the likely relationships between measurement points, should be developed. These relationships depend on the specific leachate collection system design.

Step 4 - Record and Store Data: A system should be developed for plotting or recording data so that it is easy to observe trends at related measurement points. A leachate level recording sheet should be developed in conjunction with the visual inspection recording sheet (Figure 12). In addition to providing space for recording leachate level at inspection points and observation wells, this sheet should include a record of weather conditions on the day of the inspection, accumulated precipitation since the previous inspection, and depth of snow pack.

In most cases a single absolute measurement of leachate level may not provide significant information when taken out of context, since leachate levels will vary across the facility and with time. As a result, it will be important to develop a recording procedure which will allow the facility operator to readily identify situations where areal and temporal trends are not consistent. The data are multidimensional and therefore require careful presentation to ensure trends can be readily identified.

The recording of leachate level data is an ideal application for a personal computer. Using commercially available spread sheet programs a facility owner/operator can develop a site-specific data management procedure. A carefully designed system would allow direct entry of field data in the order in which the measurement points have been inspected. The data could then be automatically converted to depth above liner and plotted against historical data in order to provide an easy means for evaluating changes with time. Similarly, the data could be automatically plotted on a grid with contour lines to allow for evaluation of areal trends. Incorporating data in a computer data base would permit manipulations such as three point running averages to identify trends more clearly. Further, a program could be developed which would automatically compare the leachate level trends in measurement points which are expected to have similar leachate levels. This automatic comparison could provide a readout of situations in which the temporal trends observed at adjacent measuring points are inconsistent.

In situations where a personal computer is not available for data management, or where the number of measuring points is very small, the operator may wish to plot the liquid-level data for each point against time in order to observe changes with time. In any case, the operator should plot the data for a given inspection on a site map to allow quick evaluation of areal inconsistencies, and to provide a consistent format for data presentation.

Leachate Level Measuring Devices

A number of methods can be used to measure the level of leachate at measurement points throughout a facility. Some methods measure the distance from the surface and others measure the depth of leachate above a fixed point (e.g., bottom of the manhole). In either case the raw field data will have to be calibrated to a level above the liner for analysis.

Methods which measure distance from surface to leachate level include:

• Conventional Tape Method

A weight is placed on the end of a measuring tape. The last several centimeters of the tape are marked with chalk before it is lowered into the measuring point. When a splash sound indicates that the weight has reached the leachate, the tape is lowered an additional few centimeters into the measuring point and a reading is taken against a reference point on the surface. The tape is then brought to the surface. The distance the tape extended into the leachate (as noted by the chalk becoming wet or washing away) is subtracted from the first reading to give the distance from the reference point to the leachate level. An alternative conventional tape method is to use a cylindrical weight, or "popper", which makes a distinct "pop" noise when the weight reaches the leachate. Depth to that level can then be measured from the tape. Both methods are fairly inaccurate compared to other methods, described below. If used, the procedure should be repeated several times and the results averaged for a more precise measurement.

• Electronic Gauge

An electronic gauge can be used in combination with a measuring tape to more accurately identify the liquid level. The device, which may have both float and conductivity level detection systems, is attached on a measuring tape and lowered into the well or manhole. When any liquid is encountered the float light is activated. When a conductive liquid is encountered the conductivity light is also activated. Using this device it is possible to determine whether an oily, nonconductive layer is on top of the leachate and to estimate its thickness. The lights are located directly on the gauge and are viewed by looking down the well. When the lights are activated the operator takes a reading of the tape against the fixed reference point on the surface.

● Automatic Level Measurement

An automatic mechanical float or conductivity gauge can be used to provide continuous leachate-level measurements. As the liquid level rises the float or gauge also rises and the slack in the wire is taken up by a spring mechanism on the surface. The spring mechanism is calibrated to indicate the depth to liquid level. The depth can be read as needed by an operator or continuously recorded on a graph.

Methods which measure depth of leachate above a fixed point include:

● Electronic Float Level Detector

This type of device has a float which activates a series of magnetic switches when lowered to the bottom of the observation point. A similar design can be permanently installed in a measuring point and provide an electronic readout of leachate depth. The switches are typically spaced at 2.5 cm (1 in.) intervals.

● Conductivity Float Level Detector

Conductivity switches can be placed at 0.6 cm (.25 in.) intervals rather than the 2.5 cm (1 in.) intervals described for float-activated magnetic switches. While it is possible to get significantly greater precision using conductivity switches, several disadvantages are associated with the technology. The switches can be fouled easily, it is possible to get a creeping of liquid up the sides of the gauge causing incorrect measurements, and contamination may result in incorrect measurements. Therefore, conductivity gauges are not recommended.

● Pressure Transducers

A pressure transducer can be installed in the bottom of each measuring point. The transducers are sensitive to an increase in the pressure caused by increased liquid levels. Unlike the conductivity gauge and the float gauge, the pressure transducer provides a continuous measurement rather than an incremental measurement of liquid level. Pressure transducers tend to be fairly sensitive and are therefore not recommended for portable gauges but only for permanent installations. Readouts from pressure transducers can be transmitted electronically and recorded automatically.

5.2.3   Leachate Quantity

As noted above, the Minimum Technology Guidance (EPA, 1985a) recommends that records be kept of the quantity of leachate collected. Comparing these data with the quantity of leachate expected over the same period can provide useful information on leachate collection system performance. Empirical methods can be used to analyze trends in leachate quantity data. Predictive models, such as those used in leachate collection system design, provide a more quantitative approach to the evaluation. These two techniques are discussed below.

5.2.3.1   Empirical Method

The quantity of leachate collected at a facility can be expected to follow some basic trends over the lifetime of the facility:

- Prior to and during placement of the first lift of waste, leachate generation may closely correspond to precipitation, since the precipitation falls directly on the leachate collection system.

- As the collection system is covered with waste, leachate generation should decrease or go to zero since the waste will absorb much of the precipitation.

- As the wastes become saturated with liquid (i.e., reach field capacity) leachate generation should increase, although each new lift of waste increases the capacity of the landfill to store liquid.

- At some point, a steady-state condition may be reached where a correlation can be found between precipitation and leachate generation. For example, leachate generation may be 80 percent of precipitation with a lag time of 1 week, with the other 20 percent being absorbed in the uppermost lift of waste.

- This steady-state condition may continue until the landfill is closed with a final cover. Leachate generation would then be expected to decrease since precipitation inputs to the waste mass are eliminated or greatly reduced.

- Leachate generation should eventually drop to zero, or to some small amount if the cover is not completely effective in eliminating liquid inputs.

These trends will vary depending on site-specific conditions such as the absorptive capacity of the waste, waste placement procedures, climate, precipitation patterns in a given year, and surface area of the open portion of the cell. Leachate generation records can be compared with expected patterns for a given collection point, with generation records at other collection points in the same cell, or with generation records from other cells at the same facility. Any major deviations from leachate generation trends expected at a given site may indicate problems with the leachate collection system.

5.2.3.2   Leachate Prediction Models

A number of analytical tools are now available which are used to predict leachate generation, primarily for design purposes. Gee (1983) compared leachate predictions from three water budget models and one empirical model with actual leachate generation in a field solid waste lysimeter. The results, shown in Table 17, indicate considerable variance between predictions and actual leachate generation even when aggregated to a yearly base. Figure 14 presents the same data expressed as percentages of actual leachate production. The figure illustrates that the state of the art for predicting

TABLE 17

ANNUAL LEACHATE PREDICTIONS AND MONTHLY MEAN ERROR COMPARED
TO ACTUAL LEACHATE PRODUCTION*

Prediction Method	1972	1974	1975	Overall
Rainfall Simulator Model:				
Mean Monthly Abs. Error (in.)	.40	.38	.34	.37
Total Leachate (gal.)	9,434	8,955	7,108	25,497
HELP Model:				
Mean Monthly Abs. Error (in.)	.29	.67	.38	.45
Total Leachate (gal.)	6,809	10,277	8,477	25,563
HSSWDS Model:				
Mean Monthly Abs. Error (in.)	.75	.81	.78	.78
Total Leachate (gal.)	12,212	15,123	12,803	40,138
Thornthwaite Water Balance:				
Mean Monthly Abs. Error (in.)	.44	.69	.61	.58
Total Leachate (gal.)	10,423	15,130	10.654	36,117
Actual Average Monthly				
Leachate Production Cell 1 (in.)	.69	.71	.36	.59
Total Actual Leachate (gal.)	8,998	9,184	4,740	22,922

*1 inch = 2.54 cm
 1 gallon = 3.785 liters

Source: Gee, 1983.

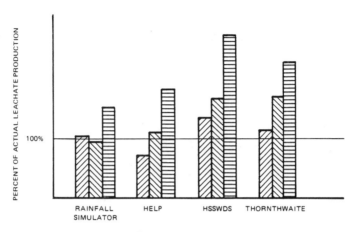

Total Annual Leachate Prediction

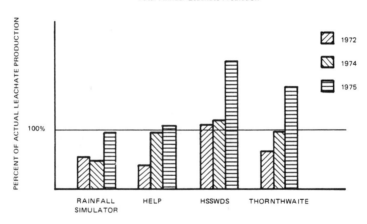

Mean Monthly Absolute Error

Figure 14.   Analysis of leachate prediction models.

leachate generation for short time intervals, even using an empirical model developed for the specific site conditions, is very rudimentary. Mean absolute errors in Figure 14 range from 40 to 200 percent of flow for the short-time period predictions which would be essential for monitoring leachate collection system performance.

Since leachate prediction techniques have been used to estimate the maximum anticipated leachate flow for sizing collection and treatment systems, these inaccuracies can be accounted for in traditional factors of safety and over-design. Except for precipitation, users of these techniques must estimate values for a number of site-specific variables. The outcome of the calculation is very sensitive to the levels assigned to each of these estimated variables. Based on the results of a sensitivity analysis of the EPA Water Balance Method to variations in the coefficient of runoff and available soil moisture, Kmet (1982) concludes "it is apparent that given the right set of assumptions practically any percolation rate (leachate generation rate) can be justified." Further, there has been limited verification of leachate prediction methods with actual leachate production records at full-scale facilities.

Because of the high degree of sensitivity of the various leachate prediction models, it would be impossible to determine whether production of leachate at lower-than-predicted levels is the result of a system failure or poor modeling. Therefore, caution should be exercised when using leachate prediction methods for ongoing monitoring of leachate collection systems.

Protocol

Precipitation data either can be collected onsite in a small meteorological station or can be obtained from the nearest U.S. Weather Service Station. Leachate generation data should be gathered from as many discrete points as the facility design permits. In most cases, leachate quantity data will be obtained from leachate pumping records. If there are a number of pumping stations throughout the facility, records should be maintained for each station separately, so that the leachate generation patterns in adjacent sections of the same facility can be compared.

To facilitate recordkeeping the site operator should develop a chart to convert leachate quantities from liters (or gallons) to centimeters (or inches) for the drainage area. Leachate generation in centimeters (inches) can then be plotted on the same graph with precipitation in centimeters (inches). Weekly records are recommended.

5.2.4   Leachate Quality

Analysis of leachate quality may provide information indicative of the potential for failure of a leachate collection system by the various failure mechanisms. The appropriate indicator parameters depend on which of the failure modes is involved. Analysis of leachate quality may be useful in determining the susceptibility of the system to pipe deterioration, sedimentation, biological growth, chemical precipitation, or biochemical precipitation.

Analysis of leachate quality may indicate whether conditions conducive to failure are present. None of the techniques discussed below, however, provides absolute confirmation of a problem; they are indications of the possibility that a problem may exist. On the other hand, the absence of a positive indication may suggest a small likelihood of failure by the mechanism being examined.

Analysis of leachate quality is primarily a conceptual technique for analyzing leachate collection system performance. Therefore, specific protocols are not provided. The technique is discussed since it may provide useful information about the failure mechanisms discussed in Section 2. It also may provide useful information about the potential for clogging of the drainage and filter layers, for which no direct inspection methods are available.

5.2.4.1 Pipe Deterioration

Pipe deterioration can be caused by a variety of mechanisms, including corrosion, oxidation, chemical attack, or other chemical reactions. The susceptibility of collection pipe to chemical attack will depend on the pipe material used. Generally, waste constituents which can damage a pipe are considered to be incompatible wastes and are excluded from disposal in the cell. Periodic monitoring of leachate pH and analysis for chemicals of concern (e.g., organic solvents) provide a check that incompatible wastes have not been disposed of in the cell. If this analysis indicates potential problems, corrective measures may be possible to prevent pipe failure.

5.2.4.2 Sedimentation

Analysis of a single leachate sample for sediment loading does not provide an indication of the potential for sedimentation clogging of the system. A low sediment-load may indicate that no sediments are entering the system, or that all the sediments are settling out somewhere in the collection pipe. Similarly, a high sediment-load may indicate a problem with the filter or drainage layer, or may show that flow is sufficient to remove sediments which would otherwise accumulate in the collection pipe over time.

A better approach would be to consider sediment loading over time and over different sampling points in the same cell. A gradual decrease in sediment load to a steady-state level indicates that the filter is working as expected. A sharp change in the sediment content of samples from a particular location, however, may indicate a change in the status of the system (e.g., sedimentation is now occurring in the pipe; the filter layer has failed at some point upgradient of the sampling location). Historical data can be used in a manner similar to leachate quantity data described in Section 5.2.3, above. For example, large differences in sediment loading at two adjacent sampling points may indicate sedimentation problems between those two points.

5.2.4.3 Biological Growth

Clogging because of biological growth occurs when naturally-occurring micro-organisms metabolize organic constituents of the waste. Slime-forming organisms can clog collection pipes and the drainage and filter layers.

Detection in the leachate of organisms known to form slimes, and nutrients, contaminant levels, and oxygen conditions within an appropriate range to support growth would indicate potential problems.

Ford (1979 and 1980) has identified three organisms associated with clogging in drain systems: <u>Vitreoscilla</u>, <u>Enterobacter</u>, and <u>Pseudomonas</u>. The last is a common soil bacteria. Conservatively, if any of these species is detected, it may be presumed that biological clogging is possible. Samples of the leachate can be cultured to determine whether growth would occur under the conditions existing in the system. The sample should be taken and cultured under the conditions existing in the system, and the culture tests should be performed with a range of conditions reflecting variations in nutrient and organic composition observed over a year. This type of laboratory work, however, can be very expensive.

5.2.4.4   Chemical Precipitation

The principal mechanism for chemical deposition is the precipitation of calcium carbonate ($CaCO_3$) or, to a lesser extent, manganese carbonate. Precipitates may form whenever the concentrations of free calcium ion (Ca^{++}) and bicarbonate ion (HCO_2^-) exceed the equilibrium concentrations at a particular pH. The equilibrium relation can be expressed in terms of the Incrustation Potential Ratio (I.P.R.) as follows (Baron, 1982):

$$\text{I.P.R.} = \frac{\text{(Total alkalinity)(Hardness)}}{10.3 \times 10^{(11-pH)}}$$

where total alkalinity and hardness are both expressed in ppm $CaCO_3$.

If the I.P.R. is less than 1, no carbonate deposition should occur. If, on the other hand, the I.P.R. is greater than 1, deposition is possible, but will not necessarily occur.

Further, other researchers have suggested ranges of these parameters for which deposition potential is positive. Shuckrow <u>et al</u>. (1981) developed the following ranges for the parameters appearing in the I.P.R. expression:

Alkalinity (as ppm $CaCO_3$):   20.6 to 5400
Hardness (as ppm $CaCO_3$):   700 to 4650
pH: 3 to 7.9

All the parameters involved can be measured with conventional instruments and methods.

In addition to determining the I.P.R. for the current sample, the I.P.R. for a leachate based on a series of samples over the past year would indicate the possibility of clogging under the highly variable conditions at a site. For a conservative indication of clogging potential, the I.P.R. would be calculated using values of alkalinity, hardness, and pH corresponding to the mean plus one standard deviation. The probability that any combination of conditions will produce a larger value of I.P.R. is about 10%. Samples taken over a period of several months should be included for an accurate indication of leachate variability. Shorter averaging times may be appropriate if overall conditions within the system are known to be changing. Seasonal averages may be more appropriate in some locations.

5.2.4.5 Biochemical Precipitation

The principal biochemical process leading to potential clogging is the precipitation of ferric oxide (hydroxide) complexes from soluble ferrous mixes by biological oxidation. Manganese can be deposited in a similar manner.

Iron precipitation is a complex process which can occur with various bacteria under a variety of conditions. Kuntze (1978) suggests that pipes are likely to clog when iron concentrations are greater than 1 ppm and pH is less than 7, if the iron is from a source other than the surrounding soils (drainage layer). Iron clogging has been observed in the field at iron concentrations as low as 0.2 ppm and at pH ranging from 2.5 to 8.5 (Lidster and Ford, undated). Concentration of dissolved oxygen and redox potential also influence biochemical iron precipitation.

Leachate samples to be used in developing data to compare with these conditions should be taken, if possible just outside of the drainage layer. If iron precipitation is occurring, the resulting iron levels in the leachate exiting the system may be so low that the test results would indicate no potential problem.

In many systems, it may be possible to obtain leachate samples only at the exit. In this case, if the presence of iron or manganese-reducing bacteria along with iron or manganese is detected in the leachate, biochemical precipitation should be considered as a possibility.

If the leachate analysis indicates the possibility, a more definitive indication can be obtained by culturing samples of the leachate, augmented by ferrous ions at the maximum concentration previously observed in the leachate. Experimental conditions should include a range of redox potential (oxygen level) and pH derived from historical leachate monitoring at the site. Iron precipitation can be quite rapid, resulting from sudden changes in pH or, more dramatically, from changes in oxygen conditions due to the introduction of air into a normally anaerobic system.

Iron deposits can also form by the precipitation of ferrous sulfide through the reaction of soluble ferrous ions in the leachate with hydrogen sulfide (H_2S) produced from anaerobic sulfate-reducing bacteria (Young et al., 1982). Anaerobic conditions can arise in the drainage and filter layers in all systems, and in the collection pipes if the exit sumps are sealed from the atmosphere. If it is possible to draw a sample from the anaerobic portions of a collection system, indications of potential clogging can be determined by culturing the leachate to determine whether the necessary bacteria are present. If sulfate is also present at levels greater than a few parts per million, and iron has been observed in that sample or in previous samples clogging should be considered a possibility.

5.2.4.6   General Considerations

The above criteria can be used to indicate whether the mechanism described is likely to occur in the facility. A negative result, however, does not indicate that the mechanism will not occur. The criteria are based on experience found in the literature and do not account for the presence of particular waste constituents, or unique site-specific conditions which may hinder or enhance the failure mechanism.

Establishing the particular range of considerations under which failure mechanisms can occur at the site would help address this problem. The validity of the I.P.R. expression, for example, depends on the absence of species that would interfere with the equilibrium processes that throw calcium out of solution. Deviations from the theoretical bounding value of unity could be determined by carrying out a set of laboratory experiments using actual leachate samples at the site. Samples of leachate with the principal parameters (alkalinity, hardness, and pH) adjusted to reflect the variations observed over a period of time would be used as a basis for determining the critical I.P.R. valid at the site. Future leachate analysis would be evaluated with respect to the site-specific criteria. This procedure would reveal, to the extent that the samples used in the experiment are representative of the full range of leachate composition, the effects of interferences and deviations from the conditions for which the criteria were derived.

Similarly, it would be possible to determine a range of conditions for the biochemical oxidation of iron, parallel to the general conditions reported above, applicable to the particular site. Experiments involving biochemistry are more difficult to systematize because the microbiological flora present are hard to characterize fully and to control. Nevertheless, it should be possible to obtain values that more closely reflect specific conditions at the site than do the general indices noted in the literature.

5.2.5   Television and Photographic Inspection

Discussion

Television and photographic inspection of sewer lines is a well developed technology for locating groundwater infiltration, root penetration, and other problems with sewer lines. The same technology is applicable to leachate collection and cap drainage systems to find clogging and inspect the condition of collection lines, provided adequate access is available.

The primary advantage of television inspection is that it allows the operator to directly observe the condition of the collection pipe and precisely locate problems. Problems in their early stages (e.g., cracked pipe, biological buildup) which do not yet affect flow or the passage of maintenance equipment can be detected. In addition, a videorecorder can be used to record inspection results. The disadvantages of television inspection are that the procedure is somewhat involved and that it can be conducted only in lines with adequate access (e.g., 15 cm (6 in.) minimum diameter, access to both ends of the pipe).

Photographic inspection is less expensive than television inspection while providing most of the same benefits. Additional drawbacks of photographic inspection, however, include decreased reliability since it is not known whether the lens is blocked until after the film is developed, and it is necessary to wait for film to be developed.

Protocol

Equipment used in television and photographic inspection of collection pipe includes (Foster and Sullivan, 1977):

1. A skid mounted camera. Types of cameras include various types of color, black and white video units and 35-mm photographic equipment.

2. A light source for the camera.

3. Television cable and steel cable (on reels) with measuring equipment to determine the location of the camera in the collection pipe.

4. Sheaves or pulleys for the cables and a winch at one end to pull the camera through the pipe.

5. A control unit with a television monitor (for television inspection), communication equipment, and a camera and/or video recorder to photograph and record key locations in the pipe.

6. An electric generator if no power supply is available onsite.

Prior to television or photographic inspection, the collection pipe should be thoroughly cleaned (see Section 6), unless the purpose of the inspection is to determine the condition of the line prior to any cleaning. Then, the camera is rigged between two access points (e.g. using a rodding machine), with the camera at one end of the line connected by cable to a winch at the opposite end, which pulls the camera slowly through the line. Television cameras monitor the line continuously and photograhic equipment can be set to take a picture at regular intervals (e.g., every meter). A meter on the winch or cable reel records the distance of movement of the cable and therefore measures the location of the camera in the line. Some units display this distance on the television monitor. Cameras are available to inspect lines from 8 cm (3 in.) to 150 cm (60 in.) in diameter (although many systems only go down to 15 cm (6 in.)), and are on the order of 300 m (1000 ft) in length.

Television or photographic inspection can be conducted annually as part of regular system inspection and maintenance. This would help identify problems which may go unnoticed by other inspection and maintenance procedures. The technique can also be used to locate or identify problems which are discovered or suspected by other methods. Television inspection, for example, can be used instead of excavation to identify the cause of pipe blockage discovered during routine flushing (assuming the pipe is not totally blocked and the camera can be rigged between two access points).

A checklist for television or photographic inspection is given in Figure 15. It is important to record the type of inspection being conducted and the precise location of collection lines being inspected. A description of all problems noted, including location, should be given. Problems which can be identified by television or photographic inspection include:

- partial clogging of the pipe;
- total or partial clogging of the pipe openings;
- deviations in the line (straightness) and grade (slope) of the pipe;
- broken or cracked pipe;
- separated or uneven pipe joints;
- foreign objects in the pipe; and
- areas of leachate accumulation.

5.2.6   Inspection During Pipe Maintenance

Discussion

Pipe maintenance techniques, discussed in Section 6, can also be used (simultaneously) to inspect collection lines. The fact that maintenance equipment can pass through the collection lines indicates that there are no major clogs or broken pipes, and that the system is continuous. The only major difference between running a low-pressure jet, for example, through a collection line for inspection as well as maintenance rather than maintenance alone is that the former utilizes a meter to measure the location of the jet in the pipe. When the progress of the jet is hindered, therefore, the location of the problem can be discerned.

Protocol

Inspection via maintenance related techniques occurs whenever maintenance equipment is run through the collection line. Regular inspection can occur quarterly, semi-annually or annually. Special inspections using this technique are discussed in Section 5.3.

A checklist for inspection using maintenance techniques is given in Figure 16. This checklist can be used for both regular and special maintenance-related inspection. The primary data inputs are the status of each section of line (defined by adjacent access points or one access point and a label) and the location of the blockage in unpassable sections. A diagram of the leachate collection system should also be provided with access points, and labels, and the status of each line should be clearly marked.

Protocols for maintenance techniques are given in Section 6.

5.3   SPECIAL INSPECTIONS

Special inspections are required at specific times in the life of a leachate collection system. The most significant times for special inspections are:

Basic Data

Name: _____

Time: _____ a.m./p.m.

Date: ___/___/___

Type of Inspection

TV ____

Photo : ____

Inspection by:

Company Name: _____

Address: _____
_____
_____

Type Record Kept

Photo ____

Video ____

Notes ____

None ____

Pipe Pre-cleaned

Date: ___/___/___

Technique: _____

By: _____

None ____

Reason:

Reason for Inspection

Annual

Problem Noted ____

describe:

Other ____

describe:

Location of Inspection*

Cell or area _____

1st access _____

last access _____

distance between

access points ____ ft

*Attach diagram of inspected
area with access points labelled,
problems and locations noted.

Comments:

Results

No problems ____

Type	Description	Location
Clogged pipe		
Clogged Slots		
Pipe line/grade		
Pipe cracked		
Pipe broken		
Pipe joints		
Ponded leachate		
Other:		

Inspector:		Approved by: _____ (print)
Signature:	Date:	Signed: Date:

Figure 15.   Checklist for television or photographic inspection.

Basic Data	Type of Inspection	Maintenance by:
Name_____	Quarter ____	Company Name: _____
Time _____ a.m., p.m.	Semi-Annual_____	Address: _____
Date ___/___/___	Annual ____	_____
	As-built ____	Technique:
	1st lift ____	
	Other ____	

First Access Point	Second Access Point or Line Label	Results* Clear	Blocked	Location of Blockage	Comments

*Attach diagram of inspected area with
access points, line labels, clear lines,
blocked lines, un-inspected lines, and
location of problems noted.

Inspector:		Approved by:_____ (print)
Signature:	Date:	Signed: Date:

Figure 16.   Checklist for maintenance-related inspection.

- after construction is completed;
- after the first lift of waste has been placed; and
- when problems are identified with system performance.

5.3.1   After Construction

After construction, inspection is needed to verify that the leachate collection system was constructed as described in as-built documentation. This inspection, called an as-built inspection, can be carried out as part of the Construction Quality Assurance Plan. The inspection can be either a maintenance-related inspection or a television or photographic inspection. Inspection protocols for these techniques are discussed above.

The main purpose of an as-built inspection is to verify that the collection line is continuous and not blocked. Television or photographic inspection can also verify that the alignment and overall condition of the line is satisfactory. Problems noted during an as-built inspection can be easily corrected since waste has not yet been placed at the facility.

5.3.2   After First Lift Has Been Placed

Inspection of the collection pipe after the first lift of waste is placed is important to ensure that the pipes were not damaged during placement and compaction of the waste. Pipes are most susceptible to crushing or displacement during placement of the first lift of waste since there is not yet a sufficient depth of waste to help diffuse equipment loading. Inspection after the first lift would be a maintenance-related or a television or photographic inspection. Inspection protocols for these techniques are discussed above. If the pipes have been inspected after construction, this inspection need only determine whether damage has occurred during placement of the first lift of waste. Problems noted can still be corrected with relative ease since only one layer of waste above the damaged section would have to be excavated.

5.3.3   When Problems Are Identified with System Performance

In order to address problems noted during inspections, it is necessary to locate and diagnose the extent and nature of the problem. Often, the location and nature of a problem will be discovered during the inspection procedure. A direct inspection technique, for example, discovers the exact location in a collection pipe where the clog begins and may be able to determine the mechanism of failure. Alternatively, high leachate-levels in observation wells do not reveal the cause of the problem, only the location of the effect.

When a problem is suspected as a result of one type of inspection, other inspection techniques described above can be used to locate the problem. Clogged collection pipe can be accurately located using direct inspection methods, provided there is adequate access to the pipe network. Problems in the drainage or filter layers can be located by examining data from various access points and leachate-level indicators. Additional observation wells can be installed in the area of concern to provide further information and document the problem. Once the cause of the problem has been located, excavation can be used, if necessary, for further diagnosis.

Table 18 provides general information on diagnosing problems in leachate collection systems.

TABLE 18

DIAGNOSING PROBLEMS

Symptom	Possible Causes
• High leachate levels above liner, constant over time	• clogged collection lines • clogged drainage layer • clogged filter layer • full sump • local ponding due to differential settling
• High leachate levels after rainfall only, leachate drains slowly during dry weather	• partially clogged collection lines, drainage layer or filter layer • undersized system
• High leachate levels, condition improves after cleaning	• clogged collection lines
• High leachate levels, condition does not improve after cleaning	• clogged drainage layer or filter layer • local ponding due to differential settling • clogged collection pipe openings
• Historical records indicate lower leachate flow than expected	• clogged collection lines, drainage layer or filter layer • ponding in waste layers • no system problems, errors in water balance modeling
• Historical records indicate higher leachate flow than expected	• no system problems, errors in water balance modeling
• Leachate levels in sump remain high even during pump cycles	• undersized pump, pump cycles too short
• Cleaning difficult or cannot be accomplished using conventional equipment	• crushed, separated or clogged (mature deposit) collection lines • bend in collection line or access point too sharp • spacing between access points too great • foreign object in collection line

(continued)

TABLE 18 (continued)

Symptom	Possible Causes
• material from drainage or filter layer in sump	• broken or separated collection pipe • collection pipe opening too large • improper particle size distribution
• No flow at inspection point when expected	• upgradient clog of collection line, drainage layer or filter layer
• "Clog" material in outflow	• partially clogged collection pipe, pipe openings or drainage layer
• Leachate ponding or seepage out of waste	• high leachate levels, see above • local leachate ponding due to impermeable waste or intermediate cover layers

6. Maintenance

Maintenance of a leachate collection and cap drainage systems is needed to ensure that liquid will be effectively removed from over the liner throughout the lifetime (and post-closure care period) of the facility. There has been little experience, however, with maintenance of these systems. Typically, collection pipes are maintained only when problems are noted; that is, maintenance techniques are used as repair measures rather than for system maintenance.

The notion that the need for preventive maintenance is obviated by the ability to repair these systems seems shortsighted for at least two reasons. First, historical evidence indicates that drainage systems of all types require preventive maintenance to operate at maximum efficiency and to prolong service life (Smith, 1976). Second, some failure mechanisms may be extremely difficult to stop once the pipe is clogged. Young iron deposits, for example, may be easily removed by preventive maintenance techniques even though the effect of the deposit may not yet be noticeable. However, mature deposits which do affect leachate flow may be extremely difficult, if not impossible, to remove by standard maintenance or repair methods (Ford, 1979).

The basic objectives of a maintenance program are (Smith, 1976):

1. To keep the system operating near maximum efficiency;
2. To obtain the longest operating life of the system; and
3. To accomplish the above two objectives at minimum cost.

Underground drainage systems, in general, require minimal maintenance (Smith, 1976). The amount of maintenance required for a leachate collection or cap drainage system will vary depending on design, construction quality, operating procedures, and leachate characteristics (quantity and quality). Collection pipes, for example, may need to be cleaned several times a year if the leachate has a high sediment load or if the system is highly susceptible to other forms of clogging. Alternatively, annual cleaning may only be a safety measure at facilities where clogging mechanisms are not active. At all facilities, regular maintenance of mechanical equipment (e.g., pumps) is required. Further research is needed to determine the cost-effectiveness of preventive maintenance in meeting the above objectives.

Mechanical and hydraulic methods for cleaning collection pipes are discussed below. These techniques were developed for maintenance of sewer pipes. Experience with these techniques for leachate collection system

96

maintenance is limited. Two major constraints on using these techniques for leachate collection systems are more limited access (e.g., risers used instead of manholes, manholes surrounded by waste) and the use of plastic pipe. Operator safety is also of greater concern for leachate collection system maintenance because of the potentially hazardous nature of the leachate. Safety considerations are discussed in Water Pollution Control Federation (1980).

Procedures are not given for maintenance of drainage layers and filter layers since no methods are currently available to mitigate failure mechanisms which may be active in these layers. Potential failure of drainage and filter layers is addressed through design, construction and system operation, including control of waste characteristics, discussed in Section 3. In addition, maintenance of mechanical equipment is not discussed. It is recommended, however, that manufacturers' recommendations for equipment maintenance be carefully followed. Information on equipment maintenance and on maintenance of drainage systems, in general, can be found in Smith (1976).

Figure 17 gives an example of a collection pipe maintenance checklist for use with the methods described in Sections 6.2 and 6.3. The checklist can be used to record the reason for the maintenance, the maintenance method used, and maintenance results. Actual checklists used should be tailored to meet the needs of a specific facility, and may include a schematic of the drainage system.

6.2 MECHANICAL METHODS

6.2.1 Rodding/Cable Machines

Discussion

Rodding machines and cable machines are both designed to power the rotation of various attachments used to clean sewer lines. Rodding machines use a series of rigid rods, joined to make a flexible line, and cable machines use a continuous cable to both spin the attachment and push and/or pull it through the collection line or sewer. A typical rodding machine is shown in Figure 18, and typical attachments for both types of machines are shown in Figure 19. Special attachments are available for use in plastic pipe.

Both rodding and cable machines can be used to clean collection lines and remove clogs. Cables are applicable to smaller lines (5 to 30 cm; 2 to 12 in.) and rods to larger lines (15 to 122 cm; 6 to 48 in.). The efficiency of rodding in lines greater than about 38 cm (15 in.) may be limited by the tendency of the rods to bend at the joints, thereby reducing their power (Foster and Sullivan, 1977). Both types of machines can be used in runs up to 300 m (1000 ft), and both have the advantage that "threading" is not required. Since the apparatus does not need to be pulled through the line, only one access point is required. Rodding and cable equipment can be used to thread the line for other equipment which does need to be pulled, such as a television inspection camera or cleaning bucket.

Basic Data	Reason	By
Name: _____	Scheduled_____	Company: _____
Time: _____ a.m./p.m.	– Period: _____	Address: _____
Date: ___/___/___	Special _____	_____
	– Specify:_____	Contact: _____

Methods Used:

1. Cable machine _____ Attachments: a. _____ b. _____ c. _____ d. _____

2. Rodding machine _____ Attachments: a. _____ b. _____ c. _____ d. _____

3. Jetting _____ psi _____

4. Propelled devices _____ Specify: a. _____ b. _____ c. _____ d. _____

5. Other _____ Specify: a. _____ b. _____ c. _____ d. _____

Results

Section Cleaned*	Method No.	Material Removed	Problems/Comments

*Schematic attached: Yes_____ No _____

Comments:

Inspector: Approved by:_____

Signed: _____ Date: _____   Signed: _____   Date: _____

Figure 17. Checklist for collection pipe maintenance.

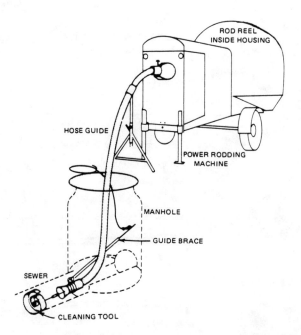

Figure 18. Power rodding machine.
(Source: Hammer, 1975.)

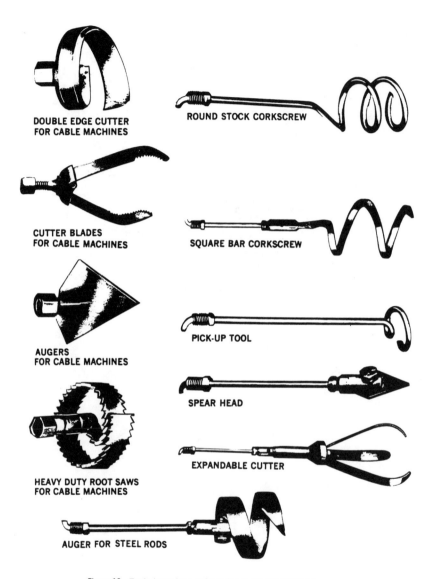

DOUBLE EDGE CUTTER
FOR CABLE MACHINES

ROUND STOCK CORKSCREW

CUTTER BLADES
FOR CABLE MACHINES

SQUARE BAR CORKSCREW

AUGERS
FOR CABLE MACHINES

PICK-UP TOOL

SPEAR HEAD

EXPANDABLE CUTTER

HEAVY DUTY ROOT SAWS
FOR CABLE MACHINES

AUGER FOR STEEL RODS

Figure 19. Typical attachments for rodding and cable machines.
(Source: W.S. Darley & Co., Melrose Park, IL.)

The primary disadvantage of rodding/cable cleaning is that the dislodged materials may not be removed from the line. Large quantities of water may be required to flush the lines subsequent to rodding or cable cleaning.

Rodding/cable cleaning will be most applicable to leachate collection or cap drainage systems in situations when flushing or jet cleaning alone is not effective or is not applicable. An example would be a line where flushing does not remove biological buildup and jetting is either not available or has been shown to damage the drainage layer because of the configuration of pipe perforations. In addition, rodding or cable cleaning may be less expensive than jetting in certain areas.

Protocol

The same protocol is used for rodding and cable cleaning. The power supply for the equipment is placed at the downstream manhole which provides access to the line to be cleaned. An appropriate attachment is selected and installed at the end of the rod or cable. The cable or rod is then placed in the line and the machines turned on. Controls include various lateral speeds to move the equipment forward or backward through the line, and rotational speeds to regulate the spin of the attachment. Maximum rotating speed should be used when the equipment is moving forward in the line (Foster and Sullivan, 1977). Specific procedures for operating rodding or cable machines can be obtained from the equipment manufacturer. It is anticipated that operators of land disposal facilities will hire an outside firm to clean collection lines by this method, although purchase or rental of appropriate equipment is possible.

Problems encountered during cleaning should be described in the maintenance record. (For example, see Figure 19.) Potential problems include sections which are difficult or impossible to clean. The location of these sections and the attachments used should be noted. Most cable and rodding machines have a meter which measures the distance of the equipment in the line. The meter should be zeroed as the equipment is placed in the line. In addition, dislodged material should be inspected before (or after) it is removed from the manhole. Pieces of pipe, drainage-layer material, or waste in the debris indicate a broken or deteriorated section of collection pipe. Chunks of biological material and chemical precipitation, or excessive sediments in the outflow indicate clogging mechanisms at work and may require further investigation.

6.2.2 Buckets

Discussion

Buckets may be used to remove large quantities of sand, gravel, and other materials from collection lines. The bucket is pulled through the line by a steel cable connected to a powered winch at the upstream manhole. When the bucket is full, it is pulled by a winch at the downstream manhole and emptied. Buckets are designed to open when pulled in one direction and to close when pulled in the other. The apparatus used for bucket cleaning is shown in Figure 20.

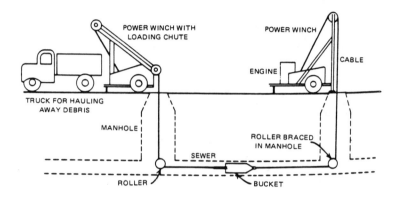

Figure 20.   Schematic of bucket machine cleaning.
(Source: Hammer, 1975.)

The primary advantage of bucket cleaning is that large quantities of material can be dislodged and removed. Various accessory tools are also available, once the equipment is set up, to remove materials not dislodged by the bucket. These tools include a "porcupine," which is similar to a stiff wire brush, and a "squeegee," made of strips of rubber (Foster and Sullivan, 1977).

The primary limitation of bucket cleaning is that access to a manhole at each end of the pipe is required, and the line must be threaded. A rodding machine, for example, can be used to push a cable through the line to be attached to the bucket, which needs to be pulled in both directions.

Buckets are available for use in lines as small as 15 cm (6 in.) and are applicable in lines up to 230 m (750 ft) long (Foster and Sullivan, 1977). It is important that the type of bucket selected be based on the construction material of the pipe to be cleaned. A bucket designed for concrete sewer pipe, for example, may damage a plastic collection pipe.

Protocol

The power winches are set up at adjacent manholes, the pipe is threaded, and the bucket is pulled through the collection pipe to dislodge and collect materials. As with other maintenance procedures, the collected material should be inspected for evidence of failure or clogging mechanisms. If materials do indicate a problem, further investigation is warranted.

6.3 HYDRAULIC METHODS

6.3.1 Jetting

Discussion

High-pressure water cleaning is one of the most effective sewer-cleaning techniques. Water is pumped through a hose connected to a special nozzle which directs the high-pressure stream of water in several directions. Various nozzle designs are available, as shown in Figure 21. The force of the water is used both to propel the nozzle through the line and to dislodge materials which may have built up on the pipe. High-pressure jets can operate at pressures of 0 to 140,000 g/cm^2 (0 to 2000 psi).

Ford (1974) experimented with jet cleaning of plastic drains clogged with ochre in Florida. He found that high-pressure jets (84,000 g/cm^2 (1200 psi) at the pump) damaged the drainage layer by displacing drainage-layer material, and recommends low-pressure (e.g., 4900 g/cm^2; 70 psi) jetting. The drainage layers tested, however, were only about 5 cm (2 in.) thick. In addition, it was found that low-pressure jets were less effective than high-pressure systems for "more seriously clogged drains," and that low-pressure systems were somewhat more difficult to use (the nozzle is no longer self-propelled). Experience with jet cleaning of leachate collection systems is limited. Jetting has been shown to be effective in removing clogs from collection pipes, but the effect of high-pressure jets on the drainage layer should be considered in selecting the optimal cleaning pressure.

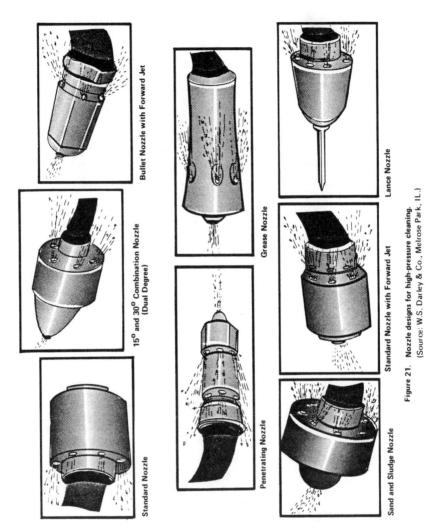

Figure 21.   Nozzle designs for high-pressure cleaning.
(Source: W.S. Darley & Co., Melrose Park, IL.)

The main advantage of jet cleaning is that it is expected to be effective in removing most types of clogs and accumulated materials from the collection pipe. In addition, it is relatively easy to use, requiring minimal setup and access only at the downstream end of the pipe.

Limitations include the need for an accessible water supply and the potential of damaging the drainage layer. Jetting may also not be effective for large or heavy debris, or for mature iron deposits. A method to remove the debris flushed out by the jet is also needed. A vacuum truck, for example, is often used to remove debris accumulated in the downstream manhole.

Protocol

Jetting equipment is set up at the downstream access point of the collection pipe to be cleaned. Nozzle type and size, pump pressure, and rate of entry and withdrawal should be based on pipe size, length, and conditions expected. More thorough cleaning is accomplished at higher pressures and slower rate of entry and withdrawal. Thorough cleaning, however, is also more expensive since more time and more water are required.

The specific protocol used for jet cleaning will depend on the design of the system and on the capabilities of the cleaning equipment available. Typical maximum lengths of pipe which can be jet cleaned range from 90 to 300 m (300 to 1000 ft) at depths of about 15 m (50 ft). Jet cleaning service should be available from local sewer cleaning firms, and the equipment is available for purchase from a variety of manufacturers. (See Foster and Sullivan, 1977.)

6.3.2 Flushing

Discussion

Collection lines can be flushed using a hose connected to a fire hydrant or other water supply. Leachate can also be used if it does not contain a high sediment load. The action of a large quantity of liquid flowing through the pipe serves to remove loosely attached debris or sediments from the pipe. Various hydraulically propelled devices are also available to increase the effectiveness of this technique. These devices include sewer balls and hinged-disc cleaners (sewer scooters).

A sewer ball (Figure 22) is an inflatable rubberized ball attached to a cable which limits the cross-sectional area available for flow at a specific point in the pipe so that water flows around the ball at higher, more turbulent velocities. Use of the sewer ball increases the ability of the water to dislodge and flush away debris which has accumulated in the pipe. Sewer balls require a certain amount of operator skill for effective use and are available in sizes as small as 15 cm (6 in.).

A hinged-disc cleaner (Figure 23) provides the same function as a sewer ball, increasing the effectiveness of flushing. The machine is pushed through the pipe by the flushing water. When debris is encountered, the machine stops, causing water to accumulate in the pipe. The operator then pulls the cable to release the top half of the disc, allowing the accumulated water to flush away

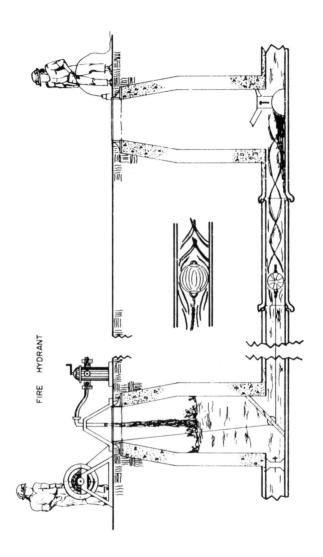

FIRE HYDRANT

Figure 22.　Sewer ball.

(Source: Water Pollution Control Federation: 1980)

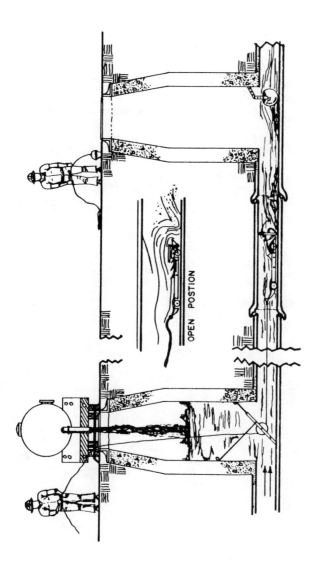

Figure 23.   The hinged disc cleaner (or "scooter").
(Source: Water Pollution Control Federation: 1980)

the debris. The velocity of the water is generally three to four times the normal flow velocity, depending on the size of the pipe. The debris is washed downstream and can be removed through a manhole or clean-out.

Simple flushing requires access to at least the downgradient portion of the pipe to be maintained, and preferably access to both ends of the pipe. Access to both ends of the pipe is required when the sewer ball or hinged-disc cleaner is used. Flushing is simpler and less expensive than other maintenance measures, but may be less effective in removing debris attached to the pipe.

Protocol

Generally, flushing is accomplished by directing the source of water into the upgradient access point. Propelled devices are designed for use from a manhole, but flushing water may be added through a clean-out or riser pipe. Debris flushed out of the pipe is removed from the downgradient access point which has been plugged to capture debris but allow the water to pass through. (See Figure 23.)

7. Repair

Leachate collection and cap drainage systems must be repaired when the mechanisms discussed in Section 2 cause the systems to fail. Failure occurs when the system becomes unable to remove leachate (or precipitation) and allows liquid to accumulate over the liner. Maintenance procedures are used to address failure mechanisms before actual failure of the system occurs. Repair procedures are used to correct the problem after it occurs, thus allowing liquid to be removed from over the liner.

Leachate collection and cap drainage systems can fail as a result of problems in the collection pipe, filter layer, drainage layer and other system components, including sumps and pumps. Problems with components of the system that are buried under the waste are of particular concern since access to these components is difficult. Evidence of system failure includes:

- no flow out of the system when flow is expected;

- high leachate levels in portions of the facility; and

- leachate ponding or seepage at the surface of the waste mass (or cap).

An investigation may be needed to gain an understanding of the cause of the problem before selecting the appropriate repair option. Locating and diagnosing problems are discussed in Section 5.3.3.

A variety of repair options are available to correct problems with failed leachate collection or cap drainage systems. The maintenance techniques described in Section 6 can be used as repair methods primarily for clogged collection pipe. Chemical methods may also be useful to remove (dissolve) material clogging a collection pipe and may be applicable to address clogging of the drainage or filter layer. Finally, the failed portion of the system can be replaced with a new system.

Selection of the appropriate repair option depends on a number of factors. Location of the problem influences the choice considerably. Some repair options, for example, are applicable only to the collection pipe and would not be of use for a clogged drainage layer. The type and extent of the problem are also important. Clogging of the drainage layer around the collection pipe, for example, might be addressed by chemical methods while chemical methods would not be applicable to extensive clogging of the drainage or filter layer away from the pipe. Also, the physical and chemical characteristics of the clogging material are important in determining the effectiveness of a repair option. In general, maintenance techniques and chemical methods are applicable to problems in and around the immediate area of the collection pipe, and replacement techniques are required for problems away from the pipe area.

Landfill design and waste characteristics must also be considered in selecting the appropriate repair option. Maintenance techniques, for example, may not be the best option for a clogged collection pipe if access to the pipe was not provided in the landfill design. Similarly, excavation and replacement may depend on the number of lifts of waste which have been placed and how "dangerous" those wastes are (e.g., explosive, reactive, volatile, unknown composition).

This section addresses the three major categories of repair methods: maintenance techniques, chemical techniques and replacement techniques. This section does not address repair of components such as pumps and sumps which are not buried by the wastes. Standard construction and system maintenance techniques can be used for repair of these components.

In some cases, the effect of leachate collection system failure can be eliminated by significantly reducing leachate generation. This would be accomplished, for example, by closing the site with a final cover to control the water balance at the site. Decreasing the quantity of precipitation and groundwater flow, and increasing runoff, surface storage and evapotranspiration can also be used to reduce the quantity of water available for leachate generation at the site (Pacey and Karbinski, 1979). The discussion below assumes that leachate generation has been minimized and repair of the leachate collection system is required.

7.2 MAINTENANCE TECHNIQUES

Maintenance techniques which can be used for leachate collection system repair include:

- rodding;
- cable tool;
- buckets;
- jetting;
- flushing alone; and
- flushing with hydraulically propelled devices.

These techniques, described in Section 6, are applicable to collection pipes clogged with sediments, biological growth, chemical precipitates and biochemical precipitates. It is also necessary that sufficient access to the pipe be available through manholes or risers. Buckets additionally require that the pipe be able to be threaded, and is therefore not applicable to totally blocked pipes.

The information provided on these techniques in Section 6 is generally applicable for their use in system repair. One major difference is that more effort may be required to remove the material which has blocked the flow in the collection pipe than to remove material that has not yet accumulated significantly. This additional effort would increase the cost of the operation since it would take longer to clean a section of pipe. Several techniques may also need to be tried before the clog is successfully removed. Care should be taken to ensure that the techniques tried do not damage the collection pipe. It is likely that the equipment operator will be most experienced with sewer cleaning and may not fully appreciate the differences between plastic and concrete pipe. It is up to the facility operator to make sure that a difficult clog is not attacked so aggressively that the collection pipe is damaged. This may require the use of tools specially designed for plastic pipe, or lower water pressures for jetting even though different tools or higher pressures may be more effective in removing the clog.

The expected success of maintenance techniques as repair methods will vary with the nature of the clog. Some clogs may be quite difficult if not impossible to remove, while others may be removed quite easily. The expected success of the technique will depend not only on the type of clog but also on its location and extent. Clogs which extend only a few centimeters are likely to be easier to remove than a similar clog which extends several meters. In one example from Section 2, biological material filled a 30 m (100 ft) section of pipe. The clog was removed by flushing with water under high pressure. Although the facility owner was concerned that the pressure might damage the pipe, the clog was successfully removed. In addition, clogs which are near an access point would be easier to remove than clogs which are midway between two access points, since the effectiveness of most techniques diminishes with distance from the access point.

7.3 CHEMICAL TECHNIQUES

Various chemicals have been used or tested for the cleaning of sewers, agricultural drainage systems, and septic drain fields. Commercially available biocides, enzymes, bacterial cultures, caustics, hydroxides and neutralizers can be used to remove grease deposits from sewer lines. Sulfur dioxide gas, dry pelletized sulfamic acid and liquid acids have been shown to be effective in removing mineral deposits and organic material from agricultural drain lines. Also, a method using hydrogen peroxide has been developed to clean septic drain fields which have been clogged with organic material. Chemical treatment is particularly important since it is applicable to mineral deposits, such as iron precipitates, which may be difficult to remove by other methods.

Discussion

Chemicals which have been used to dissolve clogs in drain lines and well points include hydrochloric acid, sulfamic acid, hydroxyacetic acid, hydrochloric acid with ammonium chloride, and sulfur dioxide gas (Grass and McKenzie, 1970). Sulfur dioxide gas and dry pelletized sulfamic acid are considered the most promising chemicals for acid treatment since they can be handled more easily and safely and have provided excellent results.

Acid treatment is applicable to iron deposits, manganese deposits, calcium carbonate incrustation, organic deposits and other materials which dissolve readily in acid. It is useful primarily for clogs in the pipe or pipe slots. Treatment, however, may also extend into the drainage layer immediately around the pipe.

The acid treatment techniques presented below were developed for use with agricultural drainage systems. Special care should be taken in applying these techniques to hazardous waste leachate collection systems. Compatibility of the acid with the pipe material, liner material and waste materials present should be carefully evaluated. Acid treatment should be used only in cells which are designed to handle low pH waste.

Protocol

The protocol for acid treatment has been derived from the protocol used for agricultural drainage systems as discussed in Grass and McKenzie (1970) and Lidster and Ford (undated).

The first step in acid treating a collection line is to clean the line by flushing or with a high-pressure jet. This serves to remove any silt or deposits which are not strongly adhered to the pipe and allows the acid to work only on the materials which are most difficult to remove. Once the pipe is cleaned, acid is introduced into the upgradient end of the pipe. When the acid reaches the downgradient end of the pipe, the downgradient end is plugged so that acid will accumulate in the pipe. For sulfur dioxide treatment, SO_2 gas and water are injected together into the pipe. The amount of water and gas used depends on the pipe size and the length of the lines. Table 19 shows the quantities of SO_2 and water for treatment of various diameter drain lines per 30 m (100 ft) length. SO_2 gas is injected from a tank through a hose extending to the bottom of the riser or manhole. Water is pumped into the drain through a hose which terminates just below the top of the riser or manhole. The tank weight is measured to determine the rate of gas flow, which is adjusted to the amount of water being pumped into the pipe to maintain a 2% solution by weight of SO_2. Water pumping rates vary between 150 and 280 liters per minute (40 and 75 gallons per minute) using 2-5 kg (5-10 lbs) of SO_2 gas per minute. Flow rates from the tank vary with temperature and with the volume of gas remaining in the tank. Nitrogen can be injected into the tank to maintain pressure at a constant flow rate of gas.

The acid solution is held in the line for up to several days if possible. Depending on the amount of clogging in the drainage layer it may be difficult to hold the acid in a leachate collection pipe since the pipe is slotted. Best results would likely be obtained when the liquid level in the leachate collection system is at the bottom of the pipe. Leachate in the area above the clog may need to be dewatered for acid treatment to be effective. Alternatively, addition of water or waiting until the collection system is saturated may be necessary if the leachate collection system is dry. The pH of the liquid in the pipe can be measured to determine the progress of the treatment. Treatment is finished when the pH in the pipe approaches that of the leachate prior to treatment. When the treatment is finished, the plug at the downgradient end of the pipe is removed to allow the leachate to drain from the pipe. The pipe is then flushed or jetted to remove deposits which are only partially dissolved or loosened as a result of the acid treatment.

Safety in handling the chemicals is a major concern in acid treatment. The primary health hazards are from inhalation of SO_2 vapors and direct contact with liquid acid. Pumping rates should be adjusted so that the acid does not overflow from the riser pipe during injection, and all contact with

TABLE 19

QUANTITIES OF SO_2 AND WATER FOR TREATMENT
OF VARIOUS SIZES OF TILE DRAINS[*]

Tile Diameter (in.)	3	4	5	6	8	10	12
Pounds of SO_2 per 100 ft	6	11	17	24	44	68	98
Gallons of Water per 100 ft	37	65	102	147	261	408	588

[*] 2% SO_2 solution: 1 lb SO_2 per 6 gal water.

  1 inch = 2.54 cm

  1 gallon = 3.785 liters

Source: Grass and McKenzie, 1972.

acid should be avoided. Personnel should be aware of proper handling procedures for the SO_2 gas and of safety precautions in conducting the acid treatment.

Acid treatment has been successful in removing iron and manganese deposits from tile drains in agricultural systems. Results of testing by Grass and McKenzie (1970) are given in Table 20. Experience with SO_2 treatment in Imperial Valley, California, conducted by Grass and McKenzie, indicate a 2- to 250-fold increase in flow rate depending on the severity of the clog in the system. Dennis (1978) reports an example of an iron clog which was not corrected either by conventional cleaning techniques, such as drain rodding or water jetting, or by sulfur dioxide treatment. The expected success of acid treatment for leachate collection systems will depend primarily on the type and extent of the clog and the ability of the acid to maintain contact with the clogged portion for an extended time. Acid treatment, therefore, may be most effective when the drainage area beneath the pipe is also clogged and may be less effective when only the pipe itself is clogged.

Additional research is needed to adapt the procedures developed for agricultural drainage systems to leachate collection systems.

7.4   REPLACEMENT TECHNIQUES

Two categories of replacement techniques are discussed in this section. The first category includes those techniques which repair, modify, or replace components of an existing leachate collection system, or retrofit a new conventional leachate collection system at a facility which previously had none. A conventional leachate collection system includes any drainage system which would be placed beneath or within the waste mass at a new facility to collect leachate. Typical leachate collection system designs are discussed in Section 3. The second category of replacement techniques involves using alternative systems to remove leachate from a facility where a conventional leachate collection system has failed or was never installed. Alternative systems include peripheral toe drains and caissons or wells installed through the waste.

Replacement techniques may be required to control leachate in a facility under a variety of circumstances including:

- a severely clogged section of collection pipe which cannot be cleaned by conventional sewer-cleaning techniques;

- extensive clogging in the drainage layer;

- extensive clogging in the filter layer;

- a poorly designed leachate collection system including inadequate access to pipes and insufficient system capacity;

- operational errors including impermeable waste material which causes ponding of leachate within the waste mass;

TABLE 20

THE SOLUBILITY OF IRON AND MANGANESE TILE
DEPOSITS IN VARIOUS CHEMICAL REAGENTS[*]

Solvent	Amount Dissolved (%)		Average (%)
	Manganese Deposit	Iron Deposit	
3.7% HCl + 2% $Na_2S_2O_5$	100	100	100.0
4.9% H_2SO_4 + 2% $Na_2S_2O_5$[**]	83	98	90.5
4.9% H_2SO_4 + 1% $Na_2S_2O_5$	57	96	76.5
4.9% H_2SO_4 + 1% Oxalic Acid	56	94	75.0
2.5% H_2SO_4 + 2% $Na_2S_2O_5$[**]	81	52	66.5
1.8% HCl + 1% $Na_2S_2O_5$	63	66	64.5
4.9% H_2SO_4 + 0.5% Oxalic Acid	38	89	63.5
10% Hydroxyacetic Acid	66	61	63.5
2.5% H_2SO_4 + 1% Oxalic Acid	51	56	53.5
2.5% H_2SO_4 + 1% $Na_2S_2O_5$	56	51	53.0
10% Sulfamic Acid	-	53	53.0
2.5% H_2SO_4 + 0.5% Oxalic Acid	29	43	36.0
4% Sulfamic Acid[***]	20	-	20.0

*1gm of deposit in 20 ml of solution.
**Equivalent to SO_2 gas.
***Above 4% concentration amount dissolved remained unchanged.

Source: Grass and McKenzie, 1970.

- construction errors including crushed collection pipe or failing to install an important system component such as a filter layer;

- differential settling that causes ponding of leachate over the liner.

Any of these problems can lead to high leachate levels or leachate seepage out of the waste mass.

Experience with replacement techniques for leachate collection systems is limited to older facilities which either did not initially have leachate collection systems or used state-of-the-art designs which have since been superceded. Replacement techniques were used at these facilities to control leachate problems which developed and/or to meet RCRA standards for landfill design. Experience with these older facilities is applicable to RCRA-designed facilities as well since the same techniques would be used when repair is required. The primary difference is that excavating through hazardous waste, especially where drummed wastes are present, is more complicated and more hazardous than drilling or excavating through refuse or homogeneous wastes.

The need for replacement techniques at RCRA facilities will likely be less than at older facilities because of the more sophisticated practices used and the measures to reduce leachate production (e.g., not accepting liquid wastes). However, replacement techniques may be required at RCRA facilities for the reasons described above. Construction errors, for example, can occur at any type of facility no matter what the design is. In addition, RCRA facilities as yet employ no standardized leachate collection system design so design features will vary. Providing access to the collection pipes, for example, is not required by RCRA and is not a feature in several recently designed facilities. Furthermore, unforeseen problems could develop with certain unproven technologies currently used in leachate collection systems. An example of this is the use of geotextile drainage or filter layers since the potential for clogging of these layers is unknown. Some design firms use geotextile materials as common practice. Others deem it wise to avoid them at this time. The potential for clogging of geotextile, however, does exist and would require replacement as a corrective measure.

The following sections discuss replacement techniques for leachate collection systems. Examples are given of six facilities which have used these techniques to correct problems with their leachate collection systems.

7.4.1   Conventional Systems

Replacement techniques which are based on conventional leachate collection system design include repairing failed portions in-place, modifying the existing leachate collection system with features not included in the original design, replacing failed portions of the leachate collection system with new components, and installing a new leachate collection system where there was none before. All these methods involve excavating through the waste to gain access to the leachate collection system or the bottom of the waste. The usefulness of these methods therefore will depend to a large extent on the thickness of the in-place waste, the availability of information about the in-place waste, and the characteristics of the in-place waste. Excavating through one lift of hazardous material is less complicated than excavating through several lifts, and excavating through a monofil of bulk material is less complicated than excavating through a mix of bulk wastes and drummed material. These factors affect the hazard involved in excavation and significantly affect the cost of the operation.

Repair or replacement of the existing leachate collection systems may be required when the problem cannot be corrected by other means. This may include fixing or replacing broken or badly clogged leachate collection pipes or portions of the drainage layer or filter layer. It also might include correcting construction errors such as placing a collection pipe, drainage or filter layer where one should have been installed.

Excavation can also be used in modifying the existing system. For example, manholes or risers can be added at collection pipe intersections or at the end of collection pipes where access is not provided. This would allow cleanout, inspection or repair of the pipe by more conventional means. It would also be possible to add new lines or connections to augment functioning of the existing leachate collection system. Alternatively, excavation can be used to install a new leachate collection system where there was none before.

The use of replacement techniques based on conventional leachate collection systems is illustrated by the following examples.

Seven Mile Creek Landfill

The Seven Mile Creek Landfill is a sanitary landfill in Eau Claire, Wisconsin. According to a letter sent to the City of Eau Claire from the Department of Natural Resources (Murray, 1980), the City had agreed to check the collection lines at the Seven Mile Creek Landfill to determine whether any sections of pipe were damaged. The City sewer crew therefore rodded a section of pipe to 35 m (116 ft) from the collection tank and hit an obstruction. This obstruction was thought to be a 45 degree elbow which the rod could not pass through. A month later the area where the elbow was located was excavated and a manhole installed to facilitate cleaning the 244 m (800 ft) run out into the fill area. The sewer crew then jetted the line to an obstruction approximately 15 m (50 ft) west of the elbow where the manhole was installed. A piece of ABS pipe was found which indicated a possible break in the line.

The garbage was then excavated in this area and a break was found between the east sidewall slope and the collection tee. A 3 m (10 ft) section of 15 cm (6 in.) ABS pipe was replaced. The area around the pipe was backfilled with gravel using No. 60 rolled roofing between the gravel and clay and mounded approximately 0.6 m (2 ft) of gravel over the pipe. Garbage was then pushed back into the hole. The cause of the break could not be determined at the time of excavation.

Maryland Chrome Ore Tailings Landfill (excerpted from MEESA, 1984)

Old chrome ore tailing cells were retrofitted with leachate collection systems at a site in Maryland for leachate removal and reuse by the generator.

Initially, the owner attempted horizontal drilling into the cells. This method proved unsuccessful because of difficulties and delays in drilling through the sandy tailings which tend to cement together over time. Leachate collection systems were finally installed by open cut trenching and laying a PVC pipe. Prior to the installation of the leachate collection system, borings indicated a 2-3 m (5-10 ft) leachate head in the old tailing cells.

Each leachate collection system consisted of a single PVC pipe header and lateral collection pipes. The laterals are 15 cm (6 in.) diameter perforated PVC pipe placed at the bottom of 1 m (3 ft) wide trenches which are excavated to the bottom of the cell. The bottom meter (3 ft) of each trench was then filled with crushed stone which was encased with a Mirafi 140 geotextile. Chrome tailings waste was then placed on top of the geotextile to fill up the trench. There are three trenches containing laterals in Area 5 and 14 trenches in Area 3. The trenches in Area 3 vary in length from 32 m (106 ft) to 79 m (260 ft). The three trenches in Area 5 are approximately 24 m (80 ft), 47 m (155 ft) and 61 m (200 ft) in length. The collected leachates flow by gravity to a sump. The sump pumps transfer the leachate to storage tanks.

Problems during construction of these systems included (1) trenching through cemented tailings in several areas; and (2) exposure of excavated tailings to rain.

Manholes were provided outside the cells on the main collection header at all bends and junctions and at spacing not greater than 122 m (400 ft). This allows closed-circuit television monitoring of the condition of the pipe, cleaning and to a limited extent physical repairs to be made to the pipe without excavation.

7.4.2 Alternative Systems

Alternative methods of leachate control are needed when it is impractical or impossible to excavate through the waste mass to replace or repair the leachate collection system or install a new system. Alternative methods include installing toe drains at the periphery of the cell and drilling caissons or wells through the waste to pump out leachate.

Toe drains are french drains typically installed at the base of the landfill. Toe drains are used to control problems with leachate seepage, and they also provide a means to retrofit a leachate collection system at a facility without excavating through the waste.

Caissons or wells can be installed through the waste at a facility to allow removal of leachate. Caissons are simply large diameter wells. They can be installed at low spots in the waste cell to collect leachate which can flow, or in areas of ponded leachate. The effectiveness of the caisson or well is limited by the ability of the leachate to flow to the well. Special care must be taken in installing a caisson or well through hazardous waste, especially if drummed materials are present. In addition, care must be taken to avoid drilling the caisson or well through the liner.

The following examples illustrate the use of toe drains, caissons and wells as repair methods for leachate collection systems.

Western Lake Superior Sanitary District Landfill (Knight et al., 1983)

The Western Lake Superior Sanitary District purchased a co-disposal landfill in 1979 which was having significant environmental problems because of leachate generation. Leachate was migrating to a nearby creek through seepage at the toe of the fill area and to groundwater contamination beneath the fill area. A toe drain was therefore designed to capture both the toe seeps and the contaminated groundwater.

The toe drain design is shown in Figure 24. The drain was designed to prevent surface water from infiltrating into the drain and causing increased treatment costs. Care was taken during construction to provide a 1 m (3 ft) interface of the sand filter with the refuse to control seepage at the toe of the fill. In addition, the drain was placed at the depth required to control the contaminated groundwater and collect the flow of groundwater from both sides.

Since no records were available about the type of waste disposed of at the facility over the years, special consideration was given to safety during construction of the toe drain.

Surface-water monitoring data for the creek, data for groundwater along the line of the drain, and leachate sampling data indicate that the collection system is performing as designed. Flow rates vary seasonally from 76 to 265 liters per minute (20 to 70 gallons per minute). The system had been in operation for 2 years in 1983.

Omega Hills Landfill (Personal Interview, Mark Gordon, 1984)

The Omega Hills landfill was the largest hazardous waste disposal site in Wisconsin. It was originally designed as a co-disposal site, accepting municipal, liquid and hazardous wastes. The facility was designed as a zone of saturation landfill, which depended on the pumping of leachate to maintain groundwater gradients toward the landfill.

The State regulators became concerned when they began to balance the quantity of liquids being delivered to the landfill against the leachate being pumped out. This concern, combined with general uneasiness about the extent and quality of groundwater monitoring, was sufficient to initiate an investigation at the site. A number of leachate head wells were drilled into the waste, and it was discovered that there was considerable leachate at the site, in some areas 9-12 m (30-40 ft) above the bottom of the waste. Further investigations indicated that the clay was not homogeneous. Around the site were sand seams that allowed leachate to migrate beyond the landfill border. It was also found that the stone-filled sump was clogged with silt, making it difficult to pump leachate out of the sump.

At this point, the State terminated all hazardous and liquid waste disposal at the facility. Approximately three years of municipal solid waste capacity remains at the site. The disposal of municipal waste has continued in an effort to help achieve a final grade which will reduce infiltration and leachate generation at the site.

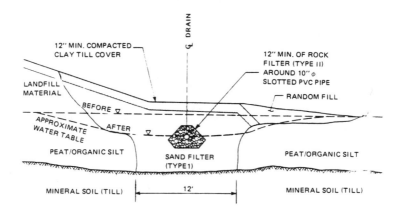

Figure 24.   Toe drain design.
(Source: Knight et al, 1983.)

The owner has been involved in a $10-14 million cleanup, consisting of the following elements:

- Construction of a leachate pretreatment facility to reduce the BOD of the leachate by 70-80%. Prior to pretreatment the average leachate BOD is approximately 30,000 ppm. Prior to construction of the pretreatment facility, leachate was trucked directly to the Milwaukee Metropolitan Sanitary District for treatment. However, because of limited capacity at the POTW, only about 45,000 liters (12,000 gallons) of the high-BOD leachate could be trucked from the landfill per day. This restriction on leachate disposal adversely affected the operation of the facility.

- Removal of waste around the perimeter and construction of new side walls as a barrier for leachate migration beyond the site. The side walls are 30 cm (12 in.) clay cutoff walls with a 2 m (5 ft) toe.

- A perimeter leachate collection system was installed in conjunction with the clay cutoff wall. This installation is at approximately the same elevation as the bottom limits of waste, and at an elevation similar to that of the existing leachate collection system. Wherever possible, piping from the old leachate collection system was interconnected with the new system.

- PVC risers have been replaced with 2 m (6 ft) diameter steel manholes. In the initial design, PVC slanted risers were to provide access to the leachate collection system. This design proved inadequate because the PVC could be crushed or distorted during the settling of the waste, and there was inadequate sump at the terminus of the risers to permit adequate pumping at these points in the collection system.

- Cleaning of leachate collection lines using a water jet.

California Co-Disposal Facility (MEESA, 1984)

Clogging, apparently the result of chemical deposition and solidification, was a recurring problem at a co-disposal landfill in California. About one-third of the waste disposed of at the facility was hazardous and about one-third was liquid waste. The clogging was very non-systematic and occurred only in certain locations while other areas within the same cell performed satisfactorily. Corrective measures included total replacement of sections of the leachate collection system. The collection system consisted of a series of well points and headers which had been installed after waste placement to control leachate. When the well points clogged they were removed from the waste, and new well points were installed (Personal Interview, J. Johnson, 1984).

Maryland Landfill (MEESA, 1984)

This landfill initially was constructed without a leachate collection system. Completed cells at the landfill, however, were retrofitted with a leachate collection system in order to facilitate leachate collection and removal. Standpipe wells were drilled at the low points in the cells and subsequently backfilled with drain rock. Leachate flows through the waste to the wells and is pumped out. The standpipe depths range from 12-24 m (40-80 ft). Because of the large size of the cells, the effectiveness of the leachate collection system is low. It was also considered prohibitively costly to excavate trenches through the waste to place leachate collection lines and to install additional leachate standpipes to enhance removal. Further, the drainage material surrounding the standpipes that were installed is filling with sediment and is expected to eventually clog the system.

References

American Society for Testing Materials (ASTM). "Soil and Rock; Building Stones." 1982 Annual Book of ASTM Standards, Part 19, 1982.

Avnimelech Y. and Z. Nevo. "Biological Clogging of Sands." Soil Sci., 98:222-6, 1964.

Baron D.M. "A Well System can be Designed to Minimize the Incrusting Tendency". The Johnson Driller's Journal. First Quarter, 1982. pp. 8-11.

Bass, J.M., J.R. Ehrenfeld, N.J. Valentine. "Potential Clogging of Landfill Drainage Systems." U.S. EPA, Municipal Environmental Research Laboratory, Cincinnati, OH. EPA-600/2-83-1090, 1984.

Bear, J. Dynamics of Fluids in Porous Media. American-Elsevier Publishing Co., New York, 1972.

Bolz, R.E., and G.L. Tuve. Handbook of Tables for Applied Engineering Science, "Properties of Commercial Plastics." 2nd Edition, CRC Press, 1976.

Canada Centre for Mineral and Energy Technology (CANMET). "Pit Slope Manual," Chapter 9, CANMET REPORT 77-1; January 1977.

Carroll, Robert G., Jr. "Geotextile Filter Criteria," Engineering Fabrics in Transportation Construction. Transportation Research Record 916, National Academy of Sciences, Washington, D.C., 1983.

Cedergren H.R. Seepage, Drainage and Flow Nets. John Wiley and Sons, 1977.

Celanese Fibers Marketing Company. "Test Procedure for Falling Head Water Permeability of Geotextiles." CFMC-FFET-1, New York, August, 1981.

Chen, Y.H., D.B. Simons, P.M. Demery. "Laboratory Testing of Plastic Filters," Vol. 107, No. 1R3, Proceedings of the ASCE, Journal of the Irrigation & Drainage Division. September, 1981.

Dennis, C.W. "The Failure of a Pipe Drainage System in an Organic Soil and Subsequent Remedial Measures." Land Drainage Service., Field Drainage Experimental Unit, Technical Report 78/3. November, 1978, pp. 1-12.

Environmental Protection Agency (EPA). "Minimum Technology Guidance on Double Liner Systems for Landfills and Surface Impoundments - Design, Construction and Operation," Draft, EPA/530-SW-85-014. 24 May 1985a.

Environmental Protection Agency. "Construction Quality Assurance for Hazardous Waste Land Disposal Facilities - Public Comment Draft" Office of Solid Waste and Emergency Response, Washington, D.C. and Hazardous Waste Environmental Research Laboratory, Cincinnati, OH. EPA/530-SW-85-021. October 1985b.

Environmental Protection Agency. EPA Version 2 of the Landfill Data, Westat Data Base. Output prepared by DPRA, Inc. For Marlene Suit. 17 November 1983a.

Environmental Protection Agency. "Lining of Waste Impoundment and Disposal Facilities." Office of Solid Waste and Emergency Response, Washington, D.C. SW-870. March, 1983b.

Environmental Protection Agency. "Draft RCRA Guidance Document for Landfill Design-Liner Systems and Final Cover." Office of Solid Waste July, 1982

Fenn, D., E. Cocozza, J. Ibister, O. Braids, B. Yare and P. Ronx. "Procedures Manual for Groundwater Monitoring at Solid Waste Disposal Facilities." EPA 530/SW-611. August, 1977.

Ford H. W. "The Problem of Clogging in Low Volume Irrigation Systems and Methods for Control." Paper presented at the Symposium on Drip Irrigation in Horiculture with Foreign Experts Participating. Skierniewice, Poland. October, 1980.

Ford H.W. "Characteristics of Slime and Ochre in Drainage and Irrigation Systems." Transactions of the American Society of Agricultural Engineers. Volume 22, No. 5, 1979. pp. 1093-1096.

Ford H.W. "Low Pressure Jet Cleaning of Plastic Drains in Sandy Soil." Transactions of the ASAE. 1974, 17(5):895-897.

Foster W.S. and R.H. Sullivan. "Sewer Infiltration and Inflow Control Product and Equipment Guide." American Public Works Association, Chicago, IL. Prepared for USEPA, Municipal Environmental Research Laboratory, Cincinnati, OH. EPA-60012-77-017c. July, 1977.

Gee, J.R. "The Prediction of Leachate Generation in Landfills - A New Method." Municipal and Industrial Waste, 6th Annual Madison Conference, University of Wisconsin - Extension, Madison, WI. September, 1983.

Ghassemi M., S. Quinlivan, M. Haro, J. Metzger, L. Scinto and H. White, "Compilation of Hazardous Waste Leachate Data." U.S. Environmental Protection Agency, Office of Solid Waste, Washington, DC April, 1983.

Giroud, J.P. "Filter Criteria for Geotextiles". Procedings of the Second International Conference in Geotextiles, Vol. 1, Las Vegas. August, 1982. pp103-108.

Giroud, J.P. "Designing with Geotextiles". Materiaux et Constructions, Vol. 14, No. 82. July/August, 1981.

Grass L.B., and A.J. MacKenzie. "Reclamation of Tile Drains by Sulphur Dioxide Treatment." Sulphur Institute J., Vol. 6(1), pp. 8-13, Spring, 1970.

Grim, R.E. Clay Mineralogy. McGraw-Hill, Inc., New York, 1953.

Haliburton, T.A. and P.E. Wood. "Evaluation of the U.S. Army Corps of Engineers Gradient Ratio Test for Geotextile Performance." Proceedings of the Second International Conference on Geotextiles, Vol. 1, August, 1982.

Hammer M.J. Water and Waste-water Technology. John Wiley and Sons, Inc., New York, 1975.

Harr, M.E. Groundwater and Seepage. McGraw-Hill, Inc., New York, 1962.

Haxo, H.E. "Lining of Waste Impoundment and Disposal Facilities." U.S. EPA SW-870, March, 1983.

Hoare, D.J. "Synthetic Fabrics as Soil Filters: A Review." Journal of the Geotechnical Engineering Division; ASCE Vol. 108, No. GT10, October, 1982.

Horz, R.C. "Geotextiles for Drainage and Erosion Control at Hazardous Waste Landfills." EPA Interagency Agreement No. AD-96-F-1-400-1. U.S. EPA, Cincinnati, Ohio. 1984

Kmet, Peter. "EPA;s 1975 Water Balance Method - Its Use and Limitations." Bureau of Solid Waste Management, Wisconsin Department of Natural Resources. October, 1982.

Knight S.K., L.R. Molsather and M.D. Bonnell. "Retrofitting an Existing Sanitary Landfill with a Leachate Collection System: A Case Study." in the Sixth Annual Madison Conference of Applied Research and Practice on Municipal and Industrial Waste. University of Wisconsin- Extension, Madison, WI. September 14-15, 1983.

Kobayashi, Hester, and B.E. Rittmann. "Microbial Removal of Hazardous Organic Compounds." Environmental Science Technology, 1982. 16(3):170A-183A.

Koerner, Robert M., and J.P. Welsh. Construction and Geotechnical Engineering Using Synthetic Fabrics. John Wiley and Sons, New York, 1980.

Kristiansen, R. "Sand Filter Trenches for Purification of Septic Tank Effluent: I The Clogging Mechanism and Soil Physical Environment." J. Environ. Quality, 1981, 10:53-64.

Kuntze H. "Iron Clogging: Diagnosis and Therapy," in Proceedings of International Drainage Workshop, pp. 452-67, May 16-20, 1978.

Lawson, C.R. "Filter Criteria for Geotextile: Relevance and Use." Journal of the Geotechnical Engineering Division; ASCE Vol. 108, No. GT10, October, 1982.

Lidster W.A., and H.W. Ford. "Rehabilatation of Ochre-(Iron) Clogged Agricultural Drains." International Commission on Irrigation and Drainage. Eleventh Congress. Q. 36, pp. 451-463. (undated).

Luthin, J.N. and A. Haig. "Some Factors Affecting Flow into Drain Pipes". Hilgardia, A. Journal of Agricultural Science, The California Agricultural Experiment Station, Vol. 41, No. 10. 1972, pp. 235-245

✓ Lutton, R.J., G.L. Regan and L.W. Jones. "Design and Construction of Covers for Solid Waste Landfills" USEPA, Office of Research and Development, Cincinnati, OH. EPA-600/2-79-165. August, 1979.

McBean, E.A., R. Poland, F.A. Rovers and A.J. Crutcher. "Leachate Collection Design for Containment Landfills" J. of Environmental Engineering, ASCE Vol. 108, No. EE1. February , 1982.

MEESA. "Corrective and Preventive Measures for Hazardous Waste Landfills and Surface Impoundments" U.S. Environmental Protection Agency, Office of Research and Development. Draft, September, 1984.

Mohammad, S. F. and R. W. Skaggs. "Drain Tube Opening Effects on Drain Inflow". Journal of Irrigation and Drainage Engineering, Vol. 109, No. 4. December 1983, pp. 393-404.

Moore, C.A. "Landfill and Surface Impoundment Performance Evaluation". Municipal Environmental Research Laboratory, Cincinnati, OH. SW-869. April, 1980.

Murray G.C. Solid Waste Superintendent, City of Eu Claire, WI. Letter to P. Kmet, WI Department of Natural Resources. File No. C.P.11-14-CT-21. January 25, 1980.

Nutting, P.E. "The Action of Some Aqueous Solution in Clays of the Montmerillonite Group." Prof. Paper 197F. U.S. Geological Survey, 1984.

Pacey J. and G. Karpinski. "Retrofitting Existing Landfills to Meet RCRA Standards for Leachate Control" in Solid Wastes Management/RRJ. February, 1979.

Peck, R.B., W.E. Hanson, and T.H. Thornburn. Foundation Engineering. Kiley, New York, 1974.

✓ Perrier, E.R. and A.C. Gibson. "Hydrologic Simulation on Solid Waste Disposal Sites." Municipal Environmental Research Laboratory, Cincinnati, OH. SW-868, September, 1982.

Schroeder, P.R., A.C. Gibson, and M.D. Smolen. "The Hydrologic Evaluation of Landfill Performance (HELP) Model." Municipal Environmental Research Laboratory, Cincinnati, OH. EPA/530-SW-84-009, June, 1984.

Sherard, J.L., L.P. Dunnigan, and J.R. Talbot. "Basic Properties of Sand and Gravel Filters." Journal of the Geotechnical Engineering Division, ASCE, Vol. 110, No. 6, June, 1984a.

Sherard, J.L., L.P. Dunnigan, and J.R. Talbot. "Filters for Silts and Clays." Journal of the Geotechnical Engineering Division, ASCE, Vol. 110, No. 6, June, 1984b.

Shuckrow, A.J., A.P. Pajak and J.W. Osheka. "Concentration Technologies for Hazardous Aqueous Waste Treatment." EPA-600/2-81-019. U.S. Environmental Protection Agency. Cincinnati, OH, 1981.

Shuckrow, A.J., A.P. Pajack and C.J. Touhill. "Management of Hazardous Waste Leachate." Municipal Environmental Research Laboratory, Cincinnati, OH. SW-871, September, 1982.

Skaggs, R.W. "Effect of Drain Tube Openings on Water Table Drawdown". Journal of Irrigation and Drainage Engineering, Vol. 104. 1978, pp. 13-21.

Smith R.A., Chairman. "Operation and Maintenance of Irrigation and Drainage Systems: Section IV-Maintenance," in J. Irrigation and Drainage Division, ASCE by Committee on Operation and Maintenance of Irrigation and Drainage Systems. Vol. 102, No. IR1, March, 1976.

Spigolon, S.J. and M.F. Kelley. "Geotechnical Assurance of Construction of Disposal Facilities." Interagency Agreement No. AD-96-F-2-A077. USEPA, Municipal Environmental Research Laboratory, Cincinnati, OH. EPA 600/2-84-040, 1984.

Terzaghi, K. and R.B. Peck. Soil Mechanics in Engineering Practice. Wiley, New York, 1967.

Tratnyek, J.T., P.O. Costas, and W.J. Lyman. "Test Methods for Determining the Chemical Waste Compatibility of Synthetic Liners". U.S. EPA, Office of Research and Development, Cincinnati, OH. August, 1984.

U.S. Army Corps of Engineers. "Drainage and Erosion Control - Substance Drainage Facilities for Airfields." Part XIII, Chapter 2, Engineering Manual, Military Construction, Washington, D.C., June 1955.

U.S. Bureau of Reclamation (USBR). Drainage Manual. U.S. Government Printing Office, Washington, D.C., 1978.

U.S. Bureau of Reclamation. Design of Small Dams. U.S. Government, Printing Office, Washington, D.C., 1977.

W.S. Darley & Co., Melrose Park, IL. Product brochures.

Water Pollution Control Federation. "Operation and Maintenance of Wastewater Collection Systems." Task Force on Sanitary Sewer Maintenance. Moore and Moree Lithographers, Washington, D.C., 1980.

Young, C.W., T.J. Nummo, M.P. Jasinksi, D.R. Cogley and S.V. Capone. "Clogging of Leachate Collection Systems Used in Hazardous Waste Disposal Facilities." Draft White Paper, prepared for U.S. EPA, Research Triangle Park, North Carolina. June, 1982.

Personal Interviews

Bander Stal, Louis. Cascade Resource Recovery, Kent City, MI. October, 1983.

Bross, Jeffrey. Deerfield Associates, D.E. October, 1983.

Gordon, Mark. WI Department of Natural Resources. Madison, WI. November, 1984.

Johnson, J. Lockman Associates, CA., November, 1984.

Kmet, Peter. WI Department of Natural Resources, Madison, WI. October, 1983.

Koch, Hank. Chemical Waste Management, Inc. Milwaukee, WI. November, 1983 and November, 1984.

Kolberg, Dan. Warzyn Engineers, Madison, WI. October, 1983.

Melia, Greg. CECOS, OH. October, 1983.

Nichols, David. Residual Management Technology, Inc., WI. November, 1983.

Pacey, John. Emcon Associates, CA. November, 1983.

Patterson, John. Emtek, Inc., Amherst, New Hampshire. December, 1984.

Peluso, Rich. Wehran Engineerings, Middleton, NY. November, 1983.

Perpich, Bill. STS Consultants, Green Bay, WI. October, 1983.

Statelmire, Jim. CECOS, NY. October 1983.

Roarback, Jom. Delaware Solid Waste Authority, DE. October, 1983.

Vetter, Bob. Department of Public Works, Madison, WI. October, 1983.

COPYRIGHT NOTICE

Other Noyes Publications

HAZARDOUS CHEMICALS DATA BOOK
Second Edition

Edited by

G. Weiss

This Second Edition of the *Hazardous Chemicals Data Book* supplies instant information on more than 1000 of the most important hazardous chemicals. The data given will provide rapid assistance to personnel involved with the handling of hazardous chemical materials and related accidents.

The compilation of hazardous chemicals is presented in a clear, concise, easy-to-locate format. It should be an indispensable source book for any library or laboratory. It is intended for use by scientists, engineers, managers, transportation personnel, and anyone else who might have contact with, or require safety data on, a particular hazardous chemical.

A large quantity of pertinent data is given for each of the chemicals, which are arranged alphabetically. **Examples** of types of properties and safe-handling-information provided are listed below.

COMMON SYNONYMS

FIRE, EXPOSURE, AND WATER POLLUTION EFFECTS

RESPONSE TO DISCHARGE
Containment
Warnings to Be Issued

LABELING
Classification
Code

CHEMICAL DESIGNATIONS
Compatibility Class
Formula
IMO/UN Designation
DOT ID No.
CAS Registry No.

OBSERVABLE CHARACTERISTICS
Physical State, Color, Odor

HEALTH HAZARDS AND TREATMENT
Personal Protective Equipment
Symptoms Following Exposure
Treatment of Exposure
Threshold Limit Value (TLV)
Short Term Inhalation Limits

Toxicity by Ingestion
Late Toxicity
Vapor (Gas) Irritant Characteristics
Liquid or Solid Irritant Characteristics
Odor Threshold
IDLH Value

FIRE HAZARDS
Flash Point
Flammable Limits in Air
Fire Extinguishing Agents
Special Hazards of Combustion
Behavior in Fire
Ignition Temperature
Electrical Hazards
Burning Rate
Adiabatic Flame Temperature
Stoichiometric Air to Fuel Ratio
Flame Temperature

CHEMICAL REACTIVITY
With Water
With Common Materials
Stability During Transport
Neutralizing Agents
Polymerization
Polymerization Inhibitor
Molar Ratio
Reactivity Group

WATER POLLUTION
Aquatic Toxicity
Waterfowl Toxicity
Biological Oxygen Demand (BOD)
Food Chain Concentration Potential

SHIPPING INFORMATION
Grades of Purity
Storage Temperature
Inert Atmosphere
Venting

HAZARD ASSESSMENT CODE

HAZARD CLASSIFICATIONS
Code of Federal Regulations
NAS Hazard Rating for Bulk Water
  Transportation
NFPA Hazard Classification

PHYSICAL AND CHEMICAL PROPERTIES

ISBN 0-8155-1072-1 (1986)   8½″ x 11″   1068 pages

Other Noyes Publications

DISPOSAL OF HAZARDOUS WASTES IN INDUSTRIAL BOILERS AND FURNACES

by

C. Castaldini, H.K. Willard, C.D. Wolbach, L.R. Waterland

Acurex Corporation

F.D. Hall, W.F. Kemner, G. Annamraju
R. Krishnan, M.A. Taft-Frank, D.N. Albrinck

PEDCo Environmental, Inc.

Pollution Technology Review No. 129

The disposal of hazardous wastes in industrial boilers and furnaces is described. Processes which convert wastes to energy continue to be of interest in energy intensive industries, and the disposal of hazardous wastes is a primary concern in today's environment-conscious society.

In the search for disposal alternatives, the USEPA has evaluated the potential use of high-temperature processes for the incineration of hazardous wastes. The feasibility of incineration in industrial boilers and furnaces is covered in Parts I and II of the book, respectively.

CONTENTS

ISBN 0-8155-1067-5 (1986)

429 pages

Other Noyes Publications

AERATION SYSTEMS
Design, Testing, Operation, and Control

Edited by

William C. Boyle
University of Wisconsin

Pollution Technology Review No. 127

Research and development activities in the field of aeration system design, operation, performance, and testing—in the United States, Canada, and Europe—are summarized in this book.

In recent years, a substantial effort has been made to search for energy efficient wastewater treatment systems. Since wastewater aeration is relatively energy intensive, R&D efforts have been aimed at improving design, manufacture, testing, operation and control of these systems. The main goals behind this R&D are aeration system energy use reduction and improved criteria for sizing oxygen transfer equipment.

The book provides a state-of-the-art document on aeration systems which will be useful to engineers and managers involved in wastewater treatment.

CONTENTS

ISBN 0-8155-1065-9 (1986)

452 pages

INNOVATIVE THERMAL HAZARDOUS ORGANIC WASTE TREATMENT PROCESSES

by

Harry Freeman

U.S. Environmental Protection Agency

Pollution Technology Review No. 125

This book contains discussions of 21 thermal processes identified by the U.S. Environmental Protection Agency as innovative processes for treating or destroying hazardous organic wastes. The intent of the information provided is to assist in the evaluation of the processes by researchers and others interested in alternative processes for treating and disposing of hazardous wastes.

Today's rapidly developing and changing technologies and industrial products and practices frequently carry with them the increased generation of solid and hazardous wastes. These materials, if improperly dealt with, can threaten both public health and the environment.

While the processes included in the book differ widely in many respects (i.e., waste streams for which they are designed and state of development), they are similar in that they offer innovative approaches to solving problems presented by the generation of hazardous wastes. Some of the included processes might be regarded as emerging technologies. Others are in commercial operation and are already well beyond any such categorization as emerging technology.

Information about the subject processes was provided voluntarily by the process developers. The criteria used for selection of a process included the innovativeness of the process when compared with conventional existing processes and the potential contribution the process could make to the evolving field of hazardous waste management technology.

CONTENTS

ISBN 0-8155-1049-7 (1985)

125 pages